# EARLY BRAZIL

*Early Brazil* presents a collection of original sources, many published for the first time in English and some never before published in any language, that illustrates the process of conquest, colonization, and settlement in Brazil. The volume emphasizes the actions and interactions of the indigenous peoples, Portuguese, and Africans in the formation of the first extensive plantation colony based on slavery in the Americas. It also includes documents that reveal the political, social, religious, and economic life of the colony.

Original documents on early Brazilian history are difficult to find in English, and this collection will serve the interests of undergraduate students, as well as graduate students, who seek to make comparisons or to understand the history of Portuguese expansion.

Stuart B. Schwartz is George Burton Adams Professor of History at Yale University. His books include *All Can Be Saved* (2008); *Victors and Vanquished: Spanish and Nahua Views of the Conquest of Mexico* (2000); *The Cambridge History of the Native Peoples of the Americas: South America* (1999); *Implicit Understandings* (1994); *Slaves, Peasants, and Rebels* (1992); *Sugar Plantations in the Formation of Brazilian Society* (1985); *Early Latin America* (1983); *A Governor and His Image in Baroque Brazil* (1979); and *Sovereignty and Society in Colonial Brazil* (1973). Professor Schwartz specializes in the history of colonial Latin America, especially Brazil, and the history of early modern expansion.

# EARLY BRAZIL

## A Documentary Collection to 1700

Edited by

### STUART B. SCHWARTZ
Yale University

Translated by

### CLIVE WILLIS AND STUART B. SCHWARTZ

CAMBRIDGE
UNIVERSITY PRESS

CAMBRIDGE UNIVERSITY PRESS
Cambridge, New York, Melbourne, Madrid, Cape Town, Singapore,
São Paulo, Delhi, Dubai, Tokyo, Mexico City

Cambridge University Press
32 Avenue of the Americas, New York, NY 10013-2473, USA

www.cambridge.org
Information on this title: www.cambridge.org/9780521124539

First published 2010

Printed in the United States of America

*A catalog record for this publication is available from the British Library.*

*Library of Congress Cataloging in Publication data*
Early Brazil : a documentary collection to 1700 / edited by Stuart B.
Schwartz ; translated by Clive Willis and Stuart B. Schwartz.
p.   cm.
Includes bibliographical references and index.
ISBN 978-0-521-19833-2 (hardback) – ISBN 978-0-521-12453-9 (pbk.)
1. Brazil – History – To 1821 – Sources.   I. Schwartz, Stuart B.   II. Title.
F2524.E275   2010
981'.01–dc22        2010006637

ISBN 978-0-521-19833-2 Hardback
ISBN 978-0-521-12453-9 Paperback

# CONTENTS

Maps begin on page xxii

# PREFACE

This collection of documents, many of which are translated here for the first time in English and some of which have not been published before in any language, has been selected to bring to students and general readers basic texts of early Brazilian history. As such, they are part of the broad topic of Europe's expansion in the early modern era and, specifically, of Portugal's role in that process and in the encounter and clash of peoples and cultures that it set in motion. After Vasco da Gama reached India and returned to Portugal in 1498, the way had been opened for trade with Asia by way of the Cape of Good Hope. A second expedition of thirteen ships sailed for India in March 1500 under the command of Pedro Alvares Cabral, but on the outward voyage, its route out into the Atlantic, taken to avoid the contrary winds and currents along the West African coast, brought this fleet to an unexpected landfall on what most (but not all) historians believe was, to Europeans at least, an unknown shore.[1] First contact with the local inhabitants was peaceful; the Portuguese carried out a little trade and exploration; a cross was erected on Friday, the first of May; and a mass was celebrated. The fleet's secretary, Pero Vaz de Caminha penned a report in the form of a letter to the king (I-1) about the new land. A ship was dispatched back to Lisbon, and the remainder of the fleet then proceeded on the Cape route toward India. Cabral called the new land the "Island of the True Cross" but that denomination was soon replaced by "Land of the Holy Cross," and then in practice by other less spiritual designations. Some of the early mariners referred to this coast as "the "land of parrots," others called it the "land of the bedsheets" because the white sand of the beaches looked as though

---

1 The so-called policy of secrecy or governmental control of information has been expounded by a number of authors. The implication is that earlier Portuguese voyages of exploration in the Atlantic had already made contact with Brazil but, for diplomatic reasons and the desire to exclude competitors, had kept the information secret. Although there is no documentary evidence of the policy, its existence would help to explain the seemingly peculiar route of Cabral's voyage and the success of including Brazil in the Portuguese sphere in the subsequent negotiations with Castile in the Treaty of Tordesillas (1494). See Jaime Cortesão, *A política de sigilio nos descobrimentos* (Lisbon, 1960); Luís de Albuquerque, *Dúvidas e certezas na história dos descobrimentos* (Lisbon, 1990).

sheets had been laid out on the shore, but the most popular name soon became *Brazil*, a word of debated etymology derived either from the legends of a mystical Atlantic island named "Brasyl" or from the valuable reddish wood that seemed the color of embers (*brasas*) extracted from the large brazilwood trees that grew in the forests of the new land. In the sixteenth century, in the age of tapestries and before the age of chemical dyes, the color red was particularly hard to produce, and so word of the new Portuguese "discovery" spread rapidly (I-2). Other Europeans, especially French merchants and sailors from Normandy and Brittany, also began to explore the Brazilian coast, contact the indigenous inhabitants, and trade for brazilwood. Despite this competition, the Portuguese crown remained more interested in the spices and riches of India than in a land of naked "gentiles," parrots, and dyewood.

For the first thirty years or so, the Crown turned to private individuals who, under royal contract, would exploit the dyewood and in return take on the task of further exploration and defense, recognizing royal sovereignty but, in effect, assuming the burdens of control. This system had been used previously on the coast of West Africa in the Atlantic islands, and the small outposts and trading stations under the direction of a manager were much like the "factories" (*feitorias*) that had organized trade in those places. The Portuguese claims, although recognized by Castile in the Treaty of Tordesillas (1494), remained in question, and both Spanish expeditions and French interlopers continued to visit the Brazilian coast despite Portuguese diplomatic protest. The Portuguese king, Dom João III, moved to eliminate the competition for dyewood by sending naval expeditions in 1527 and then again in 1532 under Martim Afonso de Sousa, whose instructions also required the establishment of settlements. The first town, São Vicente, was established by him in that year.

By that date, it was already clear that Portugal had to assume the burden of settlement if it hoped to keep foreign rivals from seizing this territory, a desire that probably became more intense when news of the exploits of Cortés in Mexico and Pizarro in Peru reached Lisbon. Still, the Crown was committed to its Indian Ocean gambit, and so it turned once again to a combination of private initiative under royal sponsorship by redeploying an institution, the hereditary seigneury, that had medieval precedents but that had already been modified and adapted to overseas colonization in Madeira and the Azores.[2] These fifteen donations or lordships along with the title of captain were awarded between 1533 and 1535 to twelve nobles (*donatarios*)

2 H. B. Johnson, "The Donatary Captaincy in Perspective: Portuguese Backgrounds to the Settlement of Brazil," *Hispanic American Historical Review*, 52 (1974), 203–14; António Vasconcelos Saldanha, *As capitanias do Brasil. Antecedentes, desenvolvimento e extinção de um fenómeno atlântico* (Lisbon, 2001).

who, in return for extensive powers and rights of taxation, were expected to colonize and develop their grants (II-1). Within each captaincy, the lord had the power to grant lands, administer justice, found towns, and collect revenues. Some of these powers were much like those of the old feudal nobility in Portugal, and even though the Crown emphasized that these grants were not feudal, the temptation for the captains was to treat them as such.

The project was only partially successful. Most of the donataries had no Brazilian experience. Some of them did not assume the challenge at all and did nothing; the four northernmost captaincies were not settled. In others, the captains squabbled with the colonists who had their own ideas of what the juridical and social character of the new settlements should be. Most of all, there was trouble with the indigenous population, who objected to the settlements that implied the taking of land, the disruption of hunting and fishing grounds, the taking of women, and eventually the imposition of forced labor. Only in a few places did the captaincy system seem to flourish, usually because of the fortuitous combination of positive relations with the indigenous people and the introduction of a major export crop, sugar. In both the captaincies of São Vicente on the southern coast and in Pernambuco to the north, alliances through marriages, trade, or military cooperation with some indigenous peoples facilitated the process of settlement. Also in both regions, sugarcane cultivation was successfully introduced. But the shift from economic activities based on dyewood collection to that of plantation agriculture altered the relationship with the native peoples from one of the barter of trade goods for the intermittent labor of felling trees to one of constant labor, which the native peoples rejected. This led donataries such as Duarte Coelho of Pernambuco (II-2) to petition for the importation of African laborers and also to increasing levels of violence between the Portuguese and the indigenous inhabitants of Brazil.

From the very first moment of contact, the Portuguese had been both attracted and repelled by the indigenous people of Brazil. Vaz de Caminha's report had stated that these people lived in a state of innocence like Adam before the fall, and his fascination with their seemingly open sexuality was repeated by many of the first Europeans who arrived. In fact, five of Cabral's crew had tried to jump ship in order to stay. During the first decades, the Portuguese and other Europeans had developed a kind of proto-ethnography distinguishing among the various groups that spoke languages of the Tupi-Guarani family, most of whom were semisedentary agriculturalists, and the many peoples who spoke languages of other families and who were, for the most part, hunters and gatherers, and thus considered less civilized by both the Portuguese and the Tupi speakers (IV-2; V-1). The endemic warfare among the Tupi, their cannibalism, their nudity, and their seeming lack of "civilization" all provoked depreciation, but neither the Portuguese nor the French could gather dyewood without them, and many Europeans took indigenous women as wives or concubines, thereby producing increasing numbers of *mamelucos*, that is, children of mixed origins.

By 1549, the continued presence of the French on the coast, growing hostility with the indigenous peoples of the coast, and the failure of a number of the captaincies moved the Crown to attempt a reorganization of the colony. In that year, a large expedition was sent out under Tomé de Sousa as governor-general to establish a royal capital. He founded the city of Salvador on the Bay of All Saints in the captaincy of Bahia, a place where the donatary had died at the hands of the Indians and where a small settlement already existed, to some extent the result of the presence of a Portuguese man who had married and settled among the Tupinambá around the bay (III-2). The expedition included royal treasury and judicial officers as well as six Jesuit missionaries. There were also about a thousand penal exiles that had been sent to colonize. The instructions (III-1) given to de Sousa authorized him to distribute lands and to promote the sugar economy, and they extended broad powers to him as governor. The successful donataries such as Duarte Coelho of Pernambuco disliked this infringement on their authority, but there was little they could do.

The royal governors, Tomé de Sousa and his successors, especially the legally trained Mem de Sá (1558–74), began to confront the central problems of the colony, brutally eliminating Indian resistance, fostering the sugar economy, and sponsoring the intensive missionary activities of the Jesuits (III-4, 5). Chief among these challenges was the continuing presence of the French, now in the form of a colony at Guanabara Bay, which included Huguenot participation and which had allied with a number of indigenous groups along the southern coast. Mem de Sá initiated a campaign against this colony of "Antarctic France" (IV-1, 2) and, after heavy fighting from 1565 to 1567, finally destroyed it (III-6, 7). In 1567, the Portuguese established their own city of Rio de Janeiro on the bay as the seat of a second royal captaincy, but at this time, it was a settlement far less important than Bahia or Pernambuco, where the sugar industry was now in full swing. By 1593, those two captaincies were producing more than 80 percent of the colony's income.[3]

The growth of that industry and its need for large numbers of laborers led to the increasing enslavement of Indians by the colonists at the same time that Jesuit missionary activities and the foundation of missionary villages, or *aldeias*, were growing. Jesuit activities throughout the colony had expanded under the leadership of men such as Fathers Manoel da Nóbrega and José de Anchieta, who led the struggle to eliminate the worst abuses of the Indians,

3 Harold B. Johnson, "The Settlement of Brazil, 1500–1580," in *Colonial Brazil*, Leslie Bethell, ed. (Cambridge: Cambridge University Press, 1987), p. 37.

improve colonist morality, and promote the religious life of the colony. Jesuit colleges were found in every major town, and eventually Jesuit sugar estates and ranches were also developed to support these activities. Even though there were only 110 Jesuits in all Brazil in 1574, their impact was enormous (V-3). Still, the colonists seeking workers objected to interference from the missionaries.

Both sides, colonists and Jesuits, sought to convince the Crown that they were best suited to make the Indians useful subjects of the Crown, and on the frontiers such as the interior of the southern region of São Paulo, an economy based on indigenous slavery persisted (V-5). However, legislation limiting enslavement of the native inhabitants in 1570, 1585, and 1609, despite loopholes, made it clear that access to indigenous laborers would be limited (V-4). Moreover, epidemic diseases devastated the indigenous populations in the 1560s, so that the expensive alternative of importing African slaves became increasingly attractive to the sugar planters in need of laborers. By the end of the century, despite colonist complaints, the transition to African labor was well on its way, and the sugar economy was booming. The number of sugar mills had reached 192 by 1612, and the colony was exporting 10,000 metric tons a year. The levels of African importation rose in the seventeenth century to approximately 7,000 to 8,000 a year. Despite this growth, Brazil still only represented a small fraction of the income of the Portuguese Crown, far behind the percentage generated by India. No wonder, then, that the kings of Portugal never included Brazil within their formal title, to the dismay of the Brazilian colonists. Still, the growth of the sugar economy was bringing increasing trade to the colony, provoking the interest and jealousy of foreign merchants and states and producing social as well as political and economic effects in the colony and throughout the empire. Among these was the solidification of a slave economy and a social hierarchy based on color. Slaves reacted to this with various forms of resistance (IX-1, 2) or sought other ways to improve their condition. Slavery as a social and economic system weighed heavily on all of Brazil's inhabitants, and virtually no one – slave, free, or former slave – escaped its effects (IX-3).

Sugar was a peculiar crop that combined agriculture and industry because of the need to process the cane and extract its juice in the field. The demands of running a sugar *engenho*, or mill, and its surrounding estate or plantation (also called, by extension, an *engenho*) demanded capital, labor, land, and a variety of skilled artisans and workers (VI-1, 3). In addition, the Brazilian industry was characterized by the presence of cane farmers who supplied sugarcane to the mills on a variety of bases, often in a kind of sharecropping (VI-2). The production and commerce of sugar created the opportunities for colonial success (VI-3). The owners of the mills and some of the larger cane farmers formed social as well as economic elite, dominating local institutions of government and social prestige. Their position rested firmly on their ability to manage their estates and to control their slave force (VI-4).

As the sugar economy flourished, political changes in the Atlantic world began to draw the colony into the vortex of dynastic and political conflicts. In 1580, just as the sugar economy was expanding, a dynastic crisis in Portugal caused by the death of King Dom Sebastião led to the assumption of the throne by Philip II of Spain. Portugal was then ruled by the Spanish Hapsburgs for the next sixty years. Although political separation between the two kingdoms was maintained and at first the situation brought Portugal certain commercial advantages, such as access to Spanish silver and markets, it also drew Portugal into Spanish geopolitical involvements and wars. The Spanish Hapsburgs imposed an exclusionary trade policy on Portugal (VI-5) that cut it off from its traditional northern European partners, the English and the Dutch. These enemies of Spain now made Portuguese shipping and colonies primary targets. In 1624, the Dutch seized Salvador and held it for a year, and in 1630, they returned to capture Pernambuco and eventually most of northeastern Brazil, which they held until 1654, supporting their operation in Brazil by also taking the major Portuguese slaving ports of El Mina (1638) and Luanda (1641–8). Dutch Brazil continued to be a colony of sugar and slaves under the auspices of the Dutch West India Company, which encouraged the resident Portuguese planters to remain in place by providing religious toleration as well as capital for their sugar operations (VIII-1). Although Portugal separated from Spain in 1640 with a "restoration" of independence and the new monarch, Dom João IV, sought alliance with the French, English, and Dutch, Portugal's colonial possessions remained at risk. The Dutch did not surrender Brazil until 1654 as a result of a local uprising against the Dutch West India Company and a financial settlement negotiated with Holland. Alliance with England was cemented by a trade agreement in 1654 and a royal marriage accompanied by an enormous dowry. Meanwhile, the war against Spain dragged on until 1668 when Spain finally recognized Portugal's independence. The war had been paid for to a large extent by taxing Brazil's products: tobacco, hides, and, above all, sugar. It was at some point in the 1640s that Brazil had replaced India as the most profitable and thus most important colonial area within the Portuguese empire, but as early as the 1620s, the governors of Portugal and many residents of the colony (VII-1) had recognized that Brazil was now the key to the empire.[4] In the colony, a vibrant culture had developed, controlled to some extent by civil

4 This shift is the central theme of Edval de Souza Barros, *Negócios de tanta importância. O conselho ultramarino e a disputa pela condução da Guerra no Atlântico e no Índico* (1643–1661) (Lisbon: Centro de História de Além-Mar and Universidade dos Açores, 2008).

and religious authority, but despite the continuing efforts of the clergy (X-1) and the watchful eye of visiting officials of the Inquisition, distance from the metropolis promoted or permitted various kinds of dissent (X-2), facilitated a disregard for law, or allowed for jurisdictional conflict or the exercise of personal power (X-1). Moreover, the inequalities and abuses inherent in a slave-based economy and society overshadowed all other aspects of the colony's organization.

As Brazil emerged from the political and military challenges of the 1640s and 1650s, it was confronted by new problems. Dutch and English colonies in the Caribbean, attracted by rising sugar prices, had set up their own plantation systems, and the competition had increased the supply of sugar and the demand for slave labor, lowering the price of the former and raising that of the latter. Brazilian planters were caught in the middle at exactly the moment that the Portuguese Crown was taxing sugar to pay for its diplomatic and military needs (VI-5). Brazil still enjoyed comparative advantages as a producer, but the conjunction of competition, prices, and international relations created a situation of crisis by the 1680s. Cut off to some extent from Spanish silver, its Indian Ocean empire and trade routes seriously reduced, and its Brazilian colony faced with a lack of revenue and specie and high taxes, the Portuguese Crown tried a variety of measures: devaluating its currency in 1688, sponsoring the exploration in search of precious metals in the far reaches of its empire, and seeking new markets in Europe for its products. Its attempts to create new plantation zones in areas such as Maranhão in northern Brazil, to exploit the resources of the Amazonian region, or to tap into the trade of the Rio de la Plata region by establishing an outpost at Colônia do Sacramento in 1680 all met with only limited success (XI-1). However, the sense of disaster disappeared after 1690. The outbreak of war in Europe in 1689 (War of the League of Augsburg; King William's War, 1689–98) and the disruption of Atlantic trade by Anglo-French hostilities once again created opportunities and new demand for Portugal's colonial products – not only sugar but tobacco and hides as well, a product of the growth of ranching in the colony (XI-2). The price of sugar increased and, with it, the industry as a whole recovered. More important, the search for metals finally produced major results with gold strikes from 1695 to 1698 in the interior of southeastern Brazil (XI-3). Gold and then diamonds began to transform the shape and the nature of the colony and its relations with Portugal. From Lisbon, the discoveries of gold seemed to be part of a providential design. As Portuguese immigrants and African slaves flooded the new mining areas and as the mineral wealth flowed back to Portugal and then into the hands of its trading partners, Brazil was recognized in Lisbon and throughout Europe as the heart of the Portuguese empire – in reality, what it had already been during much of the previous century.

In comparative terms, Portuguese Brazil shared much with the other imperial establishments of the Europeans in the Americas, but it also had distinctive features that resulted both from local conditions and opportunities and from the character and intentions of the Portuguese empire of which it was a part. Brazil had been first explored as part of an ongoing process of maritime voyaging into the Atlantic and down the coast of Africa that had eventually brought the Portuguese to the Indian subcontinent and beyond. Thus, Brazil remained for a half-century as a secondary consideration. This was a situation quite unlike the roughly contemporaneous Spanish conquest of the Caribbean, Mexico, and Peru, especially after Cortés's expedition to Mexico. Although the religious and economic motivations of both Castile and Portugal were similar, the available precious metals and large sedentary peasant populations of Mexico and the Andes provided tremendous incentives for Spanish immigration and for imperial concern and intervention. America quickly became the primary Spanish imperial venture, whereas Brazil, without apparent mineral resources and seeming to offer far fewer opportunities for wealth than the spice trade with Asia, remained something of an imperial backwater. Only after 1550 was a royal governmental presence established and, even then, the development of European institutions – convents, law courts, bishoprics, and, with the exception of the Jesuits, even the presence of the missionary religious orders – was slow to develop. Unlike Spanish America, no universities were established, no separate legal system created, no printing presses introduced; neither were the Portuguese able to use existing indigenous aristocracies as intermediaries to control the large native populations as the Spanish did in the centers of their viceroyalties. Brazil remained well integrated into metropolitan institutional life. The relative ease of contact by sea from Lisbon to Salvador probably contributed to this situation but, in general, Portugal ruled Brazil as an overseas province of slight importance. When by the 1560s the sugar economy began to develop, the colony seem to resemble the Spanish Caribbean islands of Santo Domingo and Puerto Rico, except that the availability of large indigenous populations meant that their use as labor lasted longer in Brazil than in the Caribbean. The process that led to the large-scale importation of Africans, however, was the same.

By the seventeenth century, as parts of Brazil became a full-fledged plantation colony, it attracted the interest of other empires as both a target and a model. The Dutch seizure of northeastern Brazil and their capture of the West African slaving ports to supply it was an attempt to reproduce and exploit the Portuguese success. By midcentury, Dutch Brazil's failure and the deleterious effects of the fighting on Portuguese Brazil had opened the door for the Dutch, English, and French to establish their own sugar and slave colonies in the Caribbean, sometimes closely and consciously follow-ing the Brazilian example. With the exception of Surinam, however, none of them had the continental dimensions of Brazil. The Brazilian *sertão* (inte-rior) presented both challenges and opportunities that were realized with the discovery of gold in the 1690s and the subsequent movement of popu-lation inland. The Brazilian colony was to be more than an archipelago of sugar enclaves scattered along the continent's Atlantic coast and, once large deposits of mineral wealth were discovered, its government and its charac-ter began to resemble more closely that of Spanish America, its neighbor and its major continental rival.

The documents translated in this volume have been selected to illustrate a number of the principal themes in the history just outlined. Each docu-ment is accompanied by a short introduction and information on its publi-cation history or source. Clive Willis has ably translated many of the doc-uments. Given the nature and origin of the written sources, the selection of texts tends to emphasize the Portuguese as the protagonists of this his-tory rather than the indigenous peoples of Brazil or the Africans who were brought there as slaves, but the volume is not a celebratory recitation of the exploits of the mariners, explorers, missionaries, and administrators. It seeks instead to demonstrate through these documents what the business of colonial expansion was about in a practical rather than a heroic sense. Rather than emphasizing the impressive character and skills of men such as the Jesuit missionaries Manoel da Nóbrega and Antônio Vieira, the military victories of Mem de Sá, the exploits of intrepid mariners and backwoods-men, or the literary accomplishments of observers and commentators such as Ambrósio Fernandes Brandão and Gabriel Soares de Sousa, this volume focuses the mutual perceptions and interactions of Europeans (including the French and the Dutch), Native Americans, and Africans. The theme of their interaction forms a central thread that unites these selected documents as a whole. Rather than using small snippets of many documents to cover the broadest range of topics, I have decided where possible to use entire docu-ments or extensive extracts to provide a fuller accounting of some themes but also to give the reader a feel for the nature, style, and format of the cor-respondence and literary production of the sixteenth and seventeenth cen-turies. In addition, considerable attention has been given to the political and administrative structure of the colony, its institutions, and its governance. Both the French and Dutch interludes are also represented here. Economic aspects, particularly the sugar economy, have been emphasized, given the central role of that commodity in the colony's history. Many of the docu-ments also illustrate aspects of social relations – between various sectors of

colonial society: colonists and Indians, masters and slaves, plantation owners and their dependent farmers. Unlike many of the Portuguese outposts
and enclaves in Africa and Asia, Brazil became a colony of settlement with
cities and towns, a comparatively large European population, the development of agriculture, and a large number of offspring of mixed origin, as well
as a large population of African- and Brazilian-born slaves. This was a slave
society in which European social hierarchies fused with new rankings based
on race or legal status and in which patriarchal and personal authority based
on social class combined to set the parameters of Brazilian life.

Stuart B. Schwartz
Yale University

# A NOTE ON TRANSLATION

Wherever the documents and extracts that appear in this volume have been translated into English for the first time, the sole and abiding principles have been accuracy and readability, especially from a twenty-first-century and transatlantic viewpoint. At the same time, care has been taken to maintain, as far as possible, the flavor and stylistic resonance of the original texts. Whereas the vast bulk of these texts were composed in the Portuguese language of the sixteenth and seventeenth centuries, they naturally involve a variety of styles and approaches corresponding to the standpoint and perceived duties of their authors. Some were reacting to and describing the Brazil of the initial encounters with the indigenous population and couching their reports in a form that was deferential to the Portuguese monarchy. Others were reporting on the struggle to beat back their French rivals in the sixteenth century or were setting their focus on the Dutch occupation of Pernambuco in the seventeenth century. Yet others concern themselves with the growth of the sugar economy of the Northeast and with its dependence on slave labor; inevitably there figures the involvement of the Church and, particularly, of the Jesuits in their efforts to dominate and shape Brazilian colonial society. Yet *e pluribus unum*!

# A NOTE ON PORTUGUESE CURRENCY, WEIGHTS, AND MEASURES

The basic unit of accounting was the *real* (plural: *réis*).

1 vintém = 20 réis
1 tostão = 100 réis
1 cruzado = 400 réis
1 *milréis* = 1,000 réis (written 1$000)
1 conto = 1,000 milréis or 1,000,000 réis was written 1:000

## Standard Units of Weight

*Arroba* = 14.5 kilograms = 32 pounds
*Alqueire* = 36.3 kilograms (approximately 1 English bushel; 8 gallons)
*Quintal* = 100 kilograms (the English hundredweight)

## Length and Area

*Légua* (league) = approximately 5,555 to 6,000 meters = 3 to 4 miles
*Tarefa* = 4,352 square meters (in Bahia). This measure varied regionally. It was also supposedly equivalent to the amount of land needed to produce sugarcane for one day's worth of milling.

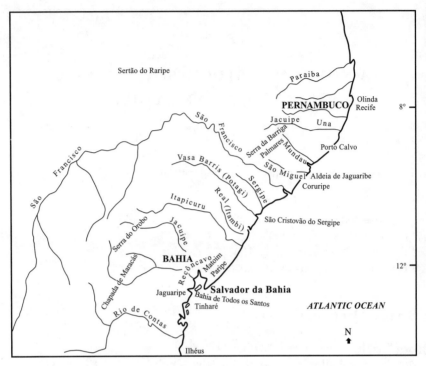

Map 1. Bahia and Pernambuco. Showing places named in the text.

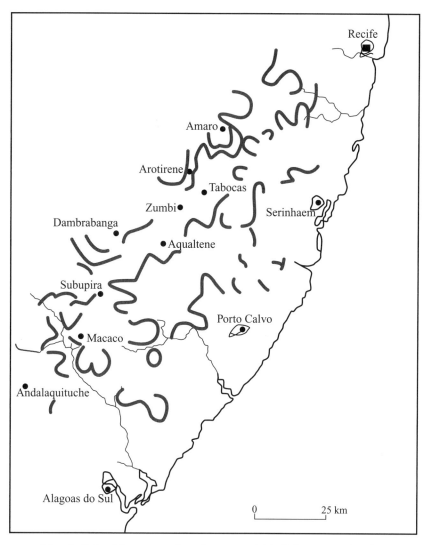

Map 2. Colonial towns and settlements within Palmares quilombo.

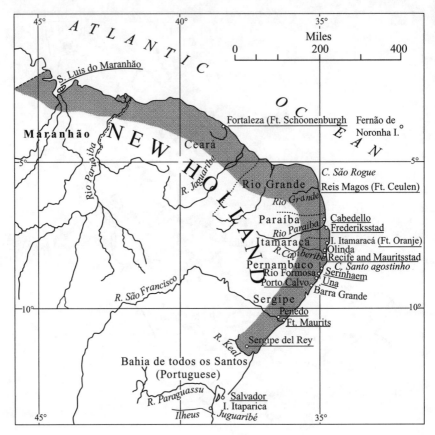

Map 3. Netherlands Brazil, 1643.

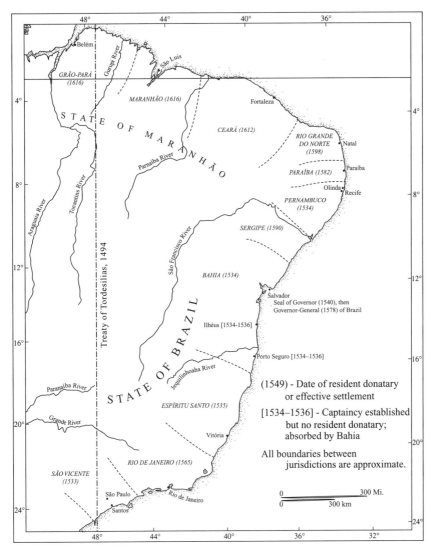

Map 4. Brazil, ca. 1650.

# 1

# THE "DISCOVERY" AND FIRST ENCOUNTERS
# WITH BRAZIL

## 1. The Letter of Pero Vaz de Caminha

*Following the return to Portugal of Vasco da Gama in 1499 after his successful voyage to India around the Cape of Good Hope, a second fleet of thirteen ships set sail from Lisbon in March 1500, commanded by Pedro Alvares Cabral, to follow the same route. In late April of that year, it made a landfall on the Brazilian coast. After briefly exploring the coast and establishing some contact with the native peoples, the main fleet continued on its way to India, but a small ship was detached to return to Portugal. It carried two letters with details on the new land and its people. The letter of Pero Vaz de Caminha is often described as the foundational document of Brazilian history. Vaz de Caminha, of a noble family from Oporto, was most likely traveling to India to take up a post as the secretary at the trading post to be established there, but he was also serving as scribe for the fleet. In many ways, his report paralleled the first letters of Columbus from the Caribbean, providing details about the geography, peoples, and conditions in the new lands. The letter of Pero Vaz de Caminha disappeared from sight until the late eighteenth century, when it was uncovered in the Portuguese royal archive. It was first published in 1817 (Aires de Casal, Corografia Brasilica [Rio de Janeiro, 1817]) and subsequently has been published in innumerable editions. (The excerpted translation presented here is from Charles David Ley, ed., Portuguese Voyages, 1498–1663, Everyman's Library, No. 986 (New York: Dutton & Co., pp. 42–45, 53–54, 56–59.)*

This same day, at the hour of vespers we sighted land, that is to say, first a very high rounded mountain, then other lower ranges of hills to the south of it, and a plain covered with large trees. The admiral named the mountain Easter Mount and the country the Land of the True Cross.

He ordered them to drop the plumb-line, and they measured twenty-five fathoms. At sunset, about six leagues from the shore we dropped anchor in nineteen fathoms, and it was a good clean anchorage. There we lay all that night. On Thursday morning we set sail and made straight for land, with the smaller ships leading the water being seventeen, sixteen, fifteen, fourteen, thirteen, twelve, ten, and nine fathoms deep, until we were half a league from the shore. Here we all cast anchor opposite a river mouth. It must have been more or less ten o'clock when we reached this anchorage.

From there we caught sight of men walking on the beaches. The small ships which arrived first said that they had seen some seven or eight of them. We let down the longboats and the skiffs. The captains of the other ships came straight to this flagship where they had speech with the admiral. He sent Nicolau Coelho on shore to examine the river. As soon as the latter began to approach it, men came out on to the beach in groups of twos and threes, so that, when the longboat reached the river mouth there were eighteen or twenty waiting.

They were dark brown and naked, and had no covering for their private parts, and they carried bows and arrows in their hands. They all came determinedly towards the boat. Nicolau Coelho made a sign to them to put down their bows, and they put them down. But he could not speak to them or make himself understood in any other way because of the waves which were breaking on the shore. He merely threw them a red cap, and a linen bonnet he had on his head, and a black hat. And one of them threw him a hat of large feathers with a small crown of red and grey feathers like a parrot's. Another gave him a large bough covered with little white beads which looked like seed-pearls. I believe that the admiral is sending these articles to Your Majesty. After this, as it was late, the expedition returned to the ships, without succeeding in having further communication with them, because of the sea.

That night there was such a strong south-easterly wind and squalls that it dragged the ships out of their position, more especially the flagship. On Friday morning at about eight o'clock, by the pilot's advice, the captain ordered the anchors to be weighed and the sails hoisted. We went up the coast to the northwards with the longboats and skiffs tied to our sterns, to see if we could find a sheltered spot to anchor in where we could stay to take in water and wood. Not that these were lacking to us, but so as to be provided with everything now, in good time. At the hour when we set sail, about sixty or seventy men had gradually come up and were seated near the river. We sailed on, and the admiral told the small ships to run under the shore and to slacken sails if they found a sufficiently protected spot for the ships.

Thus we sailed along the coast, and, ten leagues from the spot where we had weighed anchor, the aforesaid small ships found a ledge of rock which contained a very good, safe port with a very large entrance. So they went in and struck sails. The bigger ships came up behind them, and, a little while after sundown, they struck sails also, perhaps at a league from the rocks, and anchored in eleven fathoms.

Our pilot, Afonso Lopes, was in one of the small ships, and he received orders from the admiral to go in the skiff to take the soundings inside the port, for he was a lively and capable man for the work. He took up two of the men of the country from a canoe. They were young and well formed and one of them had a bow and six or seven arrows. There were many others on the shore with bows and arrows, but they did not use them. Later, in the evening, he took the two men to the flagship where they were received with great rejoicings and festivities.

They are of a dark brown, rather reddish color. They have good well-made faces and noses. They go naked, with no sort of covering. They attach no more importance to covering up their private parts or leaving them uncovered than they do to showing their faces. They are very ingenuous in that matter. They both had holes in their lower lips and a bone in them as broad as the knuckles of a hand and as thick as a cotton spindle and sharp at the end like a bodkin. They put these bones in from inside the lip and the part which is placed between the lip and the teeth is made like a rook in chess. They fit them in in such a way that they do not hurt them nor hinder them talking or eating or drinking.

Their hair is straight. They shear their hair, but leave it a certain length, not cutting it to the roots, though they shave it above the ears. One of them had on a kind of wig covered with yellow feathers which ran round from behind the cavity of the skull, from temple to temple, and so to the back of the head; it must have been about a hand's breadth wide, was very close-set and thick and covered his occiput and his ears. It was fastened, feather by feather, to his hair with a white paste like wax (but it was not wax), so that the wig was very round and full and regular, and did not need to be specially cleaned when the head was washed, only lifted up.

When they came, the admiral was seated on a chair, with a carpet at his feet instead of a dais. He was finely dressed, with a very big golden collar round his neck. Sancho de Toar, Simão de Miranda, Nicolau Coelho, Aires Correia, and the rest of us who were in the ship with him were seated on this carpet. Torches were lit. They entered. However, they made no gesture of courtesy or sign of a wish to speak to the admiral or any one else.

For all that, one of them gazed at the admiral's collar and began to point towards the land and then at the collar as if he wished to tell us that there was gold in the country. And he also looked at a silver candlestick and pointed at the land in the same way, and at the candlestick, as if there was silver there, too. We showed them a grey parrot the admiral had brought with him. They took it in their hands at once and pointed to the land, as if there were others there. We showed them a ram, but they took no notice of it. We showed them a hen, and they were almost afraid of it and did not want to take it in their hands; finally they did, but as if alarmed by it. We gave them things to eat: bread, boiled fish, comfits, sweetmeats, cakes, honey, dried figs. They would hardly eat anything of all this, and, if they tasted it, they spat it out at once. We brought them wine in a cup; they merely sipped it, did not like it at all, and did not want any more of it. We brought them water in a pitcher, and they each took a mouthful, but did not drink it; they just put it in their mouths and spat it out.

One of them saw the white beads of a rosary. He made a sign to be given them and was very pleased with them, and put them round his neck. Then he took them off and put them round his arm, pointing to the land, and again at the beads and at the captain's collar, as if he meant they would give gold for them.

We took it in this sense, because we preferred to. If, however, he was trying to tell us that he would take the beads and the collar as well, we did not choose to understand him, because we were not going to give it to him. Then he returned the beads to the man who had given them to him. Finally, they lay on their backs on the carpet to sleep. They did not try to cover up their private parts in any way; these were uncircumcised and had their hairs well shaved and arranged.

The admiral ordered one of his cushions to be put under either of their heads, and the one in the wig took care that this should not be spoiled. They had a cloak spread over them. They consented to this, pulled it over themselves, and slept.

On the Saturday morning, the admiral ordered the sails to be hoisted. We approached the entrance, which was very broad, and some six or seven fathoms in depth. All the ships entered it and anchored in five or six fathoms. The anchorage was so good and fine and safe inside that more than two hundred ships and vessels could lie in it. As soon as the ships had taken up their positions and anchored, all the captains came to this flagship. Now the admiral ordered Nicolau Coelho and Bartolomeu Dias to go on shore and take the two men and let them go with their bows and arrows. He also ordered each of them to be given a new shirt, a red bonnet, a rosary of white beads of bone, which they put on their arms, a varvel, and a bell. And he sent with them, to remain there, a banished youth of the household of Dom João Telo, named Afonso Ribeiro, who was to stay with them there and learn about their lives and their customs. I, also, was told to accompany Nicolau Coelho.

We saw them closer to and more at our leisure that day because we had nearly all intermingled. Some were painted in quarters with those paints, others by halves, and others all over, like a tapestry. They all had their lips pierced; some had bones on them, though many had not. Some wore spiky green seed-shells off some tree, which were colored like chestnut shells, though they were much smaller. These were full of little red berries which, on being squeezed, squirted out a very red juice with which they dyed themselves. The more they wet themselves after being dyed with this red, the redder they become. They were all shaven to above the ears; likewise, their eyelids and eye-lashes were shaven. All their foreheads are painted with black paint from temple to temple. This gives the impression of their wearing a ribbon round them two inches wide.

The admiral ordered the exile, Afonso Ribeiro, and the two other exiles to mix in amongst them. And he told Diogo Dias, of Sacavém, to do the same, since he was a merry fellow and knew how to amuse them. He told the exiles to stay there that night. So they all went in amongst those people.

As they afterwards related, they went a good league and a half to a hamlet of nine or ten houses. They said those houses were each as big as this flagship. They were made of wooden planks sideways on, had roofs of straw, and were fairly high. Each enclosed a single space with no partitions, but a number of posts. High up from post to post ran nets, in which they slept. Down below they lit fires to warm themselves. Each house had two little doors, one at one end and one at the other. Our men said that thirty or forty people were lodged in each house, and they saw them there. They gave our men such food as they had, consisting of plenty of *inhame* and other seeds there are in the country which they eat. It was getting late, however, and they soon made all our men turn back, for they would not let any of them stay. They even wanted to come with them, our men said. Our men exchanged some varvels and other small things of little value which they had brought with them for some very large and beautiful red parrots and two small green ones, some caps of green feathers, and a cloth of many colors, also of feathers, a rather beautiful kind of material, as Your Majesty will see when you receive all these things, for the admiral says he is sending them to you. So our men came back, and we returned to our ships.

After our meal on the Tuesday, we went on shore to fetch water and wood and to wash our clothes. There were sixty or seventy on the beach without bows or anything else when we arrived. As soon as we landed, they came up to us straight away and did not try to escape. Also many others came up later, a good two hundred, and all without bows. They came in amongst us so readily that some of them helped us to carry out the wood and put it in the boats. They vied with our men in doing this, and it gave them great pleasure. Whilst we were gathering wood, two carpenters formed a large cross out of a piece which had been cut for the purpose the day before. Many of them came and stood around the carpenters. I believe they did so more to see the iron tool it was being made with than to see the cross. For they have nothing made of iron and cut their wood and sticks with stones fashioned like wedges which they fit into a stick between two laths which they tie up very tightly to make them secure. (The men who had been to their houses told us this, because they had seen it there.) They were by now so intimate with us that they almost hindered us in what we had to do.

The admiral sent the two exiles and Diogo Dias back to the village they had visited (or to others, if they should obtain knowledge of any others), telling them not to come back to the ship to sleep in any case, even if they were sent away. So they went off.

Whilst we were cutting timber in the wood, some parrots flew through the trees. Some were green, others grey, some big, others little. It seems to me, after this, that there must be many of them in this land, even though there cannot have been more than nine or ten of those I saw, if so many. We did not see any other birds on that occasion, except some rock pigeons which seemed to me considerably bigger than those in Portugal. Many say they saw doves, but I did not see them. However, as the trees are very tall and thick and of an infinite variety, I do not doubt but that there are many birds in this jungle. Near nightfall, we returned to the ships with our wood.

The admiral had said when we had left the boat that it would be best if we went straight to the cross which was leaning against a tree near the river ready to be set up on the next day, Friday; we ought then all to kneel and kiss it so that they could see the respect we had for it. We did so and signed to the ten or twelve who were there to do the same, and they at once all went and kissed it.

They seem to be such innocent people that if we could understand their speech and they ours, they would immediately become Christians, seeing that, by all appearances, they do not understand about any faith. Therefore, if the exiles who are to remain here learn their speech and understand them, I do not doubt but that they will follow that blessed path Your Majesty is desirous they should and become Christians and believe in our holy religion. May it please God to bring them to a knowledge of it, for truly these people are good and have a fine simplicity. Any stamp we wish may be easily printed on them, for the Lord has given them good bodies and good faces, like good men. I believe it was not without cause that He brought us here. Therefore, Your Majesty who so greatly wishes to spread the Holy Catholic faith may look for their salvation. Pray God it may be accomplished with few difficulties.

They do not plough or breed cattle. There are no oxen here, nor goats, sheep, fowls, nor any other animal accustomed to live with man. They only eat this *inhame*, which is very plentiful here, and those seeds and fruits that the earth and the trees give of themselves. Nevertheless, they are of a finer, sturdier, and sleeker condition than we are for all the wheat and vegetables we eat.

While they were there that day, they danced and footed it continuously with our people to the sound of one of our tambourines, as if they were more our friends than we theirs. If we signed to them asking them if they wanted to come to our ships, they at once came forward ready to come. So that if we had invited them all, they would all have come. We did not, however, take more than four or five with us that night. The admiral took two, Simão de Miranda one whom he took as a page, and Aires Gomes another, also as a page. One of those whom the admiral took was one of the guests who had been brought him when we first arrived here; on this day, he came dressed in his shirt and his brother with him. That night they were very handsomely created, not only in the way of food, but also to a bed with mattress and sheets, the better to tame them.

To-day, Friday, 1st May, in the morning, we went on shore with our banner. We made our way up the river and disembarked on the southern bank at a place where it seemed best to us to set up the cross so that it might be seen to the best advantage. There the admiral marked the place for a pit to be made to plant the cross in. Whilst they were digging this, he and all of us went for the cross, down the river to where it was. We brought it from there as in a procession, with the friars and priests singing in front of us. There were a quantity of people about, some seventy or eighty. When they saw us coming, some of them went to help us to support the cross. We passed over the river along by the beach. We then went to set up the cross where it was to be at some two bow-shots from the river. When we went to do this, a good hundred and fifty of those people and more came up. The cross was then planted, with Your Majesty's arms and motto on it, which had before been fastened to it, and they set up an altar by its side. Friar Henrique said Mass there, and the singing and officiating was done by the others who have been already mentioned. About fifty or sixty of the people of the place were at the Mass all on their knees as we were. When the Gospel came and we all stood with uplifted hands, they arose with us, lifted their hands, and stayed like that till it was ended. After which they again sat, as we did. When God's Body was elevated and we knelt, they all knelt and lifted their hands as we did and were so silent that I assure Your Majesty it much increased our devotion.

They stayed with us thus until the Communion was over. After the Communion, the friars and priests communicated, as did the admiral and some of us. Since the sun was very strong, some of them arose whilst we were communicating, but others stayed to the end. Amongst those who stayed was a man of fifty or fifty-five years old – or rather he came up amongst those already there and also called others to come. He went in amongst them and spoke to them pointing to the altar and afterwards at Heaven, as if he were speaking to a good purpose. We took it so.

When Mass was over, the priest removed his vestments, and mounted on a chair near the altar in his surplice. He preached to us on the Gospel and about the Apostles whose day it was. At the end of the sermon, he referred to the aim of your most holy and virtuous quest, which caused much devoutness.

The men who stayed all through the sermon looked at him as we did. The one I have spoken of called others to come. Some came and some went. At the end of the sermon, Nicolau Coelho brought a number of tin crucifixes which had remained over from his former journey. It was thought well that those people should each have one hung round their necks. Friar Henrique stood beside the cross for this purpose. There he hung a crucifix round each of their necks, first making him kiss it and raise his hands. Many came for this. All who came, some forty or fifty, had crucifixes hung round their necks.

At last, a good hour after midday, we went to the ships to eat. The admiral took with him the man who had pointed out the altar and Heaven to the others; he also took a brother of his. The admiral did him much honor and gave him a Moorish shirt and his brother a shirt like the others had had.

My opinion and every one's opinion is that these people lack nothing to become completely Christian except understanding us; for they accepted as we do all they saw us do, which makes us consider that they have no idolatry or worship. I believe that if Your Majesty could send someone who could stay awhile here with them, they would all be persuaded and converted as Your Majesty desires. Therefore, if any one is coming out here, let him not omit to bring a clergyman to baptize them. For, by that time, they will have knowledge of our religion through the two exiles who are remaining with them, who also communicated to-day.

Only one woman came with those who were with us to-day. She was young and stayed throughout the Mass. We gave her a cloth to cover herself with and put it around her. But she did not pull it down to cover herself when she sat down. Thus, Sire, the innocence of Adam himself was not greater than these people's, as concerns the shame of the body. Your Majesty will judge if people who live in such innocence could be converted or no if they were taught the things that belong to their salvation.

Our last action was to go and kiss the cross in their presence. We then took our leave and went to eat.

I think, Sire, that two cabin-boys will also stay with the exiles we are leaving here, for they escaped to land in the skiff to-night and have not returned again. We think, I say, that they will stay, because, if God be willing, we are taking our departure from here in the morning.

It appears to me, Sire, that the coast of this country must be a good twenty or twenty-five leagues in length from the most southerly point we saw to the most northerly point we can see from this port. In some parts, there are great banks along by the shore, some of which are red and some white; inland it is all flat and very full of large woods. All the coastal country from one point to the other is very flat and very beautiful. As to the jungle, it seemed very large to us seen from the sea; for, look as we would, we could see nothing but land and woods, and the land seemed very extensive. Till now we have been unable to learn if there is gold or silver or any other kind of metal or iron there; we have seen none. However, the air of the country is very healthful, fresh, and as temperate as that of Entre Douro e Minho; we have found the two climates alike at this season. There is a great plenty, an infinitude of waters. The country is so well-favored that if it were rightly cultivated, it would yield everything, because of its waters.

For all that, the best fruit that could be gathered hence would be, it seems to me, the salvation of these people. That should be the chief seed for Your Majesty to scatter here. It would be enough reason, even if this was only a rest-house on the voyage to Calicut. How much more so will it be if there is a will to accomplish and perform in this land what Your Majesty so greatly desires, which is the spreading of our holy religion.

Thus, I have given Your Majesty an account of what I have seen in this land. If at some length, Your Majesty will pardon me, since my desire to tell you all made me relate it with such minuteness. And since, Sire, Your Majesty may be sure of my very faithful service in my present duties as in whatever may do you service, I beg of you as a signal favor that you send for Jorge de Ossório, my son-in-law, from the island of São Tomé – I should take this as a great kindness from you.

I kiss Your Majesty's hands.

From this Pôrto-Seguro, in Your Majesty's island of Vera Cruz, to-day, Friday, 1st May 1500.

## 2. An Early Report of Brazil

*After Cabral's landfall in 1500, a number of Spanish- and Portuguese-sponsored voyages visited the eastern coasts of South America as far south as the Straits of Magellan. News of these explorations and of the flora, fauna, and peoples they encountered began to circulate in Europe, often in the form of published correspondence or in inexpensive newsletters. The famous 1504 letter of Amerigo Vespucci is an example of the wide diffusion of information that such notices could achieve. The following text, originally published in German as* Copia der newen Zeytung ausz Presillig Landt, *had a more limited impact, but it is a good example of this type of literature. Probably written by a German merchant resident in Madeira in 1514, it describes the results of an expedition to the coasts of southern Brazil and the Rio de la Plata region of South America. Filled with a combination of erroneous, accurate, curious, and fanciful information, the document contains notable references to the indigenous peoples and their customs and to the purported existence of gold and silver. The final paragraph also reveals the reality of*

*a commerce already developing in the export of brazilwood and indicates that some
enslavement or hostage-taking of the inhabitants of the new land had already begun.
The text was originally published by John Parker, ed., Tidings Out of Brazil, trans.
Mark Graubard (Minneapolis: University of Minnesota Press, 1957), pp. 28–34.*

## TIDINGS OUT OF BRAZIL

KNOW ye that on the twelfth day of the month of October a ship arrived
here from Presillg (Brazil) to obtain provisions. This ship had been equipped
by Nono and by Cristoffel de Haro and others. There were two ships which
were given permission by the king of Portugal to chart or explore the land
of Brazil, and they have charted the land for six or seven hundred miles
in extent beyond any knowledge previously held. When they came to the
Capo de Bona Speranza (Cape of Good Hope) which is a point or promontory jutting out into the ocean at the level of Nort Assril and perhaps one
degree higher or further in latitude, and when they had arrived in such climate or region, namely around forty degrees of latitude, they found Brazil
with a cape which is a point or place extending into the ocean. And they
sailed around or passed this very cape and found that the same gulf lies as
Europe does, with the side lying *ponente levante* (west to east), that is, situated
between sunrise or east and sunset or west.

Then they saw land on the other side as well when they had sailed a distance of sixty miles along the cape in the same manner as when one travels
toward the east and passes the Stritta de Gibilterra (Strait of Gibraltar) and
sees the land of the Berbers. And when they had come around the cape as
stated and sailed or traveled northwestward toward us, there arose so great
a storm and also such a wind that they were unable to sail or travel further.
Hence, they had to sail through *tramontana*, that is, northward or midnight,
and back again to the other side and coast which is the land of Brazil.

The pilot, namely the ship's guide who sails with this ship, is a very
good friend of mine. He is also the most famous in the service of the king
of Portugal. He has made several journeys to India. He tells me he believes
that from this cape of Brazil, which is the outermost part of Brazil, it cannot
be more than six hundred miles to Malacca. He contemplates also in a short
time to undertake such a voyage from Lisbon to Malacca and return, which
will bring to the king of Portugal much profit with respect to his spice trade.

They discover also that the land of Brazil extends toward Malacca, and
as they came again to the coast or side of Brazil toward the westward, they
found many good rivers and harbors which they then navigated. All of this
region is full of people and very habitable, and they say the nearer the cape
the more prosperous are the people, being of good manners and honorable

character with no vices at all except that they wage war, one village upon another. They do not eat one another as is the custom in lower Brazil, but they do kill each other and take no captives. It is said that the people enjoy a rather good, free condition and that they are of good disposition.

The people on that coast have no laws, nor have they a king. They do, however, honor the elders among them and give obedience to them in the same manner as in lower Brazil. They are all one people although they speak another language. Also on this same coast, they cherish the memory of Saint Thomas. They wished also to show the Portuguese his footprints in the hinterland, and also to point out the cross standing in the interior. And when they speak of Saint Thomas they refer to him as the lesser god. There is, however, another god which is greater. It may well be believed that they do have memory of Saint Thomas for it is known that the body of this Saint is actually buried beyond Malacca on the coast of Siramatl in the Gulf of Ceylon. They frequently name their children Thomas in that land.

In the hinterland are high mountains. They say in some regions the snow never disappears, so they heard it reported by the natives. They visited several ports where they found many and varied kinds of unusual skins of wild animals. The people wear them raw over their bare skin as they do not know how to prepare them. There are, namely, furs of lions and leopards which are numerous in the land, lynx and genet which are caught in Spain, and also small skins that resemble genet and are excellent like those of lynx when they are rich of hair and thin of skin like a marten. The large furs of the leopards and lynx they cut up and make belts of them one span in width.

There is also to be found much otter and beaver, an indication that the land has large flowing rivers. They also have belts made of furs unknown to me. The above-named furs which to a considerable extent were raw I bought for myself, but not many of them since they brought no large quantity of such unprepared skins. They say they did not seek to obtain them because they considered them to be of no value.

They assert that the second ship which is still behind is bringing many such skins and various other things because they took more time in loading them. There is also one captain of the two ships. Among other things I have also bought three pieces of several hides sewn together. The three are almost large enough to make a lining for one coat. The Portuguese have disregarded these, but the natives cover themselves with them and have them sewn together in the same manner as we make blankets of wolfskin. It is truly an excellent lining in itself. The skins are each as large as that of a badger and have the color of a stag. There is on the skin a very coarse wool with long, pointed hair, somewhat thick, resembling sable. The fur on the inside is light as that of a marten. The skin itself has an exceptionally agreeable odor.

The country yields a wonderful abundance of fruits of good quality, and different from what we have in our lands. They also found in that country cana fistola the size of an arm's length. They also have beeswax, a gum similar to gloret, and many different kinds of birds with rough feet.

Their defensive weapons consist of hand bows, as is the custom in lower Brazil. They have no iron mines. In exchange for an axe or hatchet or knife, they give us whatever they have as is likewise the custom in lower Brazil. They have also in that land a kind of spice which burns on the tongue as pepper, even stronger. It grows in a pod with many kernels growing within it. The grain or kernel is the size of a pea.

You should also be informed that they brought sufficient evidence that, as already mentioned, they visited a port and river about two hundred miles opposite us from the cape. There they found evidence of much silver and gold, also of copper which is to be found in the interior. They say that the captain of the other ship is bringing to the king of Portugal a silver axe or hatchet which is much like their axes of stone. He also brings him a metal which they say is like brass and is not subject to rust or damage, and they do not know whether it is made of inferior gold or what it is. They have learned at the same location on the coast from the same people that further inland there is a mountain people having much gold. They wear the gold thinly plated in the same manner as an armor over the forehead and in front of the chest.

The captain also brings a man from that same land who wishes to see the king of Portugal. He claims he wants to convey to the king of Portugal evidence of so much gold and silver to be found in the land that his ships will not be able to carry it. The people of that locality assert also that at times other ships had visited them and the men were dressed like us. This, and that they have beards almost all red, the Portuguese assert as do the French from the natives' description. The honorable Portuguese would say that they are *Gezyner* who are sailing toward Malacca. There is evidence that this is true since it is known that in Malacca silver and copper can be bought to better advantage than in our countries.

Here then you have the latest tidings. The ship below deck is laden with brazilwood and above deck is full of purchased young boys and girls which cost the Portuguese little since most of them were offered voluntarily, for these people actually believe their children are traveling to the Promised Land. They also say that the natives in that land survive to an age of one hundred and forty years.

# 2

## THE DONATARIAL SYSTEM

*During the two decades after the Portuguese first arrived on the Brazilian coast, their presence remained occasional and intermittent, limited in the main to the visits of small ships loading dyewood. The Portuguese Crown made efforts to clear foreign competitors, especially Norman and Breton ships, from the coast, and to that end Martim Afonso de Sousa captained an expedition in 1532 that sought to ensure Portugal's control of the new land. Acting on his advice and that of his cousin, the powerful courtier Dom António de Ataíde, the king Dom João III divided the coast into territorial grants that could be assigned to individuals who would assume the responsibility of protecting, settling, and developing their areas. The coast was divided into fifteen parcels called hereditary captaincies, and these were assigned to twelve Portuguese courtiers and soldiers, mostly members of the lesser nobility. Each man who received an award, or carta de doação, was called a donatario. Each recipient bore the title of captain as well.*

*The apparent model for these grants was the Portuguese senhorio, or seignory, which awarded rights and privileges in perpetuity but was not based on feudal obligations. The rights of taxation, justice, administration, and the privileges to promote settlement and economic development were conceded and detailed by the king. The donation that delineated the relationship between the donatario and the king was accompanied by a foral that spelled out the obligations of the colonists to the donatary captains. In the Middle Ages, these had been granted by the lord to the people in his domain, but by the time of the settlement of Brazil, the Crown had taken upon itself the granting of these documents, thus reducing the independence of the nobility. The donatarial captaincies were an imaginative adaptation of Portuguese medieval precedents to the challenge of colonization but proved in the long term to be unsatisfactory. Some areas were never settled; others floundered because of neglect, wars with native peoples, and internal dissension. Nevertheless, the captaincies provided the first administrative structure for the settlement of the colony.*

## 1. A Royal Charter for the Captaincy of Pernambuco, Issued to Duarte Coelho on 24 September 1534

(From *História da Colonização Portuguesa do Brasil* [Oporto, 1924], vol. III, pp. 312–13).

King John [III] etc. To all those to whom this letter is addressed I wish it to be known that, with all due favor, I have now made a land donation[1] to Duarte Coelho, a nobleman of my household, for him and for all his children, grandchildren, heirs and successors, in perpetuity. This grant will ensure the due interest and inheritance relating to the captaincy and will ensure the government of sixty leagues of my territory along the coast of Brazil. This territory starts in the south at the River São Francisco, at the Cape of Santo Agostinho,[2] and ends [in the north] at the River Santa Cruz, which is in line with that cape. All this is more fully set out in the Charter of Donation that I have issued to him regarding that territory. It is highly important to have a charter stating the rentals, taxes, and other levies which have to be paid, not only those due to me and to the Crown, but also those due to the captain by virtue of his land donation. Being aware of the quality of this territory, I now once more command that it be inhabited, populated, and developed, since it is expedient that this be done in the most suitable manner and as soon as possible. I consider this decree to be in the service of God and in my own interest, as well as that of the captain and inhabitants of the territory. As I am pleased to grant them this favor, I have deemed it appropriate to order that this charter be drawn up in the following form and manner.

Firstly, the captain of the captaincy and his successors shall distribute all the territory as land grants to any persons of class and standing who are freely Christians. There shall be no charge or duty other than the tithe which the latter will be obliged to pay, as laid down by Our Lord and Master Jesus Christ, on everything that they possess on that land. The land grants shall be given in the form and manner contained in my royal decrees, but no land grants may be assumed by the captain and his successors, nor by any wife or child who are not[3] heirs to the captaincy. However, they may issue land to others of their children who are not heirs to the captaincy and, indeed to their relatives, as is set down in the Charter of Donation. A land grant may

1 This document is a royal charter (or *carta de foral*) that sets out the legal and fiscal requirements for a given territory. A land donation (or *doação*) was a concession made to the captains (the *donatários* or "donees") of vast horizontal bands of colonial Brazil. Such donations were distinct from the subsidiary *sesmarias* (or land grants) that the donees subsequently distributed.
2 This southern demarcation is vague. The river and the cape are separated by the modern state of Alagoas.
3 This negative is obviously erroneous. The system was intended to separate occupancy of the captaincy from the holding of specific *sesmarias*, or land grants.

be held by any one of their children who is not an heir to the captaincy or, indeed, by any other person, yet the inheritance of the captaincy may chance to pass to that child or person. In such circumstances, that child or person shall be obliged to relinquish the land grant to another person, after one year from the date on which it shall have been inherited. If he does not relinquish it within the said period, he shall forfeit the land grant to me and shall be required to pay a sum equal to its value. I command the factor or financial agent who represents me in the captaincy that, should this occur, he shall at once take possession of the land on my behalf. He must also order the matter to be written down in the book of my exchequer and shall establish the value of the land. Should he not do this, he shall lose his position and pay to me the value of the land from his own estate.

If there are in the captaincy, along its coasts, or in its rivers and bays, any type of precious stones, pearls, seed-pearls, gold, silver, coral, copper, tin, lead or other sort of metal, I will be paid a fifth, of which fifth the captain shall receive a tithe as laid down in his Charter of Donation. The amount of the tithe shall be paid to him at the time when the fifth is collected for me by my officials.

The brazilwood in the captaincy and any spices or drugs of any type found there shall belong to me and shall always belong to me and my successors, and neither the captain nor any other person may deal in these things nor sell them there. Nor may they export them to my realms or territories or beyond them. Whoever acts to the contrary shall forfeit his entire estate to the Crown and shall be exiled to the island of São Tomé for life. As to the brazilwood, it is my wish that the captain and the settlers in the captaincy make use of it for whatever purpose they might need it, except that they may not burn it, for if they do so they shall incur the above penalties.

Any fish caught in the captaincy that is not caught by rod incurs a tithe, being one fish for every ten so caught. It is also my wish that a further half-tithe be paid, which is one fish in every twenty, which the captain shall collect for himself, as stated in the Charter of Donation.

Should the captain and settlers and inhabitants of the captaincy themselves deliver (or arrange such delivery through other parties) to my realms or territories any type of merchandise which is available in that land (other than slaves and the other things that are prohibited above), they may do so. They shall receive welcome and shelter in any ports, cities, towns, or places in my realms or territories to which they take their goods. They shall not be obliged to unload their merchandise, nor to sell it, in any of the ports, cities, or towns against their will, should they wish to go elsewhere to make their profit. When they sell their goods in the aforesaid places in my realms or territories, they shall not pay any duty on them other than the transfer tax on what they have sold. However, under the specific charters, regulations, or by-laws of such places, they shall be obliged to pay other duties or taxes.

They may sell their merchandise to whomsoever they wish and take it outside the kingdom if they so wish, in spite of any charters, regulations, or by-laws there may be to the contrary.

All the ships of my realms and territories that travel to that territory[4] bearing merchandise on which they have paid duty here in my customs houses and that show a certificate from my officials shall not pay any duty in Brazil. Should they deliver any merchandise, taken from there to places outside my kingdom, then they shall pay me, on their departure from Brazil, a tithe of which the captain shall have his share as stated in his Charter of Donation. However, should they bring the merchandise to my realms or territories, they shall not pay anything on leaving. Those who bring the merchandise to my realms or territories shall be obliged to take or send to the captaincy within a year a certificate from my customs houses where they unloaded, stating how they unloaded, the type of merchandise, and the quantity. Should they not produce the certificate within the stated time, they shall pay a tithe on the merchandise or on that part which they do not unload in my realms or territories. Moreover, they shall have to pay the tithe in the captaincy, if they unloaded outside the kingdom. If it is a person who is not returning to the captaincy, he shall pay a deposit to the value of the tithe within the stated period of a year and send a certificate of how the produce was unloaded in my realms or territories. Should he not produce the certificate within the given time, the tithe shall be collected from the deposit.

Any foreigners who are not subjects of my realms or territories and who take or send to the territory any merchandise, though they transport them from sundry kingdoms or lands and though they have paid a tithe here, shall pay me on arrival a further tithe on the merchandise that they are carrying. If they load merchandise in the captaincy to take out of the territory, they shall pay the same tithe on the merchandise on leaving. The captain shall have his share of such tithes, as is set out in his Charter of Donation, and the share shall be given to him by my officials at the time that they are collected on my behalf.

As to supplies, weapons, artillery, gunpowder, saltpetre, sulphur, lead, and any other type of munitions of war that are taken or ordered to be taken to the captaincy by the captain and settlers or any other persons, be they my subjects or foreigners, it is my wish that they shall not incur any duty. All these items may be sold freely in the captaincy to the captain and settlers and inhabitants there who are Christians and my subjects.

All those persons, both from my realms and territories as well as those from elsewhere who travel to the captaincy, may not deal in, buy, or sell anything in commerce with the heathen native population. They shall trade only

4 The captaincy of Duarte Coelho.

with the captain and settlers and shall buy, sell, and negotiate in commerce with them alone. It is my wish that anyone who acts to the contrary shall forfeit twice the value of the merchandise and articles contracted with the heathens. Of this sum, one third shall be for my governing council, another third for the person who accuses him, and the third part for the hospital in the territory. Should there not be a hospital, it shall be for the construction of the territory's church.

Any persons who load up their ships in the captaincy shall be obliged, before starting to do so and before leaving the captaincy, to inform the captain, so that he may ensure that they are not taking out any prohibited merchandise. Nor shall they leave the captaincy without permission from the captain. Should they not obtain that permission, or should they leave without permission, they shall forfeit to me twice the value of the merchandise loaded, even if it is not prohibited merchandise. This is to be observed for as long as there is no factor or other official of mine in the captaincy. When there is one, he shall be informed of what is set down in this document, and it will be his duty to ensure that the above should take effect, as well as to give the necessary permission.

The captain of the captaincy and the settlers and inhabitants may freely trade in, buy, and sell merchandise with[out][5] the captains of the other captaincies whom I have been installing along the coast of Brazil, as well as with the settlers and inhabitants thereof, one captaincy trading with another. None of these parties shall have to pay any duty on the purchase or sale of such merchandise.

Any neighbor and settler who lives in the captaincy and who is a factor or who has an arrangement with anyone who lives outside my realms and territories may not trade with the native population of the territory, even if they are Christians. Should they trade with them, it is my wish that they shall forfeit the entire value of the merchandise in which they are dealing, of which one third is for the person who accuses them and two thirds for the construction of the walls of the captaincy.

In the captaincy, the headmen of its townships and villages shall gather and collect all duty, land tributes, and taxes that belong to my realms and territories and which, through my royal decrees, belong to and are granted to such headmen.

In the rivers of the captaincy where there is the need to install boats to cross over them, the captain shall install them and charge for them any duty or tax that his governing council prescribes for him to charge and once that charge has been confirmed by me.

---

5  The charter reads *sem* ("without"), but clearly *com* ("with") is intended.

Each one of the public and judicial notaries in the townships and villages of the captaincy shall be obliged to pay a fee of five hundred *reals* (réis)[6] a year to the captain.

The settlers and inhabitants and people of the captaincy shall be obliged in time of war to serve alongside the captain if he deems it necessary. I thus inform the present or any future captain of the captaincy. This information is also for my factor, my financial agent, and my officials, as well as for the judges and justices of the captaincy, all other justices and officials of my realms and territories, my office of justice, and my exchequer. I command all in general and each one in particular to comply with this royal charter and to see that it is fulfilled in its entirety, so that nothing set down herein can be in doubt, disputed, or contradicted, since this is my express wish. To confirm this, I have signed and sealed this charter with my seal and command it to be recorded in the books kept in the factor's office in the captaincy, as well as in my Lisbon customs-house. It will also be recorded in the books of the governing councils, townships, and settlements of the captaincy, so that all shall be aware of its content and shall wholly comply with it.

Manuel da Costa wrote this down in Évora, on 24 September in the year of Our Lord 1534.

## 2. Three Letters from Duarte Coelho to King John III

*Of the captaincies created in 1533–34, one of the most successful was Nova Lusitânia, or Pernambuco, situated on the northeastern coast of Brazil. Its Lord proprietor, Duarte Coelho, had served in India and had received the captaincy in 1534. He proved to be an active and energetic sponsor and governor of his colony. His correspondence with the king provides one of the most detailed views of the problems confronting the early colonists and donataries as well as the deficiencies of the captaincy system. These letters from the 1540s are particularly revealing of the relationship with the indigenous peoples of the region, the dyewood trade, the beginnings of the sugar industry, and the problems of governing the colonists. (From José Antônio Gonsalves de Mello and Cleonir Xavier de Albuquerque (eds.), Cartas de Duarte Coelho a el Rei [Recife, 1967], pp. 85–91, 95–100.)*

(a) Sire

Last September I sent a report to Your Majesty via the captain of the flotilla, with news of my voyage and arrival in Nova Lusitânia and of what has occurred here. Thereafter, Sire, I began to issue instructions to ensure

6 The *real* was the former monetary unit of Portugal and its overseas territories, as distinct from the modern Brazilian *real*.

calm throughout the territory, making gifts to some and peace with others, as all these things are necessary. I then ordered sugar plantations to be laid out in accordance with what, back in Portugal, I had contracted to do.[7] I have done everything I was urged to do and have provided everything I was requested to do, without any thought to my own interest or profit, save only that the work should go ahead, as is, indeed, my firm wish. We have managed to plant a large quantity of sugarcane, and everybody has worked as hard as possible, while I have given them all the assistance that I can. We shall soon complete a very large and splendid mill, and I am now ordering others to be started. May it please the Lord in His great mercy to help me in my intentions.

As regards gold, Sire, I never cease to inquire and search in that respect, and every day more news becomes available. However, its deposits lie far from here, deep within the remote interior of my territory, and we shall have to make our way across land occupied by three tribes of very perverse and savage people, each one of which is hostile to the others. Consequently, the journey is going to prove very dangerous and troublesome. To carry it out, I consider, as do all my men, that this can only be done if I go there myself. We must also ensure that the journey is properly undertaken if we are to achieve our objectives. We must not set off on wild adventures as did those on the River Plate, where more than a thousand Castilians perished, or as also did those in the Maranhão, who lost seven hundred men. The worst outcome would be to jeopardize the entire project. For this reason, Sire, I await the hour in which God shall be pleased to entrust this enterprise to me, both in His sacred service and in that of Your Majesty, for that will bring me the greatest happiness and all the reward I could wish to have.

Sire, I have made due preparations for the project and sent for the supplies that are needed for the expedition, as well as sending for a number of good men. It is also essential to leave everything here well provided for and in all respects in good order because of the French, who, if they realize that I am not present, will get up to their crooked tricks. Two weeks ago, they attempted their customary ruses but were unsuccessful. If need be, I shall forward a report on that matter so that Your Majesty can see it.

I am taking every precaution appropriate to the service of Your Majesty. May God help me and indicate to me the best time for everything to go well. Pêro de Góis and Luís de Góis, who are at present visiting this territory, will give Your Majesty any further news concerning both the territory and me. Consequently, I shall not write any more on this subject, as it will be from them that Your Majesty will acquire information about this place.

---

7   The term *engenho*, or sugar mill, by extension refers to the whole estate and is translated here with the modern term "plantation."

Since, for matters of such importance, great expense is inevitably incurred, I find myself very short of money and in debt and cannot pay the wages of as many people as I have done hitherto. Three years ago, I asked Your Majesty to do me the favor of allowing me some means of negotiating for some slaves from Guinea. Last year, I received the answer that until the original contract was completed nothing could be done, and I was given to understand that once it was completed they would be supplied. Accordingly, I wrote back to Your Majesty on this matter. I am unaware whether I have now been granted this favor, as the ships have not yet arrived. I beg Your Majesty, if this permission has not yet been granted to me, to consider how much it is in Your Majesty's interests, and how little harm or trouble it is to grant me permission to obtain some slaves, in order, Sire, to serve you better. I beseech Your Majesty to make provision for this through Dom Pedro de Moura and Manuel de Albuquerque.

From this town of Olinda, 27 April 1542
Your Majesty's servant, Duarte Coelho

(b) Sire

This year, 1546, I have written to Your Majesty three times, giving an account of matters which I felt were of interest to Your Majesty. Nevertheless, because of the uncertainties of sea travel, I have sought, Sire, to forward once again an identical report so that Your Majesty might judge what is in your best interest.

With regard to this land of Nova Lusitânia, Sire, matters have begun well (praise be to God), owing to our immense toil and great fatigue, of which God is aware. Notwithstanding that, Sire, there exist many drawbacks and hindrances that hamper the growth and development that I would have wished for in the proper service of God and Your Majesty. I devote myself very closely, Sire, to those aspects that I am able to put right here, but matters that I cannot deal with here can only be remedied by early intervention from Your Majesty, if that is indeed your wish.

I have already written to Your Majesty and explained in earlier letters that one matter that is most prejudicial to the wellbeing and development of this territory is the cutting of brazilwood. This cutting occurs at as much as twenty leagues away from the settlements that are springing up, particularly here in New Lusitânia. That is because the brazilwood, Sire, lies deep within the remote interior. Obtaining it is very troublesome, dangerous, and expensive, and the Indians work on it very unwillingly. Up to now, I have forwarded quantities of brazilwood over recent years to Your Majesty and have gathered a little for myself (with Your Majesty's gracious permission). All this has been done in accordance with your commands. It is very slow progress because of the attitude of the Indians, and in ten or twelve or eighteen months it provides merely one shipload. Although it is very costly for me, it is necessary, Sire, to put up with this because of its importance to the wellbeing of this territory. However, there are those to whom Your Majesty [also] grants brazilwood and to whom it costs little, nor do they encounter the toil and hardship nor the danger and loss of blood that we have to endure, Sire. They go through nothing that I have to go through. What I suffer they do not, nor do they know of the loss that Your Majesty will suffer. To collect brazilwood, they pester the Indians so much and promise them so many things that it is not right to promise. Where I have created order they destroy it. If they give the Indians even part of what they promise them, they destroy the orderly arrangements that I had established for the trade in brazilwood and for when Your Majesty might require it.

Sire, it is not simply that they supply the Indians with tools, as is the custom. Rather, to persuade them to gather brazilwood, they give them beads from Bahia, as well as feather headdresses and colored garments that cannot be obtained here. Worse still, they give them swords and muskets. This applies particularly to a number of men who were once in my favor and under my protection and who for the last three years have lived on the territory of Pêro Lopes,[8] which is next to mine. Under the pretense of developing estates as inhabitants of the land, they are actually exploiting the brazilwood, which they never cease to grow and to load [on to their ships]. In the last three years, they have loaded up more than six or seven ships with it.

I have commanded and executed what I have seen to be appropriate to Your Majesty's best interests, and here in my territory, Sire, I have made due provision and proclamations in accordance with the rules that Your Majesty set out in my Charter of Donation. I attempt to prevent such practices as much as possible. I have to tell you, Sire, that in the last three years, the cutting of brazilwood has been abused, and that the territory is in a consequent state of confusion. Having to deal with so much turmoil and having to put right so much malpractice are matters that have caused me great toil and upset. The cutting of brazilwood holds back the development of our estates, particularly the sugar plantations. The explanation is that [formerly], when the Indians were hungry and needed tools, they would come to clear the land and do all the other heavy work in exchange for what we gave them, and they would sell us supplies that we greatly need. But now, as they have plenty of tools, they have become worse than ever: they get all excited, swaggering around and behaving rebelliously.

The estates, in particular the sugar plantations, lie scattered about, not grouped together, and the men who come to lay out the plantations are not

8  Pêro Lopes de Sousa was the donatary whose territory lay to the north of that of Coelho.

resilient men given to resistance, but are just here to make a profit, and I have to protect and defend them daily. But who is there here, Sire, with enough money for gunpowder and cannon balls, artillery and weaponry, and all the other things that are needed? I have to tell you that it is essential that Your Majesty should remedy this situation and make due provision for it by sending me the wherewithal to prevent the cutting of brazilwood within a distance of up to twenty leagues from all my settlements. By that, I mean up to twenty leagues to the south of Olinda, where there is another Indian tribe, and twenty leagues to the north of Santa Cruz, where there is a further Indian tribe in the territory of Pêro Lopes de Sousa. This should remain in force for at least ten to twelve years, with the same penalties that Your Majesty has already imposed. In that way, Your Majesty would put right something that cannot be remedied by any other means. For anyone wanting to grow brazilwood, there exist many other harbors that can be used, without causing so much harm and damage and such disservice to God and to Your Majesty. What is planted around here, which is the very best brazilwood, will be kept for when Your Majesty wishes to make use of it, and will be most carefully attended to, when you issue the order.

Likewise, Sire, in the other aforesaid letters that I have written to Your Majesty, I reported to you and now report again that it is much in your interest, as well as for the wellbeing and preservation of good order here, to issue the following command. Namely, as we are all Portuguese and therefore your vassals and subjects, the order should go out that, whereas some behave as though they were Portuguese, others should not behave as though they were French and yet others as though they were Castilians. I say this, Sire, in respect of those people to whom Your Majesty has given land along the coast of Brazil, in order that in their territories or captaincies they should comply with, and enforce compliance with, the Letters of Mandamus[9] sent to them by the other captains and governors. They should do as does Duarte Coelho, whom Your Majesty sent here, since, Sire, you commanded him to seek to do what he should do and to carry out what is in your interest, as he has always done. I say this because matters have gone awry, and because it is most essential that Your Majesty should resolve the issue before any further turmoil arises, as Your Majesty would not be acting counter to the terms of your donations. For my part, indeed, I would not only obey Your Majesty but would see it as a favor to be the first to receive your command. Others should then follow.

I refer now to the privilege and freedom granted to me in respect of fugitives from justice, as I requested of Your Majesty in Évora. The understanding is that for crimes committed in Portugal by such fugitives, though found

---

9 These Letters of Mandamus (*Cartas Precatórias*) were authorized judicial writs.

guilty by your justices, when once they come to live with me in my territory, they cannot be summonsed or indicted for those crimes. That is how I understand the matter, but in the other territories and captaincies to which Your Majesty has given this freedom, they interpret matters to the contrary. Rather, the crimes and evil deeds committed here [in Brazil] should be met with due punishment, as is only right and just. If evildoers flee from my territory to another for fear of being punished, or from other territories to mine, the aforesaid privilege and freedom should not be applicable to them. If that were to happen, as certain other captains allow, then I have to tell you, Sire, that this territory will lose its settlers and will soon become depopulated. Everything will deteriorate. For this reason, Sire, it is most essential that everybody should have due regard for Letters of Mandamus, that everybody should comply with them, and that Your Majesty should insist on this.

Likewise, Sire, I have dispatched, via three separate routes, my reports to Your Majesty concerning the exiled convicts that have been sent out here. Moreover, I have therein described to Your Majesty my experience in my own territories. I have indicated how it is not in God's interest, nor in that of Your Majesty, nor suitable for the wellbeing and development of this land of Nova Lusitânia, that such criminals be sent here (as has been the case for the past three years). I swear and confirm to Your Majesty, on my soul, that they bring no good or benefit to this land. Rather, they cause harm and damage, and crimes are committed daily owing to their presence. We have lost any credit that we had till now with the Indians, since God and nature have not put right what I alone can do by daily ordering these criminals to be hanged. The situation causes the Indians greatly to belittle and disparage us. Moreover, such criminals are no good for any other work, they arrive here poor and naked, are unable to abandon their old tricks and are always plotting ways to escape. Your Majesty should be aware that they are worse here than the plague. For this reason I beg you, Sire, for the love of God, not to send such poison here, as it is pernicious to God's interest, to yours, to my own, and to all here with me to show mercy to such people. Even in the ships in which they come here they commit thousands of crimes, as there are more criminals on board than crew: they mutiny, they escape, they commit their crimes. We are now short of two ships, as they have disappeared because they were carrying convicts. I beseech Your Majesty once again not to send me such people and to favor me by instructing your justices not to force them on to ships bound for my territory, because, Sire, they are the ruin of me.

Similarly, I would remind Your Majesty of what I have already asked in writing, namely to command all those to whom, Sire, you have given territory in Brazil to come and live on their territories and populate them. It is in Your Majesty's interest; moreover, that was the condition prescribed. In cases where they do not come, they should send to their territories able and competent people, as well as justices of the peace who know and recognize where their duty lies. That is better than sending men of no real account, because such individuals do nothing but undo essential good work, for *mercenarius mercenarius sum.*

In the territory that belongs to Pêro Lopes de Sousa, whom God protect, and which lies next to mine, Your Majesty should command a judge to be appointed there who knows and understands what he must do. That is because there are four people there whom it would be better not to have, as they do nothing but gather brazilwood for the shipowners. When I wish to punish convicts, they flee there and do things for which all of them had already deserved to be hanged. If I send a Letter of Mandamus, I am informed that they have sanctuary there and possess privileges. These matters, Sire, should not be tolerated. Though I have tolerated them until now, through not wishing to show disrespect for the jurisdiction of others, I consider it essential, in God's interest and that of Your Majesty, to resolve this issue because of the danger and damage which could be caused by such outrages.

As to the affairs of territories and captaincies to the south, I wrote to Your Majesty last August, sending the letter via a factor of Afonso de Torres who was here. In that letter, I supplied a brief report on the situation. In the current letter, I now remind Your Majesty of the need to deal with matters in Bahia, for I feel it to be in Your Majesty's interests, as Francisco Pereira [Coutinho] is old, sick, and incompetent. Although Your Majesty is well aware of the matter, I shall nevertheless detail to you now, Sire, my inquiries concerning affairs in Bahia and what I have therefore found out. I grant that Francisco Pereira is to blame for not knowing how to govern his people as a good captain and that he is too weak to resist the insane outrages perpetrated by the crazy and stupid people who provoke uprisings and gather into factions. For such matters he cannot escape the blame. Nevertheless, it is appropriate, indeed essential, that those who have committed such crimes should be severely punished for the sheer folly, the turmoil, the crass behavior, and the acts of disobedience that they have inflicted on Francisco Pereira. I have to tell Your Majesty that these were truly dishonorable, ugly, and highly punishable offenses because the rebellions and uprisings against Francisco Pereira have caused the collapse of Bahia. I urge Your Majesty to order the arrest of the cleric who was the ringleader in this outrage, to have him transported back to Portugal and prevented from ever returning to Brazil, for my information is that he is a great scoundrel.

I also once again report to Your Majesty concerning what is happening with regard to the tithes and duties on the sugar plantations. These matters were examined in legal proceedings at the request of the people and of Your Majesty's factor. In the proceedings, it was stated that everybody at large must pay tithes on the purified sugar produced, in accord with the usage and practice of the realms and territories of Portugal. Your Majesty will find the additional arguments in the transcript of the proceedings and of the judicial decision that I am enclosing, as well as further new practices that I have ordered to be observed from now on. This is right and fair because the plantation owners were trying to fleece the people. I beseech Your Majesty to have the transcript read out in your presence. Should Your Majesty feel it right, I beg you, Sire, to ratify it. I insist to Your Majesty that it is just, and that I would normally find against the people rather than against the plantation owners, but black and worldly greed is so strong that it so clouds men's judgment as not to concede what is right and just.

I would also remind and beg Your Majesty to look to the collection of brazilwood, as recently we received news from a ship that arrived here from Portugal that people were ready to come here to collect thirty thousand *quintais* or more.[10] This has caused scandal and commotion among the people of Olinda and among all the settlers and inhabitants of my territories. They have presented me, Sire, with petitions and demands that I should not consent to this initiative, or they would abandon their estates and plantations and leave them deserted, were I to allow it. Though, Sire, I have already forbidden it, once again I have let it be known today in all the settlements and estates that nobody is to cut, grow, or talk of growing brazilwood in areas within twenty leagues of those settlements. The penalty is set out by Your Majesty in my Charter of Donation, that is, the loss of all property and permanent exile to São Tomé. This was commanded and published in Your Majesty's name in respect of my donation. Accordingly, I urge you, Sire, to send me at once your confirmation of this prohibition. That is because I have promised and sworn to the people that I shall not allow or consent to it, as it would cause so much damage to the interests of God and Your Majesty and to the wellbeing and security of all of us who are out here.

It is similarly necessary to report to Your Majesty certain other disorderly practices that occur out here in territories and captaincies lying to the south of my own. I am uncertain whether one should call the perpetrators "settlers" or "thieves." I mention this to you, Sire, as it involves the captains or those to whom Your Majesty has given land. It is their duty, through law, military custom, and usage in matters of warfare, to deliberate carefully in respect of maintaining peace or making war. It is their prerogative to make war whenever they find it appropriate and when the need presents itself. However, they should not allow people everywhere to set upon whomsoever they can lay their hands on, for that leads to all-round damage and destruction. But they are so crazily bent on this that they have created great havoc in those areas. Indeed, it is not enough for them to do it there, but

---

10   A *quintal* (plural *quintais*; Arab: quintâr) is a weight equivalent to approximately 50 kg.

they come and attack my coastlands and, indeed, wherever they can. This very year there came up from the south six huge caravels, pretending to be looking at the area, with a view to trading with my people. When they realized that I was waiting for the time when God would deem it right to enable me to go ahead with my cherished plans for the interior, and so to serve Your Majesty, they offered to come with me. I promised them great gains and set about constructing new brigantines. When I was not on my guard, they set sail and, in payment for the favors received from me, they proceeded to attack my coastal settlements before I could hurry to the rescue. I only managed to capture one ship, one that attacked the [area inhabited by the] Potiguaras, which is where three years ago I managed to ransom back twenty-five to thirty Portuguese who had got lost there. All the Indians whom they had captured I managed to rescue from them and send back to their own land, for if ever fortune casts any Portuguese on to that coast, where the harbors are dreadful, one would hope to have them returned.

I punished these attackers in the way that I felt that they deserved. I am telling Your Majesty this, since it will be imperative for you, Sire, to command all the captains in the south not to promote such actions. Indeed, I do not allow such things in my territory, nor shall I. I have sought to reveal all these matters in order to clear my conscience and to comply with what Your Majesty has entrusted to me and commanded me to do. I beg Your Majesty to intervene in these matters, for it is in your interest.

From this town of Olinda, 20 December 1546.

[Postscript] Last March in the year 1546, a box of sugar samples was selected for Your Majesty to see. It was given to a pilot from a ship belonging to Constantino de Caires. Your Majesty's factor, under my orders, delivered it to him nailed down, exactly as it had been prepared in my presence. I have now learned that it was not given to your Majesty, though I have been informed that it had been handed in at the customs-house and from there it had disappeared. I beg Your Majesty to instruct your officials that when they see something intended for Your Majesty, they should take it and present it to you, Sire. They should see that it does not disappear, for it is God's errand.

I beseech Your Majesty not to forget those matters about which you wrote to me concerning provision for the churches.

Your Majesty's servant
Duarte Coelho

(c) Sire

It is now almost a month since I sent Your Majesty a letter via a servant of mine, Francisco Frazão, giving an account of myself and of what I felt to be in your interest, as well as reporting on matters that, in my view, are of some urgency. I now refer back to that letter and beg Your Majesty to examine its contents, in order to determine what is to be done and to inform me accordingly, so that I might know where my duty lies.

In this letter, Sire, I wish to report to Your Majesty on what I learned from my friends after I wrote the earlier letter, which left here some twenty days ago. In particular, Manuel de Albuquerque has written to tell me of a matter on which he has had some conversation with certain people who understand the issue, or claim to. According to notes that I have seen, they are offering themselves to Your Majesty to settle in, or assist in the settlement of, the lost captaincies, as well as in areas to the south thereof. There are other details that I saw in the notes, according to which they request Your Majesty to grant them for twenty years all the brazilwood along the entire coastline and, most significantly, even the wood from my territory of Nova Lusitânia. They go on to request that throughout that period, they be granted all the tithes and income from the entire territory and coastline of Brazil. By that is implied the income not only from here but also from Portugal on what is exported from here, not to mention other matters that I have seen in the notes.

Although at this point I would have wished to make various comments on this issue, Sire, I shall suffer in silence, as I am unsure whether Your Majesty will accept what I have in all honesty to say. Over the past three years, I have written to Your Majesty four times to report on everything that I believed to be in your interest. Up to now, I have neither seen nor received a reply. This, Sire, would seem to derive from the little esteem in which Your Majesty holds me.

I have nevertheless sought, Sire, to deal with what, rightly and justly, affects and matters to me, though without abandoning the proper service of your interests, for that has always been my practice and intention. I have to tell you, Sire, that as to the resettlement and renewed development of the territories and captaincies to the south of here, such actions, as Your Majesty already knows, would be beneficial to your interest and God's. If Your Majesty had examined the letters I have written, you would have noted, Sire, what I reported on this matter, as I have always felt it to be in your interest to act on this, for the reasons I gave to Your Majesty in my letters. This was and is my opinion, namely, that Your Majesty should once again command the territory to be inhabited and cultivated, both in accordance with Your Majesty's wishes and with what is right and just.

However, Sire, it rankles with me that these shipowners or contractors wish to include my territory in their project. With God's mercy and by dint of loss of blood, and of immense toil and expense, I have endeavored to make this territory better developed, better ruled, better governed, and more justly administered than all the other captaincies; indeed, the others have been lost because they were so chaotic. The profit and the benefit that I have achieved and gained for Your Majesty are both a source of great pleasure and contentment to me, particularly because from now on they are bound to increase. Yet all this they now wish to have for themselves, quite apart from depriving me of that pleasure and contentment, not to mention any profit which could arise from the fruit of my own labors. It does not seem to me right or just. Your Majesty will do about it whatever you think fit. But I, Sire, shall not cease to assert what I truly understand. I believe that, on balance, it would be far better and much fairer to provide some assistance and favor to a man who has brought this land under control by dint of great toil and expense, not to say loss of blood, indeed, to a man who has raised it to the state in which it now finds itself. For things to improve still more, to multiply and increase, what this land needs is a shepherd, not some grasping profiteer like those who want to take it over. But, above all, Your Majesty must do what you think fit. Nevertheless, of my own free will, I shall not agree to the finding of some placement for me in their workshops and companies, nor do I wish to receive from Your Majesty what they want and request. However, if Your Majesty so wishes and feels it is right and just to help me and support me in a matter that I have well in hand and for which I am keen to see a successful outcome, then I shall see that as a great favor. It is outlined below.

Regarding the duties and tithes deriving from my territory, Sire, which are what these men are requesting, whether it be those collected here or those paid in Portugal, I say once again that Your Majesty should receive them in their entirety. Moreover, this continues to be what is laid down in my Charter of Donation. I ask nothing except that I should deduct payment for the priests' salaries, as is the current practice and as was commanded by Your Majesty when I first came out here. I also need money, Sire, for building work and other items for the churches, as is Your Majesty's obligation. I have written to Your Majesty on this matter three times, sending my letters via three distinct routes. I beseech Your Majesty to make due provision for this, as the need for it is very great.

But there is also a favor that I request of Your Majesty and which you may rightfully grant me. It is that, for a period of twenty years, or for the period that Your Majesty grants to these shipowners, you should deem it right to grant to me the tithes of my sugar plantations, that is, just those that I work myself, as well as what belongs to me in the plantations of third parties. Moreover, I request that the workers' pay should not be an issue for Your Majesty. My request is subject to Your Majesty's pleasure, and if this is not the case, then, Sire, let it be as you command.

Likewise, and for the same period, I wish to be granted permission to export each year, and at my own expense, some three thousand *quintais* of brazilwood, which would be free of all duty and which would help with my aforesaid expenses. This would enable me to supply once again and to refit those things that I need for our activities here, as I do not believe that there is anyone in Portugal who would give me so much money or lend it to me at any rate of interest. I would thus be able to dispatch the brazilwood to wheresoever I might wish, either east or west, and from wheresoever I might request essential supplies [in return]. The wood would be weighed here by your factor and officials, and they would give instructions for wherever it goes, with a certificate indicating what it is. If this proposal pleases Your Majesty, then I ask you, Sire, to command that this arrangement be granted to me, with the document being given to Manuel de Albuquerque, or to anyone who might request it from you on my behalf. I would cut the brazilwood in an appropriate location where it would not be detrimental. I request, Sire, three thousand *quintais*, since, owing to what it costs here and the little value it holds in Portugal, that amount would not [even] be equivalent in value to one thousand *quintais* back there.

The harvesting of brazilwood, in the chaotic manner in which [the licensees] wish to do it, is so harmful and appalling in this district of Olinda and Santa Cruz that I have already written to Your Majesty and sent you documentary proof thereof. Over the last three years and via three [separate] routes I have begged you, Sire, to act on this, as all [the shipowners] want to put into effect here the many licenses that Your Majesty has commanded to be issued. To do so would effectively destroy everything. Worse still, the territory of Pêro Lopes de Sousa, whom God preserve, is next to mine, but the shepherd himself is not present. Rather, there is some mercenary employed as an interpreter and as a factor by the shipowners. In fact, he does nothing but cut brazilwood. I have already given Your Majesty a report on this, so that you might act on it.

I beseech Your Majesty to command that from Cape Santo Agostinho [north] to the River Capibaribe, which is the limit of Potiguara territory, a distance of perhaps some twelve or thirteen leagues, and occupied by only that one Indian tribe, brazilwood be not taken there for ten to twelve years. In that way, everything can become orderly again. Apart from the coast belonging to the Potiguaras, there are so many other harbors that can be used, not only from Cape Santo Agostinho down to the River São Francisco, which is also on my stretch of coastline, but also from there [further] southwards. Indeed, such harbors belong to other tribes, who are the enemies of the Potiguaras. By their activities in those places, the licensees cannot cause us any difficulty. Moreover, any persons to whom Your Majesty deems it proper to issue due permission to do so, either in the area occupied by the Potiguaras, or in any other southern harbors may count on me, Sire, for enhanced protection. I shall readily give them all possible assistance, as, indeed, I do to the Potiguaras, who dwell [variously] some twelve, thirteen, fifteen, twenty, thirty, or even forty leagues away from here. All of it is coastline where the brazilwood is of good quality and cheaper to produce than it is here. Here we contend with a chaotic situation, with harvesting taking place ten, twelve, [even] fifteen leagues into the remoter interior, as well as with the Potiguaras' desire to proceed to my other harbors to the south of Cape Santo Agostinho, where there is a tribe that is their enemy. Just as my brigantines and the huge caravels belonging to the settlers travel along the entire length of my coastline for most of the year, so can the ships [of the licensees], and I shall assist them in every way possible. Here, they will be able to obtain interpreters and other things as they see fit. They will be able to buy from the settlers and inhabitants of the territory, sell to them [in turn], and make their profit without causing any harm, either to me or to those who are here with me.

Although I wrote to you, Sire, about a month ago and gave you an account concerning the failure to observe my Charter of Donation, I now feel it right to tell Your Majesty about this one more time and to report to you, Sire, on what is happening. The reason is this: a number of settlers here have come to me to complain that in Portugal certain people did not wish to recognize the freedoms set out in my Charter of Donation. Moreover, several people have already written to me from Portugal about this. These people had already arranged with me for them to come out here or to have plantations laid out [on their behalf]. It would appear that now they have learned that my Charter of Donation is not being observed. That has come about despite the decrees that I have issued to them. In these, I state that I consider it their right and in Your Majesty's interests, from the day on which they come here, either on their own account or through an agent, to settle on the land and establish their plantations. It is their right also to bring with them their officials, or to arrange for them to be brought, as well as all the men and objects essential for the plantations. Furthermore, they should be able to enjoy the privileges and liberties of settlers and inhabitants of my territories, as expressed in my Charter of Donation. Once the news was received here, Sire, it caused great commotion, and a meeting was held of all the people, including officials, noblemen, and men of standing. All of them took counsel in common together and formed a consultative body. They presented me with a signed petition, which accompanies this letter, vehemently pleading with me to act justly toward them. Your Majesty will see my reply written on the back of the petition. I assuaged their anger and pacified them by apologizing for the fact that Your Majesty was unaware of this matter. I promised them that I would inform you at once, Sire, giving them the hope that Your Majesty would turn your attention to this matter on their behalf.

For this reason, Sire, I beg Your Majesty to read my letter and grasp its intent. You will see, Sire, that it is entirely concerned with the service of your interests, in which I feel that I am dying, though one death would be preferable to all those "deaths" that are incomplete. Matters of this kind in lands that are so far from Portugal require different approaches from those in use back home. Your Majesty knows that I have always been careful, in matters of concern to you, Sire, to give a good account of myself, as God and Your Majesty are aware and as is widely recognized. It must be reasonable to assert, Sire, that nothing that you do should hold me back from pursuing matters that are in your interests, for the loss will be far greater as a result of failing to hold on to our privileges, whereas the profit could be enormous. I do not consider, nay, I do not believe that this change emanated from Your Majesty, or that you are aware of it, Sire, but that it derives from officials who are ready to go too far to prove their own worth. If it originates with contractors, then Your Majesty should remember what is in your best interests, for they think of nothing but their own profit.

Your Majesty knows that I came here to serve you, and that what, Sire, you granted to me in my Charter of Donation was to ensure that everything be done both quickly and well, as praise be to God is the case. Your Majesty made a number of concessions that you considered, Sire, were in your best interests, and about which I have made a full declaration to Your Majesty. Among these was the concession made to me, my heirs and successors, and all the settlers and inhabitants who came to my territories to live here and to populate this area. That was that we would not have to pay more than a single tax of ten percent on all merchandise or other items that we dispatched or delivered to Portugal. Moreover, we could sell and do with the merchandise whatever we liked. Likewise, even when they entered or arrived at any port, city, town, or other place belonging to your realms and territories and when they wished neither to sell nor to unload their goods, they would be free not to do so. In such circumstances, they would be able to go wherever they wished, without let or hindrance, despite the existence in those ports, cities, towns, and other places of charters or practices that run counter to ours. What I am told, Sire, by those who are writing to me from Portugal, and what everyone here is complaining about, is that the aforesaid concession is not being observed over here. I am told that it is being denied to settlers and inhabitants who have lived here for the last six, eight, ten, or even twelve years. These are people who have large estates, servants, and slaves. They are people who devote themselves to enhancing the quality of this land. The reason given in Portugal is that some of them have wives in Portugal and that therefore they cannot receive the freedoms and privileges expressed in my Charter of Donation.

The same applies to the noblemen and other powerful figures who live in Portugal but who have developments out here, as it applies also to others in respect of sending their factors, men, and slaves to lay out plantations.

This is a worthy objective that greatly leads to the growth and development of the land, for they bring Your Majesty great profit and will bring still more in the future if the land continues to improve as, praise God, it is doing.

Similarly, Sire, there are people in Portugal who have their own idea of what settlers and inhabitants should be like, as opposed to those whom, through my orders and diligent toil, I regularly recruit for this land. Indeed, such people are listed in my registration book and in the records of the territory as settlers and inhabitants. Your Majesty's factor, your financial agent, and your secretary have issued certificates to such settlers and inhabitants, but not to others. It is also said in Portugal, and this causes another problem, that the settlers and inhabitants who dispatch sugar and cotton from here should not enjoy the concessions unless the produce is their own work and harvested by them. Sire, this seems to be born of malice, since in every country of the world it is the normal practice to do as I do and as I have established. By that, I mean that among all the settlers and inhabitants there are some who develop sugar plantations, for that is what they are skilled at doing; but others plant hemp, others plant cotton, and others grow food, which is vitally necessary for the territory, while yet others are fishermen, which is also essential. Some have ships that sail off to collect supplies and ply their trade throughout the territory, in accordance with rules that I have laid down. Others have special skills on the sugar plantations, in sugar production, in carpentry, in the forges, and in pottery; others are craftsmen in creating molds for the sugar; and there are yet other craftsmen as well. All these I constantly strive to recruit at my own expense. The territory needs them, and I make sure that such men are sought after in Portugal, Galicia, and the Canary Islands. There are others who have been brought over by those who come to develop the sugar plantations. They also settle here and inhabit the country. Some of them are single, others have got married out here. Every day I succeed in getting some to marry, while I work constantly at persuading others to do so. This, Sire, is because we have such sound practices in order to populate the new territories which are so far from the kingdom, which are as large as this is and from which so much profit is expected, both in God's interest and in that of Your Majesty. Accordingly, for the good of all your realms and territories and for other reasons, Your Majesty sent me out here. While I work and do all I can and ought to do, I beg you, Sire, not to permit people to tamper with what is laid down, for this is no time to do so. Indeed, our freedoms and privileges ought rather to be increased than curtailed.

I beg your Majesty to read this letter and to reach an early decision on all these matters. I urge Your Majesty to recognize the honesty of what I intend, for you know, Sire, that it is in my character and is my firm intent to act sincerely and to speak the truth to everyone, most of all toward Your

Majesty and in your interests. I constantly work hard in this regard, for it is both essential and appropriate to do so. If this were not the case and if I did not recognize it as such, I swear on my soul that long ago I would have returned to Portugal. I declare this because I am a man of complete honor in your service and one who wishes to do still better than I have done up to now. I know for sure that I shall give as good account of myself as any man has done or ever will do.

Once again, I beg Your Majesty to act on these matters about which I have written and reported, so that I might know what my duty is and so that matters do not drift, for time lost is the greatest loss of all. Anything else can be recovered, but time cannot.

May God in His mercy protect Your Majesty and all your interests and give Your Majesty victory against all those who seek to act against those interests. Amen.

Olinda, 15 April 1549

[Postscript] As to brazilwood, I beg Your Majesty to reach a decision regarding this issue, not only because of the turmoil, but also because it gets stolen amid the turmoil. It causes me great anger and displeasure to report this. When I seek to resolve the matter, Sire, people do the opposite of what I have determined, in my attempts to serve Your Majesty and to curtail the confusion. Indeed, I cannot find anybody who does not think that he has some right to deal in brazilwood as though it were some vegetable to be sold on the market. I have punished some who have disobeyed my orders, but I cannot interfere in the jurisdiction of others, except by sending requests and Letters of Mandamus, to which no more attention is paid than if they were so much idle chatter. I have already informed Your Majesty of this, and the fault will not lie at my door.

Your Majesty's servant
Duarte Coelho

## 3. A Letter from Felipe Guillén to Queen Catarina, Giving News of Porto Seguro and of Mem de Sá's Victory at Rio de Janeiro

*Most of the captaincies were plagued by a series of problems stemming from mis-management and resistance by the indigenous peoples. In this letter of 1561, a some-what later period after royal government had been established in the colony, Felipe Guillén, a Spaniard in the service of Portugal, provides a discussion of the situation in the captaincy of Porto Seguro in which he gives considerable attention to the rela-tions between the settlers and the local indigenous peoples. He notes the difference between various tribes and the threat that one group, the indomitable Aimoré, had caused to the captaincy. He also notes how alliances with some groups can provide protection to the colony. In addition, he notes events taking place to the south where the Portuguese were driving a French settlement from Guanabara Bay, the site of modern Rio de Janeiro. As a Spaniard, Guillén uses the Spanish experience in America to compare colonization practices in Brazil.*

*The original document is found in Arquivo Nacional da Torre do Tombo [ANTT Corpo Chronologico, part 1 maço 104, doc. 83] and is translated here from Joaquim Verissimo Serrão, O Rio de Janeiro, 2 vols. (Rio de Janeiro, 1967), II, pp. 44–46. (Note: The original of this letter is damaged in sundry places. Text in square brackets is therefore inferred.)*

Madam

I sent a letter to Your Majesty via Dr. Pêro Borges both about the circumstances prevailing in this country and concerning certain matters that I felt were, of necessity, significant to the interests of our lord the king.[11] After Pêro Borges left, Mem de Sá pondered the fact that, as governor-general,[12] he had brought peace to this entire coast and its people, that he had restored, reformed, and made safe the captaincy of Ilhéus, and that he had defeated the French and ousted them from Rio de Janeiro. He then took the view, along with everyone else, that [only one objective remained,] in order to complete his service to our lord the king, [and that was] to expend every effort to discover gold.

He gave orders that the project be given the strongest [support]. He himself gave it due priority and assembled more than one hundred men, equipped with everything necessary for such an expedition. He also dispatched with them a number of native tribesmen[13] from the area around the town of Salvador, not only as a protective force but also to carry their baggage and supplies. They all set out together and made their way inland for some sixty leagues, traveling in peace and safety, being welcomed everywhere by the native population. They came upon a people known as the Tupinambás, who displayed pleasure at their arrival. However, as the trusting Christians made their way onwards, without their weapons at the ready, they were treacherously ambushed by the Tupinambás. The outcome of the incident was that the Christians were routed and [many] men were killed.

---

11  King Sebastian (r. 1557–1578) was at that time merely seven years of age. His grandmother, Queen Catarina, the Spanish widow of John III, acted as regent of Portugal from 1557 until 1562.

12  Mem de Sá was the third governor-general of Brazil, holding that office from 1558 until his death in 1572.

13  The original Spanish text reads *negros* at this point, but it is clear that the tribesmen were American Indians, not blacks. The term *negros da terra* (blacks of the land) was often used for Indians.

Although they themselves killed many of their native [opponents, it did not prove] appropriate to allow the expedition to proceed. Consequently, they returned to the town.

As I have seen from various letters, the governor remained determined [to serve] the king and Your Majesty and ordered that the expedition should set out once more. That is because, once [gold] is found out here in Brazil, there will be few in Portugal who will not wish to profit thereby. Once gold is found, this land will bring major advantages to Portugal and to Castile. This will be in sharp contrast to the toil and privation of those of us who are now here and who live in wait of its discovery. There are, indeed, grounds to believe that it does exist, and that, if it does, then it can be found. Nothing can be achieved without toil, but everything can be achieved with perseverance. It is right that we should all desire this outcome, because I assure Your Majesty that when Queen Isabella, your grandmother (may she live in heavenly glory), commanded that the Antilles be discovered, she nevertheless remained in doubt. Her counsellor advised her as follows: "Madam, Your Majesty must surely order their discovery, because your [current expenditure] thereon is some twenty to thirty cruzados. If they are not discovered, the loss will not be [great]. Should they be [discovered], then the gain will be infinite." Indeed, such was the [outcome]. Consequently, I assure Your Majesty that in this regard this land must be explored [and by] one of two methods: either by sending so small a contingent that the native population through whom they pass will have no fear of them, or by sending so large an expedition that by sheer weight of arms they will pass through and arrive at their appropriate objective. It is, however, inappropriate to send a small party, because any slight setback could be fatal to them, whereas a large force of two hundred expeditionaries is ample if they take with them fifteen hundred to two thousand native tribesmen. After all, the latter can easily be found among the tribesmen that live around this bay.[14] I shall not mention anything further to Your Majesty on this subject.

[Rather,] I wish to say that, having traveled around this captaincy of Porto Seguro, [I have noticed] that it is subject to the encroachment of a tribe known as the Aimorés. As [a people] they behave routinely, except that on one day they are in one place and on the next in another. They lead [a nomadic existence], living off fruit and what they can hunt down. They set ambushes for all other people and seek out ways of killing any person with impunity. If they do kill anyone, they strip the best flesh from them, eat it, and then decamp. In so many places on the estates, this captaincy has been attacked by them. One of the three townships has been subjected to so much daily aggression that its population has fled. In the other two, the

14  The Tupiniquins.

Aimorés have slaughtered men, women, and large numbers of slaves, and did so in such a way that all the settlers were on the point of abandoning this captaincy. We sent letters with information about the situation to the city[15] where the governor-general[16] and the chief justice, Brás Fragoso, both reside. We urged that the chief justice should hurry to the aid of the captaincy, which he [did]. Not only did the inhabitants of the captaincy, for all their fear of the Aimorés, rise up and strengthen their defenses, but also the judge dealt out corrective punishments to the Aimorés, as well as bringing justice to bear on other issues. [Indeed,] by 17 January this year, he had established such good order by meting out both punishments and justice, that the settlers no longer have differences to resolve, nor do they have any fear of the Aimoré tribe.

I assure Your Majesty that on both counts, had he not come to impose order on us, then this captaincy of Porto Seguro would have been abandoned. Everything was achieved with that measured skill that is so evident from his intellectual grasp of the issues. He was greatly moved by the extreme poverty of the settlers here and set about his task as if driven by paternal concern for us. He has already [arranged] that the Tupiniquins may dwell among us and has [so motivated] them that they act for us as a defensive shield. He has also sent for many other [soldiers] whose arrival we expect any day now. Accordingly, this captaincy will now be secure, and its settlers will no longer fear the obvious dangers. I ask Your Majesty to believe that this man has no lack of dedication, commitment, and willpower when it comes to serving both our lord the king and Your Majesty.

As for me, having regard to place, time, and due need, I [earnestly] beseech Your Majesty, during the life of our lord the king, whom God preserve, to extend to me your favors. After I quit this life [I beg] Your Majesty not to dash my hopes [of being counted] among those whom Your Majesty considers to be your willing servants.

Written in this captaincy and township of Porto Seguro, 12 March 1561.

Your Majesty's servant
Felipe Guillén

15  Salvador.
16  Mem de Sá.

# 3

## ROYAL GOVERNMENT

### 1. Instructions Issued to the First Governor-General of Brazil, Tomé de Sousa, on 17 December 1548

*The failure of the captaincy system to provide a firm basis for settlement or to clear the coast of European rivals finally moved the king of Portugal, Dom João III, to establish more direct control. In 1549, he sent Tomé de Sousa, a Portuguese comman- der with experience in North Africa and India, as governor of Brazil. The Governor- General sailed with an expedition of more than one thousand men and created a city, Salvador, on the Bay of All Saints in the captaincy of Bahia, where the donatary had died and there was thus no significant legal obstruction to the establishment of royal control. The expedition also included a senior judge and a royal treasurer. The new governor received his charter, or <u>regimento</u>, in December 1549. It included instructions on the organization of government as well as specific instructions on the creation of Salvador, which became the capital city. The governor was granted considerable powers to establish towns, encourage immigration, collect taxes, and promote trade. The document also demonstrates that the Crown was well aware of the Indian peoples and of previous Portuguese relations with them. The expedition also included six Jesuit missionaries, who immediately began to assume the task of converting the Indians. The instructions contained in this first <u>regimento</u> were often repeated in later instructions to senior officials so that this document served as a model for royal government in Brazil. (From História da Colonização Portuguesa do Brasil, vol. III, pp. 345–50.)*

I the king make it known to you, Tomé de Sousa, gentleman of my household, that I deem it essential, both in the service of God and in my own interests, to maintain and ennoble the captaincies and settlements of my territories in Brazil. It is essential too to instill order and to effect some means by which men may more safely and effectively go over there to populate the territory, thus to glorify our Holy Faith and to bring profit to my realms and territories and to their inhabitants. I have commanded that in that territory a fortress should be built, as well as a large and sturdy township[1] in a place suitable for that purpose. I have ordered that assistance be given by that township to the other settlements, that justice be administered, and that attention be given to those matters that are in my interest and in that of my treasury, not to mention the good of the country. I have been informed that the bay known as Bahia de Todos os Santos[2] is the most suitable place along the Brazilian coastline for such a township and settlement to be located. Accordingly, because of the nature of the harbor and the rivers that flow into it, as well as the productive and healthy characteristics of the land and, indeed, other aspects, I deem it to be in my interest that this township should be constructed in Bahia. For that purpose, a fleet is to sail out there with men, artillery, arms, munitions, and everything else that is necessary. Because of the great faith that I have in you and because I trust that you will know how to serve me with all due loyalty and diligence in a matter of such major importance, I deem it appropriate to send you as governor-general of my territories in Brazil. In that role, you are to build the fortress in the manner set out below and you will be both captain of the fortress and of the territory of Bahia.

You are to go as captain-major of the fleet and will travel directly to Bahia de Todos os Santos. On the voyage, you will observe further written instructions.

As soon as you arrive in Bahia, you are to take control of the stockade there that was built by Francisco Pereira Coutinho. That, I am told, is currently inhabited by subjects of mine and in receipt of assistance from certain indigenous pagan tribesmen. For that reason, you will be able to disembark peacefully, without any resistance, and to settle there with the men who are going with you. Should you find that not to be the case, and if the stockade turns out to be inhabited [solely] by native tribesmen, you will do everything in your power to capture it and with the least possible danger to our people there. You will, however, do battle with any who resist you and you will take control of the stockade. This task is to be accomplished as soon as you arrive or when once you see it to be in my best interests.

As soon as you are in control of the stockade, you will order any damage to be repaired and have a second stockade built nearby. It shall be built of wood or wattle and daub and surrounded by defense ditches, as you deem appropriate, and within it people shall be securely protected. You will then issue orders with a view to the provision of sustenance from the land and will command that plants be sown. That is to be done both by the men whom you are taking with you and by the tribesmen or, indeed, according to any other method that will bring about the best harvests. Should it seem to be

---

1   The site of the future Salvador.
2   Literally, "Bay of All Saints."

in my greater interest to disembark in the place where the fortress is to be constructed, then you are to take that course of action.

When you arrive in Bahia, you must find every means possible of reporting your arrival to the captains of every captaincy along the Brazilian coastline. You must also tell them that it is my wish that, as soon as they learn of your landfall, they are to give you all assistance possible in providing men, supplies, and any other things that they have at their disposal and which you might need. They are also to inform all persons in their captaincies who possess land in Bahia de Todos os Santos that they must go to Bahia in the first ships available, with a view to inhabiting the area and to working the land. Should they not travel on the first ships, they shall lose the right to any place on those ships, and their places shall be given to others. The captains are to issue decrees on these matters and are to send copies to you.

I am informed that the natives of Bahia belong to a small group of Tupinambás, of whom there are perhaps five or six thousand warriors. I am also told that they live along the coast to the north as far as Totuapara, which is six leagues away, and that their territory stretches into the interior as far as Paraguaçu, which is some five leagues away. Moreover, in Bahia they possess the island of Itaparica and three smaller islands, all of which those tribesmen inhabit. In addition, I have learned that the land and the islands would easily lend themselves to being captured in short order by a small company of well-organized men. That is because the area has few trees, is of easy access, and has little by way of high ground or undergrowth. I have been told that in 1545, when Francisco Pereira Coutinho was captain of Bahia, some of these tribesmen went to war against him, ejected him from his territory, and destroyed the estates, as well as causing much further devastation to the Christian population. Others followed their example and wrought similar havoc in other captaincies. However, certain pagan tribesmen around Bahia did not consent to such activity and refused to participate in the uprising. Instead, they are living peaceably alongside the Christian settlers and are helpful to them. That is also the case with all the other coastal tribes in Brazil. Indeed, they are waiting to see what punishment is to be inflicted on those who began the devastation.

Consequently, it is in God's interest and in my own that those who rebelled and waged war should be punished as rigorously as possible. I command you to take such action when once you arrive in Bahia. You are to seek out the pagan tribesmen who kept the peace and so favor them that, should you need their help, you can rely on it. As soon as the stockade has been repaired, and when you have at hand all that you need and the time is right, then you should come to an agreement with those who have a good grasp of the issues. Thus, you will determine how you should punish the guilty while maintaining the greatest security and with the least risk to your inhabitants.

Once that has been done, you will restore order by destroying the villages and encampments of the guilty parties and by killing and taking captive a number of them sufficient, in your view, to constitute both due punishment and a discouragement to them all. They will then sue for peace, which you are to grant them, and then you are to pardon them. That presupposes their recognition that they are my subjects and vassals and that every year they are to provide supplies to the people in the township. When they sue for peace, you must also seize some of the leaders of the uprising and order them by law to be hanged in the villages in which they were leaders.

I have been informed that the people known as the Tupiniquins that dwell in these captaincies are enemies of the tribesmen around Bahia. I am told that they wish to be present when you are ready to go to war, so as to assist you and to inhabit some part of the land of Bahia. They are prepared for this, and I am writing to the respective captains, asking them to send you some men from that tribe. You are also to write to the captains instructing them that they must inform you about the lie of the land and about what people, arms, and munitions the Tupiniquins have, whether they are living in peace or are at war, and whether they need any help from you. You are to give a warm welcome to the Christians and to the pagan tribesmen from those other captaincies and you should so assist them that they will be happy to assist you in turn whenever you need it. However, the pagan tribesmen should be given shelter in places where they are unable to do anything contrary to our interests. That is because you should not place too much faith in them, lest greater trouble should arise. You should send them back when once you can dispense with them. If any of these pagan tribesmen wish to remain in Bahia, you will give them land on which to build their homes and where they should be content to stay.

I am also told that the place where the stockade stands at present is not suitable for the construction of a fortress and township. I therefore command that the fort be constructed elsewhere, further into the interior of Bahia. I also recommend and order that when you have pacified the territory, you work with those who know which location is the most suitable for the building of a sturdy fortress that can be well defended. The chosen area should display appropriate characteristics for the future construction of a large town. The town itself would be such that the other captaincies might receive their provisions from it. It is, moreover, my earnest hope that it should be a healthy place where the air is good and where there is ample [drinking] water. There should be a harbor where ships may be moored and, when necessary, where they can be beached. All these points, or as many as are feasible, mean that the fortress and the township will be able to assist and supply all the other territories in Brazil.

Accordingly, in what seems to you to be the best place, you are to order a fortress to be built of a size and design appropriate to the site that you choose. You are to follow the plans that you are taking along with you and you are to work with the craftsmen whom I am sending out, not to mention any other persons with competence in such matters. Craftsmen such as stonemasons, carpenters, and others will be accompanying you. It will be their job to prepare the mortar, bricks, and roofing tiles. Indeed, in order that the fortress can be started, quantities of building materials are also to be taken in the ships of your fleet. If you do not find materials over there for raising a fort built of stone and mortar, then you are to make it out of stone and clay or wattle and daub or even wood, as best you can, provided that it is strong. The fortress is to be built so well that you will be able to assemble and lodge there with the men that you are taking along with you. Within the existing stockade, there should also be left a sufficient number of men to inhabit and defend it.

I wish the township to be as I have above described it. It is to extend for six leagues in every direction. However, if a given direction cannot extend to six leagues because the land runs out, then it is to stretch as far as the captaincy's land allows, and you are to mark out its boundaries so that everybody knows its full extent.

As soon as you have ensured that the land can safely be put to use, you are to issue land grants, within the established boundaries, to those who ask for it, provided that it has not previously been given to others who wish to live and work on that land. This is to be done within a period that will be notified. You are to grant such land free of any cost. The recipients are to pay only a tithe to Our Lord Jesus Christ, subject to the conditions and obligations set out in the royal charter that was given to that territory and which is recorded in the fourth book of my *Ordinances*, in the chapter entitled "Land Grants."

They are to live for three years in the town of Bahia or on the land granted to them, during which time they may neither sell the land nor pass it on to others. You must not grant to anyone more land than you consider that they will be able to work properly. [I now turn to] those who already possess land within the [above] boundaries and those who are already in Bahia, quite apart from those who are yet to go out there. If the first-named express the wish, within the period that is to be notified to them, to work the land that they previously held, then you are to restore that land to them to work it anew, subject to the requirements set out above. If, however, some of those who are absent do not return, within the period to be notified, to work the land that they possessed earlier, then you are to grant it to those who will put it to good use. This condition will be incorporated into the deeds of the land grants conferred.

The land grants shall stipulate that water from the streams that lie within the boundaries of land where it is possible to lay out sugar and other plantations is to be provided free of charge. Such water as you grant for sugar plantations is to be given to those who are able to lay out the plantations within a time limit that you are to determine. To ensure that the sugar plantations function properly and are suitably run, you are to supply as much land as is needed for that purpose. The beneficiaries will be obliged to build a [fortified] tower or blockhouse, of a design and size to be established by you in the deeds. Such constructions are to be as you think right for each site and must be large enough and secure enough for the plantation and its inhabitants. They shall be required to settle there and to put the land and water to good use. For a period of three years, they shall not be permitted to sell or let either of these to other people. This stipulation shall be incorporated into the aforesaid deeds of their land grants.

Not only will you confer land to be properly run, but you will also determine its limits. The owner of each parcel of land shall provide work on the sugarcane to sharecroppers who shall work within his boundaries for at least six months of the plantation's working year in the production of their crops. Such owners shall receive from the plantations that portion which, from information given to you, you deem appropriate, so that the sharecroppers in turn receive a fair share for themselves and so are content to work the land. This obligation and declaration in respect of the sharing out of the cane crop shall be set down in the deeds of the land grants.

There are those who were given water within the boundaries before Bahia was abandoned. Some may still be present, others absent. If they wish to undertake an obligation to receive water under the conditions set out above, you are to grant it to them if they request it within the time-limit to be established. If they do not request it within that time-limit, then you are to bequeath it, subject to the same conditions, to those who are able to lay out the plantations in accordance with the above stipulations.

You are to reconnoitre such land and water in the captaincy as lies beyond the boundaries that I have established [in these instructions]. By that, I mean the land that extends from the boundaries of the town as far as the River São Francisco, at which point the captaincy of Duarte Coelho begins. You are to investigate how many rivers and watercourses there are and whether the land is suitable for the planting of sugarcane and other crops. If anybody requests such land from you, you are to find out how much land each one requires and what crops he undertakes to produce. You are to write everything down for me, expressing your opinion thereon, so that the conferring of such land shall be seen to be in my best interests. In that way, the land will best be peopled and put to good use. You are also to state how much land is to be given to each applicant and under what legal requirements, so that I can then instruct you as to how I consider that you should proceed.

I deem it right that for a period of five years, new land grants or water grants in the captaincy of Bahia may not be conferred on those who are currently settlers in any other captaincy. Nor may such people come to settle in the captaincy of Bahia during that period. The only exceptions are those who had previously received land grants in the captaincy. They alone will be permitted to return from the other captaincies, wherever they may be, to put their land to good use.

It is in my interest to install in Bahia a number of ships, plied by oars, both to serve my territory and as a maritime defense system. It is therefore my wish and command that as soon as possible and as well as you are able, you should give orders for the construction of such ships as you deem necessary and of the size and design that you see right for the purpose. You are to take the appropriate craftsmen with you, as well as the necessary stores and equipment from my warehouses. When once the ships have been built, you must see that they are armed and fitted out for duties wherever needed and you will find a suitable place for them to be beached when not required at sea.

I have been informed that the pagan tribesmen that live along the coast of the captaincy of Jorge de Figueiredo, from the township of São Jorge as far as Bahia de Todos os Santos, are members of the Tupinambá tribe. They have rebelled at times against the Christians and caused them much damage. They are still in a state of rebellion even now and are waging war against us. It would greatly serve God and my interests if they were to be ejected from that area, so that it might then be inhabited both by Christians and by pagans from the Tupiniquin tribe, who are said to be peaceful. The latter are offering to assist in the expulsion of the Tupinambás and are prepared both to inhabit and to defend the territory. I therefore command you to write to whoever is acting as captain in the captaincy of Jorge de Figueiredo and to Afonso Álvares, the *provedor*[3] of my treasury, and to any others that in your opinion should gather in Bahia. As soon as they arrive, you are to consult with them and with any others who understand the best means of expelling the pagans from the territory. You will reach an agreement to do as much as you can, as time allows, to deal with the pagan tribes of Paraguaçu and Totuapara and with any other pagan tribesmen that are to be found in your captaincy of Bahia. You will agree to peace terms and you will work to preserve and keep the peace, so that Christians may live safely in the territory and put the land to good use. Whenever there is any uprising, you will move swiftly to quell

---

3  A *provedor* was a comptroller or financial officer. Hereafter, the term is rendered as "comptroller."

it and, by punishing the guilty, you will strive to bring peace as effectively as you can.

When once you have sufficiently completed your duties in Bahia as to enable you to leave them aside, you are to visit the other captaincies. In your place as captain, you will select a man of such ability and prudence as you believe suitable and you will issue him with instructions as to what his duties will be during your absence. Meanwhile, you will choose ships and men with which to travel to the other captaincies. As the captaincy of Vasco Fernandes Coutinho, namely Espírito Santo, is in revolt, you will head there as soon as you possibly can. You will find out from Vasco Fernandes and any others who know anything about this matter just what has caused the pagan tribesmen to rise up. You must discover what it is necessary to do in order to bring about reforms in the captaincy, as well as to attract more settlers. Whatever you decide shall be put into effect so as to ensure the safety of the territory and its future peace. You must also discover means of preventing any further rebellion on the part of the pagan tribesmen. Indeed, you are to remain in the captaincy of Espírito Santo for as long as you deem it necessary to bring this about.

You are to visit each and every one of the captaincies and hold conversations with the captains thereof, as well as with the comptroller-in-chief of my treasury, as he is to accompany you on your tour of the captaincies. You will also discuss matters with the judge of each captaincy, as also with such officials of my treasury as are present therein and with any other men of standing in the territory. You will discuss with them how best to maintain order and security. You are to command that settlements in the captaincies that are not yet enclosed by a stockade should now be protected in that way, and that existing stockades should be repaired. They should be provided with everything necessary for their fortification and defenses. You must, on agreement with the aforesaid officials, issue an edict to all those to whom water and land grants have already been given and to those on whom they will henceforth be conferred for the laying out of plantations. That edict shall stipulate that the plantations are to be laid out within the time-limits established by the captain who issues the grants. Moreover, in the settlements adjacent to the plantations, there are to be built fortified towers or blockhouses. Boundaries are to be set for such areas, just like those established above for the territory of Bahia.

Those in receipt of land to be worked on may neither sell nor let it for three years and they are to work that land for as long as the grant stands. I also order the captains that when they grant water and land, it is to be subject to the above requirements, and that they must write those requirements into the deeds of the land grants that they issue. Those who already hold land are also to be notified of this edict, which is to be copied into the book of the governing council of each captaincy in order to ensure its observance. Furthermore, it is detrimental to estates, plantations, and settlements to be established at no little distance from the townships from which they are meant to receive help and supplies when there is need for that support. You are therefore to order that henceforth they must be established as close to the towns as possible. As for those that you consider to be indeed distant, you must give orders that they are so to be fortified that they can be properly defended when the need arises.

You are to give orders that once a week (or more frequently, if you feel it necessary), a market should be held in every town and settlement. To that market the pagan tribesmen may go to sell whatever they have and to buy whatever they need. You are to order that no Christians other than the landowners and the plantation workers are to go into the pagan villages to trade with them. Such people may deal at any time with the pagan tribesmen of the villages that lie within the bounds of the area occupied by their plantations. However, if it should seem a problem to you for all those from every plantation to have the freedom to trade with the pagans under these terms, then it would be preferable to order that only one person from each plantation should do so.

When any Christians need to buy anything from the pagan tribesmen on days that are not market days, they are to tell the captain. He may grant permission for them to go and buy, when and where he deems it appropriate.

Nobody may go into the interior to trade without your permission or, if you are not present, without that of the comptroller-general of my treasury or that of the captains. That permission shall only be given to those who appear to be going for the right motives and whose journey and business are unlikely to cause trouble. They may only travel from one captaincy to another by land if they are granted permission by the comptroller or the captains. Moreover, in order to avoid any trouble, they must go across land that is peaceful. The punishment for transgression is a flogging for a common workman, while an individual of higher standing shall pay twenty cruzados, half of which shall be for [the ransom of] captives and the other half for his accuser. The comptrollers shall only give permission in the absence of the captain.

Since the principal reason why I gave orders for the settling of land in Brazil was the conversion of its people to our Holy Catholic Faith, I strongly recommend that you discuss with the captains and officials the best way to achieve this. You are to tell them on my behalf that I shall be truly grateful to them if they take special care to persuade the pagans to become Christians. To ensure that they are content to be Christians, those who live in peace should be treated well and given all due help. Your captains and officials must not consent to subjecting them to any oppression or heavy-handed treatment. If that should occur, it is to be put right so as to ensure their contentment, while any who acted against them must be justly punished.

I wish you to come to an agreement with your captains and officials concerning the prices that you believe all goods produced in the territory are genuinely worth. You are also to establish the value of produce from Portugal and from elsewhere, so that there come about clear and reasonable prices based on the nature of each territory. Those shall be the prices at which they are to be sold and exchanged.

When you travel to visit the captaincies, you are to be accompanied by António Cardoso de Barros, whom I am sending out as comptroller-general of my treasury in Brazil. In each of the captaincies, you are to discover whether officials of my treasury are still there and under what arrangements they are working. If there are no such officials, you are to discover whether they are needed. If, indeed, they are, then, having heard the views of the comptroller of my treasury, you are to appoint temporary officials to serve until I can provide others.

You are to discover what dues and income are owed to me in each captaincy and how they have till now been both collected and disbursed. That task shall be carried out jointly with the comptroller-general. Furthermore, you are to comply with everything set out in his instructions, where such matters are expressed in greater detail.

I have been informed that in the territory and townships in Brazil, there are certain men who have ships and caravels in which they sail from one captaincy to another and that in every way possible they attack and rob peaceful pagan tribesmen. They trick them into going aboard their ships and they take them elsewhere, selling them to their enemies. That is why pagan tribesmen have been rebelling and waging war on the Christians, and it has been the main cause till now of any harm done. It is in God's interest and in mine that the matter be dealt with, so that it no longer occurs. Henceforth, I command that no man, regardless of his class or standing, is to attack or wage war on the pagan tribesmen without due permission. Even though the pagan tribesmen should rebel or wage war, nobody shall do so, either by land or by sea, using either their own ships or those of others, without your prior permission or that of the captain of the captaincy under whose jurisdiction they happen to be. The captain shall only give permission when he believes the time is right, and it must only be given to a man whom you trust to do his duty and to carry out what he is instructed to do. Should any of these men set off without permission or exceed the orders given to them by the captain when he grants permission, they shall incur the death penalty and loss of their entire estate, half of which shall be for the ransom of captives and the other half for their accusers. This edict is to be proclaimed and published in all the captaincies and copied into the books of their governing councils, with a declaration of how it came to be made.

There are those who, to trade their goods, go by sea from one captaincy to another, either in their own ships or in those belonging to others. When they start to load up and before leaving the port, they must report to the [local] comptroller of my treasury who is stationed in that captaincy and tell him where the ship is being got ready. That will enable him to make the checks required in his instructions regarding merchandise to be loaded and the way in which it is to be unloaded in the places to which they are being taken.

It is my wish that from now on, no man should build any ship or caravel in Brazil without due permission. That permission you are to give in those places where you are present, in accordance with the instructions issued to the comptrollers of the various captaincies. Whenever you are not present, it is my command that the license shall be granted by the comptrollers. Moreover, you are to tell those who ask you for a license for building such ships that they are to be fitted with oars. They should have at least fifteen benches, and there should be a gap of three handspans between each bench. They shall pay no duty in my customs-houses in Portugal in respect of the munitions and equipment necessary for such ships. If they fit them with eighteen benches or more, they are to receive a grant of forty cruzados. This grant for their construction is to be issued by my treasury, as set out in the instructions held by the comptrollers. The sum is to be paid from my income from Brazil, this being specified in the instructions borne by the comptroller-general.

Should you feel that in any of the captaincies a ship fitted with oars should be built at the expense of my treasury, you are to order this to be done, and the comptroller-general shall give orders as to how it is to be built. Your duty shall be to order the artillery necessary for it to be well armed. The cost is to be debited from my account by my financial agent in accordance with the instructions held by the comptroller-general.

Through law and the *Ordinances* of these realms, I have commanded that no arms should be given to Muslims or to any other infidels, since, if they were to receive such weaponry, it would be against the interest of Our Lord and be harmful to Christians. Thus, I command that no man of whatever class or standing is to give to the pagan tribesmen of Brazil any of the following items: artillery, arquebuses, muskets, gunpowder, munitions, crossbows, lances, swords, daggers, cleavers, wood-handled scythes, German knives, or anything of that sort. Indeed, they are not to receive any other arms of whatever kind, either offensive or defensive. Any man who acts to the contrary shall pay with his life and lose all his possessions, half of which shall be for [the ransom of] captives and the other half for his accuser. I also command the justices of every township in the captaincies in Brazil that when they draw up their obligatory annual report on their officials, they should make inquiries about the above matter. Should they find any guilty parties, they are to exact the penalty indicated, in accordance with my *Ordinances*. The prohibition will also imply the following items: axes, hatchets, round-handled scythes, pruning hooks, wedges, small tack knives, and small shears. That is because such things might be handed to the pagan tribesmen in our trade with them and in exchange for money, as has occurred up to now at specific prices. The edict is to be published in each of the captaincies and recorded in the books of the governing councils, together with a declaration as to how it came to be made. Though the edict does not specifically prohibit axes, hatchets, round-handled scythes, pruning hooks, wedges, small knives, and shears, nevertheless I wish these items to be included till I send you a dispensation from the Pope.

It is essential for the fortresses and settlements in my territory in Brazil to have at their disposal artillery, munitions, and defensive and offensive weapons for their security and protection. It is therefore my wish and command that the captains of the captaincies in the territory, as well as the owners of the plantations and the settlers there, should have the following artillery and weaponry available. Every captain shall be required to have in his captaincy at least two cannon, six mortar, six bombards, twenty arquebuses or muskets, as well as all the necessary gunpowder. He shall also have twenty crossbows, twenty lances or spears, forty swords, and forty cotton-padded jackets, such as are used in Brazil. The estate and plantation owners who under the current instructions are to have fortified towers and blockhouses shall have at least four mortars and ten muskets with the necessary gunpowder, as well as ten crossbows, twenty swords, ten lances or spears, and twenty cotton-padded jackets. Every settler in Brazil who has a house, land, or water there, or a ship, shall have at least one crossbow, some muskets, a sword, and a lance or spear. This edict is to be proclaimed and displayed in each of the captaincies, with the declaration that those who do not have such artillery, gunpowder, and weaponry are to obtain them within a year of its publication. After that time, if they do not have them, they shall pay twice the cost of the weapons that they lack, of which half shall be for [the ransom of] captives and half for their accusers.

When the comptroller-general makes his tour of the captaincies, he shall take care to find out whether the persons listed above have the necessary weaponry. He is to impose the punishments described above on those who incur them. When he does not tour the captaincies, that task shall be carried out by the [local] comptroller of my treasury in each captaincy. What the latter comptroller discovers shall be set down in a written report. That report is to be forwarded to the comptroller-general so that he can act on it in accordance with this edict. Should any of the persons mentioned need to equip themselves with all or just some of the weapons, then it is my express wish that such items should be issued to them from my storehouses at the prevailing prices. The comptroller-general or the [local] comptrollers shall oversee the provision of artillery and weaponry that the captains are required to have. In respect of other persons, the captains are to carry this out, but it is my firm wish that the comptroller-general or the [local] comptrollers should oversee the exercise.

In accordance with the charter that was issued to the captaincies of the territory, all brazilwood is my property. No man may trade in it without my permission. I have been informed that those to whom I have duly given licenses for them to deliver certain quantities of brazilwood are having to barter it at a cost much higher than was customary and much greater than its true worth. Because they seek to acquire it as swiftly as possible, that very fact drives the cost upwards. It can and does result in all kinds of problems. It is therefore my express wish that in every captaincy, you should hold discussions with the comptroller-general of my treasury, the captain, the officials, and any others that you deem appropriate in order to determine what needs to be done. That will be to enable the license-holders to acquire the wood with the least possible disruption in the territory. You must impose a limit on the barter value that they are to pay for the goods circulating in the territory in place of money, and the decision reached is to be recorded in the book of the governing councils on order to ensure future compliance.

I have been informed that many people in Brazil move from one captaincy to another without permission from their captains. Problems result from such actions. To counteract this, it is my express wish that any persons who live in a particular captaincy must seek permission from their captain if they wish to move to any other captaincy. He is to grant such permission provided that, at that time, he has no need of the individuals who request permission. Otherwise, he must refuse. When he is inclined to give permission, he must first find out whether that individual has ever worked with or for any other person or has entered any form of contract with any other person and that he has fulfilled his obligations. If he finds that he has fulfilled them and is not bound to anyone, he is to grant him permission and give him a certificate to that effect. The recipient is to take the certificate with him, and it shall be collected from him in any other captaincy to which he might go. If the captain of that captaincy does not collect it from him, then he cannot admit him. Moreover, if he does admit him [in such circumstances], it is my express wish that he should incur a fine of fifty cruzados, to be divided equally between [the ransom of] captives and his accuser. This stipulation does not apply to exiled convicts, for they must always remain in the captaincies in which they disembarked when they were banished from this kingdom. They are not permitted to transfer to other captaincies. This edict is to be made public in every captaincy and recorded in the books of the governing councils.

One of the main objectives to be carried out in my territories in Brazil, so that they may be populated more effectively, is to issue the command that all pirates who venture to that land should be punished in such a way that they never dare to return. Furthermore, I recommend that you take special care so that as soon as you discover that there are pirates on any part of the coast, you are in a position to attack them with as many ships and men as you think appropriate. You are to make every effort to capture them and, once they have been captured, you are to take proceedings against them, as contained in a decree issued by me concerning this matter and that you are to take with you. If you are not able to go in person, or if for some reason closer to my interests, you believe that you ought not to go, then you are to choose and send a trustworthy person in your stead, to whom you will issue instructions as to what he must do.

For such things to be carried out effectively, and for the best defense both by land and by sea, it will be necessary to station a number of ships propelled by oars in the captaincies to which the pirates usually sail. You are to discuss matters with the comptroller-general of my treasury, as well as with the local captains, comptrollers, and officials of the various captaincies, not to mention others whom you may consider to be experienced in such matters. You will determine with them how best to build such ships, how big they should be, and in which captaincies they are to be built. You must also determine how, when need arises, they can best be supplied and armed, and how many of them there should be. You will need to decide at whose cost they are to be built and which captaincies are to enjoy the privilege of making a contribution to the necessary expenses. Your decisions are to be set down in a report that is to be forwarded to me, so that I might use the information to make due provision according to my best interests.

When you go to Bahia, you are to write to the captains of the other captaincies that as soon as they know that there are pirates along the coast, they are to write back to you. First of all, they are to ascertain what ships the pirates have, how big they are, how many men they are crewed by, and where they have anchored. That will enable you to act in such matters either as set out above or in a way that you consider to be in my best interests. Meanwhile, have them proceed with their tasks with all the equipment necessary to accomplish them safely.

I deem it to be greatly in my interests for you to discover what lies within the remoter interior of my territory of Bahia. Consequently, I recommend that as soon as there is both the time and the opportunity to carry it out effectively, you should order the dispatch of a number of well-supplied and covered brigantines along the rivers of Paraguaçu de São Francisco. Their crews shall be trustworthy and include local interpreters. They are to sail westwards upriver as far as they can and, wherever they go, they are to plant stone pillars and other markers. They shall provide reports of exactly where they have placed them, of the routes that they have taken, and of everything that they discover. You are then to write a detailed report to me concerning your role in all this and everything that takes place.

It is my recommendation and command that you carry out everything contained in these instructions. You should also ensure that others comply with them, just as I trust that you will. Jerónimo Correia wrote this in Almeirim, 17 December 1548.

[Postscript]

If any convicts that go to Brazil to serve me, either aboard ships of my fleet or in any capacity on land, and if you believe that they should therefore be trained to carry out other duties, be they juridical or financial, then you should indeed give them such duties when you need more men to serve you. That does not, however, include anyone exiled for theft or fraud.

Provided that you consider them to be worthy thereof, it is my express wish that you should confer knighthoods on any men who have served, in time of warfare, either aboard ships of my fleet or on land. You are to issue a document to each one stating the reason why they have deserved their knighthoods.

When you deem it appropriate and in my best interests to pay anyone an advance on their salary or wages or to make a gift to anyone, then you may do so, provided that the gift does not exceed one thousand cruzados in any one year.

In edicts within these instructions, I have commanded you to wage war on the pagan tribesmen in the manner set out therein. I have also commanded you to punish those among them who are guilty of past misdemeanors. Owing to the poor grasp of such matters that, till now, such pagans have shown (and this greatly lessens their guilt), it is my express wish that should they now recognize their guilt and seek to be pardoned, then such pardon should be granted to them. Furthermore, it is my wish that you should steer them in that direction as best you can, as it is my firm intent that they be converted forthwith to our Holy Faith. It is therefore reasonable that you should apply all possible measures to bring that about. The principal measure is to avoid waging war on them, since otherwise there could be no communication with them that would lead to their conversion.

You are to take with you a copy of my *Ordinances*, as I have given orders therein that in my realms and territories nobody, of whatever standing, may wear brocades, silks, or other material mentioned in my *Ordinances*.[4] As soon as you arrive in Bahia, you are to order this to be made known and are to send copies of the *Ordinances*, countersigned by you, to the other captaincies, so that there they can be made public and fully observed. This notification is to be decreed in every captaincy and copied, along with the *Ordinances*, into the book of the governing council. Any punishments contained in them are to be observed with effect from the day of the notification.

It is my view that it would be highly undesirable for members of pagan tribes who become Christians to live in settlements mingling with those who have not. It would be greatly in God's interest and in my own to keep them apart. It is my recommendation and command that you ensure that those who become Christians should live together, close to the settlements of the captaincies, so that they might mix with other Christians rather than with pagans. In that way, they can be taught the doctrine of our Holy Faith. As for their children, because they can be more easily taught doctrine, you must give urgent orders that they should become Christians, duly educated and removed from the company of pagans. On my behalf, you are to tell the captains of the other captaincies that you would be grateful if they were to take care to do the same in every captaincy. The children will live in the Portuguese settlements, and it would give me great pleasure for them to be taught in the way that I have explained to you.

When anything occurs that is not covered by these instructions, and if you form the view that it is in my best interests to act, then you should discuss the matter with my officials and with any others who are able to give you information or advice. Then you should take action. If there is disagreement as to what should be done, then it is my wish that your view should prevail. A report should then be drawn up, indicating both your opinion and the opinions of those with whom you have conferred. The report should then be forwarded to me along with the first letters that you send to me after the discussion.

## 2. The Capital: The City of Salvador and the Captaincy of Bahia. The Treatise of Gabriel Soares de Souza

*Tomé de Sousa created the colonial capital at Salvador on the Bay of All Saints. We know a great deal about that city and its environs from the excellent account of Gabriel Soares de Sousa. Born in Portugal in approximately 1540, Soares de*

---

4 Sumptuary laws were designed to maintain social hierarchies. In the case of early Brazil, where capital was in short supply, they may have also been designed to discourage the purchase of luxury items.

*Sousa arrived in Brazil in 1569 and settled in Bahia, where he established a sugar mill in the Recôncavo, the lands surrounding the Bay of All Saints. In hope of gaining support for exploration into the sertão (interior), he traveled to the court in Madrid (Portugal was ruled by the Spanish Hapsburgs from 1580 to 1640). There, in 1587, he penned a number of promotional texts to support his project, hoping to influence important courtiers. These texts have come to be known as the Tratado descretivo. He received a commission and returned to Brazil, where he led an unsuccessful expedition into the interior in search of mines. He died somewhere near the Paraguaçu River in 1591 and was eventually laid to rest in the Benedictine monastery in Salvador under a tombstone that read simply: "Here lies a sinner." The account of Soares de Souza is valuable for the level of detail it provides about the land, the flora and fauna, the indigenous peoples, and the growing colony. His long residence in Brazil, his intimate knowledge of the sugar industry, his familiarity with the indigenous peoples and their customs, and his own curiosity and powers of observation all make his account particularly valuable. The Tratado circulated in manuscript for centuries and was consulted by many historians but was only published for the first time in 1825 in a poor edition. The translation presented here is based on Gabriel Soares de Sousa, Tratado desccretivo do Brasil de 1587, edited by Francisco Adolfo de Varnhagen in 1839, which has been the basis of most modern editions of the work. (From Gabriel Soares de Sousa, Tratado Descritivo do Brasil em 1587, 4th ed. [São Paulo, 1971], pp. 129–42; 144–63.)*

## Chapter III. How the City of Salvador Came to Be Built

When Tomé de Sousa had finished disembarking the members of his fleet and had settled them in Vila Velha, he gave orders for the bay to be explored, with a view to finding, at some point where the bay stretched further inland, a more sheltered anchorage than that in which the fleet lay. He was keen to remove it from the harbor of Vila Velha, in which it was far from secure, owing to its exposed position. As there was a [suitable] harbor and anchorage, that nowadays is be found facing the city [of Salvador], he had the fleet transferred to that spot, because of its straightforward and sheltered characteristics. Once the fleet had been duly safeguarded, he ordered the land around to be carefully reconnoitred. That done, he decided that the area facing the harbor was indeed the best for it had been inappropriate to build fortifications at the harbor of Vila Velha. His reasoning was that facing the [new] harbor there flowed a great stream that came down to the shore. The stream was ideal for the provision of a supply of fresh water both to the ships and for use in the city. All the members of his advisory council readily concurred with his opinion, and the decision was duly taken to proceed.

Steps were then taken to go ahead with the building enterprise. First of all, they built a very sturdy stockade of wattle and daub to protect the workmen and the soldiers from the native tribesmen. When it had been completed, the city was laid out inside it. Streets were neatly set out with houses covered with roofs of palm branches after the manner of the native population. These were for the time being the dwellings of the youths and soldiers that had arrived onboard the fleet. When once they had all been housed, Tomé de Sousa gave orders that the city be surrounded with ramparts of stone and gravel, a task that he completed very promptly. This fortification had two bastions facing the sea and four facing inland. On every one of the bastions there were sited cannon of the highest standard that he had brought for that specific purpose. As a result, the city was very securely fortified against attack from the native tribesmen. Then the governor-general immediately founded, within the city, a college of the Jesuit Fathers, as well as other churches and major buildings. These included buildings for the governor and his entourage and for the city council. Also constructed were a prison, a customs house, counting houses, treasury buildings, warehouses, and other workshops appropriate to the service of His Majesty.

## Chapter IV. How the King Came to Send a Second Fleet in Support of Tomé de Sousa

In the following year, 1550, a further fleet, with men and supplies, was dispatched as additional aid to the new city. Its captain was Simão da Gama de Andrade, who sailed in a very famous old galleon and was accompanied by several merchant ships. In this fleet, there journeyed Bishop Pedro Fernandes Sardinha, an exemplary figure of great authority and a distinguished preacher. He traveled with a full complement of clergy, church ornaments, bells, silver plate, and other ecclesiastical furnishings, as well as everything else appropriate for the celebration of the Mass. His valuation of the expenditure on the foregoing, as well as on the outlay on artillery, munitions, supplies, wages, and officers' salaries, was that it came to more than three hundred thousand cruzados.[5]

Then, in 1551, yet a third fleet was sent by His Majesty in support of the city. It was captained by António de Oliveira, who was accompanied by married settlers and a number of exiled convicts. Aboard the ships, the late Queen Catarina sent a number of young unmarried women of noble

---

5  A cruzado was normally a silver coin, equivalent to 400 reals (réis) in a system in which the real was the unitary copper coin.

stock. She had arranged for them to be brought together and reared in the convent for orphan girls in Lisbon. In letters to the governor-general, she greatly commended them with a view to his marrying them to men who were then prominent. As dowries, the young women bore with them offices in the treasury and in the legal service. In this way, the city gradually gained a noble character.

His Majesty also sent to the new city slaves captured in Guinea, as well as cows and mares. These were to be distributed among the settlers, in return for payment from their wages and salaries. In addition, he sent out goods to be sold at the same price that they cost in Lisbon. That was because at that time, traders did not travel to those parts, nor was there any incentive for them, owing to the fact that there were not yet any men in Salvador that they could take on as employees. Accordingly, every year His Majesty dispatched a fleet in support of the settlers: such fleets carried exiled convicts, young orphan women, and all manner of goods. In that way, the city very progressively enhanced its character and increased its population. The other captaincies also benefited from this aid and were visited by the governor-general. In that way, they were brought more closely into the king's service, all of which promoted the administration of his justice and enhanced his treasury.

### Chapter V. How Dom Duarte da Costa Became Governor-General of Brazil

When Tomé de Sousa completed his stint as governor-general (a period that he had spent so well in the new State of Brazil), he requested His Majesty to recall him to Portugal. That request was granted when the king sent out as governor-general Dom Duarte da Costa, a member of his advisory council. He provided him with an appropriate flotilla for the journey to Brazil, aboard which he arrived safely in Bahia de Todos os Santos. He went ashore in the city of Salvador, which was the name that His Majesty commanded him to give to it. The coat of arms of the city, given by the king, consisted of a white dove on a green field, with a white circlet around it and with letters of gold proclaiming *Sic illa ad Arcam reversa est*.

The dove holds three olive leaves in its beak. The new governor-general was installed by Tomé de Sousa, who then set sail in the same flotilla. It bore him back to Portugal, where he served as chamberlain both to King John and to his grandson, King Sebastian. In that very post he also served Queen Catarina for as long as she lived.

As regards Dom Duarte, once he had taken up the reins of government, he worked as hard as possible to fortify and defend this city from the native tribesmen, particularly as they rose up during his period in office. They committed great outrages that in some instances he put right through prudent diplomacy, whereas in others he punished them by waging savage war against them. That fight was led by his son, Dom Álvaro da Costa, who accompanied him in such undertakings and proved himself to be a most valiant leader of men.

Throughout the time when Dom Duarte was governor-general of Brazil, he benefited from the assistance provided by fleets that were sent out from Portugal. Onboard these there were transported not only many settlers but also exiled convicts, as well as all necessary supplies. Dom Duarte was succeeded by Mem de Sá, whose deeds we have already touched on. Mem de Sá was likewise appointed governor-general of the State of Brazil by King John III. Good fortune favored him for the fourteen years that he held office: he defeated and subjugated all the pagan Tupinambá tribesmen in the captaincy of Bahia, as well as all other tribesmen as far down as Rio de Janeiro. Indeed, a whole and very remarkable treatise could be devoted to what he accomplished.

Nevertheless, Mem de Sá received very little help from Portugal, firstly through the immediate death of King John[6] (who had so devotedly worked at building up and adding to the State of Brazil), and secondly, though Queen Catarina imitated him for the [short] period in which she reigned over Brazil, because many benefits ceased when she relinquished the regency.[7] The annual aid that the new city received was gradually reduced to a trickle, to the point where the only vessel to arrive was the single galleon on which successive governors-general came out to take up their posts. As a result, the once flourishing State of Brazil flourished no more. Though this city of Salvador has grown in the numbers of its inhabitants, in its buildings, and in its output, those factors are due to the great fertility of the soil that has been such a boon to the settlers. Consequently, within its present boundaries, as they stretch inland, there are now forty sugar mills, with buildings that proclaim their very prosperity, not to mention slave quarters and sundry other workshops. Indeed, there would have been many more sugar mills, if the settlers had received the appropriate backing that they have deserved for their hard efforts. It was with their assistance that Mem de Sá defeated and laid low the native tribesmen who lived in the area of Bahia, burning down and razing to the ground more than thirty of their villages. Those tribesmen who escaped death or captivity fled into the interior, putting more than forty

---

6  Although he appointed Mem de Sá, John III died in June 1557, several months before the new governor-general's departure for Brazil in 1558.

7  Queen Catarina became regent during King Sebastian's infancy, but her rule was to last only from 1557 until December 1562, when she was succeeded in that office by John's brother, Cardinal Henry.

leagues between themselves and the sea. With those selfsame settlers, Mem de Sá went to the aid of the captaincies of Ilhéus, Porto Seguro, and Espírito Santo, who were clearly separated from the tribesmen of those areas. Again with the help of the settlers, on two occasions he ejected the French from Rio de Janeiro, which he then went on to fill with inhabitants. Many of the settlers met their end there, yet even now no recompense has been made to their children. They all took part in these and many other undertakings at their own cost. Nobody paid them wages nor gave them supplies, unlike the practice in India and elsewhere. In recognition of the great sacrifices made by the settlers of this city, not a single honor and not a single favor has been bestowed on any one of them, at which they remain greatly scandalized and disappointed.

### Chapter VI. The Climate of Bahia, the Winds That Blow along Its Coast and the Direction of Its Seawater

Bahia de Todos os Santos is located at thirteen degrees, thirty-three minutes south, as was mentioned earlier. All year round the days are roughly the same in length as the nights. Summer days are from an hour to an hour and a half longer than winter days. Winter in this province begins in the month of April and ends in the latter days of July. That season is not so cold that it makes people huddle round the fire, though the natives feel the cold because they wear no clothes. Throughout winter, the waters flow along the coast and for a hundred leagues out to sea. They flow from south to north for four to five months. Sometimes the winds blow from the south, southwest, and east-southeast, creating a fierce headwind along the coast from Porto Seguro to Cape Santo Agostinho.

Summer begins in August (whereas in Portugal it begins in March) and lasts until the latter days of March. Throughout that season, the winds blow from the northeast and east-northeast. The waters flow along the coast, driven by the winds from north to south. That is why one can only sail along the coast helped by the normal trade winds. The whole year round, when it rains, the skies of Bahia display the most beautiful, multicolored clouds. Their splendor has no equal anywhere else and is a source of surprise and admiration. Also noteworthy is the fact that in the area around Bahia, the first light of day is simultaneous with the first rays of sunlight, and that this feature is true both in winter and in summer. Similarly, at the setting of the sun in the evening, darkness falls instantly, and night closes in. Let the mathematicians provide explanations to anyone interested in penetrating this secret. Certainly, the seafarers and philosophers who have reached this land, not to mention other men of sound judgment, have yet to hit on the reason why this should be.

## Chapter VII. The Location of the City of Salvador

The city of Salvador is located in the Bahia de Todos os Santos (Bay of All Saints), one league within the entrance to the bay. It stands on a cliff and faces west, overlooking the bay. Ramparts and towers were built around it at the time of Tomé de Sousa, the builder of the city, as mentioned above. The ramparts have collapsed because they were of rough stonework and because they were never repaired. The explanation is that either the governors-general were knowingly negligent in this or that the city gradually extended well beyond the ramparts. Whichever is the case, nobody now recollects the precise position of the ramparts. The city has approximately eight hundred inhabitants. Beyond the city, in all the surrounding territory of Bahia, there probably live in excess of two thousand more. Taking both groups together, it is possible to amass, when needed, a force of five hundred men on horseback and a further two thousand on foot, not counting the men from the ships that are always in the harbor.

In the middle of the city, there is a fine square, in which are held occasional bullfights. On the south side stand a number of noble buildings that house the governors-general. On the north side there stand the treasury, the customs house, and warehouses. On the east stand the city hall, the prison, and sundry houses belonging to settlers. The area surrounded by these structures is square in shape, and the pillory is at its very center. On the west there is an unimpeded view of the sea. Along this side are ranged a number of sturdy cannon. Beyond them the land falls steeply away down rugged cliffs to the sea. From the corners of this side of the square, two pathways sweep down, round sharp bends, to the shore. One begins on the north side and leads to the stream known as Pereira and to the landing stage for those coming off the ships. The other, which begins on the south side of the square, leads to the chapel of Our Lady of the Immaculate Conception, close to where the general landing stage for merchandise is to be found. That landing stage is also approached by a cart track, along which goods and other things that have been unloaded from the ships are taken by cart up to the city.

If one goes back to the main square, one finds running out of its northerly side a splendid row of shops that leads to the cathedral. At the end of that street, on the side overlooking the sea, stand the Misericórdia and its hospital. The church of the Misericórdia is not large but it is beautifully built and very ornate. The Misericórdia does not possess large offices and wards for the sick, owing to its lack of funds. It receives no income from His Majesty or from private individuals, being entirely dependent on alms from local residents. Though the latter donors are numerous, the needs of the Misericórdia are greater. That is due to the many seamen and exiled convicts who leave Portugal in great penury. The only solution they can find for their plight is to turn for help to the Misericórdia. The alms it receives amount to roughly three thousand cruzados annually. This sum is meticulously spent on tending the sick and helping the needy.

## Chapter VIII. The Layout of the City around the Cathedral

The cathedral of the city of Salvador is situated facing the sea, overlooking the ships' anchorage. In front of its main door there is a flat and spacious area, from which there is a fine view and a sheer drop to the landing stage.

The cathedral church has three naves. It is a tall building of splendid size and fine appearance. It possesses five very ornate and well-constructed chapels and two altars to either side of the main chapel. The cathedral is girt about with an open space on all sides. As yet uncompleted are its belfry and clocktower, and still lacking are a number of very necessary ancillary buildings. The cathedral, however, is lacking in financial resources. Its annual building fund comes to no more than one hundred milréis,[8] and even that sum is amassed with great difficulty.

Divine service is provided in the cathedral church by the dean and four archdeacons, six canons, two deputy canons, four chaplains, one priest, one coadjutor, four choristers, and one choirmaster. Many of the ministers are not priests.[9] Though their numbers are so small, the divine office is carried out with great solemnity, and they take up a large portion of the bishop's resources. This is disbursed on keeping the able priests happy, as each one requires a share appropriate to his being a canon or archdeacon or dean, posts that other clergy avoid. That is because each canon gets only thirty milréis, the archdeacons only thirty-five, and the dean a mere forty, though these amounts are not even enough to pay for their vestments. For that reason, most clergy prefer to be chaplains to the Misericórdia or to certain sugar mills, where their contract amounts to sixty milréis, along with board and lodging. In such places, their orders and altar fees bring in as much again.

The cathedral is in great need of ornamentation, and the ornaments that it does have are much damaged. As a result, on the major feast-days, ornaments are borrowed from the chapters of the lay brotherhoods. It is clear that His Majesty cannot have been informed of this, for if he had been, he would already have given orders to remove this deficiency in the celebration of the divine office. As he requires payment of tithes by this, his State of Brazil, whose very head is so damaged, then it is only right that due remedies should be brought to bear as soon as possible.

---

8   A *milréis* was a silver coin equivalent to a thousand réis.
9   This clearly means that such ministers were only in minor orders.

## Chapter IX. The Layout of the City Beyond the Cathedral

Beyond the cathedral and also running in a northerly direction lies another very broad street, likewise occupied by rows of merchants' shops. That street ends in a large and spacious open area where horse tournaments are held. That is because it is bigger than the main square, which is hemmed in by noble houses. The open area is occupied, on the side looking toward the sea, by a sumptuous college belonging to the Jesuit Fathers. It possesses a fine and splendid church, where the divine office is celebrated with very rich ornamentation and which the Fathers always keep very clean and fragrant.[10]

This college possesses splendidly built dormitories, some of which have a wonderful view of the sea. It is constructed of whitewashed stone with many carved staircases, windows, balconies, and doors. The cubicles are separated by well-lined partitions and have excellent stone flooring. The college owns large enclosed cisterns bordering the seashore, with excellent water in them,[11] while along the shore it possesses warehouses, in which are stored goods that the Jesuits import from abroad. The college normally houses eighty religious, some of whom are occupied in preaching and hearing confessions, while others teach Latin, philosophy, science, and theology, as well as dealing with cases of conscience, in which work they have borne great fruit in this region. The college is very wealthy because it receives an annual grant of four thousand cruzados. In addition, further income that it derives from the land amounts to as much again. That is because it owns many cattle farms, in which it is reported that there are two thousand cows that give birth every year. The college also possesses many other estates and plantations, where many new forms of vegetable produce are amply harvested in this fertile land of Bahia.

## Chapter X. The Layout of the City in the Same Direction, as Far as Its Perimeter

Another very long street runs beyond the college in the same northerly direction. It is a very broad street and is full of residents' houses. Further on, on the very outskirts of the city, perched on a hill, stands a monastery of Capuchins devoted to Saint Anthony.[12] The monastery was founded quite recently from the alms of the people, with which this site was purchased. Other devotees gave them further adjacent pieces of land on which the residents built a church. With the church and its secluded monastery, it has proved possible to accommodate up to twenty religious. In the future,

10 This church is nowadays the cathedral of Salvador.
11 This was freshwater diverted from the nearby stream mentioned in Chapter III.
12 The Capuchins were a branch of the Franciscans that had been founded in 1529. These particular Capuchins had a devotion to Saint Anthony of Lisbon and Padua, himself a Franciscan.

further monastic buildings will be added in line with the priests' wishes. Within the monastery, they have an enclosed water supply. The water runs down to the sea from above, where the monastery stands. If one returns from the monastery to the main square and to the land side, one finds that the city has very fine streets, lined with residents' houses and their fruit gardens. The gardens are replete with fertile coconut palms and date palms, with orange trees and briers, with fig trees, pomegranate trees, and vines. All this gives a fragrant air to the city. On the land side and coursing along its entire edge, the city has a ready stream of water, which is available both for washing clothes and for watering the kitchen gardens that run alongside it.[13]

## Chapter XI. The Layout of the City to the South of the Main Square

If we go back to the main square and face south, we encounter another very fine residents' street, at the end of which stands the chapel of Saint Lucy. There is also a cannon emplacement alongside. The street is splendidly set out, with numerous traders' shops, and at the top end is situated the beautiful church of Our Lady of Succor, with its vaulted chapel. When the city was first built, that site was occupied by the cathedral.

Farther to the south, on the outskirts of the city, on a hill and in an open position, there stands the Benedictine monastery, with its cloisters, ample workshops, and dormitories. Twenty religious reside in the monastery. They have at their disposal their own enclosure, with its kitchen garden and a stream of water that rises at that very spot. It is, in fact, the stream that encircles the whole city, as has been mentioned earlier. This Benedictine monastery is very poor and is maintained by the alms that the monks beg from the settlers' profits. It receives no income from His Majesty, though such an income would be well employed, in view of the monastery's needs. That is because its religious lead holy, decent, and exemplary lives and are greatly loved and appreciated by the people. They arrived in the city three years ago, with permission from His Majesty to found this monastery. The residents built it at their own expense and did so with the greatest enthusiasm.

The other streets of this city receive no special mention here, as to do so would be an endless task.

## Chapter XII. Other Notable Parts of the City

The city has great landing stages, with three streams running down to the shore alongside them. The seamen make full use of the water from these

---

13 As explained in Chapter XII, the stream was, however, no longer used as a source of drinking water.

streams at the very edge of the sea, just as most of the city makes use of it, as the water from the streams is of very good quality. Next to the main landing stage stands a humble chapel to Our Lady of the Immaculate Conception. This chapel was the very first house of prayer and the first construction with which Tomé de Sousa concerned himself.

The view of the city from a distance is very agreeable. That is because the houses have gardens full of trees. The trees are palms that soar above the rooftops, and orange trees that are laden with oranges the whole year round. The view of the latter trees from afar, especially from the sea, is delightful. That is because the city, on its cliff-top, stretches out alongside the sea.

The city has no higher ground [to its rear] from which it could be attacked if the city were appropriately surrounded. An attack is feasible, though the city has a brook running through it. The brook rises from a nearby spring and runs round the whole city, but it is no longer used as drinking water because the ground where the spring rises has been trodden down by oxen who drink there, as well as by pigs. Though its water is [still] clear and of very good quality, the settlers no longer use it because there are many other springs from which each individual drinks according to preference, though they usually resort to the nearest one, as they are all of good-quality water.

The land available to the city stretches for between one and two leagues beyond the city's edge and is almost entirely given over to farms that greatly resemble those in Portugal. On these are cultivated all manner of foodstuffs, both fruit and vegetables. These are supplied to all those in the city that do not grow them in their own gardens. They are sold in the street markets, which are always well stocked. Most of the time, there is a good supply of bread. This is made from the grain that is normally shipped from Portugal to Bahia. Also transported are many wines from the island of Madeira and from the Canaries. These wines are more delicate, more fragrant, better colored, and sweeter than those that are drunk in the very islands from which they are imported. The wines are sold on stalls in the street, along with other goods imported from Spain, as well as light woollens, silks, and all manner of fabrics, not to mention the more usual merchandise.

## Chapter XIII. How the [Wealthy] Residents of the City of Salvador Regale Themselves, and Some of Their Characteristics

Within the city limits of Salvador, there are many wealthy property-owning residents, owners of gold and silver ornaments, stables full of horses, and ample domestic furnishings. There are also many that possess two to three cruzados' worth of beautifully wrought gold and silver jewelry. In Bahia, there reside more than a hundred settlers whose annual income goes from one thousand to five thousand cruzados. There are others who are wealthier still and whose property ranges in value from twenty to fifty or sixty thousand cruzados or even more. They regale themselves richly, with many horses, servants, and slaves, not to mention owning an excess of clothing, especially the women. They dress entirely in silks, because this land is not cold, and spend a fortune on them, [parading them] among people of lesser condition. For any mean individual wears doublet and hose made of satin or damask, while the womenfolk wear skirts and doublets of the same fabrics. The wealthy, as they have every opportunity, keep their houses in fine array, with silver service on their tables and bedeck their wives with choice clothes and golden jewelry.

The city has fourteen heavy cannon and roughly forty light cannon. The heavy cannon are located in the emplacements previously mentioned, as well as in another one that stands at the Ponta do Padrão.[14] That emplacement exists to defend the entrance to the harbor bar from attacks made by pirate ships. Its sole purpose is to try to cause them sufficient damage to drive them off course, preventing them from seizing the harbor with their very first broadside. That is because the entrance to the harbor bar is very wide, enabling them to make off with any carracks they might wish, without the [remaining] artillery causing them any upset.

## Chapter XIV. How Bahia Could Be More Easily Defended

It is not inappropriate to mention at this juncture that our master the king has the duty to insist that all due assistance be given to the city to remove its vulnerability by his ordering that it be fortified and girt about with ramparts. That would be only right in the interests both of service to him and of the security of its residents. The city runs the risk of being ransacked by a handful of pirate ships that could [so easily] attack it. That is because so many of its people are scattered around outside the city, while those within the city have no point from which they could defend it, while waiting for help to come from those people who live on the estates and plantations. But as long as it has no encircling ramparts, it has no better means of defending itself from any pirates entering the bay than by the resort to a handful of galliots that could be constructed at little cost and could always be fully armed. To fight in support of the galliots there could also be vessels from the plantations, as well as other boats. [Light] cannon could be taken aboard for that purpose. Such an armada could gain further support from the carracks from Portugal. There are always eight to ten of those in the harbor, and from now on there will be as many as fifteen or twenty that will be loading sugar and

---

14  Literally, "Landfall Pillar Point." A *padrão* was a commemorative stone pillar, bearing the royal arms, erected by Portuguese navigators as a mark of possession.

cotton. Men from the city could be put aboard them to defend them, as well as some cannon with which to attack the enemy. As for the latter, if they were not to capture the city at the first onset, they would be unable to force their way in later, owing to the help of up to two thousand Portuguese approaching both by land and sea. The latter could be supported in the battle by ten thousand slaves: four thousand black slaves from Guinea and six thousand native Indians, who are very fine bowmen. All these, together with the men from the city, would constitute a very reasonable fighting force. Such a force, if well led, could inflict heavy losses on any armed aggressors landing on the shore. The aggressors would find themselves harassed and attacked in the dense undergrowth and would be forced to retreat in great haste. God forbid, however, that such should be the outcome, owing to the vulnerability of the city.[15] The English are certainly aware of that weakness, as they have already visited the city. They could seize much booty. If, as of now, they were to attack the city with any flotilla, they would find many ships laden with sugar and cotton and great quantities of the same stored in the warehouses that lie alongside the traders' wharves. Not only would they find such merchandise, but they would also find large amounts of ready cash, many gold and silver pieces, and many household items.

### Chapter XV. The Great Qualities of Bahia de Todos os Santos

The late John III of Portugal was so attached to the State of Brazil, and especially to Bahia, that if he had lived for a few more years, he would have built there one of the most remarkable countries in the world. He would so have enhanced the city of Salvador that it could have been counted among the most outstanding cities in his [many] kingdoms. The city was well capable of receiving such enhancement. Indeed, it is nowadays even more suitable for such development, because it dominates this bay, which is the biggest and most beautiful bay that we know of in the whole world, both in its grandeur and in its rich fertility. This bay is huge; it has very fine, clear, and healthy air; it has excellent fresh water; and is rich in the natural vegetable produce of the land, in its plentiful game, and in the abundance of its tasty fish and delicious fruit. The lie of the land is as follows.

The bay extends from the Ponta do Padrão to the promontory of Tinharé. The distance between the two is of some nine to ten leagues, though the captain of the captaincy of Ilhéus asserts that the bay extends only from the tip of the island of Itaparica to the Ponta do Padrão. However, a court ruling has established that it indeed runs from the Ponta do Padrão to the promontory of Tinharé, as stated above. The ruling was issued in order to remove any uncertainties between the land lessors of the captaincies of Ilhéus and

15  The fear is that the retreat might be through the city.

Bahia, as to which party owned the tithes derived from the fishing that takes place in the vicinity of the promontory of Tinharé. The ruling was that the tithes belonged to the lessor of Bahia, as it was ascertained that the bay runs inwards from that hill, as should be the true interpretation. [. . . . ]

## Chapter XVIII. The Stretch of Sea within the Bay, Its Capacity for Carracks under Sail and Its Islands

From the city on one side of the bay to the opposite mainland (which is known as Paraguaçu), one has to sail a distance of nine to ten leagues. In the middle, there is an island called the Island of the Friars [Ilha dos *Frades*]. It is two leagues long and one league wide. To the north of that island lies another, called the Island of the Tide [Ilha de *Maré*]. This island is one league long and half a league wide. The two islands lie three leagues apart. From the Island of the Tide to the mainland to the west, there is a distance of roughly half a league. From the Island of the Friars to the island of Itaparica, there is a distance of four leagues. The city lies six leagues away from the Island of the Tide and there is a similar distance from the city to the Island of the Friars. There is a stretch of sea running from the tip of the island of Itaparica to that of the Island of the Friars and on to the Island of the Tide, and from there to the mainland by the River Matoim and on again to the city. Throughout that entire stretch of sea to the entrance to the harbor bar, carracks of every tonnage may tack against the wind. They will not encounter any shallows, as long as they keep the distance of a light cannon shot away from the shore.

The Island of the Friars belongs to a certain proprietor named João Nogueira. He settled on the island with six or seven other farmers who work for him. They each have their own small-holdings where they grow food and rear cattle and pigs. The island has many streams, though they are too tiny for sugar estates, and the earth could not sustain the canes. The Island of the Tide has excellent soil for such plantations, for cotton, and for all other forms of vegetable produce. There is a cane plantation tilled by oxen. It belongs to Bartolomeu Pires, who is choirmaster at the cathedral. He has a workforce of more than twenty settlers. They have a well-designed church dedicated to Our Lady of the Snows. It has its own priest to administer the sacraments to the settlers.

## Chapter XIX. A Description of the Captaincy of Bahia, from the City to the Tip of Tapagipe, as Well as of Its Islands

As stated above, it is a journey of one league from the city to the Ponta do Padrão. It is now appropriate for us to cover the whole surrounding area that constitutes the captaincy of Bahia, in order to show how much there is to see and how much is noteworthy.

If we begin by traveling from the city to the tip of Tapagipe, which is a league distant, then, halfway along, a water-mill is under construction on a stream called "The Children's Brook." It cannot be very productive as it is too near the city. The mill is being built by one of the major settlers in Bahia, namely Cristóvão de Aguiar de Altero. At the tip of Tapagipe are a number of potteries and a cattle corral belonging to Garcia de Ávila. At the very end of the tip of Tapagipe, there is a gap in the reefs, permitting an entry for the caravels, and these for some time have made use of it. From the mouth of the bar there is a channel along which the caravels and other ships can find a safe haven. When the city was first founded, there were views expressed that this channel should be dug at the tip of Tapagipe, on the grounds that it would be a safer and surer arrangement. It runs north and south in relation to the Ponta do Padrão.

To the right of the Ponta do Padrão there is a very deep inlet along which carracks of four hundred tons make their entrance. This inlet is called Pirajá. There are great bends in it as it makes its way inshore. On one of them, the shore allows ships to be beached very easily, permitting caulking in harmony with the tides, because the receding water lays bare the keel, facilitating the firing and caulking.

Along this inlet, after we pass the point, we come upon three small inhabited islands on which work takes place on cane plantations and small-holdings. On the land at the point, there are two more potteries. They are very productive because the clay here is plentiful and of very good quality. This clay is supplied to most of the sugar mills, for they use it in the process of purifying the sugar.

## Chapter XX. A Description of the Sugar Plantations along the River Pirajá

If we go up the inlet, keeping our eyes on the land, there is a fine view of three sugar plantations, as well as many other estates that have a splendid appearance when viewed from the sea. When the saltwater comes to an end, there begins a fine river of freshwater that is used in the grinding process by a mill belonging to His Majesty. Alongside the mill is a church dedicated to Saint Bartholomew, as well as its surrounding parish. The output of the mill amounts to six hundred and fifty arrobas[16] of white sugar every year. Inland from this plantation, half a league away, there stands another mill. It is the property of Diogo da Rocha de Sá and uses a different watercourse in its grinding process. It has a splendid set of buildings, along with a well-appointed church dedicated to Saint Sebastian. To the left of the mill

16  An arroba was a weight equivalent to approximately 15 kg.

belonging to His Majesty stands another mill. It is the property of João de Barros Cardoso and lies half a league away, on the city side. The inlet bends inward toward it and is used by its barges. This mill is highly productive and employs many slaves in its output. It has immense buildings and plentiful vegetable fields, cane plantations, and cattle farms. It also possesses a chapel dedicated to Our Lady of the Incarnation, which is very well appointed with all necessary fixtures.

Between the plantations, there is a very productive apiary, rich in honey, belonging to António Nunes Reimão. To the right of the plantation belonging to His Majesty is yet another plantation, owned by Dona Leonor Soares, wife of the late Simão da Gama de Andrade. The mill on this plantation uses again a different watercourse in the grinding process. It too is very productive and is very well built.

The River Pirajá is full of fish and shellfish. The city and the estates in the area greatly rely on these. There are always seven or eight fishing boats at work there with their nets, catching large quantities of fish. In winter, when the weather is stormy, the fishermen fish there from rafts belonging to city residents as well as to estate owners for two leagues around. They always succeed in catching fish, and all needs are satisfied.

## Chapter XXI. The Location of the Estates That Run from the Mouth of the Pirajá as Far as the River Matoim

Down the River Pirajá and then, from its mouth, up along the side of the bay, there is a whole series of fine estates that are so delightful to behold from the sea that our eyes never tire of looking at them.

At the outset there stands an estate belonging to António de Oliveira de Carvalhal, who was the mayor of Vila Velha. It has a chapel dedicated to Saint Blaize. This beautiful shoreline follows the bay until it reaches the church of Our Lady of the Stair, a very fine and well-appointed building belonging to the Jesuit Fathers. Sometimes certain Fathers go there to convalesce from their illnesses, as it is ideal for that purpose. The church stands a league away from the River Pirajá and two leagues distant from the city. Farther up from Our Lady of the Stair, the land doubles back to the harbor at Paripe, a league away. The harbor is known as "the Great Beach" (Praia Grande), because it is such a delightful sight. All along it are splendid estates, not forgetting a well-constructed sugar mill that uses oxen for the grinding process. Its owner is Francisco de Aguilar, a prominent figure and a Castilian by birth. Some five hundred *braças*[17] inland from the harbor at Paripe stands another mill worked by oxen. It formerly belonged

17  A *braça* was a linear measure equivalent to 7 feet.

to Vasco Rodrigues Lobato, is totally encircled by cane plantations, and produces many *arrobas*.

From the harbor at Paripe, the land spears its way into the sea and runs along like that for the best part of a league till it reaches a chapel dedicated to Saint Thomas on a patch of higher ground. Close to the hillock, footprints can be seen imprinted on a flat piece of rock. According to the native tribespeople, their ancestors claimed that the marks were left there long ago by the feet of a holy man. All the land in this area is very fertile, full of cane plantations and brier patches, fruit from Spain, and local fruit. From here, the land sweeps back on itself, forming another beautiful beach full of fertile estates. Above them all there stands the Church of Our Lady of O,[18] the parish church of the township of Paripe, which lies nearby, complete with streets and full of residents. It is the oldest township and judicial district of Bahia.

From this beach, the land once again darts away like a spear toward the sea. Its farthest projection is known as Toquetoque Point, from which it again doubles back till reaching the mouth of the River Matoim, overlooked by fine estates. From the harbor at Paripe to the River Matoim is a distance of two leagues, while from the Matoim to the city the distance is five leagues.

## Chapter XXII. A Description of the Dimensions of the River Matoim and of the Cane Plantations along It

The tide sweeps up the River Matoim for four leagues. The mouth of the river, from one bank to the other, is no wider than a light cannon shot. For more than a league from its mouth, the river is lined by the most fertile farms. It has many twists and turns, inlets and creeks, and after that first league, the river greatly widens from one bank to the other. On the right, and up a certain arm of the river, lies the famous cane plantation of Paripe. It formerly belonged to Afonso de Torres and is now the property of the merchant Baltasar Pereira. Dues are paid to this plantation by all the farms adjacent to the harbor at Paripe (which is also known as the Shark [*Tubarão*]), by those that run on to the mouth of the Matoim and by those extending for two leagues upstream.

Beyond this plantation there are yet many more estates running up the right-hand side of the river. On the estate belonging to Francisco Barbuda is to be found a chapel dedicated to Saint Benedict. Further on, on another estate, the owner of which is Cristóvão de Aguiar, there is another chapel, dedicated to Our Lady. The land runs on like this as far as the mouth of the River Salgado, with numerous noble estates that have elegant and spacious

---

18  This unusual name is sometimes rendered as "Our Lady of Expectation of Childbirth."

farmhouses. Along the bank of that river, there is situated a sugar mill driven by oxen. It has two cane crushers and belongs to Gaspar Dias Barbosa. It is a property of immense value and has on its land a church dedicated to Saint Catherine. Close to this sugar mill there runs a stream on which there could be erected an excellent mill powered by water. However, this has not been done, as there is a dispute about the water between contending claimants.

On the other side of this cane plantation there lies yet another one, which is said to belong to Sebastião da Ponte. There the crushing [of the cane] is effected by a river named Cotegipe. This plantation is very rich in well-designed buildings. If we go back downstream for about half a league on the right-hand side, we come upon an island belonging to Jorge de Magalhães. It is a remarkable sight because it is entirely covered with cane plantations, and in the middle of it is higher ground on which there are noble buildings surrounded by rows of orange trees and other trees. It is a wonderful sight to see. A league downstream from the Cotegipe plantation, there runs a river known as Aratu: there, Sebastião de Faria has been erecting a splendid mill powered by water, with imposing buildings both for habitation and for the purification of the sugar, as well as a church dedicated to Saint Jerome. All these buildings are of whitewashed stone, and he has spent more than twelve thousand cruzados on the project.

Half a league farther downstream from this last plantation is a watercourse named Carnaibuçu, on which no sugar mill has been built, owing to litigation about the water. At the mouth of this river, there is a very fertile island belonging to Nuno Fernandes. A league from there, one comes on a mill driven by oxen: this is the property of Jorge Antunes. It is well-equipped with numerous buildings and has a church dedicated to Our Lady of the Rosary.

It is roughly a league from this plantation to the mouth of the River Matoim. This stretch is full of very large estates. Their buildings and cane plantations are within sight of the river, and it is a river that is very beautiful and very wide throughout its entire course.

Opposite the mouth of the River Matoim lies the Island of the Tide. The island stretches upward from there along its entire length. Anything [else] that could be said about it has already been mentioned.

### Chapter XXIII. A Description of the Lie of the Land from the Mouth of the Matoim to the Mataripe Inlet and of the Plantations to Be Found There

If we leave the mouth of the Matoim and turn right, we see that for half a league the land is full of farms and cane plantations, among them another plantation belonging to Sebastião de Faria. It possesses two cane crushers

powered by oxen and has imposing buildings comprising the mill, the purification sheds, the residence, and sundry other workshops. There is a beautiful church dedicated to Our Lady of Piety, which is the parish church to this
area. Seen from the sea, this estate is of such grandeur that it resembles a
small town.

If we follow along the bank of the Salgado for half a league, we find
that it too boasts many estates. At its mouth there is an estate that belonged
to the dean of the cathedral, with a well-constructed chapel dedicated to
Our Lady, situated on a spit of land. Facing the spit of land and close to the
mainland lies an island, which reportedly belongs to Pedro Fernandes. He
once lived there with his family. It possesses sundry cane plantations and
small-holdings and has its own supply of water.

From the dean's estate, there takes shape the creek known as Jacarecanga.
Halfway along it lies a splendid sugar mill driven by oxen. It belongs to
Cristóvão de Barros. Up to that location there are many, many farms and
cane plantations. This particular plantation has vast buildings and a church
dedicated to Saint Antony. The creek is halfmoon-shaped and, in line with
the lie of the land, extends for two leagues. On it there is a watercourse on
which a mill could be sited, but no such construction has been attempted,
owing to the uncompleted litigation surrounding it. All around the creek,
overlooking the water, there are numerous farms and fine cane plantations.

On leaving the creek and turning to the right toward the spit of land,
we notice how the land bends back after half a league. On this stretch of
land are located two ox-powered sugar mills. One of these belongs to Tristão
Rodrigo and is close to the spit at the end of the creek. Facing it and close
to the Island of the Tide is an islet known as Pacé, from which the nearby
land and parish have taken their names. The plantation belonging to Tristão
Rodrigo has a fine chapel dedicated to Saint Anne. The other sugar mill and
its plantation are situated at the end of this tract of land and are the property
of Luís Gonçalves Varejão. On the plantation there stands another church. It
is dedicated to Our Lady of the Rosary and is the local parish church.

The land then carries on from the plantation till it forms a sharp point
surrounded by sea. This it does for half a league. At the end of this tract is
the spit of land known as Tomás Alegre. All along it are many farms and
cane plantations, including an apiary devoted to making honey and belonging to Marcos da Costa. Facing this spit of land is the tip of the Island of the
Tide. From there, the land again doubles back inland, creating a kind of creek
in the space of one league. It is full of noble estates and great cane plantations. At the end thereof there stands a fine sugar mill powered by water and
belonging to Tomás Alegre, along with a well-constructed chapel dedicated
to Saint Antony. A league away from this sugar mill, we come to the end
of an estuary called the Petinga, where all around there are cultivated many

splendid cane plantations. The Petinga is a sort of river or stream where one could have constructed a fine sugar mill powered by water, but this has not been done because of contention about the river and its ownership.

From here, one can reach the plantation of Miguel Batista, which lies half a league inland. It possesses elegant buildings and a well-built chapel dedicated to Our Lady. If we head back to the estuary and harbor of Petinga, the land stretches out to sea for about half a league, forming a rounded extremity. There we find an attractive estate belonging to André Monteiro. Then the land recedes for half a league along another inlet, named Mataripe. There we encounter an apiary producing honey. It belongs to João Adrião, a merchant. Following the inlet, we come to the church and judicial district of Tayaçupina. It lies half a league inland on higher ground with a view of the sea. It is a village inhabited by many settlers who work the land, growing cotton and other vegetable produce. The church is dedicated to Our Lady of O.

## Chapter XXIV. A Description of the Lie of the Land from the Mouth of the Mataripe Estuary to Marapé Point and of the Sugar Plantations to Be Found There

From the Mataripe estuary to that of Caípe is about a league, or less. It is all under cultivation and abundantly covered with cane plantations laid out by the local settlers. Hard by the Caípe estuary there is a sugar mill with two cane crushers, driven by oxen. It is a highly regarded development and belongs to Martim Carvalho. It also includes a well-appointed chapel dedicated to the Most Holy Trinity, as well as the other necessary outbuildings.

Facing the Caípe estuary lies a small rocky island, about half a league out to sea. Its name is Itapitanga. From the estuary, the land runs in a straight line for a league or more, at the end of which there is another mill driven by oxen. It stands on an estate rich in both slaves and cane plantations. Its buildings are very imposing and it possesses a new and elegant church dedicated to Our Lady of the Snows. The estate is the property of André Fernandes Margalho, who inherited all the land from his father. Running parallel to it, a mere light cannon shot away, stretches the island of Cururupeba. It is half a league in length and belongs to the Jesuit Fathers, who have rented it out to seven or eight settlers who live there.

Between this island and that of the Friars are two quite small islands belonging to António da Costa. On each of these lives a single settler, who cultivates it. Beyond the estate of André Fernandes, the land forms a creek of about a league in length, at the end of which is the Parnamirim estuary. Opposite the creek and close to the mainland, there are to be found three islands. The first of these faces the great estate and also belongs to André

Fernandes. It is about half a league long. A number of settlers live there and grow sugar cane and other vegetable produce. Close to this island is another smaller one, and it too belongs to André Fernandes. From it he takes the firewood needed for the mill. Further on from Parnamirim lies the third island, known as the Island of the Springs (Ilha das *Fontes*). It belongs to João Nogueira, is half a league long, and likewise is inhabited by seven or eight settlers. On all three islands, the land stands high and is very fertile.

At the mouth of the Parnamirim estuary, there stands a sugar mill driven by oxen. It belongs to Belchior Dias Porcalho and has a chapel dedicated to Saint Catherine. The sea flows in along the Parnamirim estuary for half a league, at the end of which there stands another ox-driven sugar mill. It is the property of António da Costa and is very well appointed. The estuary itself is lined on both sides with cane plantations and numerous fine farm buildings. In the middle of the estuary stands an island belonging to Vicente Monteiro. It too is cultivated and has a very imposing farmstead. If we return to the mouth of the estuary and walk for about a league, we find that the land is inhabited by many settlers. There they possess excellent estates planted with sugar cane and cotton. This area is known as Tamarari. In the center of that area there stands a parish church dedicated to Our Lady. At its end, the land forms a spit. To the right thereof, the land sweeps backward till it reaches another estuary, called Marapé. Here begins the territory [formerly] belonging to Mem de Sá. Nowadays, it is the property of his son-in-law, the Count of Linhares.

## Chapter XXV. A Description of the River Seregipe and of the Land around It as Far as the Mouth of the River Paraguaçu

As one leaves behind the area known as Tamarari, there begins that of the estate of the Count of Linhares. It curves back deep inland, creating a kind of creek called Marapé. This runs on till it reaches the mouth of the River Seregipe and is roughly two leagues long. It is filled with very fertile estates. The sea sweeps up the River Seregipe for more than three leagues, where it is joined by a tributary named Traripe. In that area, there once was to be found a plantation laid out by António Dias Adorno, but it was abandoned because a dike burst that had been very costly to build. As a result, it is at present deserted. This situation is unlikely to continue for long because the land is very fertile and because much capital has been expended on it.

After making our way down the estuary for a league and a half on the right-hand side, we come upon the celebrated estate of Mem de Sá, which now belongs to his son-in-law, the Count of Linhares. It has a well-constructed defensive tower and fine buildings for the purification of sugar. There are substantial slave quarters and sundry other workshops, as well as a church dedicated to Our Lady of Piety. Not a single settler lives on this side of the estate, or for as far as the river bar, a distance of some two leagues. That is because the land is needed for the running of the estate and because, near to the sandbar, there is a stream on which there could be built another very fine sugar mill. However, all along the other side of the river, there are many splendid estates with fine cane plantations. Among those there is one that once belonged to Gonçalo Anes, who went on to become a Benedictine monk. There, the Benedictines have been building a church dedicated to their saint, along with a monastic retreat, and it is to the church that those in the vicinity go to hear Mass.

At the mouth of the river, beyond the sandbar, lies an island called Cajaíba. It is roughly a league in length and half a league wide. It is inhabited by ten to twelve settlers who cultivate sugar cane and grow other forms of vegetable produce on their small-holdings. The island is the property of the Count of Linhares. Next to the island is another. It is small and unpopulated but has very fertile soil. Very close to the mainland and at the end of the river, on the same side as the estate, is to be found yet another island. It is a half a league square. Between it and the mainland, a boat can barely squeeze through. This island, as well as the other two, belongs to the Count of Linhares.

From the mouth of the River Seregipe, if we turn to the right on leaving it, we note that the land is broken into a series of major creeks for a distance of four leagues until we reach the area known as Acum. The stream there has the same name and flows directly into the sea. Two sugar mills could well be built on it, but that has not happened because the land is also part of the estate of the Count of Linhares and because he has no desire to sell or rent it. For that reason, few settlers live on it. Indeed, the count has a fine cattle corral there. From the boundary of this territory belonging to the count as far as the mouth of the River Paraguaçu is a distance of three or four leagues. Here, we find no estates because the land is not very fertile and is fit only for cattle-rearing. Indeed, there are a number of cattle farms here.

For four leagues up the River Paraguaçu, this stretch of territory was given as a land grant to Brás Fragoso. Later, it was sold to its current owner, Francisco de Araújo. He has laid out a number of estates on it. The land here is fertile and extends upstream.

## Chapter XXVI. A Description of the Vastness of the River Paraguaçu and of Its Nearby Sugar Plantations on King's Land

The River Paraguaçu has a huge volume of water and, at its mouth, a heavy cannon shot separates the two banks. The tide sweeps up the river for six leagues. For two leagues upstream and along both banks, as far as the Island of the French [*Franceses*], the land rises high, is of poor quality, and is barely settled, except for a handful of cattle farms. Stretching upstream from the sandbar of the river, there lies an island that is half a league long and five hundred *braças* wide, though some parts are of lesser dimensions. Its land is low-lying and infertile and it is named after Gaspar Dias Barbosa.

If we head upstream for the two leagues that take us to the Island of the French, we find that it towers up very high and that it has a circumference of six hundred *braças*. In times past, the French used to sail up as far as this point in their carracks, since the anchorage was deep enough. On this island, they were safe from the local tribesmen and were able to trade with them freely. Beyond the island upstream, there opens out a beautiful bay that stretches for two leagues until it reaches the mouth of the freshwater river. Facing the Island of the French is the apiary belonging to António Peneda. If we go beyond the island, we encounter on the right-hand side a broad inlet that extends for three leagues. It is very beautiful and is known as Uguape [currently, Iguape]. On its left, there is a stretch of nearly two leagues, along which there lie three small undeveloped islands. They are, however, covered in trees and could be put to use. There is also an island belonging to António de Paiva that has been sown with cane plantations. There, the mainland starts to close in, and upstream from the island the width of the river is [only] half a league.

However, if we go back to António Peneda's apiary, turn to the right and follow the Uguape inlet for two leagues, we find that there the soil is very poor and is of little use other than for cattle rearing. Halfway along this track, we come upon a flat island that António Dias Adorno has developed for the plentiful cultivation of vegetables. Farther on, there is another island known as Oyster Island [*Ilha da Ostra*]. Such an enormous quantity of oysters has been harvested there that they have been able to make more than ten thousand *moios*[19] of whitewash [from the shells]. Every day, they harvest an amazing and unending supply of them.

After those two leagues, the soil becomes more fertile. For about a league, as far as the estate of António Lopes Ulhoa, there are numerous cane plantations and many splendid farms. The Ulhoa estate grinds huge quantities of sugar cane and has many fine buildings of whitewashed stone. The tributary that powers the grinding is called Ubiripitanga. If we proceed upstream from this estate, then we note that on the right-hand side, along the saltwater part of the river, the land is replete with farms and cane plantations, as well as an apiary farm belonging to António Rodrigues. By continuing to the freshwater part of the Paraguaçu, a distance of some two leagues, we come upon the remarkable and well-located estate of João de Brito de Almeida. It enjoys

---

19 A *moio*, based on the Roman *modius*, was the equivalent of 1,200 liters.

a fine panoramic view of the bay. Its immense buildings are constructed in whitewashed stone, including a beautiful church dedicated to Saint John. The estate is highly productive and uses a stream for grinding the cane that depends on a millrace that stretches back for a league. The powerful millrace courses along a specially hacked-out stone channel, complete with weirs, as well as whitewashed stone retaining walls and buttresses, but, before we reach this estate, there are three small nearby islands of sand. These are full of mangrove swamps and are a regular source of shellfish.

About a light cannon shot farther upstream from this estate, there enters the very bay that it forms with the saltwater section of the River Paraguaçu. From one bank to the other at its mouth is roughly the distance of a shot from a heavy cannon. Upstream it is navigable, with quite large boats, as far as a waterfall that lies about three leagues inland. Journeying up the river, we note few farms on the right, as it is land belonging to the estate of João de Brito. Before reaching the waterfall, we catch sight of the estate of another well-built sugar mill that is driven by water power. It was built, on his own initiative, by a certain Rodrigo Martins, a *mameluco*,[20] as well as by Luís de Brito de Almeida. Nearby live many *mamelucos* on their farms.

## Chapter XXVII. A Description of the Land Adjoining the River Paraguaçu, with Special Reference to the Captaincy of Dom Álvaro da Costa

In the last chapter, we noted the vast size of the River Paraguaçu, which stands on king's land. We shall now continue to describe the river with appropriate reference to the land on its far side. This falls within the captaincy of Dom Álvaro da Costa, who owns ten leagues of the land that ascends that bank of the river, as well as land along the shore of the bay as far as the River Jaguaripe, and then for a further ten leagues up that river. King John [III] granted him that land, along with the title of captain and governor thereof. That will be the subject of this chapter.

Let us begin with the waterfall on the River Paraguaçu. Descending from there, on the right-hand side, we find that it has numerous inlets along which live many settlers. In their turn, streams pour into these inlets, yet no sugar mills are to be found there. We leave the mouth of the river at the place where the saltwater reaches into it from the bay and head to the right for about a league. We pass the islands mentioned earlier till we come upon the branch of the river known as Igaraçu. Upstream from here, the river is very broad for some two leagues. The land on its left is poor and flat and has few farms,

---

20   A *mameluco* is the name given to the offspring of a white and an American Indian; the equivalent of *mestiço*.

but down the right bank there is fertile soil, despite the rocks and boulders, and there are plenty of farms.

At the end of the two leagues, the river branches into three where the sea flows in. By the right-hand branch of the river lies the impressive estate of Lopo Fernandes. Its mill and the other buildings are of whitewashed stone, as is the majestic Church of Our Lady of Grace. They are girt by highly productive sugar plantations. The sea courses up the middle branch of the river for two leagues, at the end of which there flows into it a fine tributary known as Igaraçu. Here, there lies the opportunity for a further mill. Along both banks, there are to be seen so many cane plantations and small-holdings. On the spit of land formed by one estuary and another stands a chapel dedicated to Saint Joseph. Along the second of these estuaries, that is, the one on the left, there stands a prosperous estate with great whitewashed stone buildings, including the main residence, the purification building, and a splendid church. This estate is most productive, as are the others along the river. It was built by António Adorno, though it has now passed to his heirs.

On the River Paraguaçu and its surrounding area, wherever there is saltwater, there are to be found all manner of shellfish. In particular, there are huge oysters, and, when the tide goes out, four blacks can fill a boat with them. It also has great opportunities for fishing, either by net or by line, especially in the bay that it forms at its delta. That is because one bank thereof is two leagues in length, and other banks are some two leagues apart. In the whole area adjacent to this river there is also plentiful game.

*Chapter XXVIII. A Description of the Lie of the Land from the River Paraguaçu, along the Seashore of Bahia as Far as the Mouth of the Jaguaripe, and Then up That River*

From the mouth of the River Paraguaçu, where it issues into the vast bay, the land is for two leagues edged by sandy creeks. Along these are to be found cattle farms and fishermen. At the end of that stretch, the land runs out to a sandy spit of land that sticks well out into the sea of the bay. The tide regularly cuts it off. When the tide is in, part of the spit of land is turned into an island, while at the other end, there are seven or eight sandy islets covered in mangroves. As the coast sweeps away toward Jaguaripe, it forms a series of inlets for some three leagues. Along these, as far as opposite the Island of Stone [*Pedra*], there are numerous cattle farms and other farms belonging to poorer people who just plant vegetable crops for their own sustenance. The Island of Stone is little more than half a league in length and is much less in width. Further on, there is another island that is more than a league long. It is known as the island of Fernão Vaz. Behind them, the coast of the mainland runs closely parallel to these islands. It runs on for three leagues till it reaches the River Jaguaripe. This land is uninhabited, flat, and infertile. Through it a stream known as Pujuca runs into the sea. It could be used for a mill, though the water is somewhat shallow at its mouth, and a mill would need to be erected farther inland in order to be truly productive.

Turning upstream for two leagues from the mouth of the Jaguaripe, we find that the soil is very poor and only fit for cattle grazing and growing vegetables. After those two leagues, the land is reasonably good as far as the waterfall. It is traversed by five streams that flow into the river, on all of which mills could be built. Such mills have not, however, been constructed because the captain of this territory does not wish to grant waters that would produce less than two percent of their rent value. That is because at the end of a year, their output would amount to eighty to one hundred *arrobas* of sugar, with each *arroba* being worth eight hundred reals.

The River Jaguaripe is similar in size to the Douro but preferable because of its fertility. It is navigable as far as the waterfall. The waterfall lies five leagues upriver from the sandbar, and for two leagues below it the water is freshwater, though the power of the incoming tide of saltwater forces the freshwater as far back as the waterfall. At that point, if we turn downstream to the right, we encounter a water mill belonging to Fernão Cabral de Ataíde. It is a handsome building and possesses splendid living quarters and sundry workshops, as well as a fine church dedicated to Saint Benedict. This estate was built on king's land that is exempt from any rental of the sort that the captains habitually impose. Below this estate, there dwell a number of settlers who own their small-holdings and cane plantations along the river. These enhance the appearance of the river. Into it, some two leagues downstream from Fernão Cabral's estate, there flow three small tributaries on the same side, all of them capable of powering mills. However, the land on this side is bare and sandy and is incapable of providing more than firewood for the mills. This stretch of land terminates in a narrow spit opposite the island of Fernão Vaz. That spit has a small island at its tip, and it is there that the River Irajuí joins the Jaguaripe.

## Chapter XXIX. A Description of the Dimensions, Beauty, and Surroundings of the River Irajuí

If we follow the land upriver, on the right-hand side, for two leagues from the place where the two rivers meet, we find that the land is poor and is only of use for providing firewood for the estates. Farther up from here, a league away from the waterfall, we encounter many cane plantations and farms that belong to settlers. These stretch as far as the spot where the saltwater courses inland along two inlets. There, two streams join the saltwater, and on them stand two sugar mills, to which we shall return. Let us first consider the River Irajuí: it extends for a quarter of a league at this point, and on its banks there stand numerous cane plantations and farms. Amongst them is an apiary belonging to Gaspar de Freitas, and beyond it, close to the waterfall, is situated the estate of Diogo Correia de Sande. This is one of the finest estates in Bahia because it is splendidly designed, with large living quarters and workshops, plus a new church dedicated to the True Cross.

If we go back downriver to the right-hand tributary, known as Caípe, and then proceed upstream, we come upon an elegant estate boasting a residence, purification buildings, and many other workshops, as well as the beautiful Church of Saint Laurence. Close by, there live many neighbors in the village known as Graciosa. It is a very fertile village and is rich in vegetable crops and has many sugar plantations. It is the property of Gabriel Soares de Sousa.[21] From this estate to that of Diogo Correia, it is a mere four hundred *braças* along the cart track. There are two bridges across the tributaries here. Cart journeys across them connect the two estates, and both estates have a view of one another.

If we return to the other inlet that lies on the other bank of the River Irajuí, we come across the tributary known as Jaceru. This is also used to power another recently built sugar mill owned by the selfsame Diogo Correia. It is very well appointed and equipped and has all the necessary workshops. All along this tributary are numerous farms worked by settlers. They have splendid cane plantations. Then, if we go downstream, following the right-hand bank for more than a league, we note that the land on that side is similarly inhabited and cultivated. Indeed, the river resembles the Tagus from Vila Franca [de Xira] upwards.

Proceeding straight on from the spit of land that divides the River Jaguaripe, we see that the land is of poorer quality. There are three estuaries that sweep up it for two leagues. Into these there discharge streams on which mills could be built for grinding cane. But the soil is incapable of sustaining cane for more than a few years. Below one estuary, there lies a little island that is known as Salt [*Sal*] Island because the native tribesmen, when they lived nearer to the sea, used to harvest it there. Opposite lies another little island, at the tip of the spit of land that separates the two rivers. From this island to the sandbar is a distance of about half a league, but it is soil of very poor quality.

Then, from that spot to the island of Fernão Vaz is roughly a further league. That island, the island of Itaparica,[22] and the mainland form a sort of bay that is roughly a league square. Located there is the sandbar just mentioned: it is known as the bar of Jaguaripe.

21 The author.
22 The text refers to *Taparica*. This is the island of Itaparica.

**Chapter XXX. A Description of the Land between the Bar of Jaguaripe and Juquirijape, followed by That of the Land from There to the River Una**

From the Jaguaripe bar, it is a distance of four leagues along the coast to the River Juquirijape. It is dotted with creeks as one proceeds roughly from north to south. The land is low-lying and of poor quality. It has little woodland and is crossed by four shallow streams that issue from the plains. Such land is only fit for cattle rearing. The River Juquirijape has a small and low-lying sandbar. Only coastal vessels can cross it, however, as it extends for a league across the entire river mouth. Yet the water between the bar and the waterfall is very deep, and ships of a hundred tons or more could sail up it. The distance between the two is some four leagues. This river is as beautiful as the Guadiana but is a lot deeper. As we head upriver, we notice that on both banks and for two leagues, the land is of poor quality and is mainly bare prairie, though with ample water meadows, which are good for cattle. Even farther upriver, we come upon two tributaries on which two sugar mills could be erected.

On the further of the two tributaries, along the bank leading to the waterfall and for a good league of meadowland, there is soil that is very fertile for the planting of sugar cane. Along the other bank, the soil is of poorer quality. Near the waterfall flows a very productive stream on which Gabriel Soares has started to build a mill. By so doing, he has brought great benefits to the area, has established a village for slaves, and has put a steward in charge of them. Close to the sandbar of the river is a farm where vegetable produce is grown and where there is a workforce to harvest it. The river itself is rich in fish and molluscs, and [along its banks there is] plentiful game and wild fruit.

Along the seashore from the sandbar of the Juquirijape to the cattle farm of Sebastião da Ponte is a distance of five leagues. The land is unoccupied and is characterized by a creek into which flow three streams that rise on the prairies of the interior and which are only of use for cattle rearing. In the rainy season, the whole of the shoreline is very exposed all the way to the sandbar of the Jaguaripe. Powerful headwinds blow from the east and east-southeast, driving huge waves onto the shore and sending them surging over the sandbar. However, they miss the mouth of the Juquirijape, failing to collect inland. They simply batter the shore, which means that there is no danger to people because there is nothing there but sand.

The cattle farm belonging to Sebastião da Ponte stands on a spit of land sticking out into the sea. It faces the promontory of Tinharé. Beyond the spit of land, the shore rushes back inwards, forming an estuary as far as the River Una, sweeping round for three leagues along the shore. The tide sweeps up the river for more than two leagues, at the end of which there lies the estate of Sebastião da Ponte. There, a sugar mill is driven by a stream and propels two cane crushers. This is a big and powerful estate: its residence, purification building, and other workshops are very well constructed. It possesses a beautiful church that is dedicated to Saint Gens and has three vaulted chapels. Along the River Una, there dwell sundry settlers who have been creating splendid farms that produce sugar cane and vegetable crops.

## Chapter XXXI. A Description of the Land from the River Una to Tinharé, and of the Island of Itaparica and Other Islands

A league away from the mouth of the River Una another river flows into the sea, namely the Tairiri. The tide courses up it for two or three leagues to where Fernão Rodrigues de Sousa built an estate with a large workforce. It possesses a fine and well-equipped sugar mill, along with the usual workshops and the well-designed Church of Our Lady of the Rosary. It is also defended by a large body of soldiers who protect it from the accursed Aimoré tribe, owing to the great damage that the latter have already inflicted. If we go round the mouth of the river, which is very close to the island of Tinharé, we see that it flows as far as the promontory, creating a creek of some three leagues before it reaches the spit of land around it. It is there that what is understood to be the Bay of All Saints [*Bahia de Todos os Santos*] terminates. The island gives shelter to the land for as far as Corral Point [*Ponta do Curral*]. That is because the land rises up quite high, which is inopportune for cane plantations. Numerous settlers live there, having been recruited by Domingos Saraiva, the owner of the island. He used to live there and owns the farm there. On it are many cattle and a chapel where Mass is said at his behest. From the mouth of the River Tairiri to this island is about a heavy cannon shot. In the sea between the island and the mainland, there are abundant fish and molluscs. Frequently also, in the rainy season, the sea casts ashore excellent ambergris both on the island and on the adjacent beaches as far as the River Juquirijape.

If we return to the aforesaid island of Itaparica, then we find that on the Tinharé side there is no harbor where landing is possible, owing to surrounding rocky shallows where the sea regularly pounds. However, on the side facing the bay, there are ample harbors where boats may land at any time. On that side also, the island has many inlets and spits of land. The inlets are ready refuges in stormy conditions for shipping that is heading to the city from other parts of the bay.

On the tip of the island of Itaparica that faces the bar of the Jaguaripe, there is a nearby small island belonging to Lopo Rebelo. It is covered with trees and is a plentiful source of timber. From its tip and well inland, the island of Itaparica is inhabited by a number of settlers. These settlers live close to the seashore, grow sugar cane and vegetables, and rear cattle.

From the island of Itaparica to the island of Tamaratiba, the coast extends for about two leagues. The distance between the latter and the shoreline is a good heavy cannon shot. Tamaratiba is one league in length and half a league wide. Its soil serves only for the cultivation of vegetables. Six or seven settlers live there, on land that is the property of the Count of Castanheira. Close to Tamaratiba, on the mainland side, lies the small isle of Saint Gonçalo. It is flat and covered with trees, and its soil is poor and sandy. Most of the time it is used by fishermen working with nets, as there are numerous good spots for casting. Facing this island are three flat islets that jut out into the sea opposite the spit of land that sticks out from the mouth of the Paraguaçu. The distance between them is probably about a league. On the sea side of the tip of Itaparica, there is another small, flat island covered with trees, and this too is only of profit to fishermen using nets. At the end of Tamaratiba Island, between the island and Itaparica, there are three tiny, sandy islets and, close to them, there lies the small isle known as the Isle of Pigs [*Porcos*]. It is only about six hundred *braças* square. There is yet another small island further on, named João Fidalgo. It belongs to a solitary settler. Even further on still, along a large creek formed by the island of Itaparica, there is situated the estate belonging to Gaspar Pacheco. Its sugar mill is operated by oxen, and its harbor is used by the settlers who live in the interior of the island. There stands the Church of the Holy Cross. Two leagues from this estate, we come upon the tip of the island of Itaparica, which projects well out into the sea and is known as the Point of the Cross [*Ponta da Cruz*]. Along that stretch of the island live numerous settlers, who grow vegetables and a certain quantity of sugar cane there. One league to the north of the Point of the Cross lies an island known as the Island of Fear [*Medo*]. Its surface is flat and uninhabited because it is all sand and has no [fresh] water.

From the tip of the island of Itaparica, the coast sweeps back, facing the city [of Salvador]. This area is entirely inhabited by settlers who grow an abundance of vegetables and cultivate cane plantations. On the estate of Fernão de Sousa, there stands a well-appointed church, dedicated to Our Lady, where residents on this side of the island attend Mass on Sundays and holy days.

We have now completed the circuit of the bay of Bahia and its islands, of which there are thirty-nine, that is to say, twenty-two islands and seventeen islets. That does not include the islands that are found upstream in the rivers. There are sixteen of the latter islands, both large and small. These bring about a grand total of fifty-five. If we omit going up any of the rivers, the distance around the bay from the Ponta do Padrão to the Tinharé Promontory comes to fifty-three leagues.

### Chapter XXXII. The Number of Churches, Sugar Estates, and Vessels to Be Found in Bahia

Now that we have completed our description of the vastness of Bahia and its surrounding areas, it is appropriate for us to quantify its great resources, not counting the number of its inhabitants, for these we wrote about earlier.

Let us begin by totalling up the number of sugar estates. We have supplied some details about each one individually, noting especially how their mills are powered. Currently, there are thirty-six of them: twenty-one resort to water power, and fifteen are driven by oxen. Another four are under construction. There are eight very productive apiaries with ample workshops. The sugar estates of Bahia export annually more than one hundred and twenty [thousand] *arrobas* of sugar and many preserves. Bahia and its surrounding areas have sixty-two churches, if we include the cathedral and three monastic houses. Of those churches, sixteen are parish churches, that is to say, nine are livings paid for by His Majesty, whilst in seven parishes the priest receives his income from his parishioners. The majority of the other churches have chaplains and charitable brotherhoods, as in Lisbon. All the churches are clean, well-appointed, and amply supplied with ecclesiastical ornaments. On the days of their patron saints, there are great celebrations.

Whenever it is appropriate in the service of His Majesty, one thousand four hundred vessels are able to assemble in the Bay of Bahia. With keels ranging from forty-five to seventy hand-spans, there are one hundred mighty vessels, capable of bearing three heavy cannon at the bows and two light cannon on each broadside. With keels ranging down from forty-four to thirty-five hand-spans, we can add eight hundred vessels on which at least a single light cannon can be mounted at the bows. Were we to add the smallest vessels, then there would be three hundred boats with keels of thirty-four hand-spans or less, plus two hundred canoes. All these latter are well provided with oars. Bahia possesses so many vessels because all the estates and farms depend on service by sea. There is no individual without his own boat, or canoe at the very least, nor is there a single sugar estate without four vessels or more. Even those are not really enough to service them fully.

### 3. A Letter from the Governor-General of Brazil, Tomé de Sousa, to King John III, with Information about the Towns and Settlements That He Had Visited on the Coast of Brazil

*Tomé de Sousa governed Brazil until 1553. He proved to be an active leader who devoted his considerable energy to shoring up the defense of the coastal cities and bring the Indians under Portuguese control. He traveled extensively along the coast,*

*visiting the donataries and trying to stimulate the development of the captaincies,*
*but at the same time making clear the authority of the Crown. He also gave consid-*
*erable support to the Jesuits who had arrived in his fleet in 1549. In 1552, in the*
*company of Jesuit father Manoel da Nóbrega, the governor visited the southern cap-*
*taincies, where he helped to establish towns, improve fortifications, and support the*
*missionary effort of the Jesuits. This letter reports on that trip and makes clear his*
*desire to find mineral wealth, his preoccupation with the threat of foreign interlopers*
*or settlers, especially the Spanish in the Rio de la Plata.* (Translated from *História*
*da Colonização Portuguesa do Brasil*, vol. III, pp. 364–6.)

Sire

I reached this city of Salvador after sailing down the coast, as I explained
in my letter to Your Majesty on 1 May this year. Here, I found Manuel da
Fonseca and the light craft in which he had brought his money and possessions to Salvador. He arrived safe and sound, as I have already mentioned in
some detail to Your Majesty. I dispatched him at once to transport cargo to
Pernambuco because that seemed to me to be a sensible procedure, as well
as being in the interests of your treasury. I have remained here to refit the
flotilla in which I arrived. It consists of one carrack and two wooden caravels. Their bombards needed to be rehoused and repaired, not to mention
other matters carried out on the advice of the shipyards back in Portugal.
It has occurred to me that by now there must have been some delay in the
dispatch of the carrack that Your Majesty wrote to say would be sent out to
me for my journeys [along this coast]. Moreover, the flotilla here has been
at some risk through our not having all the equipment expected from Portugal with which to repair it. In addition, the carrack now seems likely to
reach this coast in our winter, a troublesome season for shipping. Indeed, it
seems to me to be both advisable and in your treasury's best interest to send
back Pêro de Góis aboard the [carrack's] flotilla, along with the necessary
timber.[23] When the carrack arrives, we shall do as Your Majesty commands.
It is my opinion that everything out here is duly ready for that purpose.

I have traveled along the entire coastline and believe that by so doing
I have performed a considerable service both to your Majesty and to this
territory. At all events, I have done everything that I deemed to be feasible
and have spent all that I had. I am not telling you of my expenditure as some
kind of hint to Your Majesty concerning my outgoings, but, rather, so that
Your Majesty should be aware of the pleasure I have had in spending money
in your service. In fact, were I to dare to break with normal practice, I would
put to sea in a caravel in order to inform Your Majesty of many concerns that
cannot be put in writing. Such matters are of great import for the good of

---

23 It later becomes clear from the text that Góis is the bearer of this letter to the king.

this land. As such a journey is out of the question, I shall confine myself to outlining those concerns as briefly as possible. The rest I am entrusting to Pêro de Góis. Quite apart from knowing this land better than anyone else, he has also traveled with me and has seen everything that I have.

Along this coastline, I have ordered the construction of mud ramparts, complete with battlements, around all townships and settlements that have plantations. Those that were not close to the sea I have had transferred close to the sea. I have supplied them with all the artillery that I have felt necessary. That artillery I have entrusted to your royal comptrollers, since the captains declined to receive it, despite their obligation to do so. Neither have the captains established their estates in such places as were required in Your Majesty's instructions. I have commanded court-houses and prisons to be installed in every town, as well as the laying out of streets. All these things have been carried out without undue pressure being placed on the residents. Indeed, they were very pleased to do so and to play a major role in this activity.

As I have stated to Your Majesty, I shall draw attention solely to matters essential for the survival of this land, just as no man can survive without his head. Your Majesty should order the captains to reside in their captaincies. If there exist good reasons for them not to do so, then they should install people in whom Your Majesty might have confidence. Most of those now serving as captains are not known to Your Majesty, nor is their parentage. Indeed, I have removed one from the captaincy of Ilhéus. That captaincy is the richest in estates along the entire coast and is the most productive for Your Majesty. Nevertheless, the man is a New Christian, has been accused by the Holy Inquisition, and is inappropriate for the post. He was appointed by the son of Jorge de Figueiredo, whom God preserve. I have appointed an honest and wealthy captain [in his stead]. He is of good family and resides in the captaincy. His appointment will last until Your Majesty should decide otherwise. Alternatively, the captaincy could be awarded to João Gonçalves Dormundo, who is a nobleman and has been granted a coat of arms by Your Majesty.

Your Majesty should also provide an honest and wealthy captain for this city of Salvador, as its very nature requires it. Moreover, the governor-general should not have to reside in one particular place. Rather, he should take up residence wheresoever he judges that there is the greatest need of him.

Your Majesty's rule of law applicable in Pernambuco and in all the captaincies down the coast is a separate matter and should not apply to Your Majesty's treasury in the captaincies nor in the rule of law applicable thereto.

The captaincy of Espírito Santo ought to be the richest along the coast, but it is as ineffective as its captain, Vasco Fernandes Coutinho. I acted in good faith in appointing him, but Your Majesty should command another captain or, indeed, Vasco Fernandes himself, to go there as soon as possible.

I have sent Your Majesty frequent letters requesting you to send up to ten honorable and dedicated servants of Your Majesty to act in the captaincies as officials of your treasury or to act as captains or in other capacities as the need arises. I have visited [the bay of] Rio de Janeiro, farther down this coast. It is located in the captaincy of Martim Afonso and is fifty leagues away from São Vicente and fifty from Espírito Santo. I am forwarding a sketch thereof, as it would be pointless to write anything about some river without a picture. The river is named Janeiro.[24] I am of the view that Your Majesty ought to establish there a fine and noble settlement, as along this coast this is the only river up which the French sail. They take large quantities of pepper away from there. I have been informed that one year they took away fifty casks of it, and that they will take away as much as they can market. The woodland is of similar quality to that found here. Your Majesty should already have received information about it and would not need to have it now, if this point along the coast had a fortified settlement. I beg Your Majesty not to delay in this matter because, quite apart from the reason that I have mentioned, there should be installed there a further senior Crown judge. He is needed to cover the whole coast, to provide justice both there and in this city. The appointment needs to be made early because of the trade winds. The reason why I installed no fortress by that river this year, as laid down in your [general] instructions, was that I was unable to do so. That was because I had few men at my disposal and because it did not seem sensible to deploy them too diffusely. That principle applies to another bay, namely the one called Angra dos Reis, about which Pêro de Góis will supply you with detailed information.

São Vicente, Martim Afonso's captaincy, is very good land and has vast water resources, plains, and mountain ranges. [The township named São Vicente] is situated on an island three leagues long and one league wide. Another township, however, has been built on the island, and that is called Santos. It was built because São Vicente did not have such a good harbor, whereas that at Santos, located one league away from São Vicente, has the best possible harbor, where all the ships in the world could lie with their bows beached on land. This island seems too small to me for two towns, and I felt it better to have only one, covering the entire island. It is true that São Vicente was the first township to be built along the coast, and there is a beautiful church there as well as whitewashed stone houses and a college run by the Jesuits. Santos, however, has a better harbor and position, which are two factors in its favor, and there is already a royal customs house there.

24  In fact, the river (*rio*) is no more than an extended bay.

I shall need Your Majesty's decision on this matter, as I am apprehensive about dismantling a township belonging to Martim Afonso, for all that I have added a third one for him, namely Bertioga. That township was ordered to be built by Your Majesty and is located some five leagues away from São Vicente, at the mouth of the river. As the Indians were causing a lot of trouble there, I had ordered it to be built along the lines that I had earlier described to Your Majesty. It cost nothing apart from the work carried out by the settlers. However, now that I have seen it with my own eyes, as well as studying Your Majesty's letters, I have ordered changes and enlargements to its construction. Everyone here agreed that this was better, as you will see from the enclosed sketch. I have also ordered another township to be built on the plain inland from the town of São Vicente, where a number of settlers were fairly scattered. I have had them enclosed and brought together within a stockade. In that way, all the settlements will be able to benefit from the land around it. The township is called Santo André. That is because there is a small chapel dedicated to that apostle on the spot on which I built it. I have made João Ramalho from Coimbra its captain. He was already living here when Martim Afonso arrived. He has so many children, grandchildren, and great-grandchildren and other descendants that I dare not tell Your Majesty. He has not a hair on his head or on his face, and he walks nine leagues before dinner. I have ordered a further settlement, named Conceição, to be sited on the edge of this plain. It too is populated by other settlers, scattered over the same stretch of plain at the seaward end. Likewise, I have brought them together within an enclosure where they can live in a more organized way. Apart from these two settlements being essential for the common good of the captaincy, I was glad to do this for an additional reason that I shall come to later. The two townships of São Vicente and Santos are not enclosed, and their houses are scattered in such a way that they could only be enclosed with great difficulty and at great expense to the settlers. The settlers possess whitewashed stone houses and large estates, all of which have been laid out haphazardly. Consequently, the only good solution that has emerged for them is for each establishment to build a fortified tower in the best defensive position available. In that way, they will be as secure as the nature of their land permits. This strategy must be put into effect, for otherwise they will come to harm.

A flotilla with about three hundred people aboard had left Castile, bound for the River Plate; part of the flotilla reached the island of Príncipe in the Gulf of Guinea, while another part [was approaching] the coast between the River Plate and São Vicente. Some sixty leagues from the latter, in the vicinity of the river known as the Rio dos Patos, [this part of the flotilla] was almost totally lost. Only some sixty people were rescued, of whom nearly half were women. One of the women is the wife of the governor, Fernando de Sarabia.

He too was lost, along with daughters and relatives of his, some nine or ten noblewomen, among others. The Indians saw that they were people who were like us and, when they told them that they were our brothers, they did them no harm whatever. Rather, they looked after them, as they were in such distress. A captain from their party, one João de Salazar, made his way to São Vicente. He was formerly in the service of the Duke of Aveiro, who had made him take the habit of the Order of Saint James. When I too arrived, he asked me to send for the shipwrecked men and women. I held it to be a service to God and to Your Majesty to dispatch a ship to bring them to São Vicente. It occurred to me that the women would arrive so distraught at their suffering that they would marry any men who would give them something to eat, while the men would each settle down to farming the land. I shared with them what little poor resources I had. It was not so little as to be less than what I have called my own these last thirty-five years.

Along the River Plate, three hundred leagues from the bar to the north and northeast, there is a large settlement of Castilians who were taken there by Don Pedro de Mendoza. It lies at [latitude] twenty-five and a quarter degrees, whereas São Vicente lies at twenty-three and three-quarters. It gradually became apparent that their town, which is named the city of Asunción, is very close to [the captaincy of] São Vicente and cannot be more than a hundred leagues from there, since it can clearly be seen from the highest point in São Vicente. We all feel that this town lies within Your Majesty's boundaries and that should Castile deny this, then it would be hard to prove that the Moluccas are theirs. If these words seem to Your Majesty to be those of an incompetent astronomer or even worse cosmographer, then, Sire, you would be quite right, for I know nothing about it except to wish that the whole world belonged to Your Majesty and to your heirs. I have discovered that the inhabitants of São Vicente have frequently been in contact with the Castilians, so much so that last year your customs house earned a hundred cruzados in duty on goods that the Castilians bring in to sell. Since I consider that at no point will Your Majesty be able to disentangle our people here from the Castilians, I have imposed heavy penalties to prevent this [trade] route being used. This I did even before informing Your Majesty about the situation and before installing large patrols. I have taken great pleasure in building the aforementioned townships on the plain of São Vicente, and that is why I think it right that the route should be blocked. I beg Your Majesty to dispatch a prompt reply to this section of my letter, with orders as how best we can serve you. That is because I cannot determine what decision to take with regard to these new developments in the light of the clear intention of the Castilians to head for our township.

The Brothers of the Society of Jesus are doing much for God in this country and in so many ways, as I have from time to time reported to Your

Majesty. They are very keen to penetrate into the interior, to build their homes in the remoter parts and to settle among the natives. I have expressly forbidden this in words that must be used to prohibit such activity. I have explained to them that as Your Majesty's territory expands, then too they may advance. But, if two or three of them, along with interpreters, wanted to go into the interior and preach to the heathens and make their homes among them, then that would only seem reasonable if they were accompanied by our men.

I regret this very much, especially as they have taken my decision as a form of martyrdom. I beseech Your Majesty's prompt help in this matter because I am loath to be at loggerheads with men who are so virtuous and such good friends of mine. That is because I always doubt my own judgment and, were it not for the fact that people all along this coast held a contrary view, I would not have dared to prevent this enterprise.

Castilian markers have been found in certain places between the River Plate and São Vicente: I have had them removed and thrown into the sea and ordered they be replaced by the arms of Your Majesty.

While traveling along the coast, I heard fresh news from the natives about gold. I shall only believe this when I see it, for all that I wish it were true. Nevertheless, I have given orders to twelve men and a Jesuit priest who are ready to go by land via Porto Seguro and up into Pernambuco, where some other men had already gone. Our Lord will want Your Majesty to share with Him whatever might come from these men bringing news of some great treasure.

From the city of Salvador, 1 June 1553. Tomé de Sousa.

## 4. The Governorship of Mem de Sá

*Mem de Sá, the third governor-general of Brazil (1556–72), was in many ways the royal official who during his long service defined the nature of the colony and firmly established Portuguese rule. Trained as a jurist at the University of Salamanca in Spain, he had served in Portuguese judicial offices before coming to Brazil. He became a strong supporter of the Jesuit missionaries, but he also initiated military campaigns against the Indians of Bahia, Porto Seguro, and Espírito Santo. As governor, much of his attention was focused on destroying the French colony in Guanabara Bay, where under Nicholas Durand de Villegaignon a settlement had been established in 1555. In two major campaigns, the French were finally driven out in 1567, and the Portuguese established the city of Rio de Janeiro on the bay. Mem de Sá died in Salvador in 1572, leaving two sugar mills and a considerable fortune to his heir. By the time of his death, the colony's government had been regularized, Indian resistance had been broken along the coast, foreign rivals had been expelled, and the sugar economy was beginning to flourish.*

*In the three texts presented here, we see the governor-general at work. In a letter of 1558 (a) to the queen, Mem de Sá describes his difficulties in controlling the Portuguese settlers and the Indians under their control and seeks adequate compensation for his efforts. In another letter of 1560 to the queen (b), he details the precarious situation in some captaincies and the personal sacrifices he has made. Finally, in a report (c) on his service composed in 1570, various persons present depositions on his actions. This document is interesting not only for its details of the governor's actions but also because it demonstrates the form in which testimony was gathered according to a fixed set of questions that judges developed before witnesses were called to depose.* (Translated from *Annaes da Biblioteca Nacional do Rio de Janeiro,* vol. 27 [1906], pp. 225–6.)

## (a) Letter from the Governor-General, Mem de Sá, to the Regent, Queen Catarina, Concerning the State of Affairs in Brazil, with Particular Reference to Rio de Janeiro and Espírito Santo

Madam

After Dom Duarte [da Costa] left, I received the enclosed letter from Vasco Fernandes Coutinho. His captaincy was in revolt, and the heathens there had reduced the Christians to such straits that unless they received assistance, they would have been unable to escape being killed and eaten. The captaincy is now very peaceful, and the heathens have been duly punished. So many of them, particularly their leaders, have been killed that I trust that they will not readily rise up again. I give thanks to God that my son, Fernão de Sá, survived the campaign in the service both of God and Your Majesty. The potential danger for this country at the present time is whenever a captain is both old and poor. It follows, as Your Majesty will understand, that the shipowners are the mainstay of Brazil and that any captaincy that does not have them cannot survive.

I believe that Your Majesty should take over the territory belonging to Vasco Fernandes and dispatch him to São Tomé. The land should be given to rich men desirous of coming out here. They are in search of honors and a ship, and some of them should be sent to this captaincy, others to Espírito Santo. They should be granted once again their due privileges, even though the royal charter specifies these for all such as wish to come here. I intend to go and establish another city. It is my belief that, with God's help, I shall very soon be able to build a city much like Salvador. It will be the city of Espírito Santo. This land will then be totally secure both from the heathens and from the French. It is very clear that the latter rate highly their chances of making an attack there and that they are greatly to be feared.

By going in person to establish a settlement there, I may well be able to thwart their designs. Indeed, the city may well not need, for the present, any other fortress to defend it.

Vasco Fernandes is also going there. He is so exhausted and distraught that all he wants is to be relieved of his captaincy.

I am sending Your Majesty a letter that I have received from Espírito Santo with the news that a caravel and a brigantine from the flotilla that I sent as part of the rescue mission have found a number of Frenchmen in Rio de Janeiro. They even went so far as to see whether they could capture any of the sloops that they sail along the coast, in order to find out the truth about how many men they have and what their intentions are.

Others who have come from there have told me that they are building eight craft powered by oars. Three are built like galleys and the rest like brigantines. However, they have not seen these vessels and only have the natives' word for it. Yet they are strongly built, carry many men, and are well armed. Their harvest will be solely pepper. May it please Our Lord to dispel such plans from their minds. May Our Lord add unto Your Majesty's life and royal wellbeing.

From your city of Salvador. 1 June 1558. Mem de Sá.


## (b) A Letter from the Governor-General, Mem de Sá, to the Regent, Queen Catarina, Concerning the State of Affairs in Brazil

(From *Annaes da Biblioteca Nacional do Rio de Janeiro*, vol. 27 [1906], pp. 227–9.)

Madam

By a different route I have sent Your Majesty a letter about what happened to me in the conflict I had with the heathens of Paraguaçu as well as with the French in Rio de Janeiro, to which end Bartolomeu de Vasconcelos was appointed. He arrived as captain-major of the flotilla and also took part in the conflict. He and all the other captains and men, who all fought well, likewise deserve to be rewarded.

The captaincy of Bahia was greatly at peace when I left it. The natives were also very quiet and more peaceful than ever.

The city is growing all the time. With the territory that has now been pacified, a kingdom could be created around Bahia, and the land is extremely fertile for any purpose to which it might be put.

The Jesuit fathers have written to Your Majesty about how successfully they are propagating the Christian faith among the native tribesmen of Bahia. I believe that the time has come when, owing to their work, these pagans will share in the grace of Our Lord.

On 12 November last year, four hundred and seventy people were baptized on one day in the Church of the Holy Spirit, which is situated seven leagues away from the city. Many more could be baptized daily. These people know their doctrine better than many [existing] Christians do. In other churches, many more have either been baptized or are being baptized. In the schools, three hundred and sixty children already know how to read and write.

I would have built many more churches if I had had the wherewithal to do so. Your Majesty might see your way to pardon the mistakes I made when I first arrived here because the penalties affected such construction. Indeed, the other judicial penalties meted out according to the law back in Portugal are those that are applied to the natives here. This land should not and cannot be ruled by the laws and practice of Portugal. If Your Majesty is not slow to pardon, then you will have no subjects in Brazil. [I say this] because I have acquired a new concern that this land should be preserved.

I wrote to Your Majesty last year setting out the ways in which this needs to be done. I reminded you how essential it was to install honorable and conscientious captains in the captaincies. Recently, when I was sailing down the coast, I saw what can happen. Porto Seguro is losing its population because of its captain. As for Ilhéus, if I had not gone to its aid, it would have been lost and they would have killed the captain. In Espírito Santo, there are three sons of Vasco Fernandes Coutinho, all young and still without beards, yet all of them are captains. In São Vicente, the population is close to rebellion. As I have already written to say, if Your Majesty wishes Brazil to remain populated, it is essential to ensure true order in the captaincies.

When I reached the captaincy of Espírito Santo, I found a letter from Vasco Fernandes Coutinho. In it he asked the judge in the captaincy to revoke his title to the captaincy. Moreover, he was providing adequate proxy. The settlers were already ready to leave and, when they heard this news, they came to see me, accompanied by their wives and children, begging me to take over the captaincy on Your Majesty's behalf. This I did, as Your Majesty can see from a document that I have drawn up. I did so with the agreement of the captains that the matter should be brought to Your Majesty's attention. I took this action in order to prevent the loss of a good captaincy and because of the work that the Jesuit fathers have carried out with the native population. For, indeed, there are many well-indoctrinated Christians among them. Furthermore, the land is good and is very productive in excellent brazilwood. When the shipowners hear that you have issued the necessary decrees, they will return to their work should Your Majesty command that they be told to.

I have not written to Your Majesty about the particular duties that needed to be carried out by the numerous men that I requested for the provision of townships for the natives. Now, and at less cost, and owing to the great need I have of them, I have given orders that each township of natives shall have a magistrate drawn from their own ranks, for they like this kind of honor and are easily contented with little. If they are given clothes annually, and if the women receive a cotton smock, that should be ample. Your Majesty should command that these be issued to them.

I also ordered stocks and a pillory to be placed in every township, just to show them that they have all the things that the Christians have. Their magistrate is to put the children in the stocks whenever they play truant from school or when they commit other minor misdemeanors. It is done on the authority of teachers living in the township, and they are content to acknowledge it, accepting punishment better than we do.

The powers that I requested from Your Majesty were sought on the grounds of my experience of this land and because they are essential for governors. Your Majesty should remember that you people this land with convicts and criminals, the bulk of whom deserved to be put to death and whose sole trade is a life of crime. If a governor-general does not have sweeping judicial powers to punish or to pardon them, then there is little purpose in his being here, and the Crown judge has much greater jurisdiction. Such judges, however, do as they see fit and, when challenged, reply that everything lies within their jurisdiction or competence. I showed the officials of the governing council the decisions taken by the Court of Conscience[25] with regard to the ransom of natives and commanded them to be set down in the council's book. They took this very badly, as they have no other source of profit in this country. They are writing to Your Majesty about it. It is my belief that if those of conscience were better informed, they would be more generous in certain matters.

I brought with me a secretary to write down the decrees that I issue, as well as other essential matters that it would be impossible for me to write down myself. I did not request a secretary from Your Majesty as it was my belief that such a post was normal, for Tomé de Sousa also had one. However, till now he has received no pay. I request Your Majesty to order that he

---

25 *Mesa da consciência* was instituted by King John III to supervise the overseas activities of military orders, of hospitals, and of all those who had positions of profit under the Crown. It was not extinguished until 1833.

be paid for the time that he has been in my service, just as the secretary of Tomé de Sousa was paid. That would obviate my having to pay him from my own resources. The administration of Brazil is constantly increasing, and a governor-general really needs two secretaries.

I beg Your Majesty that in recompense for my services, you recall me to Portugal and replace me with another governor-general. I assure Your Majesty that I am not right for this land. I spend far more than I receive in salary, and I am paid in goods that are of no use to me. I am forever engaged in warfare and similar conflicts, in which it is my duty to supply food to men who fight and die without wages or sustenance. Yet these things are not available [for me] to give to them.

I am an old man. I have children who are bereft of support. One daughter, who was in the convent of Saint Catherine of Siena in Évora, was ordered to leave by Brother Luis de Granada. I cannot grasp how it is of service to God or to Your Majesty that the daughter of one who is serving God in Brazil should be turned out of her convent and into the street. May Our Lord add unto Your Majesty's life and royal wellbeing.

From Rio de Janeiro, 31 March [1560]. Mem de Sá.

## (c) Depositions on the Rule of Mem de Sá as Governor-General of Brazil, Written in Salvador, September to December 1570

*(Translated from Annaes da Biblioteca Nacional do Rio de Janeiro, vol. 27, pp. 130–218 [excerpts].)*

### (1) The Deposition of an Unnamed Witness [Annaes, 27, p. 130]

Governor-general Mem de Sá has declared that it is necessary for him to report on the work he has carried out on His Majesty's behalf since leaving Lisbon, arriving in this country, and journeying by sea and land. It is important that people in this captaincy and in the others along the coast should be aware of the widely known fact that he left Lisbon at the end of April 1557. For eight months, he sailed into very bad weather, putting in at the island[s] of Cabo Verde and again at the islands of São Tomé and Príncipe. Of the three hundred and thirty men with him, forty-two died. They were all provided with chickens and everything they needed. That was the reason, along with the Grace of God, why many survived. He always provided food for His Majesty's servants and for other men of worth. While at sea, he also supplied the female orphans with all necessary sustenance.[26] Once they reached this city, he ensured that they got married. Indeed, they are all now married, have social standing, and are well-to-do.

Mem de Sá was under orders to curtail litigation and to prevent gambling, and so he has done. Yet the land was in rebellion, and the settlers were keeping scant control of their estates, both for fear of the heathen natives and because they were short of artillery. [Accordingly,] he made military incursions into Revelados. I myself took part in the expedition to the township of Boca Torta. He has worked hard to increase His Majesty's income. He has devoted himself too to the development of the sugar plantations, as well as to the cathedral, the Misericórdia, the Jesuit house, and the fortifications around the residence of the governor-general. Shortly after his arrival, he dispatched his son, Fernão de Sá, to go and help out Vasco Fernandes Coutinho. I recall what happened there, as well as what he did to rescue the captaincy of Ilhéus and bring it under control. On receiving a message, he then left Ilhéus and hastened to quell a rebellion of the natives in Paraguaçu, where many white men had been slaughtered. He then headed for Rio de Janeiro on receipt of a message brought by a certain Monsieur de Bolles, attacking with a small flotilla and relatively few armed men. He went on to provide assistance at Espírito Santo. Afterwards, he sent his nephew, Estácio de Sá, to Rio de Janeiro. In 1566, His Majesty sent a flotilla for him to sail in as governor-general. What happened at Rio de Janeiro is now much acclaimed. He now requests that detailed reports be sought from witnesses so that the truth be known. Furthermore, he requests reports on what took place in Espírito Santo when he went back there, as well as on all the other matters to which he draws attention. He trusts that these reports will be made public, thus ensuring that he receive his just reward. [....]

### (2) *Mem de Sá's Own Deposition (Annaes, 27, pp. 134–6)*

At the time when I was preparing to leave Ilhéus, there arrived from the captaincy of São Vicente a French gentleman by the name of Monsieur de Bolles. According to the French, he was a man of noble family who had come from France to establish a settlement at Rio de Janeiro, along with another nobleman, Monsieur de Villegaignon, who had built a very strong fortress there. Owing to disagreements between them, he had left Villegaignon and made his way to São Vicente. From there, he came to me and disclosed to me a number of Villegaignon's evil intentions that would be to the detriment of this country and of His Majesty's interests.

---

26  These were the *órfãs del-Rei*, orphan girls of marriageable age sent to the colonies at the Crown's expense. Their dowries were often minor government posts.

I decided to go in person, as His Majesty had commanded. I set sail with a very small flotilla and relatively few men directly from Portugal, my main force being composed only of seamen. At midday, I attacked the fortress from all sides. This was against the wishes of those in the flotilla who had come directly from Portugal, as well as of their captain-major and the other captains. The fortress was located on high ground in the middle of the bay. My ships were in a position to surround it, but our approach was hindered by their constantly heavy cannon fire. We disembarked and attacked the two forts that they had built on the island. We encountered more than one hundred and twenty Frenchmen and fifteen hundred Indians. Twice they made forays against us, fighting furiously. However, many French fell, one of their forts was captured, and the other one was incessantly attacked. For those reasons, they left at night in canoes, leaving to us one of the strongest fortresses in Christendom. It possesses many fine bronze cannon and many others of cast iron, as well as large quantities of gunpowder. There are other munitions too, not to mention vessels powered by oars, that they use for traveling along the coast. All this I inspected with the captain-major. Witnesses will confirm how much I was at odds with him, owing to my relentless onslaught on the fortress. I laid waste a number of strong townships and killed many Indians. Then I left for São Vicente, where the native heathens were in revolt. I restored peace and for a full year gave all food necessary to those in need of it. [....]

While I was in this captaincy of Bahia, the natives of Rio de Janeiro were far from peaceful. Accordingly, I sent a small flotilla back to Rio de Janeiro. As this captaincy was not entirely peaceful either, and as the people in the captaincy believed that I should not abandon them, I sent Estácio de Sá, my nephew, as Crown judge, or, rather, I dispatched my nephew as captain-major, with Brás Fragoso as Crown judge. Their undertaking was to create a settlement, but they did not succeed. However, Estácio de Sá went back again and built a township that he kept in being for two years. He endured a lot of fighting and many setbacks, without any help from any source other than from God and from what support I was able to give him, always at my own expense. He provided food for many people.

Then, in 1566, His Majesty was informed that the French were building many fortresses both in the interior and along the coast. They had taken control of the Indians and were already very powerful and had many cannon at their disposal. Accordingly, he sent another fleet to Rio and ordered me to go there in person.

I made my way as best I could and at great personal expense, as I had to feed all those who accompanied me. I fell ill in Espírito Santo and was still sick when I reached Rio, being at death's door. However, I ordered an attack on the fortress belonging to Piraçu Mirim, a formidable and warlike chieftain. His fortress was perched on lofty crags and defended by many French, with ample cannon at their disposal. The assault on the fortress was fought with great courage. Many Christians were either killed or wounded. Yet, as much fervor was felt at the end as at the beginning, for our forces overcame and captured nine or ten Frenchmen and killed sundry others. Estácio de Sá sustained an arrow wound from which he subsequently died.

A few days later, I ordered another onslaught on another fortress at Parnapaçu, where there were more than one thousand soldiers and plentiful cannon. The fighting went on continuously for three days. Finally, by dint of immense efforts and even greater risk, they managed to force their way in. A number of whites died. After a grim defensive struggle, they surrendered and were all taken prisoner. Our men were now ready to go on to another fortress that was stronger than all the others and in which there were many French. However, the latter did not dare to await [their arrival] and abandoned the fortress. It has three very strong baileys, with battlements and defensive towers. Yet at once they came to me to sue for peace. That I authorized, on the understanding that they became His Majesty's vassals. Indeed, that place had been built by Estácio de Sá as a stronghold in time of war.

With the agreement of the captains and others who were in Rio de Janeiro, I chose a site that seemed more appropriate for the construction of the City of Saint Sebastian.[27] This place was a large dense area full of massive trees. It involved a great deal of work in felling them and clearing the ground. I set about building a large city girt with towers some twenty handspans wide and forty handspans high, all to be enclosed within a lofty rampart provided with sturdy battlements and plentiful cannon. I built the Jesuit church. It has a tiled roof, is well appointed, and is where the Fathers now reside. I have also constructed the cathedral, complete with three naves and likewise well appointed. I provided an imposing, two-storey city hall, again with a tiled roof. The prison, the warehouses, and His Majesty's finance department are also two-storey buildings with tiled roofs and galleries. I also gave orders and help for the construction of many other two-storey houses with tiled roofs. When this had been done, as I had become aware of a number of chieftains, all installed in forts with sundry defensive walls, I duly attacked them and laid them low. Many were slain, and for that reason they again sued for peace. I ordered many settlers to come with their livestock to live in the city. The cattle are doing well and breeding successfully.

I received news that the heathen tribesmen in the captaincy of Espírito Santo were in revolt and had killed many whites. Consequently, I felt it necessary to go and provide assistance. This was with the agreement of the captains and settlers of the territory. I left behind my nephew, Salvador Correia

27  The full name of Rio is Cidade de São Sebastião do Rio de Janeiro.

de Sá, as captain of the city of Rio de Janeiro and I am still supporting him at my own expense. When I reached the captaincy, I very swiftly quelled the tribesmen who wanted peace. As for those who did not, they were punished and many of them slain. Those who got away left the territory, which became more peaceful than it had ever been. All of this I did at my own expense.

Three ships arrived here from India. I gave orders for them to be well supplied and sent them on their way.

Francisco Barreto arrived here afterwards with more than six hundred and forty men. The territory was lacking in supplies and everything else, yet he too was given provisions that could not have been bettered in Portugal. This was at the expense of the settlers and was done in the service of His Majesty. [ . . . . ]

### (3) *The Deposition of João de Araújo, Knight (Annaes, 27, pp. 141–4)*

Concerning article seventeen, the witness said that when the governor-general was in the captaincy of Ilhéus, a certain Frenchman had arrived there from the captaincy of São Vicente. His name was Monsieur de Bolles. He was a nobleman, as later became apparent. The Frenchman told him that he had been stationed in a fortress at Rio de Janeiro. The fortress was held by the French and was very strong. He had had a disagreement with Monsieur de Villegaignon, who was the commander there. Consequently, he had secretly left without his permission and had made his way to São Vicente and to the Portuguese who were there. From there, he had proceeded to meet the governor-general, as mentioned above. He had revealed to him the intentions of Villegaignon and of the havoc that he intended to inflict along the coast. The witness said nothing more on the matter.

As for article eighteen, the witness stated that after the governor-general had been informed of what was happening at Rio de Janeiro and of Villegaignon's strong position there, he had duly decided to go there. That he had done, with a fleet that had come from Portugal, of which Bartolomeu de Vasconcelos was captain-major. Moreover, the governor-general had also assembled as many men and ships of his own, though those were few. He did that because the fortress was strong and because the fleet from Portugal had brought no fighting men, only captains and seamen. The governor-general had reached Rio with this fleet and had at once surrounded the fortress. As it was located on an island, he posted ships where they could receive assistance from the Indians.

When he had established his fleet at Rio, he received many suggestions as to how to attack the fortress from those accompanying him, as well as from men of standing who had come up from São Vicente. There were many of them offering advice, including the captain-major, Bartolomeu de Vasconcelos, and sundry other nobles and high-ranking men. All declared that he ought not to attack the fortress as it was too strong and as his resources were so few. The fortress appeared to be impregnable. Such advice continued to be given to him right up to the eve of its actual capture. Nevertheless, he gave the order to everyone to attack, declaring that whatever the outcome, it would be as Our Lord wished it to be. The captain-major had pleaded with the governor-general that as our master the king's principal representative, he should hold back from besieging the fortress, as it was certain that many men would be lost even if, by some miracle, God did not wish to preserve it. Despite the advice given by all these men to the governor-general, he had refused to abandon his decision to attack the fortress. The captain-major and all those present told him that since as governor-general, that was his final decision, they would all assist him to the very best of their ability as, indeed, they did.

The following day, once the action was agreed, the governor-general attacked the fortress with the men who accompanied him, except for those who remained aboard the Portuguese ships that were surrounding the fortress. The advance began in the afternoon, with the governor-general landing on the Palmas islands, where he commanded a light cannon to be placed. This was used to begin the attack on the fortress. When night fell, the governor-general and those with him closed in on the fortress. During the night, he ordered more cannon to be unloaded from the ships and emplacements to be set up, so that by morning everything was in readiness. They managed to cause substantial damage to the fortress, by dint of the gun emplacements and because they were already very close to it. That same day, the French burst out, with many pagan tribesmen in their ranks, and fought with the Portuguese. The latter forced the French to retreat, causing heavy losses both to them and to the Indians. This they continued to do until the French abandoned the fortress and sailed for the mainland. In the fortress were found large quantities of cannon, both of bronze and of cast iron, ample munitions and gunpowder, plentiful provisions, and many other things.

After capturing the fortress, the governor-general attacked a number of townships, destroying them and inflicting considerable damage. He also captured a French ship that was anchored at Rio. Once everything was destroyed, he made his way to São Vicente, as requested by the people there. He brought peace to the territory because the heathen tribesmen were in revolt against the Christian population. The governor-general spent many months there before his return to this city and he always supplied food to many people. That concludes all that the witness said on this subject.

As regards article nineteen, the witness said that while the governor-general was returning to this captaincy, he called at the captaincy of Espírito

Santo, where the pagan tribesmen were in revolt. The governor-general had worked hard and done everything necessary to quell them and to ensure that they made peace with the Christian population. He also did the same in Porto Seguro. The witness had no more to say on this article.

Concerning article twenty, the witness stated that following everything already declared, the governor-general dispatched his nephew, Estácio de Sá, to Rio de Janeiro, as well as the comptroller-general, Brás Fragoso, because the heathen tribesmen were at war. They sailed for Rio in a small flotilla. There they fought against the tribesmen, but they were unable to effect a settlement there, and so continued to São Vicente. From there, Estácio de Sá made his way back [to Rio] without Brás Fragoso. In spite of the heathen tribesmen, he built a sturdy stockade of wattle and daub, from which he made regular forays against the Indians. He remained there until the governor-general went there to support him. All this the latter did at his own great risk and expense. That was all the witness said as regards article twenty.

In respect of article twenty-one, the witness declared that in 1566, Cristóvão de Barros arrived in the captaincy with a fleet of which he was captain-major. The fleet brought a message to the governor-general from our lord the king. In it, he instructed him to proceed to Rio de Janeiro with as many men as possible and to make every effort to destroy the French who were there. That the governor-general did, but at first he had traveled via the captaincy of Espírito Santo, where he fell ill. Despite his illness, he had gone on to Rio, where he was very ill on arrival. Yet, as soon as he arrived, he ordered an attack on a fortress where there were very many Frenchmen with ample cannon, not to mention many sturdy Indians. These were attacked by the Portuguese. The fortress was captured, many Indians were killed, and the French were taken prisoner. They were brought before the governor-general, who commanded that justice should be done. During the onslaught, his nephew, Estácio de Sá, was struck by an arrow and died, as did many other white men. The witness said no more concerning this article.

In respect of article twenty-two, the witness said that after the settlement had been destroyed, the governor-general gave orders for the destruction of another settlement mentioned in that article. This settlement was very strong and possessed a considerable population. After three days, the Portuguese attacked it, making use of plentiful artillery, and entered the settlement. They captured and killed many Indians. All those that they took prisoner they brought before the governor.

Thereafter, the governor-general was informed that there existed a second fortress where there were many Frenchmen. He decided to go there. However, before he could put this into effect, not only Frenchmen but also Indians came to him suing for peace. This the governor-general granted. The fortress had been the stockade that Estácio de Sá had built. The governor-general then decided to construct a large and noble settlement in a good position, complete with baileys and fortifications. That, indeed, is what he did. It is both imposing and of good quality. It possesses houses with tiled roofs and walls either of wattle and daub or of gravel and crushed stones. He gave orders for the construction of a large, well-appointed, and noble cathedral, of a sturdy prison, of a courthouse, of a city hall, and of other buildings that he considered appropriate for the attractive layout of the city. This is the City of São Sebastião. There are many settlers already to be found there and it is very peaceful. That concludes the deposition of the witness on that article. [....]

# 4

## THE FRENCH INTERLUDE

*The Portuguese had been troubled by the presence of French ships on the coast throughout the first half of the sixteenth century. The competition for dyewood lay at the heart of the rivalry, and both the French and the Portuguese mobilized indigenous allies to attack their rivals. In 1555, the French established an outpost at Fort Coligny on an island in Guanabara Bay. Although the colony established good relations with the local indigenous population, eventually squabbling between its Huegenot and Catholic members and the authoritarian rule of its leader, Nicholas Durand de Villegagnon, weakened the colony. The Portuguese destroyed the colony in 1560 and established their own settlement, São Sebastião do Rio de Janeiro on the shores of Guanabara Bay, in 1563. In the following letter, the seriousness of the French threat is made clear.*

### 1. Letter from Francisco Portocarrero to King John III Concerning the Abuses Committed by the French in Bahia, the Maladministration of the Governor-General, Dom Duarte da Costa, and the Presence of Pirates at Rio de Janeiro

(From *História da Colonização Portuguesa do Brasil*, vol. III, p. 377.)

Salvador, 20 April 1555

Sire

Some days ago I wrote to Your Majesty, via Pernambuco, to report on the circumstances of the mission on which you sent me to this land, along with the governor-general, Dom Duarte da Costa, whom I serve here as captain-major. I also mentioned that till then I had never left this city, for there are Frenchmen marauding along the coast and stealing both boats and ships. One carrack was in the land of the Potiguaras and had [almost] no men on board. The reason for that was that in that territory, our people were very hungry. [Meanwhile,] the French were cutting down brazil-wood some fifteen to twenty leagues inland at the most. The carrack had only six or seven men on board, and other carracks were in the same state.

I therefore requested the use of the well-equipped caravels that had come with the governor-general, as well as two galliots that tow an assault boat by its bows. Each of the galliots has six light cannon, as well as ten bombards. Another ship tows a mortar, plus all the ammunition and all the men that we would need to make an easy job of capturing the French or at least of giving them a fright. That way, they would know that Your Majesty has quite a fleet deployed here.

In the reefed inlet belonging to Dom Rodrigo, they loaded up two carracks, and I have learned that three more were loaded up in the French port. We heard this from eyewitnesses. From that inlet, they ply their trade, for this year their twin-masted ships came as far as Totuapara, and that is only twelve leagues from the said inlet. As mentioned above, I requested the ships from the governor-general, since they were lying idle and causing expense to Your Majesty without performing any service. All they do is travel to Tinharé, Paraguaçu, and Jaguaribe to trade in chickens, pigs, and other supplies, just for a handful of settlers. Yet he refused to release them to me, for all that I requested them many times, both in public and in private.

Then a ship arrived from São Vicente, bearing the Crown judge and another man, Gaspar Gomes by name, who is a settler in Ilhéus. The latter told us how when he was sailing up from São Vicente and put in at Rio de Janeiro, he had come upon a French carrack. By this ship he had been arrested and held for two months until it had completed loading. He declared that the carrack was carrying a ton of pepper, as well as a cargo of brazilwood. At the same time, there was another carrack at Cabo Frio that was full of casks [of pepper]. At Rio de Janeiro, where they had done much trade, interpreters and factors were preparing cargo for yet another carrack.

Meanwhile, there arrived one Luís Álvares, a settler from São Vicente, who was traveling in his own ship. He had encountered the carrack, for it was expected to show up. From what he said about its appearance, it was the last of those mentioned above, as it must have weighed some three hundred tons. It had pursued his ship, but he sought shelter from it in a bay protected by reefs. He ordered his longboat to attack it while he bombarded it. As our ship possessed a quantity of cannon, it was able to defend itself. As soon as this news arrived, on behalf of Your Majesty, I once again asked the governor-general for the use of the ships that were lying expensively idle in the harbor here, as I have mentioned above. I would have been able to seek out those carracks because it was the monsoon season, which comes in the middle of October. Even those reasons were not enough to enable me to go after them.

Then Vasco Fernandes Coutinho arrived here and went close to the reefed inlet of Dom Rodrigo to trade from one of his boats. There, he saw a carrack entering the bay with a longboat at its stern, but he was able to escape them because he was in another bay. Again, I reported this on Your Majesty's behalf to the governor-general, but he paid no heed. Then another boat came from Pernambuco and likewise saw the carrack, as well as two more in the port used by the French. I decided to ask for boats propelled by oars since they were lying idle. I requested that they be made available to me because I would be ready in twenty days' time. His answer was that the men did not want to go, as they were not being paid. I replied that all the men were prepared to go, both soldiers and sailors alike, but his answer then was that he had no supplies. I replied that I would provide them, and when he realized that he could not refuse, he fell silent and gave no answer. He did not like the idea and became resentful at my demands. On his way from church, all the people began to raise a huge clamor, crying out that they were all prepared to go at their own expense. Indeed, if I were to find two ships in partnership with them, then I could simply set off. However, I had only one, the one belonging to João Rodrigues Pessanha, and, although he was prepared to make it available so that I could be of service to Your Majesty, I held back for that reason.

Owing to my demands for such things, the governor-general now hates me. Nevertheless, he has now released to me two caravels. These are so essential here. Partly because he does not wish me to seek out the aforesaid carracks, it is all the more important that the caravels should set sail. I am reporting all this to Your Majesty so that you can take whatever steps you think appropriate. I also thought it right to tell Your Majesty just how much this land is in decline and falling short of the levels of defense and protection that pertained in the time of Tomé de Sousa. There are so many matters in demand here, and from each one there spring up twenty more. They are all caused by the greed here for the emoluments of office. It would be a great service to Our Lord if Your Majesty were to resolve these matters before this land is lost, for it is such good territory. May Our Lord add years to Your Majesty's life and enhance your wellbeing.

From this city of Salvador, today, 20 April 1555. Francisco Portocarrero.


## 2. Jean de Léry: Excerpts from *History of a Voyage to the Land of Brazil*

*The French settlement in Guanabara Bay destroyed by Mem de Sá in 1560 had been created under the leadership of Nicolas Durand de Villegagnon in 1555. It was only one of a number of French attempts to create settlements in the Americas in the sixteenth century that were opposed by other European powers. The Brazilian settlement called "Antartic France" produced two important chronicles: one by the*

*Catholic friar André Thevet and another by the Protestant Jean de Léry, who had been sent by Calvin from Geneva to write about the settlement. He arrived in 1557 and stayed for about a year. His account is neither unbiased nor free from errors, but it does give a thorough report of events in the colony as well as detailed observations on the indigenous peoples encountered. In the excerpts reproduced here, the motives of the settlers and the challenges they faced, the impression made by the land and its peoples, and especially the tensions created by the religious differences among the colonists are made clear.* (From *History of a Voyage to the Land of Brazil* [Berkeley: University of California Press, 1992], pp. 3–6; 25–32.)

## OF THE MOTIVE AND THE OCCASION THAT MADE US UNDERTAKE THIS DISTANT VOYAGE TO THE LAND OF BRAZIL

A number of cosmographers and other historians of our time have already written about the length, width, beauty, and fertility of that fourth part of the world called "America" – or the land of Brazil, together with the islands near it and the lands adjacent to it (lands completely unknown to the Ancients) – as well as of the various navigations in the eighty years since it was first discovered; therefore, I will not pause to summarize those matters at length or in a general fashion. My intention and my subject in this history will be simply to declare what I have myself experienced, seen, heard, and observed, both on the sea, coming and going, and among the American savages, with whom I visited and lived for about a year. And, so that the whole enterprise may be better understood by everyone, beginning with the motives for our undertaking so arduous and distant a voyage, I will speak briefly of what occasioned it.

In the year 1555, a certain Villegagnon, Knight of Malta (that is, of the Order called "St. John of Jerusalem"), discontented in France and having had some unpleasant dealings in Brittany, where he was living at the time, let it be known to several distinguished personages of various ranks throughout the realm of France that he had long yearned to withdraw into some distant country, where he might freely and purely serve God according to the reformation of the Gospel, and, moreover, that he desired to prepare a place for all those who might wish to retire there to escape persecution: which, indeed, at that time was such that many persons, of both sexes and of all stations of life, in all parts of France, by edicts of the king and by decrees of the Parlement were being burned alive, their goods confiscated, on account of the Religion.

Villegagnon declared, moreover, both by word of mouth and by letter, that having heard so many good reports of the beauty and fertility of the part of America called the "land of Brazil," he was ready to set forth in order to settle there and to put his plan into effect. And, in fact, under this fine pretext, he won the hearts of some of the nobility who were of the Reformed Religion, who, with the same motives that he claimed to have, wished to find such a retreat. Among them was Gaspard de Coligny of blessed memory, Admiral of France, who enjoyed the favor of King Henry II, the reigning monarch at that time. Admiral Coligny proposed to the king that if Villegagnon made this voyage, he might discover great riches and other commodities for the profit of the realm; thereupon the king gave Villegagnon two fine ships fitted out and furnished with artillery and ten thousand francs for the voyage.

Before leaving France, Villegagnon promised several honorable persons who accompanied him that he would establish the pure service of God in the place where he would reside. After providing himself with sailors and artisans to take with him, in May of 1555 he embarked on the sea, where he underwent many tempests and tribulations; but, finally, in spite of all difficulties, he reached his destination the following November.

Upon his arrival, he disembarked, and at first considered settling on a rocky islet at the mouth of an arm of the sea and a saltwater bay called by the savages *Guanabara*, which (as I shall describe) is located twenty-three degrees beyond the Equator – that is, right under the Tropic of Capricorn; however, the heavy seas drove him away. He advanced about a league toward land and set himself up on a previously uninhabitable island. Once he had unloaded his artillery and his other gear, so as to enjoy greater security against both the savages and the Portuguese, who already have so many fortresses in that country, he began to build a fort.

Furthermore, still pretending to be burning with zeal to advance the reign of Jesus Christ, and attempting to persuade his people of the same, when his ships were loaded and ready to return to France, he wrote and sent a man to Geneva expressly to request that the Church and its ministers help him as much as possible in his holy enterprise. But, above all, in order to pursue and speedily advance the work that he had undertaken, and which (he said) he desired to continue with all his strength, he urgently entreated them to send him not only ministers of the Word of God, but also to send a number of other persons well instructed in the Christian religion to accompany the ministers, the better to reform him and his people, and even to bring the savages to the knowledge of their salvation.

When the Church of Geneva received his letters and heard his news, it first rendered thanks to God for the extension of the realm of Christ into so distant a country, even into so strange a land, and among a nation that was indeed completely ignorant of the true God.

The late Lord Admiral, to whom Villegagnon had written for the same reason, solicited by letter Philippe de Corguilleray, Sieur du Pont (who had retired near Geneva, and who had been his neighbor in France near

Châtillon-sur-Loing) to undertake the voyage in order to lead those who wanted to join Villegagnon in that land of Brazil. The same request was made by the Church and the Ministers of Geneva, and although he was already old and feeble, the Sieur du Pont, out of the strong desire that he had to employ himself in so good a work, agreed to do what was asked of him, postponing all his other business, even leaving his children and his family to go so far away.

That being done, it was next a question of finding ministers of the Word of God. Du Pont and other friends of his spoke of this to a number of students of theology in Geneva, and several of them, including Pierre Richier (already more than fifty years old) and Guillaume Chartier, promised him that if they were recognized according to the ordinance of the Church to be fitted to that charge, they were ready to take it on. Thus, after these two had been presented to the ministers of Geneva, who heard them expound on certain passages of the Holy Scripture and exhorted them concerning the rest of their duty, they willingly accepted, with the leader Du Pont, to cross the sea to join Villegagnon and undertake to spread the Gospel in America.

Now there still remained to be found some other persons instructed in the principal articles of the faith and also, as Villegagnon had ordered, artisans expert in their craft. But so as not to deceive anybody, Du Pont told of the long and tedious path to be taken: that is to say, about a hundred and fifty leagues by land and more than two thousand leagues by sea. He added that upon arrival in that land of America, one would have to be content to eat, instead of bread, a certain flour made from a root; and as for wine, not a trace, for no grapevines grow there. In short, just as in a New World (as Villegagnon intones in his letter), one would have to adopt ways of life and nourishment completely different from those of our Europe. Therefore, anyone preferring theory to practice in these things, and unwilling to undergo a change of air, or to endure the waves of the sea and the heat of the Torrid Zone, or to see the Antarctic Pole, would by no means choose to accept such a challenge or to enlist and embark on such a voyage.

Nevertheless, after several summonses and inquiries on all sides, the following men, more courageous, it would seem, than the others, presented themselves to accompany Du Pont, Richier, and Chartier: Pierre Bourdon, Matthieu Verneuil, Jean du Bordel, André La Fon, Nicolas Denis, Jean Gardien, Martin David, Nicolas Raviquet, Nicolas Carmeau, Jacques Rousseau, and I, Jean de Léry, who, as much out of an earnest desire that God had given me to serve His glory as out of curiosity to see this New World, was of the company. So we were fourteen in number who left the city of Geneva to make this voyage the tenth of September 1556.

We wended our way to Châtillon-sur-Loing, where we met with my Lord Admiral, who not only encouraged us to pursue our enterprise but also, promising to help us in naval matters and offering much good advice, gave us hope that by God's grace we would see the fruits of our labors. From there, we set forth for Paris, where during the month that we stayed there, several gentlemen and some others, who had heard why we were making this voyage, joined our company. From there, we passed on to Rouen and went to the seaport of Honfleur, which was our appointed place in Normandy; there we remained for about a month, making our preparations and waiting for our ships to be ready to set sail.

## OF THE SIGHTING AND FIRST VIEW THAT WE HAD BOTH OF WEST INDIA OR THE LAND OF BRAZIL AND OF THE SAVAGES THAT INHABIT IT, TOGETHER WITH EVERYTHING THAT HAPPENED TO US ON THE SEA UP TO THE TROPIC OF CAPRICORN

After that, we had a favorable west wind, which lasted so long that on the twenty-sixth of February 1557 (as determined with the astrolabe and planisphere), at about eight o'clock in the morning, we sighted West India, the land of Brazil, the fourth part of the world, unknown to the Ancients: otherwise called "America" (from the name of him who first discovered it in about 1497). You can well imagine that when we saw we were so near the place that we had set out for, with some hope of soon putting foot to ground, we were filled with joy and gave wholehearted thanks to God. Indeed, since we had been tossing and afloat on the sea almost four months without putting in to port, it had often occurred to us that we were in exile out there, and it seemed as though we would never escape it. After we had ascertained that what we had sighted was, indeed, dry land (for you can often be deceived on the sea by the clouds, which then vanish), having a fair wind and heading straight for the land, the same day (our Admiral having gone on ahead), we cast anchor a half a league from a mountainous place that the savages call *Huuassou.*

After we had taken the boat down out of the ship and, according to the custom in that land when one arrives, had fired the cannon several times to warn the inhabitants, we suddenly saw a great number of savage men and women on the seashore. However (as some of our seamen who had been there before recognized), they were of the nation called *Margaia,* allies of the Portuguese, and therefore such enemies of the French that if they had had us at their mercy, we would have paid no other ransom except being slain and cut to pieces, and serving as a meal for them.

We also began to see for the first time, even in the month of February (just when over here, and in almost all of Europe, everything is closed up and hidden in the womb of the earth because of the cold and frost), the forests, woods, and plants of that country as green and flourishing as those of our France are in May and June. And it is that way all year long, and in all seasons in that land of Brazil.

Notwithstanding this enmity of our Margaia with respect to the French, which both they and we dissimulated as best we could, our master's mate, who could stammer out a few words in their language, got into the ship's boat with a few other sailors and went over to the shore, where the savages continued to assemble in big troops. However, since our people put no trust in them except for some express purpose, they stayed beyond an arrow's reach from land so as to avoid the danger of being seized and *boucané* – that is, roasted. From a distance, our sailors displayed for them knives, mirrors, combs, and other trifles, and called out to them asking for food supplies in exchange; some of the savages, who had drawn as near as they could, upon hearing this did not wait to be asked again but hurried off to get food for them. So when he returned, our master's mate brought back flour made from a root (which the savages eat instead of bread), hams, and the meat of a certain kind of boar, with an abundance of other food and fruits that are found in that country. Not only that but, to present themselves to us, and to bid us welcome, six men and one woman embarked straightaway to come see us on the ship. And because these were the first savages that I had seen up close, you can well imagine that I looked at them and studied them attentively. I will postpone describing them at length until a more appropriate place, but still even now I want to say something in passing.

First, both the men and the woman were as utterly naked as when they came out of their mother's womb; however, to bedeck themselves, they were painted and blackened over the entire body. The men had their heads shaved close in front, like a monk's tonsure, and wore their hair long in back; but, in the style of men's wigs over here, their locks were clipped around the neck. Furthermore, they all had the lower lip pierced, and each one wore in the hole a green stone, well polished, carefully placed, and mounted in the lip as in a setting; the stone was of about the size of a testoon, and they would take it out and put it back whenever they pleased. They wear such things thinking to be the more handsomely adorned; but, to tell the truth, when this stone is removed and this great split in the lower lip appears like a second mouth, they are greatly disfigured. As for the woman, besides not having a split lip, she wore her hair long like the women over here; her ears were so cruelly pierced that you could have put a finger through the holes; she wore great pendants of white bone in them, which swung almost to her shoulders. I will wait until later to refute the error of those who would have had us believe that the savages were covered with hair.

However, before these visitors left us, the men, and especially two or three elders who seemed to be the most important men in their parishes (as we say over here), claimed that their region grew the finest brazilwood that could be found in the whole country, and they promised to help us cut and carry it; furthermore, they would provide us with food – in short, they did everything they could to persuade us to load our ship right there. But because, as I have said, they were our enemies, all this was merely to lure us and trick us into coming ashore so that afterwards, having the advantage over us, they could cut us to pieces and eat us. So aside from the fact that we intended in any case to go elsewhere, we had no mind to stop there.

After our Margaia had taken a good look at our artillery and at whatever else they wanted to see in our ship, since we wanted neither to detain them nor to offend them (bearing in mind the consequences of our deeds for other Frenchmen who would come there unwarned in the future and who might suffer as a result of our acts) and since they were asking to return to their people who were waiting for them on the shore, it was a question of paying them what they wished for the food they had brought us. And because they have no use of currency, the payment we made them was in shirts, knives, fishhooks, mirrors, and other merchandise and small wares fit to peddle among this people. But here was the best of it. Upon their arrival, these good people, all naked, had not been sparing in showing us everything they had; and now at their departure, not being in the habit of wearing undergarments or, indeed, any other kind of clothes, when they put on the shirts that we had given them and came to seat themselves in the ship's boat, they tucked them clear up to the navel so as not to spoil them, and, revealing what should be hidden, insisted that we see their behinds and their buttocks as they took their farewell of us. Were these not courteous officers, and was this not a fine ambassadorial civility? For notwithstanding the proverb that is so common to us over here, that the flesh is nearer than the shirt, they on the contrary, as if to show us that they were not of that mind, and perhaps as a display of their magnificent hospitality, favored their shirts over their skin by showing us their behinds.

After we had refreshed ourselves a little there (for although the food that they had brought us seemed strange, nonetheless out of necessity we ate heartily of it), the next day, a Sunday, we weighed anchor and set sail. Skirting the land, and working our way toward our destination, we had not sailed more than nine or ten leagues before we found ourselves at the place of a Portuguese fort, called by them *Espirito santo* (and by the savages *Moab*). Recognizing both our equipage and that of the caravel that we had in tow (which they judged correctly that we had taken from their countrymen), they fired three cannon shots at us, and we fired three or four at them in reply. But because we were too far for the reach of their shot, they did us no harm, and I think we did none to them, either.

Then going on our way, still skirting the land, we passed near a place called *Tapemiry*, where at the entry to the land and at the mouth of the sea, there are some little islands; I think that the savages who live there are friends and allies of the French.

A little farther on, at around twenty degrees, live other savages called *Paraïbes*, in whose land, I noticed as we passed, you can see little pointed mountains shaped like chimneys.

The first of March we were at the latitude of the Little Shallows, that is, an area of reefs and points of land mingled with small rocks that stick out into the sea, which mariners avoid as much as possible lest their ships hit against them.

At these shallows, we had a clear sighting of a flatland that for about fifteen leagues of its length is possessed and inhabited by the Ouetaca, savages so fierce and wild that just as they cannot live in peace with each other, they wage open and continual war against all their neighbors as well as against strangers in general. They are so swift of foot and run so fast that not only do they evade all risk of death when they are pressed and pursued by their enemies (who have never been able to vanquish them or tame them), but also when they hunt they catch certain wild animals – kinds of stags and does – by running them down. Although like other Brazilians they go entirely naked, nonetheless, contrary to the most ordinary custom of the men of that country (who, as I have already said and will later expand upon, shave the front of their head and clip their locks in back), these wear their hair long, hanging down to the buttocks. In short, since these devilish Ouetaca remain invincible in this little region, and furthermore, like dogs and wolves, eat flesh raw, and because even their language is not understood by their neighbors, they are considered to be among the most barbarous, cruel, and dreaded nations that can be found in all the West Indies and the land of Brazil. Furthermore, since they neither have nor wish to have any acquaintance or commerce with the French, Spanish, Portuguese, or with any from our side of the ocean, they know nothing about our merchandise.

However, according to what I have heard since then from a Norman interpreter, when their neighbors have goods that they want, this is their manner of bartering. The Margaia, Cara-ia, or Tupinamba (which are the names of the three neighboring nations), or one of the other savages of that country, without trusting or approaching the Ouetaca, shows him from afar what he has – a pruning-hook, a knife, a comb, a mirror, or some other kind of wares brought over for trade – and indicates by a sign if he wants to exchange it for something else. If the other agrees, he shows in turn a bit of featherwork, or some of the green stones that they set in their lips, or some other thing that they have in their region. Then they will agree on a place three or four hundred steps from there; the first, having carried the thing that he wants to exchange and set it on a stone or log, will then withdraw, either back or to one side. The Ouetaca then comes to take it and leaves the object he had displayed at the same spot; then he too will retreat and will allow the Margaia (or whoever it may be) to come and get it: so that up to that point they keep their promises to each other. But as soon as each one has returned with his object of exchange, and gone past the boundaries of the place where he had first come to present himself, the truce is broken, and it is then a question of which one can catch the other and take back from him what he was carrying away. You can well imagine that the Ouetaca, who can run like a greyhound, has the advantage, and presses hard on the heels of the one he is chasing. Therefore, unless the lame, gouty, or otherwise slow-footed folk from over here want to lose their merchandise, I do not recommend that they negotiate or barter with the Ouetaca.

Now it is similarly true of the Basques that they have an entirely separate language and that, as everyone knows, being lively and nimble, they are held to be the best running footmen in the world; since on these two points they could be compared with our Ouetaca, it seems that they might well be a match for them on the field. You could also rank with them certain men who live in a region of Florida, near the Palm River, who (as someone writes) are so strong and light of foot that they can overtake a stag, and run for a whole day without rest; then too, there are great giants on the river La Plata, which also (according to the same author) are so agile that merely by running and using their hands they can catch certain deer of the region. But to these coursers I will let go the reins; to these two-footed hounds I will let slip the leash: let them run as swift as the wind though they fall thick as rain (tumbling onto their noses) in their three places in America (places nonetheless far from each other, for the regions of La Plata and of Florida are over fifteen hundred leagues apart) or their fourth place back in our Europe. These I will leave to return to the thread of my story.

After we had sailed along the shore of the Ouetaca territory and left it behind us, we passed into the view of another neighboring country named *Macaé*, inhabited by other savages of which I will say nothing except that, for the reasons I have mentioned, you can guess that they do not have an easy time of it and have no mind to be lulled to sleep next to such brusque and fidgety alarm-clocks as their neighbors are. On the shore of their land there can be seen a big rock shaped like a tower, which, when the sun strikes it, glistens and sparkles so brightly that some think it is a sort of emerald; indeed, the French and Portuguese who travel there call it the "Emerald of Macaé." They say, however, that the site cannot be approached with ships because of the innumerable rocky points just above the water, which project about two leagues into the sea; they also maintain that it is inaccessible from the land.

There are also three little islands called the "Islands of Macaé," near which we cast anchor and slept for a night. The next day, setting sail, we thought that we could arrive at Cape Frio that same day. However, instead of advancing, we had such a contrary wind that we had to give up and turn back to where we had come from that morning, and stay there at anchor until Thursday evening; and, as you will hear, we nearly stayed there for good. For Tuesday the second of March, the day called "Shrove-Tuesday," after our sailors had made merry according to their custom, it happened that around eleven o'clock at night, just as we were about to retire, a storm came up so suddenly that the cable holding the anchor of our ship was unable to sustain the violence of the furious waves, and it suddenly snapped. Our vessel, tossed about by the billows and pushed toward the shore, came in to where we had only twelve feet of water (which was the least it could float in even when it was completely empty), and we very nearly ran aground. In fact, the master and the pilot, who were sounding the depth as the ship was drifting, instead of being more confident and giving courage to the others, when they saw that we had come to that point cried out two or three times, "We are lost! We are lost!" Our sailors, however, speedily cast another anchor, which thanks to God held firm, and we were prevented from being carried onto the rocks of these Islands of Macaé, which without a doubt would have entirely wrecked our ship, and – with the sea being as high as it was – would have left us with no hope of saving ourselves. This fright and shock lasted around three hours, during which time there was not much use in shouting, "Larboard! Starboard! Raise the helm! Luff! Haul the bow line! Let go the sheet!" – for all that kind of yelling goes on out on the high seas, where the seamen do not fear a storm as much as they do close to land, where we were at that time.

Since our drinking water was spoiled, when morning came and the storm had ceased, some of us went to get fresh water in these uninhabitable islands. We found the land covered with eggs and birds of various kinds, utterly different from our own; and because they were unaccustomed to seeing men, they were so tame that they let themselves be caught by hand, or killed by blows of a stick. We filled our bark with them and brought back to the ship as many as we pleased. Although it was the day called "Ash Wednesday," nonetheless our sailors – even the most Roman Catholic among them – who had a good appetite from their work of the night before, had no scruples about eating them. And, after all, since he who (contrary to the doctrine of the Gospel) has forbidden Christians to eat meat on certain days has not yet set foot in this land, where consequently no one has heard of observing the laws of such superstitious abstinence, it seems that the place gave them sufficient dispensation.

The Thursday that we left these three islands, we had such a favorable wind that the next day, around four o'clock in the afternoon, we arrived at Cape Frio, the best-known port and harbor for French navigation in that country. There, after casting anchor and firing several cannon shots as a signal to the inhabitants, the captain and the ship's master, with some of us others, went ashore. First, we found on the shore a great number of savages called *Tupinamba*, allies and confederates of our nation, who brought us, along with their courtesies and welcome, news of *Paycolas* (for so they called Villegagnon), which made us very happy. In this same place we caught, both with a net and with hooks, a great quantity of several kinds of fish, all different from those over here; but among the others, there was one, perhaps the oddest, most deformed and most monstrous that one might ever see, and for that reason I wanted to describe it here. It was almost as big as a yearling calf, and had a nose about five feet long, and a foot and a half wide, armed with teeth on each side, as sharp and cutting as a saw: so that when on the land we saw one of them suddenly move this great nose, we all were wary of it, lest we be marked by it, and cried out to each other, "Watch your legs!" Its flesh was so hard that although we all had a good appetite, and we even boiled it more than twenty-four hours, still, we could never eat it.

It was there, too, that we first saw flocks of parrots flying high above, like pigeons and crows in France; they are always joined together as couples in the air, almost like our turtledoves.

Having thus arrived at twenty-five or thirty leagues from our destination, we desired nothing more than to get there as soon as possible, and for that reason we did not make as long a stay at Cape Frio as we might otherwise have done. So the evening of that same day, having made ready and set sail, we cut the water so swiftly that on Sunday the seventh of March 1557, leaving the high sea on the left (to the east), we entered the inlet of the sea, the saltwater estuary called *Guanabara* by the savages, and *Janeiro* by the Portuguese (who gave it that name because they discovered it on the first day of January). So, as I mentioned in the first chapter of this history, and as I will describe hereafter at more length, we found Villegagnon settled, as he had been since the preceding year, on a little island situated in this estuary. When we had saluted him with cannon fire from about a quarter of a league off, and he had answered us, we drew near the shore and cast anchor. So that, in sum, was our navigation, and what happened to us and what we saw on our way to the land of Brazil.

## 3. Corsairs: French Interlopers at Bahia (1614)

*Not only did the French and the Dutch seek to establish their own colonies on the Brazilian coast but, beginning in the sixteenth century, corsairs and contrabandists also visited Brazil on a regular basis. Sometimes they found colonists willing to trade and officials willing to turn a blind eye to illicit trade, but in other instances, the exclusionary policies of the Portuguese Crown were rigidly enforced and the inter-lopers turned to piracy and violence. Most of the reports we have of these foreign interlopers come from their own accounts of their activities but, in this document, we have a local view of such events. In this account of a disastrous engagement with French corsairs in 1614, the municipal council of Salvador writes to Gaspar de Sousa, the governor of Brazil, who at the time of the attack had been absent in Per-nambuco, Brazil's richest captaincy at the time. This extract from its letter reveals the way in which such maritime actions affected the society and political organiza-tion of the colony, but it also indicates the frustrations of the residents of Salvador with the lack of leadership. From Pernambuco, Gaspar de Sousa had been directing the conquest of the northern area of Maranhão and the expulsion of another French attempt at colonization there, and the town councilors of Salvador did not hesitate to voice their displeasure at his distraction.* (From Arquivo Histórico Ultramarino (Lisbon) [AHU] Bahia, papéis avulsos, caixa 1.)

To Governor Gaspar de Sousa:

We have advised Your Lordship in our letter of the disastrous events suffered by Captain Balthesar de Aragão which we sent to you some ten days ago by land; and because there may be delays in so long a journey, we wish to advise you again by means of this present ship and to recount the incident and what has happened after we had written [and sent] by land.

On the 17th or 18th of February [1614], there appeared close to the mouth of this Bahia three corsair ships. They appeared every morning and chased the boats and small fishing vessels, and in the afternoon they returned to sea toward the hill of São Paulo. Afterwards, the lookouts warned that there were five ships and that they were corsairs, Captain-Major Balthesar de Aragão decided to fight them and clean the coast, so that in the same week he organized an armada of six ships and two caravels, sending as the flagship [*capitania*] his own ship, which was in the port loaded with three hundred chests, of sugar. Everything was made ready in four or five days, and he sailed accompanied by close to two hundred men, including the most noble and honored young men of this land and people very "clean" [of impecca-ble origins] and distinguished. Sunday, at nightfall of the 23 of February, he sailed from this bay with the whole armada, sailing far to sea through the whole night of São Mathias and in the morning appearing before the shore in front of the São Paulo hill. Meeting the enemy, he ordered his ships attack. The *capitania* caught a contrary wind [*calcavento*] and, being a great sailing ship and the captain not wishing to see the enemy escape, ordered the lower gun ports opened in order to fire and sink the enemy. As the ship closed with the enemy, it took water through the open gun ports and turned over and, in an instant, it sank to the bottom with all hands, which on seeing this happen, the remaining ships returned to Bahia. Manoel de Pina had taken a small pinnace [*pataxo*] and Vasco de Brito who had gone as admiral had taken another with great loss of life on both sides, but mostly by the enemy. And wishing to come to help when the ship went down, his soldiers would not allow it for they had neither powder nor shot and because they were far away and against the wind. And they said they could not save anyone, a thing of such grief and general loss which caused such great confusion and lament in this land that it was impossible to console the people, and it was, in truth, the most notable and painful loss that could have happened in this land, and it touched everyone.[1]

When the news arrived, your Lordship's commissioners gathered in council with some of the principal persons of the land where some of us were also found and they decided that the armada should be resupplied with munitions and should return with another ship to seek out the enemy because it was now with two pinnaces less and it was said that its flagship was taking water.

They elected as the captain-majors of four ships, Vasco de Brito and the admiral of the Philippines who was here. Vasco de Brito asked for a ship that in the first effort had been captained by Bento de Araújo as his ship because his own was unsuitable and was the worst in the fleet. One of the Commissioners in charge refused to comply and, because Vasco de Brito complained, he was placed under house arrest. And they elected Afonso de França as captain-major of the whole fleet. And despite all the haste because they did not have a captain-major, they did not sail until March 3, forcing people to embark by arresting them. Your Lordship should note that the people did not lack courage, but men were beside themselves with grief and pain because of the loss of their captain-major, their relatives and friends; some wept for their parents, others for their children and brothers. And also because of the general revulsion that all the people have for one of Your Lordship's commissioners, for everyone knows he is a man who wishes the people ill and wishes to destroy them – and when he who governs wishes his subjects ill and is hated by them, he will never be obeyed especially when they must risk their lives. . . .

It is a great shame to see this city and all the people cry out. All this is the result of the absence of its governor and [it must be] our own sins that Our Lord having given us such a good governor have not permitted that we have him with us to govern and defend us in so many tasks. It is a thing that we lament with passion that the capital of this state is allowed to be lost without government or order so that new and uncertain conquests which will never

---

1 Frei Vicente do Salvador, *História do Brazil* (1627) bk. v, chap. vi, reported that most of the men drowned at sea, and the few who survived were rescued by the enemy. See *História do Brazil*, ed. Maria Lêda Oliveira (Rio de Janeiro: Versal, 2008).

end and be carried out, and that the sure thing from whence His Majesty derives benefit and where so many loyal and noble vassals reside be ignored in order to search for that which is of doubtful benefit.

We now ask Your Lordship to gaze on this people and the miserable state in which it has fallen, which is naught but pure confusion and disorder and that you leave everything and come to this land.

# 5

# INDIANS, JESUITS, AND COLONISTS

*During much of the second half of the sixteenth century, Portuguese colonists and Jesuit missionaries struggled over the best way to control, convert, and employ the indigenous inhabitants of Brazil. Both the colonists who, with the development of a sugar industry, began to enslave the native peoples, and the Jesuits, who wanted to bring them into missionary villages, hoped to convince the Crown that they were best suited to bring the Indians under Portuguese authority and make them subjects of the king useful to the colony. The Crown issued laws limiting or prohibiting the enslavement of Indians in 1574, 1595, 1609, and 1680, but there were always considerable loopholes in the legislation. During the struggle over control of the Indians, both colonists and Jesuits became highly critical of their opponents, but both sides also wrote in some detail about the indigenous peoples of Brazil.*

## 1. The Tupinambás

*Of all the indigenous peoples on the coast, the Tupinambá of Bahia received the most attention from early European observers. In this excerpt, the sugar planter, Gabriel Soares de Sousa, presents an extensive and detailed ethnography that demonstrates the curiosity of the early Portuguese observers but also the limitations in describing Native American cultures imposed by European preconceptions and understandings. His account maintains the usual Portuguese distinction between the Tupi-speaking peoples and the tapuyas, or groups that spoke non-Tupi languages. Although he notes the barbarism and cannibalism of the latter, his account also reveals a familiarity and, at times, admiration for their skills.* (From Gabriel Soares de Sousa, *Tratado Descretivo do Brasil* em 1587, pp. 299–322.)

## Chapter CXLVII. The Original Inhabitants of Bahia

According to information gleaned from Indians of very great age, the first inhabitants of Bahia and the surrounding area were the Tapuyas. They are a very ancient tribe, and more will be revealed about them in due course. They were expelled from Bahia and areas close to the sea by an opposing tribe, the Tupinaés, who swept down on them from inland, attracted by reports about the fertility of the land and about the plentiful seafood that characterize this province. One tribe waged war on the other until finally the Tupinaés defeated and routed the Tapuyas, forcing them to abandon the coastal areas and retreat into the interior without any real chance of recapturing their former territory. The Tupinaés dominated and ruled over that area for many years, continuing to repel attacks launched from inland by the Tapuyas, the original inhabitants of the coast.

News of the fertility and productive nature of the area came also to the notice of the Tupinambá tribe. They gathered together and likewise descended on the region around Bahia from lands beyond the River São Francisco. They gradually gained control of it, waging war on the resident Tupinaés and destroying their farms and villages. Without quarter, they killed anyone who offered resistance, till finally they expelled them from the coastal area. The Tupinaés retreated inland, abandoning their territory to the Tupinambás, who now held sway over it. The Tupinaés then confronted their old enemies, the Tapuyas, but the latter fought a ferocious war against them, forcing them even farther inland as they recoiled from the onset of the Tupinambás, who now controlled the coast. Always presenting a strong front to their adversaries, the Tupinambás remained the masters of this land for many years, until the arrival of the Portuguese. This information has been gathered from both the Tupinambás and the Tupinaés, for they pass the story down from generation to generation.

### Chapter CXLVIII. The Physique and Nature of the Tupinambás and the Divisions between Them

The Tupinambás are of average height, are very dark-skinned, and are sturdy and amiable. Facially, they appear to be very cheerful and they smile readily. They all have good, small, white teeth that never suffer decay. Their legs are strong and they have small feet. They always shave their faces. They also never allow hair to grow on other parts of their bodies and remove it whenever it appears. Their strength is notable and they work hard. They are a warlike people and fight bravely even when ambushed. They enjoy novelty. Their libido is excessive, but they are great huntsmen and fishermen, as well as being dedicated farmers.

Having become masters of the territory around Bahia, the tribe then divided up into sundry groups, owing to the sundry differences that grew up between them. They split into separate villages, and finally enmity developed. Those who had settled between the River São Francisco and the River

Real proclaimed themselves enemies of those who had established themselves between the River Real and the coast at Bahia. Fierce battles took place daily. Both sides ate some of their captives, while the remainder became their captors' slaves.

Those Tupinambás in Bahia who dwelled where the city now stands declared themselves enemies of those who lived at the other end of Bahia, where it is bounded by the River Paraguaçu and the River Sergipe. They fought ferociously against one another at sea, in naval battles aboard canoes. Between the islands, they laid ambushes for one another. The death toll was very heavy everywhere, cannibalism took place, and both sides took captives as well. That situation continued until the arrival of the Portuguese.

## Chapter CXLIX. Further Divisions among the Tupinambás, with Some Settling on the Island of Itaparica and Others along the River Jaguaripe

Among the Tupinambás who lived on the spot where the city is, there also broke out dissension between one group and another because a young woman was forcibly taken from her father without any intention of returning her. As a result of the disagreement, there broke away all her father's relatives, people who were prominent among the Indians. They made their way to the island of Itaparica, which is in the middle of the bay. Many others joined them, and they also made common cause with their neighbors along the River Paraguaçu. They waged war on those who lived where the city stands, the boundaries of which they called Caramurê. The Tupinambás ambushed one another daily, and even today there is a small island known as the Island of Fear because they used to lie in wait behind it. They would emerge from behind it in their canoes, ambushing one another. Every day, they killed one another in large numbers.

Of the Tupinambás who settled on the island of Itaparica, some went on to populate the banks of the Jaguaripe, [the island of] Tinharé, and the coast of Ilhéus. So united in hatred were these people, all because of the young woman, their forebear, that even today, among the few that survive, the hatred is such that the mutual slaughter continues whenever the opportunity arises. Indeed, if they come across some old grave belonging to their enemies, they dig up the skulls and smash them to pieces. Their practice then is to give themselves new names. The hostility, moreover, constantly renews itself.

Once, after the time when the Portuguese had settled along the River Jaguaripe, in their very township there assembled a great village gathering of the nearby Indians, intent on smashing skulls on open land, amid great festivity. Those who smashed skulls were to take new names, and the skulls had been dug up in an abandoned village. It was an act of revenge for the death of the very parents or relatives of those who smashed the skulls. The skulls were [first] decorated with birds' feathers, in typical fashion, and the festivity was characterized by great drunkenness: the gathering had been arranged by the Portuguese settlers precisely in order to scandalize the relatives of the dead and to provoke further hatred. That was because the Portuguese feared that the Tupinambás might all make common cause in order to wage war against them. It was effective in preventing that from happening, and in that way, the Portuguese who lived alongside the river guaranteed their own safety.

## Chapter CL. The Customs and Language of the Tupinambás

Despite the fact that the Tupinambás have split up into different and mutually hostile groups, they all speak a language that is almost generalized along the whole of the Brazilian coast. Moreover, they all have the same customs, living habits, and pagan rites. They do not have any entity to worship, they have no concept of truth, and all they know is the fact of life and death. Anything that they are told is simply accepted. They are more barbarous than any other people that God has created.

They are very amusing when they speak, especially the women. Their speech is rather verbose, as are their prayers. However, it is notable that three letters are missing from their alphabet, namely F, L, and capital or double R. The fact that they have no F is due to their lack of faith in anything that they might worship. Not even those born among Christians and catechized by the Jesuit Fathers have any faith in Our Lord God, nor have they any regard for truth or any loyalty to anyone who does them a favor. Moreover, the lack of the letter L in their pronunciation is due to the lack of any law to keep or any principles by which to govern themselves. Each one of them makes his own law solely to suit himself. There do not exist any laws between them by which they could govern themselves, not even in their dealings one with another. Their lack of the letter R in their pronunciation is due to the fact that they have no king to rule over them, no king whom they might obey. Indeed, they show no obedience to anyone: children do not obey their parents, and they all live as they think fit. To say "Francisco" they say "Pancico"; "Lourenço" comes out as "Rorenço," and to say "Rodrigo" they pronounce it as "Rodigo." This is how they utter all the words that contain these three letters.[1]

---

1  The reasoning here is based on the initial letters of the three elements of culture that the Tupinambás are said to lack: *fé* (faith), *lei* (law), and *rei* (king).

## Chapter CLI. The Location and Layout of the Tupinambá Villages and the Number of Their Leaders

In every Tupinambá village there exists a headman, but they only follow him when at war. Then they show a degree of obedience toward him, according to the trust they have in his vigor and experience. But in time of peace, everyone does as he sees fit. The headman has to be a man of courage for them to appreciate him, as well as being a man who is well loved by his relatives, so that he can have people to help him to till his fields. Nevertheless, when he tends them with the help of relatives and friends, he must take the lead in being the first to set to work. When such a headman decides where to locate his village, he always looks for a raised site that is exposed to the wind, so that their houses can be constantly aired. There must also be water close at hand, and the land around the village must be of a quality that enables them to plant out their crops. The headman also chooses a spot that will please the more elderly. His own house is a very long building, covered with branches of the pindova palm, which is the name the Indians give to that tree.[2] The other houses in the village are also very long and are laid out in such a way that an open square is left in the middle. This open area is for dancing and for other gatherings.

Every village has [such] a chief. He must be an elder among the Indians and a man with a family. For that reason, the other villagers show him respect. They inhabit the village for as long as the palm branches on their houses avoid rot: they last for three or four years. When once the branches let a lot of rain into their houses, the Indians transfer their village elsewhere. The houses are not divided into rooms other than by the crossbeams. In the spaces below and between the beams, there is an individual section for each family to inhabit. The headman chooses his living space first. There he installs himself, along with his wife and children, his concubines, unmarried male servants, and any elderly women who serve him. Then, similarly, they take up their living spaces all the other families that are to share his house. They cannot move elsewhere, except in the case of a young unmarried man who is to marry. In that case, he goes to share the living space of his wife.

Over the crossbeams in the houses they stretch poles, set close together, which [*the resulting platform*] they call a *jirau*. On these *jiraus*, they store household utensils and their vegetables. They smoke the vegetables to prevent them from rotting. The same procedure is followed in the other houses. In all the houses, every section of living space is occupied. They eat squatting on the floor, all at the same time, whilst the headmen stretch out in

---

2   The branches of the pindova palm (*Attalea humilis*) were woven into mats to create thatched roofs.

hammocks. It is in these houses that these pagan people have sexual intercourse, though without any wrangling between them, as each male has his own female.

Whenever this kind of village is at odds with its enemies and is situated in an area where hostile attacks are likely, then they build a very sturdy wattle and daub wall around their village. The wall has doorways and arrow slits. At a distance of some twenty to thirty hand-spans from the wall, they build a wooden palisade with means of escape back inside the [inner] wall. If their enemies get inside the palisade, the defenders can in that way elude them. As the defenders withdraw, they bar themselves inside so as to be able to fire arrows at their assailants and in that way to rout them, as is often the case.

## Chapter CLII. Love and Marriage among the Tupinambás

The true wife of a Tupinambá is the first woman that he has taken and to whom he has paid court. In their marriage ceremony, the father simply hands over his daughter to his son-in-law. Once they have sexual union, they are deemed to be married. However, the headmen have more than one wife. Indeed, the one who has most wives is considered to be the most worthy of esteem. Moreover, the wives all show obedience to the first wife and serve her. She hangs her hammock next to that of her husband, and there is always a burning fire between the two hammocks. The other wives hang their hammocks further away and sleep in them, with a fire between each pair. Whenever the husband wishes to have intercourse with any one of them, he leaps into her hammock with her and remains there just long enough to satisfy himself. He then goes back to his place. There is always jealousy among the wives, and the first wife is particularly possessive. That is because the first wife is usually older than the rest and less modest, for intercourse takes place in full public view.

Whenever the headman is not the major figure in all the houses of an Indian village, it is when the man who has most children is the richest and most highly esteemed. That is because his daughters are greatly sought after by suitors among the young men. The young men serve the fathers of the young women for two or three years before their fathers hand them over as wives. Furthermore, they will hand them over only to those who have served them best. The suitors till the land for them, they also go fishing and hunting for the fathers-in-law that they wish to please, not to mention bringing firewood from the forest. When once the brides are handed over by the fathers-in-law, the bridegrooms go and lodge with their wives in the living space of their fathers-in-law. They leave behind their fathers, mothers, siblings, and any other relatives with whom they previously lived.

In no circumstances is a bride handed over to her husband until she has started her menstrual cycle. Once it has started, the young woman is obliged to wear a cotton thread attached to her waist and another one on each of her upper arms, to make it known to everybody. When once her husband deflowers her, the bride is then bound to break the threads, for everyone to know that she is now a true woman. Even if one such young woman is deflowered by a man who is not her husband, for all that the act takes place in secret, she is still bound to break the threads of her virginity, for she believes that otherwise the devil would snatch her away at once. Mishaps of that kind often occur. Nevertheless, the father does not get angry on that account because there is no shortage of suitors, despite the setback. If a village headman asks another Indian for his daughter's hand, the father gives it even if she is still a girl. In such circumstances, the precept mentioned above is not followed because he takes her off to his own living space and rears her until her menstrual cycles begin. Under no circumstances may he touch her before that.

### Chapter CLIII. How These Pagans Adorn Themselves

The young men among the Tupinambás customarily remove all bodily hair other than the hair on their heads. That hair they clip in a variety of ways. Indeed, they did so even before they acquired scissors, using well-sharpened canes. Some of them wear their hair cut back and very neatly trimmed above their ears. They cover their genitals with some adornment for its own sake and not out of any specific need to cover them. They paint themselves with black markings made with genipap ink.[3] Their girlfriends, if they have them, carefully do the painting for them. On their heads they wear yellow feathers, fixed at the base with wax. From their ears hang earrings fashioned from bone, and from their necks dangle great white beads that they make from seashells. Their girlfriends scrape away the hair from their foreheads for them, using little canes. They also remove the hair from their beards, their eyelashes, and their eyebrows, as well as the rest of their bodily hair, as mentioned above. Whenever the youths want to make themselves appear especially elegant, then they apply mastic resin to make their hair stand upright. Then they attach tiny yellow feathers to their hair and also hang white beads under their armpits. They respectively adorn their arms and legs with armbands and garters of yellow feathers and place a diadem of the same feathers on their heads.

The young women likewise use genipap ink to paint themselves with many markings in their own style and make themselves very attractive.

---

3   The bark of the genipap tree (*Genipa americana*) yields an ink-like tannin.

They decorate themselves with great strings of beads of all kinds. They wear them dangling from their necks and around their arms. On their legs, below their knees, they wear leg-bands made of cotton thread and painted red. The bands are three fingers wide. They are fastened round their legs by their mothers when they are still little girls. That is to ensure that while they are growing up and their legs are thickening around their calves, they should still wear them during courtship, though in such a way that only with difficulty can they take them off. While they are still unmarried, their mothers paint them. After they marry, their husbands do so, if they truly love them. The equivalent of all the hair that the youths remove is, in the case of the young women, shaved off by other women. Such Indian women also treat their hair to make it long, thick, and black. To achieve that, they frequently anoint their hair with wild coconut oil.

### Chapter CLIV. What the Tupinambás Do at Childbirth and How They Bring up Their Children

When these Indian women start to feel the pangs of childbirth, they do not seek out midwives, nor do they protect themselves from the open air, nor do they perform other ceremonies. An Indian woman gives birth in the fields or elsewhere, just like a wild beast. When it is over, she goes to the river or stream and washes both herself and her newborn baby. She then returns home, where her husband immediately takes to his hammock, lying there, well covered up, until the baby's navel heals. Relatives and friends then visit them, bringing presents of food and drink. The wife pays fond attention to her husband during the aftermath of childbirth, and he remains well wrapped up, in order to avoid any infection from the air. According to their belief, if he were to catch any such infection from the air, then that would greatly harm the baby. Furthermore, were he to get up and carry out any work, their baby would die, and he would suffer great abdominal pain. Nobody can remove from the husband's head the notion that no danger exists on the woman's part, but only on his. His belief is that the child issued from his loins, and that the wife's sole contribution has been to keep his seed in her belly, where it grows into a baby.

When a Tupinambá child is born, it at once receives an appropriate name. The names that they give are those of wild beasts, fish, birds, trees, foodstuffs, weapons, and sundry other things. A hole is made under the child's lower lip, and there they set an ornamental stone, once the child has grown up.

The Tupinambás never punish their children, give them no rules to live by, and never rebuke them for anything they do. The boys are taught to use bows and arrows, firstly how to hit a target and then how to shoot down birds. They carry their children, both male and female, on their backs till the age of seven or eight. Boys and girls suckle at their mother's breast until she gives birth again. The mothers teach their daughters how to adorn themselves, just as Portuguese women do, how to spin cotton, and how to do the housework according to custom.

### Chapter CLV. How the Tupinambás Make Themselves Appear Elegant

To make themselves appear elegant, the Tupinambás resort to many strange and outlandish practices. For instance, once the boys are grown up, three or four holes are made under the lower lip, and there they insert stones with pointed ends sticking outward. Others make holes above their upper lip, as well as their lower lip, and there they likewise place stones. These stones are round, green, and brown. They are inserted right up into their cheeks and look just like rubber mirrors. Yet others have two or three holes made in their cheeks in which they put stones with pointed ends projecting outward. There are even some who have all such holes, with stones in all of them, with the result that they look like demons. They suffer the pain caused by this in order to terrify their enemies.

They also wear headdresses of red and yellow feathers. Once they are placed on their heads, they pull them right down to their ears. They also fashion necklaces from their enemies' teeth and altogether wear up to two or three thousand of them. To their feet they attach chestnut-like bells fashioned from certain plants; their jangling can be heard quite far off. For further elegance, these Indians also adorn themselves with circlets of ostrich feathers that they fasten round their hips. The resultant bulk is so large as to cover their backs from top to bottom. To give themselves a sinister appearance, they smear themselves all over with genipap juice to the point where they resemble blacks from Guinea. They stain their feet and their cheeks with a fine red ink. Under their armpits they hang large numbers of beads made from seashells, whilst on their arms they wear smaller beads made out of feathers. Once adorned with all these items, they carry a wooden sword decorated with the shells of birds' eggs. The shells are of various colors whilst the sword hilt is adorned with large bird feathers, as well as with bells made from yellow feathers. They hang the sword on their backs and tied to their necks. In their left hand, they carry their bow and arrows tipped with sharks' teeth. In their right hand, they hold a rattle that consists of a gourd full of pebbles and fitted with a handle. They walk along shaking it to accompany their chanting. They dress up in this gaudy fashion when there are festivities and the drinking of wine in their village or in an adjacent one. On these occasions, they chant and shake their rattles at first on their own and then in groups. Thus adorned, they make themselves both feared and respected.

## Chapter CLVI. The Barbarians and Their Libido

The Tupinambás are so libidinous that there is no sin of lust that they do not commit. Even when quite young, they have relations with women, including women more advanced in years. Indeed, the older women, no longer desired by grown men, entice such boys with gifts and caresses. They teach them things that they do not know and do not leave them day or night. These heathens are so lustful that they seldom have any respect for their sisters or aunts. However, as that sin is against even their customs, they sleep with them out in the forest. Some even do so with their own daughters. Nor are they content with one woman but have many, as mentioned earlier. In consequence, many of them die from exhaustion.

When the men converse, their only topic is the filthy activity that they commit hourly. They are so given to the [sins of the] flesh that to satisfy their appetites, they are not content with the natural dimensions of their penis. That is because many of them are in the habit of placing on it the hair of some animal, hair that is so poisonous that it causes the penis to develop an immense swelling. The very painful effect lasts for more than six months, which loses them a considerable interval. But then each man's penis is so abnormally huge that their women cannot bear to wait for it and then they can barely endure it. These savages are not even satisfied with their pursuit of such sinful yet natural carnality. Rather, they are also much given to committing the unspeakable sin. Nor do they regard it as an outrage. Indeed, any man who has intercourse with another male considers himself to be a valiant brave, and they regard such bestiality as a great feat. In their inland villages, there are some that set up brothels for those who desire to have intercourse with men as though they were whores.

When the fathers and mothers see that their sons are developing sexual urges, they seek out women for them and teach them what to do. Young females likewise desire males, especially those who live among the Portuguese. Yet the Tupinambá males are not possessive. Even if they find other men with their women, they do not see that as a reason for killing anyone. At the very most, they give the women a thrashing. As for the women, if they love their husbands and wish to keep them contented, they seek out young women for them to enjoy. They even steer them toward their husband's hammocks, begging and bribing them to lie with their men. Such actions are alien to all other races except these barbarians.

## Chapter CLVII. Tupinambá Family Relationships and Practices

The custom of the Tupinambás is that when a married man dies, his eldest brother must marry his widow. If he has no brother, then the lot falls to his nearest relative on the male side of the family. Moreover, the widow's brother must marry the [dead] man's daughter if he has one. Whenever the mother of that girl has no brother, then the daughter takes as husband the nearest male relative on her mother's side. If that relative does not wish to marry his niece, he must not prevent anyone from sleeping with her and will give to her whatever husband she wishes.

The uncle who is the brother of the girl's father may not marry his niece nor, if they are following the custom, may he touch her. Rather, he must treat her as though she were his daughter, and she must obey him as though he were her father. Indeed, after the death of her father, she must call her uncle "father." Whenever such a girl has no uncle that is her father's brother, then that place is taken by the nearest male relative. Indeed, all relatives on her father's side are to be called "father," and their duty is to call her "daughter." Yet her obedience is always owed to the nearest male relative.

Grandchildren address the brothers and cousins of their grandfather in the same way, just as they similarly address the grandchildren and the children of the grandsons and granddaughters of their brothers and cousins. On the mother's side likewise, her brothers and cousins address their nephews as sons, and they address their uncles as though they were their fathers. Nevertheless, they do not hold them in quite the same respect that they show for their uncles on their father's side.

These pagans greatly prize their relatives. Indeed, a man with many relatives, both male and female, is greatly respected and feared. He constantly strives to tighten the links between them and to be as one with them wherever they live. Whenever an Indian who has relatives offers hospitality to them in his house and living space, and there is food available, he lies down in his hammock and the food is placed in a pot that is [first] passed to him. Then they all squat round, mothers and children and all their relatives, young and old, and they all eat together from the pot, for it is placed in their midst.

## Chapter CLVIII. *How the Tupinambás Eat and Drink*

As stated above, when the headman eats, he lies down in his hammock, and his relatives also eat with him. He makes them all welcome, including the servants and slaves, and the latter pay him no particular respect. Indeed, when the meat or fish is not very plentiful, the headman divides it up into equal portions and quite often he is left with nothing for himself. [Apart from the headman,] they all eat squatting down. The dish from which they eat is placed on the ground in their midst. While they eat, they drink neither water nor wine and only do so after they have finished eating. When the Tupinambás eat at night, they do so seated on the ground, as mentioned above, and with their backs to the fire, so that they are all in darkness. They never speak while they are eating, leaving that until after the meal. Whenever they have food in plenty, they spend the night hours doing nothing else, until they are overcome by sleep. On the other hand, these pagans sometimes survive without food and go without eating for two or three days. Indeed, the slaves among them give little service to their masters in the preparation of food. Rather, they normally serve them by working on their crops and by hunting and fishing for them.

These pagans, if reared among their own people, do not eat pork. They only do so if they are slaves reared among the whites. But they do eat the flesh of peccaries. Only the shrewd ones among them use olive oil. They do not skin their game but singe it all over or remove the skin in hot water. They then eat it roasted or baked, scarcely washing the innards. They do not scale or gut their fish. Whether the fish comes from the sea or from rivers, they roast or bake it. They use salt to season their food and to preserve their meat and fish. They make it by boiling down saltwater in a pot over the fire until it sets and goes hard. They also use it as a remedy, smearing it on their injuries, though that causes smarting.

These barbarians, both males and females, are very fond of wine. They make it from their root vegetables and from edible flour, though their main wine is made from a root that they call *aipim*.[4] First they cook it, then they tread it before cooking it again. When once it is well cooked, they seek out the most attractive young women of the village. Their task is to squeeze out the cassava with their hands or even by chewing it. After squeezing it, they place it in a dish. According to their pagan beliefs, they are putting their virtue there with it. The water and juice from the roots is poured into great pots specially kept for the purpose. The wine is cooked in them until it acquires a sharp taste. Once it is right, they drink it and sing heartily. Indeed, they sing and dance the whole night before the day on which the wine is ready. Then, the next morning, the drinking, singing, and dancing really begins. The young unmarried women of the village distribute the wine in great gourds that they call *cuias*. They give it to those who are singing. The latter eat nothing while they are drinking and carousing until they fall to the ground intoxicated. The man who performs the craziest actions during such binges is highly regarded by the rest. Quarrels break out among them, as their jealousies are recalled on such occasions. They then punish their womenfolk on that account, at which their friends dash to their aid. They also resort to games with blazing firebrands.

It is their custom to have something to eat before they go to work on their crops. They eat not a thing while doing that work, only eating again when once they have returned home.

4 Sweet cassava (*Manihot aipi*).

## Chapter CLIX. *Farming and Other Skills Employed by the Tupinambás*

When the Tupinambás go off to tend their crops, they just work from seven o'clock till noon. Only the truly diligent work until evening. They do not eat during their working hours but only after they arrive home again. The men normally work in the woods, burning them down and clearing the land, whilst the women plant the crops and keep them clear. The menfolk go in search of firewood with which to keep themselves warm and which they use to provide a fire also while they sleep in their hammocks, which are their beds. The womenfolk go in search of water from the stream and prepare the food. The men also normally take the hammocks down to the rivers to wash them when they get dirty.

The Tupinambás' only masterpieces are when they fashion baskets from palm leaves, as well as when they make other containers from the same leaves for their own use and in their own special style. They make their own bows and arrows. They produce very skillful artifacts from straw padding and from woodcarvings that they decorate in black and white. They make wicker baskets that they call *samburás*. They also carve other containers, like those found on the route to India. They fashion headdresses and capes from birds' feathers, not to mention other items that they make from feathers for their own use. They know how to apply red and yellow dye to white feathers. They alter the feathers of their parrots by using frogs' blood. They pull out the green feathers, and that causes others to grow that are yellow. The headmen among the Indians also have their hammocks decorated with patterns of woven rushes, fibers, and threads of cotton that they call *muçuranas*,[5] similar in their design to halters from Fez.

When these heathens seek to catch a lot of fish either from freshwater rivers or from saltwater inlets, they stretch a net of canes across such waterways and drive the fish downstream toward them. Then they throw into the water a large quantity of crushed herbs called *timbó*.[6] That serves to poison the fish that then float to the surface, and in that way they catch vast numbers of them.

The women of these pagans do not do any cooking or any washing. They merely spin cotton, yet they do not form a weft from it, though they could, as they simply do not know how to weave. From the yarn they fashion the hammocks in which they sleep, though they do not embroider them. They also use the yarn to make braided ribbons of varying widths with which to adorn their hair. It is the older women who have the task of preparing the flour for their food and of carrying the manioc on their backs, fetching it from

5 Named after the mussurana snake (*Oxyrhopus claelia*) because of its markings.
6 The woody vine (*Paullinia pinnata*).

their fields to where they live. As for those women who are very old, they have the job of fashioning earthenware containers, for example, the pots in which they make their wine. Some pots that they make are so big that they hold as much as a whole cask. In these and in smaller ones, they boil the wine that they drink. These elderly women also fashion pans, mugs, and bowls in which they cook their flour, as well as other bowls into which they pour it, from which they eat and which are decorated in colored dyes. This pottery is baked in a hole in the ground by placing firewood on top. These Indian women firmly believe that if the pottery is baked by any other person than the one who has shaped it, then it will shatter in the fire. The elderly women also help to prepare the flour, making it in their own living space.

These heathen women are very fond of rearing dogs for their husbands to take with them when hunting. Indeed, when the women go out with them, they carry the dogs on their backs. They also get pleasure from breeding chickens and other birds in their houses. They customarily clean themselves with a stick that they always keep by them for that purpose and, when they leave the house, they carry it with them. They are unashamed to clean themselves in front of other people nor do they mind others seeing them eat lice, a thing that they do when they inspect one another's heads. The one that finds the lice hands them over to the one who had them in her hair. The latter then crunches them between her teeth. They do not do this simply in order to eat them but as a way of avenging themselves for the bites that they have suffered.

### Chapter CLX. Other Tupinambá Skills and Customs

The Tupinambás are great archers, with regard both to wildfowl and to swine, deer, and other animals. Many of them use that skill to shoot both freshwater fish and sea fish. In that way, they kill more than their anglers do. Nor are they afraid to attack and kill huge snakes. They also attack water lizards as big as they themselves are, capturing them alive in their arms.

Moreover, these Indians, when they return from hunting or fishing, normally share what they bring back with the headman of the house in which they dwell. What is left they hand over to their womenfolk or to whomsoever has the task of sheltering them in their living space.

These Indians consider themselves to be sparely built, nimble at jumping and climbing, to be fine runners, and to be skilled sailors whenever they board boats and ships, in which at no time can anyone excel them at working their sails. They are also great oarsmen when they propel their canoes. These are dugouts in which twenty or thirty Indians row standing up, driving the canoe forward at immense speed. They are also very shrewd at grasping whatever the whites teach them, contrary to what might have been expected from such barbarians. They are swiftly adaptable when getting to know sundry tasks on the sugar plantations, such as wielding an axe in carpentry, or working a saw, or making pottery, or driving a cart. When it comes to breeding cows, they reveal great skill and care. In one respect, the Tupinambás have something that would make them good Franciscan friars, namely that everything that they have is held in common ownership, and all those in their house may make use of it. This applies equally to their tools (which are what they value most), to their clothing (what little they have), and to their food supply. When they eat, any person whatsoever may partake of their food, even if he is their adversary: they will not stop him or even scowl at his doing so.

The young Indian women who are reared and taught alongside the Portuguese women adapt very well to cooking and needlework. They carry out all the tasks with a needle that they are taught to do and show great skill. As to the preparation of sweetmeats, they make excellent cooks. However, they are very prone to have love affairs with the white men, both tempting them and being sought by them.

The Tupinambás are fine swimmers and divers and, when it matters to them, will swim three or four leagues. Such men are they that when at night they have nothing with which to fish, they plunge into the water and, when they sense that a fish is nearby, they dive down and catch it with their hands. Similarly, along the coast, they drag octopuses and lobsters out from their holes on the seabed.

### Chapter CLXI. The Tupinambá Sorcerers and Those Who Eat Earth to Kill Themselves

These Tupinambá pagans have great sorcerers among their number. They gain this repute among them through filling their heads with countless untruths. Each sorcerer inhabits a house that is set apart from the rest. It is very dark inside and has a tiny doorway such that nobody dares to enter the house or to touch anything pertaining to it. In the main, these sorcerers have no knowledge of anything but take to their trade as a means of making themselves respected and feared, as they realize just how easy it is to make these people believe anything whatsoever. There are some that communicate with demons. The demons frequently give them a thrashing and cause them to feel in debt to them for what they say. For this reason, the sorcerers are not so much believed by the Indians as feared.[7] The Tupinambás call their sorcerers *pajés*. A sorcerer becomes very indignant with any Indian who does not surrender to him his daughter or anything else that he demands from him,

---

7  It is fairly clear from this text that the sorcerers also masqueraded as demons.

telling the Indian, "Be off with you, for you are going to die." That is what they describe as "casting the spell of death." The Indians are so barbarous that they then take to their hammocks, panic-stricken and refusing to eat. They are so overcome that as a result they die, without anyone being able to persuade them that they can evade the sorcerers' spells. So, out of fear for their lives, some Indians surrender their daughters to them to be their wives. It often happens that a demon appears to the Indians in some dark location and proceeds to thrash them, so that they run away panic-stricken. But others remain unharmed by the demon and receive information from him about matters that are well known.

These Indians have another very barbarous habit, such that if they are stricken by something that greatly irks them, they become so depressed that they decide to end their lives. They start eating earth, a small amount every day, until they begin to waste away, and their faces and eyes swell up. Finally, they die from the effects, without anyone being able to help them or to dissuade them from their determination to kill themselves. They assert that their demon urges them to do so, when appearing to them, whence their determination to eat earth.

### Chapter CLXII. Sad Longings among the Tupinambás, Their Weeping and Their Singing

The Tupinambás have the custom that whenever one of their number returns from an absence, then, the moment he comes through the doorway, he immediately goes and lies down in his hammock. Then one or more old women go at once to him, squat down in front of him, and begin to wail aloud on his account. In their laments, they tell him about how much he has been missed during his absence and about all the troubles experienced by various other members [of the tribe]. Then the men respond by wailing in return, though without adding further words, until they grow weary of it all and tell the old women to be quiet, at which the latter duly obey. If the recipient of the wailing has come back from far away, then all the women of his household come to bewail his absence, not to mention his female relatives that now belong to other households. When once their wailing is over, they welcome him and bring him food in a great bowl. On it they place fish and meat and flour and put it all together for him [in the bowl] on the ground. He eats it lying down [in his hammock]. When he has finished eating, all the villagers come forward to welcome him, one by one. They ask him about his experiences in the places where he has been. When one of their leaders returns from an absence, even if he has only been to his plantation, all the women of his household come to lament his absence. They come forward one by one, or sometimes in pairs, bringing him presents of things to eat and carrying out the above-mentioned ceremonies.

When an Indian dies, his wife, his mother, and his female relatives bewail his death in a very piteous tone and go on doing so for several days. Their wailing is filled with countless laments that greatly affect anybody who understands the situation. The men, however, do not weep, for it is their custom never to weep over any of their people who die.

The Tupinambás regard themselves as good at making music. They sing reasonably well in their own way and possess good voices. But they all sing in unison. Their music makers improvise the themes of their songs, as well as the variations, and the last-named always end with the refrain from the main theme. One singer begins the song, and the rest join in with the refrain. They sing and dance together in a circle, in the midst of which one of them strikes a tambourine with simple blows. Others carry maracas in their hands: a maraca is a dry gourd with pebbles inside it and is attached to a handle with which to hold it. In their dancing, they do not have sequences and, when at a standstill, their only activity is to tap one foot on the ground in time with the tambourine. They all join in the dancing together and then visit one another's houses, where wine is at the ready with which to invite people in. Sometimes, in their midst, a couple of young women will sing together. Indeed, some of the young women are also skilled at making music and are highly regarded on that account.

These pagans greatly respect their music makers and give them a warm welcome wherever they go. In fact, many of them have made their way into the interior and traveled through areas controlled by their enemies without being harmed by them.

### Chapter CLXIII. The Manner in Which the Tupinambás Look after Their Guests

Whenever a guest enters a Tupinambá house, at once the owner of the specific section of living space at which the guest arrives offers him his hammock, and his wife places food before him. They refrain from asking him who he is, [or] where he comes from, [or] what he has come for. While the guest eats his food, they ask him in their language, "Have you just arrived?," and he replies, "Yes." All those who wish to do so also come to welcome him and afterwards they converse with him slowly.

Whenever a guest who is not a Tupinambá enters one of these villages, he calls out as he goes and makes his way through the entire village until he comes upon the headman's house. Without speaking to anyone, he lies down in some convenient house, where at once he is brought something to eat. When he has finished eating, the headman has a hammock put up for him next to the doorway of his living space and on one side, whilst the headman places his own hammock on the opposite side. In that way, the doorway is in the middle as a way in for anybody wanting to enter. Accordingly, the villagers come forward to welcome him, just as above. In this area, the headman converses, very slowly, with his guest, while the other Indians of the village sit round, eager to hear news. Nobody gives an answer or asks a question till the headman has finished speaking. Once he has finished speaking, he tells his guest to rest at his leisure. Then the headman takes his leave of the guest, and others then come forward to speak to him, to find out what news there is from the place he has come from.

The next day, the headman gathers with the village elders in a different house to discuss the arrival of this Indian who is not a Tupinambá and to talk about the matters he has related concerning where he has come from. They then vote by tokens to decide whether or not he has come in good faith. Even if he is their enemy, the miracle is that he can leave without their killing him and that they fulfill their obligations [as hosts] to him with all due festivity. The old women even utter their laments to him before he eats, just as above.

### Chapter CLXIV. The Practice and Ceremonies of the Tupinambás When They Meet in Council

Whenever the village headman wishes to discuss some issue of importance, he sends a message round to all the Indians of standing. They duly assemble in the central area of the village. There, on stakes that have been placed in the ground for that purpose, they hang up their hammocks around that of the headman. All those who wish to listen to their deliberations also gather round, as there is no secrecy among them. They all squat down and, when quiet falls, the headman states his case, to which they all listen intently. When he has finished speaking, the elders then respond, each one in turn. While one of them is speaking, all the rest keep silent till the time comes to decide what they are going to do. Quite frequently, there are differing views on this.

Some of the leaders who take part in the council bring with them pipes full of smoke, which they inhale. The headman does this first. For the purpose, he has a youth with him who hands him the lighted pipe. Once the youth has taken the tray back from him, he then orders the pipe to be passed round on it to one who has not had it and then in turn to all those who have not received the pipe. These Indians establish their authority in this way, just as those in India do when they eat betel-nuts in similar gatherings.[8]

---

8  Strictly speaking, "betel-nuts" are areca nuts wrapped in betel leaves.

This is also the practice among many white men and among all half-castes. They inhale the smoke as [though] a form of sustenance and cannot go about without it in their mouths, though it both fouls their breath and very greatly discolors their teeth. The pipe from which they smoke is a tube made out of a dried palm leaf. Inside it are three or four leaves of dried tobacco leaves, which the Indians call *petume*. The pipe is tied with a thread near the tightest end, where the *petume* leaves are, and that is the end that is lit. Once it is alight, they place it in their mouths and inhale the smoke. The dense smoke goes up into their nasal cavities and down their throats and is vigorously expelled through their nostrils. When they can no longer tolerate the smoke, they remove the pipe from their mouths.

## Chapter CLXV. How These Barbarians Cure Themselves of Their Illnesses

The Tupinambás are very susceptible to buboes.[9] They mainly catch it off one another when children because they never take precautions. They consider that they are bound to catch it sooner or later, and that it is preferable to catch it when they are children. Their sole remedy is to get the buboes to dry out, when once they make an appearance. That they do by painting them with genipap juice.[10] If that does not work, then the bubo pustules are treated with jacaranda leaves. When once the pustules dry up, they consider that they are cured from the disease. Indeed, they experience no further pain in their joints when the pustules have dried.

Sometimes and in certain places more than in others, these Indians are prone to tertian or quartan fevers. These are brought about by their going about in the heat without anything to cover their heads. They are also caused by their perspiring greatly after bathing in the cold water of rivers and streams in the heat of the day. A further cause can be through tiredness and perspiration as a result of working. Their sole remedy for these fevers is to eat gruel in the form of manioc porridge, as mentioned above, and which is both light and wholesome. They also smear themselves with genipap juice, which blackens their skin and to which they have a strong attachment.

These Indians cure themselves of boils and pimples by applying the juice of medicinal herbs that they have at their disposal. Indeed, they bring about some quite remarkable cures, as stated earlier. Whenever their heads become feverish, they scarify themselves in a stream. However, in the case of children, they are subjected to a dry scarification on their legs. The exercise is

---

9 Swollen lymph nodes in the groin or armpits. The chronic form is bubonic plague.
10 Genipap is the edible orange-sized fruit of the genip tree (*Genipa americana*).

carried out by older women, using a special very sharp tooth taken from an agouti.[11]

They treat major injuries and arrow wounds by applying a miraculous remedy that they call *cabureíba*.[12] They also use other herbal remedies whose qualities have already been mentioned. They use them to heal their wind-pipes, for these frequently swell up with cancer. As for deep arrow wounds and other injuries by which they are imperiled, they treat them in a strange way. Above a fire they fashion a bed made of poles of varying widths, lay-ing the injured on top, with their wounds facing downwards over the fire. With the heat, all the blood and moisture in their wounds run out. When all the moisture in them has gone, they then treat them with oil and balsam, as already mentioned. After a few days, they regain their health. There are no physicians of distinction among these barbarians, yet their charges make a very good recovery. Owing to the fact that these Indians always go about naked, and owing to their hardy approach to sleeping on the ground, they often fall victim to discharges that they attribute to the "evil eye." Such dis-charges are accompanied by pains in their joints. With regard to the "evil eye," their sorcerers cast themselves in the role of great physicians. They place their mouths at the painful spot and suck at it, sometimes using their teeth as well. They then take out of their mouths some piece of iron or some other thing that they scheme to remove from the spot where they were suck-ing: it had "emerged" from where the pain was. They then paint the spot with genipap juice, declaring that all is now well.

### Chapter CLVI. The Tupinambás' Great Knowledge of the Land

The Tupinambás have a great knowledge of the land on which they set foot. They turn their heads toward the sun, from which they take their bearings. In that way, they hit upon good routes through wild areas across which they have never previously journeyed. That is clear from what happened in Bahia, when two Tupinambá prisoners, duly convicted for their crimes, were dispatched by sea to Rio de Janeiro. Each one escaped in turn and made his way back here, always avoiding inhabited areas for fear of attract-ing enemy attention. All the time they made their way through the forest. In that way, they came back to Bahia and reached their own native village, safe and sound, after a journey of more than three hundred leagues.

When these barbarians journey through the forest without knowing where the inhabited areas are, their practice is to lie down on the ground and sniff the air to discover whether they can smell fire, because they can

11  A rabbit-sized burrowing rodent of the genus *Dasyprocta*.
12  The oil of the *cabríuva-do-campo* tree (*Myrocarpus fastigiatus*).

detect fire by its smell at more than half a league away. That fact we have learnt from a man who is very familiar with their habits. When they smell fire, they climb the highest trees they can find in order to see the smoke, which is something that they can make out at a very considerable distance. They then head toward the smoke if it suits them to do so, or they head away from it if they judge it better to get away before their presence can be noted. As the Tupinambás possess this knowledge of the land and of fire, they are greatly appreciated when the Portuguese propose to wage war in some quarter. The Tupinambás are always sent on ahead to reconnoiter the terrain, to guide the rest of the party along the route that they should follow, and to show them the best place for them to spend the night.

## Chapter CLXVII. The Tupinambás' Preparations for War

As the Tupinambás are a very warlike people, all their basic tenets are concerned with how to wage war on their enemies. With that in view, their leaders gather in the central area of their village and discuss the matter together, as has been indicated. There, they decide in what place and at what time the war is to be waged. To that end, they notify all the men to be ready with their bows and arrows and body-shields. These shields are fashioned from light, soft wood. Their womenfolk are all competent at preparing the flour for them to take with them. It is known as "war flour" because it has to last throughout the conflict, hence its name. When once they are all ready with their weaponry and provisions, on the nights before they set out, the headman goes around calling out to the houses, telling them where they are bound for and proclaiming their duty to avenge themselves on their enemies. He stresses their duty both to do so and to fight courageously. He promises them victory over their enemies, proclaiming that no danger will befall them and that they will be commemorated by those who in later times will sing their praises. Finally, he tells them that they will begin their journey the next morning. At daybreak, once they have eaten, each man heaves on to his back his flour ration and the hammock on which he will sleep and takes his body-shield, bow, and arrows in his hands. Some also carry a wooden sword around their necks in a sling. Noise-makers carry tambourines, and others carry trumpets, playing them along the route and creating a huge din with them when they come in view of the enemy.

The leaders of these barbarians take their wives along with them, loaded down with their provisions. The leaders themselves merely carry their hammock and other weaponry on their backs and their bows and arrows in their hands. Before they set out, the headman takes the lead, a task that they deem to be a very great honor, and he it is who shows them the way and indicates where they shall spend each night. The battle order in which they advance is simply one in front of the other because they know no other way of doing it. Once they have crossed their own boundaries and have entered enemy territory, they normally send their scouts ahead on reconnaissance. The scouts are always nimble young men who know very well what they have to do. As they advance with the greatest circumspection, the daily progress [of the Tupinambá force] is no more than one and a half to two leagues, which is as far as they can proceed by nine o'clock in the morning. They then pitch camp close to a water supply and erect grass shelters that they call *tejupares*. They lay them out in rows, with a path through the middle. That is where they pass the daytime, making fires inside their *tejupares*.

## Chapter CLXVIII. How the Tupinambás Attack Their Enemies

As soon as the Tupinambás arrive at a point two days away from the enemy village, they cease to make fires during the daytime so that their distant smoke should not be noted by the enemy. They form up in order to make a dawn raid on their adversaries. They use the full moon to make their final journey by night, in order to spring an attack on their opponents, catching them unawares and unprepared. The moment they reach the village, they all let out a terrifying roar, adding to it with blasts on their trumpets and much rattling of their tambourines. So begins their onslaught on the enemy. From the very first attack, they give no quarter to adults or children. They rush forward, armed with spiked clubs that smash to pieces an opponent's head with the very first blow. Some of these barbarians are so bloodthirsty that they lop off the genitals of their dead adversaries, both male and female. They take them back to their womenfolk who shrivel them up in the fire and keep them as mementoes to give to their husbands to eat on festive occasions. It takes a long time to eat them. As for their adversaries whom they did not kill in the conflict, they take them back as prisoners, in order to kill them in the central area of the village as part of the usual festivities.

As for the spoils of such warfare, the headman makes off with nothing in particular; rather, every man seizes whatever he can. When the victors withdraw, they set fire to the houses of the village they have raided, houses that are covered in palm leaves right down to the ground. They make their way back immediately, marching at a vigorous pace for the rest of the day and right through the night. Their scouts bring up the rear, lest a large number of the enemy should group together to take their revenge for what has happened to their neighbors, as happens on a daily basis. If the Tupinambás find that their adversaries are ready for them with a palisade and if the Tupinambás are bold enough to surround it, then they build around it an outer palisade of branches and thorns and link it all together with timber that they ram into the ground. This they call a *caiçá*.[13] For as long as [the vegetation in the palisade] remains green, nothing can break through and harm them. As a result, they are safe from enemy arrows. The *caiçá* is built quite close to the enemy palisade. The night is rent by a thousand taunts and shouts of bravado, till either the Tupinambás smash down the [inner] palisade or raise the siege if they dare not proceed or because they have run out of food.

## Chapter CLXIX. Counterattacks from the Tupinambás' Enemies When They Withdraw

Frequently, when the Tupinambás are making their way back home from a raid on their enemies, a large number of the latter assemble in an effort to catch up with them to the point where they can no longer get away. It then becomes essential for the Tupinambás to lie in wait for them. They do this alongside a watercourse, where they dig in, resorting to a rampart of *caiçá*. They work in great haste so that they can sleep there, safe from their opponents, though they post an ample number of sentinels. They are often surrounded and hemmed in by their adversaries. But the besieged Tupinambás can see from behind their palisade those who are on the other side of it, and can freely fire all their arrows at them, whereas those on the outside cannot see those that are firing at them. If [their would-be assailants] have not come equipped to overthrow them or have brought insufficient supplies to be able to prolong the siege, then they withdraw again, through not being able to defeat the Tupinambás as they had wished.

This kind of attack that the Tupinambás inflict on the Tupinaés and on other enemies is often inflicted on them as well. If they receive no prior warning or are otherwise unprepared, they suffer very greatly. However, on most occasions, they are the ones who launch attacks on their enemies. Moreover, they show more foresight with regard to such raids, in that they send messengers to get help from their neighbors, and the latter rush at once to their assistance.

When the Tupinambás find themselves besieged by enemies, those of greatest authority among them go round at night calling out to them to make every effort to fight nobly and to have no fear of their opponents because they will swiftly take their vengeance on them, and help will not be long in coming. They regularly utter the same encouragement when they have surrounded the enemy and are keen to overthrow them. Before they launch their attack, they all assemble on the preceding night. The headman walks

13   Or, more usually, *caiçara*.

around and tells his men in a loud voice what their duties will be. He counsels them to be prepared and alert. He utters the same words, when they get ready the *caiçá* palisades, to encourage them and to get them to complete the work as quickly as possible. Whenever the Tupinambás fight on open ground, they leap about from side to side and never fall quiet, constantly whistling and striking their chests with their fists, ducking the arrows fired at them by their opponents and vehemently firing their own back at them.

## 2. Jesuits and Go-Betweens

*In the two letters translated here, Father Manoel de Nóbrega, writing from southern Brazil, makes clear the strategies of the early Jesuit missionaries as well as the many moral and spiritual challenges facing them, not only from the unconverted native peoples but from the unruly and unrestrained settlers as well. In the first letter (a) from Nóbrega to his Jesuit superior, he makes clear the dependence of the Jesuits on an early Portuguese go-between or intermediary who had become a key figure among the native peoples of southern Brazil. He also discusses the state of sexual liberty in which the early settlers lived and the moral and theological challenges that this created for the Jesuit missionaries. The following document (b) reveals the close Jesuit relationship with the governor-general but also a general frustration with the sins and avarice of the settlers.*

### (a) Letter from Father Manoel da Nóbrega to Father Luís Gonçalves da Câmara (31 August 1553)

> (From Serafim Leite, ed., *Cartas do Brasil e mais escritos de Manoel da Nóbrega. Opera omnia* [Coimbra, 1955], pp. 180–6.)

I write to your Reverence from the *sertão* of this captaincy of São Vicente where I have remained this year after arriving with the fleet. The fruit that is made in this land according to the Brothers who are in São Vicente you will already know about because they will write with more knowledge. Yesterday. The festival of the martyrdom of São João Bautista, I came to a village [*aldeia*] where those who are converted have been gathered and where I have placed two Jesuit Brothers to indoctrinate them. I solemnly made fifty catecumens and I have much hope that they will be good Christians and will merit baptism, and this will be shown by the works of faith they now undertake.[14]

---

14 This is a reference to the village of Piritininga, the original site of the town of São Paulo.

I am moving on to search for some chosen by Our Lord among these gentiles: there I will stay while I wait for news from Bahia of the Fathers that I believe are on their way. Pedro Correia has gone on ahead to call for penitence as remission for their sins.

I use every means that seems to us the best way to win the goodwill of the gentiles. The youth are the principal ones who come to us from everywhere.

In this country, there is a certain João Ramalho, the oldest man in these parts. He has many children and is related throughout the *sertão*, and I am bringing the eldest with me throughout the interior to give more authority to our ministry. Because he is very well known and venerated among the gentiles and he has daughters married to the principal [Portuguese] men of the captaincy, and all of these sons and daughters are the children of one Indian woman, daughter of the greatest and most important [chief] of this land.[15] Thus, in him and her and in their children we hope to have a great tool for the conversion of the gentiles. This man, for even more help, is a relative of Father Paiva and here they have gotten to know each other.

When he came from Portugal about forty years ago or more, he left his wife there alive and never more heard of her, but it seems that she must be dead many years now. He wishes very much to marry the mother of his children. He has already written to Portugal but has never had a response on this matter. Therefore, it is necessary for Your Reverence to write to Vouzela, the land of Father Mestre Simão, for the business of Our Lord requires it; because if this man was in a state of grace, Our Lord would do much for him in this land, because when he is in a state of mortal sin, much was done on his behalf. And since this is a matter of such importance, I have sent to Your Reverence the best information of all that I have said.

In this land are many men living in sin [*amancebados*] and who wish to marry the women, and this would be a great service to Our Lord. I have already written that we have obtained from the Pope the jurisdiction to take over these cases of the men who are here in these heathen lands. Because some sleep with two sisters and then later when they have children with one want to marry her and cannot. Others have impediments of affinity and consanguinity and for the good of all and the remedy of many, this should be halted to bring peace and tranquility to many consciences.

And what we have said for the gentiles should also be applied to the Christians of these parts, or at least until the Pope offers a general pardon. If the nuncio had the power, he should make a special dispensation for this João Ramalho so he can marry this Indian woman, despite the fact that he may have known her sister or some other relative of hers. And the same

15    The reference here is to Chief Tibiriça.

should apply to two or three *mestiços* who wish to marry Indian women who have born them children, despite any affinity there might be between them.

This would be a great service to Our Lord and if this costs anything, he [João Ramalho] will send sugar from here to pay for it. Perhaps there is some virtuous soul there who can loan the amount. Because I find this very necessary and because of my great desire to see so many souls rescued, I write to Your reverence so that in the first returning ship you can send an answer to this captaincy of São Vicente. The rest I will write when the ships arrive if I am in the right place, and if not the Fathers and Brothers [of the Jesuits order] will assume that task. To a letter sent to this São Vicente I have already responded. To those that come by way of Bahia, I have not seen them yet. It is easier for a message to come from Lisbon to this captaincy than from Bahia.

Vale Pater. From this far *sertão*, the last day of August, 1553
The worthless son of Your Reverence
Nóbrega

## (b) A Jesuit Report: A Letter from Manuel da Nóbrega S.J., in São Vicente, to the Inquisitor-General, Simão Rodrigues S.J., in Lisbon (10? March 1553)

(From Serafim Leite S.J., ed., *Cartas do Brasil* [São Paulo, 1955], pp. 154–63 and 181–5.)

Pax Christi

I have written to Your Reverence earlier, although I believe that this letter will be delivered to you first. In the former letter, I explained to you that we were making ready to venture among the heathen people, adding that for that reason I was remaining in this captaincy this year and was not planning to return with the governor-general in his fleet. Moreover, it is our belief, based on our experience of this territory, that we can expect the undertaking to be highly fruitful, since we know for certain that the less close they are to white [lay]men, the more trust the Indians have in us. Every day they demand to know why it is taking us so long to go and teach them.

On the governor-general's departure, some settlers were either unhappy with the governor-general or they had received some news or nurtured some hope that there may be gold or silver in this territory. They were aware that we planned to go into the interior to set up a [professed] house, and almost everyone in this captaincy or many of its leaders had decided to go exactly where we were intending to settle. This came to the governor-general's attention. He told me what was happening in the territory, informed me of the obligation that we had to our virtuous king, and forbade us to go ahead with our plans, and with good reason. Quite apart from opening the gates to dreadful outrages, it would mean that people would be leaving the captaincy. We therefore agreed not to set forth until His Majesty should send a message to the governor-general, concerning which the latter will either send word or write to us if he goes to Portugal this year. The way in which we serve Our Lord in this captaincy and in others depends very much on the decision taken.

I requested permission from the governor-general to allow us to go inland via some other captaincy along the coast where there are no problems such as there are here. The difficulties here arise from the discovery of mines thought to contain silver, though, owing to the shortage of people to do the digging, it is uncertain what it is. The mines were found and explored by the Castilians from Paraguay, who reside a hundred leagues away from this captaincy, and it has been ascertained that the mines are within territory allotted to the king of Portugal. Owing to this and other matters, the governor-general closed the route both to Portuguese and to Castilians. A pagan tribe in this region has also provided information about the existence of much gold, and the Castilians are traveling through Peru to find it. I learned of this and other matters after our departure [into the interior] was prevented, although these restrictions have ceased to apply in other captaincies.

The governor-general's answer to that is that he would not consent to our opening a house among the heathens in any captaincy, declaring that, should they inflict any harm on the Christians, this could not be avenged if we were in the interior. He also claimed that every wrongdoer would seek refuge with us. Such arguments would disappear were we to go to other heathen tribes dwelling beyond the captaincy. All in all, we are virtually held captive and have no freedom to serve Our Lord as we believe that we should.

The governor-general told us that we may proceed to preach the Gospel by returning to the captaincies and townships inhabited by Christians. The heathens here do not have the characteristics of the pagans of the early Church, who, on the one hand, either mistreated or immediately killed those who preached to them against their idols, or who, on the other, so believed the Bible as to be ready to die for Christ. But, these heathens do not have idols for whom they would lay down their lives; and they believe everything that they are told. The only difficulty lies in eliminating their evil customs by transforming them into good deeds that are pleasing to Christ. That means remaining among them so that they can see our good example. It means living alongside them and educating their children from an early age in doctrine and good habits. In this way, we are certain that they will all become Christians, better even than the white men who are here. It is of little value to go and preach to them and then return home. That is because, though they believe to a certain extent, it does not take much for them to be led back into their former ways. They believe in them just as they believe in their sorcerers. At times they lie to the latter, at times they happen to tell the truth. Owing to that situation, unless we are able to dwell among them, our efforts will bear no fruit.

Among the Christians, fruit has already been harvested, and this was easily achieved. Indeed, I believe that there are some among them who were predestined by Our Lord. But others have hardened their hearts so much as to be steeped in sin. Yet, through the teaching that their slaves and the native Indian women receive, such people desire to keep well clear of sin. They come to us and say that they fear God. Their [white] masters are of such a nature that some order them not to come for instruction. Others tell them that one should merely live as one wishes in this world, since in the next life the soul feels nothing. Others tell them we do not know what we are saying, and that it is they who are the true men and who are telling them the truth. Yet others tell them lies about us to discredit us with all the heathens, which is often the result. Indeed, I ordered Brother Pêro Correia to write to Your Reverence to notify you of this. For this reason, not only do we achieve nothing while they are around us but also we lose credit among the Indians and heathens, and more in this captaincy than in the others.

I believe that the reason is that the [white] people here are backward in understanding, badly brought up and for so long prone to the worst habits, not to mention their being people of the lowest caliber. There are also many Indians in this territory who are subjected to forced labor and others who are attacked and robbed. We help the Indians and preach against those who subject them to forced labor. Some Indians have escaped. Meanwhile, we give no absolution to their captors unless they set them free. As a result, *commota est universa gens contra nos.*[16] I am referring to those [whites] who are affected by this scourge, since the others, who are free of it, hold us in loving esteem. Accordingly, our current efforts are directed toward instructing Indian children in the various captaincy houses. We bring them up well and also bring on the slaves, both male and female. In spite of so much opposition from the white population, all they can do is to persist in discrediting our ministry.

In addition to the above, the bishop and his visitor are resorting to another procedure in accordance with their wishes and their grasp of the situation. That procedure may well be the best one and what Our Lord desires but it runs completely counter to the system that we had adopted in this country. We could have achieved so much more among the Christians, given

16  Matthew 21:10.

the fear that we instilled in them concerning impending ecclesiastical justice, than we can do now that it is here. I shall limit myself to declaring just one thing in general to Your Reverence, and that will give you cause to weep. It is that wherever there is a chance of financial gain, even if there is no wrongdoing, there is the closest investigation, whereas wherever that is not the case, even though great sins are committed, the matter receives scant attention. I have particularly protested about this to the visitor. He replied that this approach was in pursuit of the bishop's instructions. This scandal has so much spread along the coast that I believe that it will resound there. The bishop is not a particularly erudite man and is very trusting. A well-educated and experienced vicar-general ought to be sent out to assist him.

The governor-general has achieved a great deal along this coast, so much so that we never cease to praise Our Lord for giving such knowledge and virtue to one man. He did all he could during the visitation of this coast. But only Our Lord is perfect, and this man cannot do everything. I say this because when a thing is well done, it is in the service of Our Lord God (as well as with the king, our lord on earth). One cannot deny that the governor-general accomplishes what few men could. But when he is able to discern that a given activity, even when [apparently] right, might be detrimental to the interests of the king, he draws back from carrying it out and forbids others to do so. His avoidance of inappropriate actions is highly praiseworthy. I have come to recognize this aspect of his work on a daily basis, notably in what follows.

Nearly all the men who inhabit the coastal areas, particularly in this captaincy, possess Indian slaves. The slaves demand their freedom and know nothing of the law other than to turn to us, taking refuge in the Church's embrace as though we were their parents and protectors. For our part, we have learned from past experience and have no wish to provoke any scandal, nor do we wish to be stoned. As a result we can do nothing for them, nor do we dare to preach to them. This means that through lack of justice, they remain captives, and their masters remain in mortal sin. Moreover, we are losing all credit among these pagans because we cannot give them what they hoped for.

I told the governor-general that he should do something about this. He does everything only after taking counsel, but some of his advisers also have Indians in their houses. As a result, he believes that he should not meddle because of the harm it could cause to many men [i.e., Indians], and that it is better for them to remain slaves and work on the estates. He also believes that it is in the interests of the king and for the greater good of the territory and its settlers. The contrary approach, as it would affect almost everyone, would be very bad for the country. He also gives other similar reasons. But despite all his arguments, my view was that he should not hold back from taking the right and just course of action, since, where there is no justice, there comes no favor from Our Lord. Rather, for the greater good of the country, I believe that everyone should be given what is his. That is preferable to a system sustained by sin, for that is something from which they [i.e., the settlers] will never escape. I also believe that it would mean that the plantations would produce more sugar and [therefore] more tithes for His Majesty.

This land, which is the best in the world, is little favored by Our Lord because of these and similar sins. If a virtuous man were selected to set these men free and if he were to marry the men to the women, permitting them to live among the Christians and making them obey Christian law and customs, that would be far better for the territory. All the heathens would know the truth about Christians. That truth arrived with the arrival of the governor-general and the Jesuit Fathers. Nevertheless, they have experienced so much the untruths uttered by them [i.e., the settlers] that such a course of action would be the best way for our reputation to be restored and for them [i.e., the Indians] to become Christians.

However, since that appears at first sight not to be in the king's best interests, everyone is opposed to it. It pains me to see them [i.e., the Indians] so justifiably complaining about their harsh captivity, yet there is nobody to protect them. Owing to the great prevalence of this problem here (and nowhere else have I been so aware of it), I am writing to Your Reverence so that you can advise His Majesty of your view of the matter.

Although these issues are set down in a rather haphazard way, I know that Your Reverence will consider them carefully and, after discussing them at length with His Majesty, will write back to tell us how to proceed. The fact is that if we are not allowed to go and find the heathen tribespeople, there is very little else left for us to do.

For the above reasons, I have now decided to leave this house in the hands of two stewards and its financial officer. I shall remove the Jesuit Fathers from all temporal administration, leaving them solely in control of the teaching and catechesis of the children. Moreover, they shall show extreme obedience to the rector, who is to be placed in authority over the children. I have put in place the Brotherhood of the Name of Jesus. All of this has been carefully carried out. In that way, I have removed of the opportunity for evil gossip which, while not true, was not without cause.

I shall return to Bahia on the first available ship, which will be soon, and shall take with me the new lay brothers whom I have found here. Among them there is one, Pêro Correia, who has achieved more than any of us here, as he speaks the language and is both wise and virtuous. We hope not to lose time and, wherever we go, we hope to harvest much fruit through the authority and credit that he enjoys among the heathens.

This house has fifty children and with all the people here could sustain [another] fifty or hundred more. It is in very great need of help from Portugal. The governor-general has given me reason to hope that His Majesty would grant to us the rice tithe of this captaincy, for it does not bring him a very great profit. It would, however, be most useful for this house and would support many children, as I shall explain to Father Pedro Doméneco in greater detail. The supplies and clothes that His Majesty has commanded to be distributed here bring us no satisfaction. Indeed, supplies given to us for ten people who came with us from Portugal are not enough to support and clothe even three, with the result that we continue to rely on charitable contributions that we ourselves brought with us from Portugal.

## 3. The Jesuit Establishment

*By the 1570s, the Jesuits had become the principal missionary order in Brazil and had established a firm material and administrative basis for their multiple religious, educational, and economic interests in the colony. In this report of 1577, Father Belchior Cordeiro, returning to Rome after five years in Brazil, presented an overview of the Jesuit establishment in the colony and their activities to Everardo Mercuriano, the Father General of the Jesuit Order.* (From Belchior Cordeiro S.J., *Emformação dalgumas cousas do Brasil*, ed. Serafim Leite S.J., in Anais da Academia Portuguesa da História, 2nd series, 15 [1965], pp. 182–201.)

There are three colleges and five residences in this province or, put another way, there are eight residences if we include the villages inhabited by Christian Indians, where our Jesuit Fathers inhabit buildings that they likewise describe as residences.

All these colleges and residences are situated along the seacoast, wherever the Portuguese have settled. Placing them not in the order in which they were founded but in the order in which they run down the coast, the college of Pernambuco is the first. The second college is that of Bahia, which is located one hundred leagues from Pernambuco. Some ten, fifteen, or twenty leagues around the college in Bahia lie three or four villages of Christian Indians with three or four religious living in each, and we can also call these residences. Next there is the residence of Ilhéus, which is thirty leagues south of Bahia. After that comes the residence of Porto Seguro, which is a further thirty leagues from Ilhéus. Up to this point, all the residences are attached to the college of Bahia and come under the jurisdiction of the rector of that college. That is where the diocese of Bahia ends.

There then follows the residence of Espírito Santo, which is sixty leagues from Porto Seguro. Next there is the college of Rio de Janeiro, which is, I believe, sixty leagues or more from Espírito Santo. The residence of Espírito Santo is attached to it. Then there come the residences of São Vicente, which, if I am not mistaken, are forty leagues distant from the college of Rio de Janeiro. Finally, there is the residence of Piratininga, which lies some fifteen to twenty leagues south of São Vicente.

Until now, the Portuguese have lived along the coast, and our houses run from one end to the other in the order that I have set down: Pernambuco, Bahia with its [Indian] villages, Ilhéus, Porto Seguro, Espírito Santo with its villages, Rio de Janeiro with one village, and Piratininga.

## Some Particular Aspects of Each of These Colleges and Residences of Pernambuco

The first college along this coast, which is closest to Portugal and which is the one most easily reached by sea, is that of Pernambuco. The town in which it is situated is called Olinda. The entire captaincy, which is under the aegis of one donatary [i.e., Duarte Coelho], is called Pernambuco. The captaincy comprises many other townships, villages, and sugar plantations.

The College of Pernambuco has an endowment of one thousand *cruzados*, but, since sugar brings a very favorable return, at a price set by the king himself, the college's income is more than a thousand *cruzados*. It has to support a community of twenty religious. It also possesses a [square?] league of land, which a lady bequeathed to it. However, our community has not yet made use of it, nor do they expect to profit much from it, as it is some distance away [from the college] and is not very fertile.

There is a course on the humanities. There is also a law course.

All twenty members of the Society could be needed here, and many more would be so, since many people live in the captaincy and others sail there to join them. But the income is not enough to support the community, nor is it possible for them to fully to carry out the work of the Society, no matter how diligently they have been devoting themselves to it. It is therefore important for Your Paternity to decide what ought to be done.

As a general rule, the Fathers neither preach nor hear confessions other than in the town, where the college is situated. As the town is not very large (since normally the settlers live outside on their estates, and the town is inhabited solely by traders and officials), one pulpit is enough. If, therefore, we preach in our [professed] house, then we do not preach in the town's church and vice versa.

There is a reason why our Jesuit Fathers do not usually go off to preach and hear confessions in the other townships and settlements. It is that in this captaincy, it is not possible to travel in the summer, as it is so hot, nor is it possible in winter, except by journeying on horseback, as there are so many rivers. We would need two horses and we do not have any, nor are we likely to have. We cannot easily find anyone who has horses to lend to us, especially because two slaves would have to accompany the horses, and because their masters do not wish to lose their services, not to mention the wear and tear on the horses.

However, on certain occasions during the year, a number of parishes send a request for a preacher to preach on their feast day and for that reason they send two horses. Sometimes it happens that in order to come back [to Olinda], the Fathers have to issue a personal entreaty for horses, simply because, as often happens, those who provided the horses for the outward journey are less inclined to provide them for the journey back again. However, nowadays the owners of the horses provide them without any fuss, and one of our priests performs this service on certain days in the year.

On the feast day or Sunday, the visiting priest hears the confessions of the Portuguese of the given parish and then preaches to them. If he knows their language, he also does the same for the Christian Indians who are there, though as a rule there are only a few.

The Indians of the captaincy are made to work hard by their masters on the sugar estates. That means that during the week it is impossible to instruct them in the Faith, since there is no moment when their owners are willing or able to release them from their work. When Sunday is reached, the wretched slaves just want to rest. Their recreation is simply to go to the seaside or to go hunting or just to drink in groups, so that not even their masters can keep them back on that day, as that is already their entitlement. As a result, there is no opportunity to instruct them in the Faith either on Sunday or during the week. That means that hardly any of the slaves in Pernambuco are Christians. They live and die in mortal sin and are sunk in the deepest barbarism without being able to remedy the matter. That is because their masters want nothing more from them than work and simply treat them as animals.

However, since there are some landowners, though very few, who are God-fearing and sometimes take some of their slaves with them to church, the priest is able to instruct them, hear their confessions, and unite them in marriage, after he has completed his missionary visit to the Portuguese.

In the town, where the college is located, instruction is provided, and we preach to the slaves of the town. Indeed, usually there is a gathering of a hundred, a hundred and fifty, even two hundred of them.

That is why we have so few missions in this captaincy. It is impossible to provide instruction to the slaves other than to those who live in the town and work within its gates. As for those who live outside on the plantations, they are as barbarous as they were when living among the [other] heathens. Quite apart from not receiving instruction in the Faith from either their masters or the Jesuit Fathers, they are by their very nature extremely wild and remote from godly matters.

Everything in Brazil costs so much, not only products from Portugal but also those that are produced here. However, the college receives, beyond its regular income, much in the way of charitable contributions left in wills worth ten or twenty or even a hundred *cruzados*, not to mention other small amounts. Without these, it would never have been possible to support the community of twenty, though the truth is that they do not usually eat bread or drink wine. Some, however, receive a glass of wine with their water. They live in great poverty and need.

Variously, five, six, seven, eight, ten, or twelve students attend the regular Latin course. As for the law course, they are told to come a thousand times, but there are only two, three, four, or five of them. They might attend one in four classes. Our pleas are not enough nor are the penalties imposed by the bishop.

The members of our community have to have reasonable amenities, which is usual in the Society. It could be possible for them to have such amenities there, and it is right that they should have. However, the income of this college is not enough, even with regular almsgiving, to support a community of more than ten or twelve. Any more than that number are unnecessary in such a college. Ten or twelve are quite enough, and all the others are excessive. For example, we need only four or five priests, one or two of whom should preach to the people, with one of them helping the other and going off on the missions, whenever they occur. The reason is that so much preaching to the people as there is at present is quite unnecessary. Indeed, even the professed house in Rome does not afford so much preaching. The preaching loses its value by being so excessive, as do we in the entreaties that we make in them. As for one of the preachers, he need have no more than average education to provide counselling to resolve any problem that might occur. With regard to law courses and Latin classes, these should be abandoned, as their sole effect is to take up and waste the time of two men.

It is important that one or two of these selfsame priests speak the local tongue. At the very least, one priest and one lay brother should be able to do so. Indeed, they are improving in this respect, with a view to one of them working away while the other remains behind.

With four Father confessors in the college, there are enough of them to say Mass and to hear everybody's confession, because the numbers of those going to confession are usually very small. As for the sea fishermen, their number is growing. In Holy Week, they still appear to be few in number but that number is growing all the time. In that way [the Fathers] will have the great satisfaction of leading busy lives, avoiding idleness, and carrying out necessary duties.

It is clearly unnecessary to want to provide courses of study just for the purpose of saying that there is a college. In the same way, it is unnecessary to have people who have not enough with which to occupy themselves, simply seeking to avoid losing an income that is insufficient in any event. All these factors generate numerous problems that I shall touch on later.

One outcome that the college achieves very successfully is its provision of education for children. There are classes where they learn to read and write and where they receive excellent instruction. The college works just as hard at preaching and hearing confessions, for all that *vilescunt ibi nostra ministeria*,[17] simply because there are too many of us and too few of the faithful.

## Bahia

The College of Bahia, which was the first to be founded in that area, is in the city of Salvador, which is commonly called Bahia de Todos os Santos.[18] In Salvador live the governor-general of all Brazil, the Crown judge, the bishop, and our provincial. It is obliged to have a certain number of religious (for each one of whom the king gives fifty *cruzados*). I understand that there are sixty such religious. If I am not mistaken, the college has an endowment of five thousand *cruzados*. It possesses a great deal of good land, part of which is already productive, part of which can be worked if need be. It has a large herd of cattle and owns many slaves. It is well supplied and can provide as much as is needed.

The college offers a course in Latin, sometimes two. There is also a law course and another in theology. In addition, the arts[19] are studied. There is a children's school where reading and writing are taught. Though this captaincy does not have as many inhabitants as Pernambuco, it is more suitable for the work of the Society, since the people are more devout and friendly, and all the settlements and estates are close to the sea. Owing to the frequent arrival of ships, not only are horses needed, just as in Pernambuco, but it is also less arduous than going into the interior.

The slaves of this captaincy are more easily susceptible to instruction in the Faith, both because they are close to those of our villages where there are Christian Indians and, of course, because they have less hard work to do than those in Pernambuco. That is explained by the fact that they produce

---

17  Our efforts in that regard become devalued.
18  Bay of All Saints.
19  The humanities and philosophy.

less sugar, that their masters are gentler with them, and, last of all, that they receive regular instruction from our catechists.

However, this captaincy is not so different from what I have said about Pernambuco as to prevent me, in due proportion, from saying the same about this college. Your Paternity must understand that what we [in Brazil] call a city is [in Europe] a [mere] township or large village and needs no more than a single preacher. By that, I mean that there are only enough people to fill a single hall. Moreover, those who are described as settlers in the city actually live on their estates and only return to the city for Lent.

It is my opinion that this college needs no more than a community of thirty religious: six priests to say daily Mass (and they would also act as confessors), two who would take turns to preach and two priests who speak the local language, one to work outside the college and one to remain there. There would thus be ten priests for all the work of the college and for all potential missions in the field, such as to the Portuguese on their estates and in the parishes and to the Indians who are their slaves. The college is provided with an ample, not to say too large a community, since, as I said, the city is small and has a bishop, his canons, and many other priests.

It is appropriate that the college should offer a course in law, as it does, not because there are those who attend and those who are reluctant to do so, nor because the penalties that the bishop imposes are insufficient, but because this is the center not only of the diocese but also of the whole of Brazil. It must not be said that on our account there is no such course. The course can be taught by either of the two preachers.

For the same reason, the class in humanities is appropriate. Those who customarily attend amount to some fifteen or twenty, though I would prefer them to be thirty. As for the study of philosophy and theology, that is attempting the impossible and has no useful purpose, for reasons that I shall give later. As for all the other parts of Brazil, Latin should be eliminated for at least the next ten years.

In each of the villages that the college has in its charge, it is important that there should be two or three of our religious, one of whom should be a priest, as, indeed, has been the practice until now. The villages are not very far apart, and it is easy for their inhabitants to gather to make their confession. Furthermore, since we possess our own horses, one of the Father Superiors goes to visit them and hears their confession every fortnight, as well as checking the cattle that we have there. Therefore, none of this is very difficult to achieve.

With [just] twelve or thirteen priests in this college, it is well provided for. There is someone to organize the missions as well as others to live in the villages. In that way, they will satisfy their temporal needs, have plenty to do, and the problems that have been wont to beset Brazil will disappear.

## The Residences in Ilhéus, Porto Seguro, Espírito Santo, São Vicente, and Piratininga

In each of these captaincies, four of our religious are enough because there are few people, almost all of whom are poor and honest farmers. Two or three of the religious should be priests, one of whom should be a preacher and another able to speak the language. However, in São Vicente, I believe that five or six are needed since, from what I hear, there are various settlements, though they are small and their people very humble farmers. In Piratininga, there are usually only two, and that is sufficient because there are [virtually] no people there, though we do have cattle and small-holdings in the vicinity. A few Indians and white men live there, but, as it is never visited by ships from Portugal and as there is never any produce with which to trade, it amounts to nothing.

The Fathers in these captaincies should be suitably provided for in temporal matters by the colleges to which they belong. That is because apart from being poor, they live lonely and dispiriting lives, wishing they were back in their colleges. For the same reason, it would also be appropriate to change them round every two years, as well as to prevent them from forming close friendships, for those are so easily made in such a small place. With these [small] numbers, these residences are not only sufficient to carry out the work of the Society but also suffice to ensure that our religious live among their fellows. That is because formerly they lived there, moving every two years; yet, if they took a dislike to the place, they would only stay for a few months.

## Rio de Janeiro

The third college is located in the City of São Sebastião, commonly called Rio de Janeiro. The college there is smaller than that in Bahia but larger than the one in Pernambuco. In accordance with the endowment that was granted to it, the college is obliged to have a certain number of workmen. At the outset, there arose a problem that in turn gave rise to another. It was believed that the land was very rich, but now it is said not to be. Therefore, as navigation is very difficult and perilous (because one must sail round Cabo Frio, which is a very dangerous procedure), only one ship a year travels out there from Portugal. Sometimes it fails to arrive since it is easier to sail twice from Portugal to Pernambuco, less dangerously and in less time, and even to Bahia, than to journey just once to Rio de Janeiro. For that reason, the few people who went to live in that city are gradually leaving it again. At the present time, it is a city which is really only a village. Its inhabitants are merely poor peasant farmers. Therefore, we should not attach any more importance to it than to any other residence. It should have one preacher and another priest who knows the language. It should have up to four priests in all and as many lay brothers: then it will grow. Latin classes on no account should be taught, but there should be classes in reading and writing for the children because those classes should be kept going just as in all the other colleges and residences. That is because such classes are very practical, there are a good number of children, and the settlers approve of them. The religious that live here are also very desirous of changing places, and that facility should be allowed them every two years, as they are a very long distance away from Bahia and live alone. The distance between Portugal and Bahia is much the same as that between Bahia and the southern areas [of Brazil]. Should there be the above number of religious, they would be sufficiently provided for in temporal matters. I believe that there will be enough work to keep them all busy, which is precisely what is needed for them to live happy and peaceful lives, for if they are allowed to be idle in Brazil they will become discontented.

## General Matters

If the number of religious in the colleges and residences were to be reduced, it would be essential to have the [prior] consent of the king.

Brazil is a hot country and does not favor study, as at least seven or eight months are like an Italian summer. Under no circumstances is it right to send our religious out there just in order to study because apart from the great heat, there is a great shortage of other facilities for that purpose. The Fathers usually ask for religious from Portugal, and students are sent out along with others who go out to Brazil. There they are admitted, not because they are needed for the work of the Society, but simply to perpetuate study in Bahia, Pernambuco, and Rio de Janeiro and to make up the numbers that the king requires us to have. That means that quite apart from other drawbacks, they do not receive a proper education because the land is not conducive to it. Furthermore, they lead a miserable existence, as the Society does not keep them occupied, and as they are unable to pursue their studies. Thus, some of them leave, while others are expelled.

I say, then, that none of our religious should study in Brazil, nor should there be any record kept of such activity. For the reasons that I have mentioned, the exceptions to that are the courses in Latin and in [canon] law at the College of Bahia. As for our religious, they should go out from Portugal fully trained. In Brazil, there should be admitted [to the College of Bahia] the sons of Portuguese who are born out there. That is appropriate because they [also] speak the local language. There are not many of them, and it is not difficult for them to learn enough Latin and law to enable them to carry out their ministry.

It seems to me to be quite absurd for the Society to require two hundred of its religious to be there, merely to ensure that the colleges should qualify for their income, when there is no need for more than fifty. If it is intended that our religious should lead meaningful lives, then [at best] there is only enough work to keep half of that number occupied. It is quite insufferable to request that religious be sent out and to receive individuals who are so unnecessary and who go out there to study in a place that is so unsuited to that end.

Those who should live in Brazil ought to set out from Portugal or from here [Rome] as fully trained priests of thirty-five to forty years of age, or they should be lay brothers of a similar age. As the settlers in Brazil are usually of humble and lowly farming stock, there is no need for men of learning, except in Bahia and Pernambuco. Members of the nobility and merchants live in those two places. Thus, it is appropriate that each of those places should have one or two able preachers who are also capable of resolving matters of law. Elsewhere all that is needed are men of virtue and strength.

No religious should be dispatched to Brazil unless they intend to become proficient in the local language. That is because the few that have that intention reveal that they have both the persistence and the ability. Those that are born here know the language well, but it is right that a few more should be sent out to join them.

There are two main reasons for the unhappiness of our religious out in Brazil. One is that there are so many of them that they become idle, with nothing to do or with which to occupy their time. In particular, those who have been admitted from any other place where the Society works regard themselves as having been deceived, for things run counter to what they expected. I mean by this that they believed that there would be many conversions to perform, whereas in fact there are few of them and they are of scant importance. When I say "of scant importance," I mean that the people are both very rustic and very barbarous. Apart from the innocent few who are baptized and earn salvation (which is greatly to be prized), the majority of them are spiritually incapable of any such thing. Moreover, having been fully occupied in their [previous] provinces, [the newcomers] now find themselves with their hands idle. That is because there are few confessions to hear and because those are made by certain very devout persons who regularly go to hear our preaching. So [the newcomers] become bored. I believe the situation to be due to an excess of preaching, certainly more than there normally is in Portugal. What is worse is that, in Brazil, if one's spirit does not warm to the task, then the effort is wasted. That is a common complaint made by all our religious. It arises from the country being so hot and from the food being so lacking in nourishment that their bodies become neglected. They have nothing with which to occupy themselves, they become idle, and cannot even devote themselves to prayer. From this, Your Paternity will understand the extent to which this land is suitable for study.

The second thing that upsets our religious arises from the notable lack of temporal necessities, namely food and clothing. Throughout Brazil, bread is neither eaten nor wine drunk, except when some of the Fathers and a few of the lay brothers are allowed a glass of watered-down wine, more or less as is our practice in Rome. That has been the case for some years there, for formerly even fewer received it, and even now not all are allowed it. Bread, as I mentioned earlier, is only eaten in Pernambuco. That is because it is closer to Portugal and because there are many traders and people who eat bread. In consequence, devout women sometimes send out bread by way of almsgiving. Other bread is actually on sale there, so that sometimes there is placed on the table a third of what is on offer here, though it is not available to all. That is why one can say that, broadly speaking, bread is not eaten nor is wine drunk. Meat is in short supply, except in Bahia. Generally speaking, there is a great deal of suffering because of the food, not just because of the lack of it but also because of its [poor] quality, for in Brazil it is tasteless and lacking in sustenance. Doubtless, those out in Brazil would choose to fast continuously and would greatly rejoice thereat – always provided that they were to receive what we eat here on a fast day! Yet they are not particularly discontented on that account. The truth is that they are not even allowed all that is available out there and which they could have, as would be only proper, for that certainly is our practice here [in Rome]. I believe that it either all stems from the procedure to which our Father Superiors have subjected Brazil or from the poverty in which those of us from Portugal have been brought up. In the main, the problem gets worse when decisions are made by a Father Superiors who has not been brought up in a world of plenty.

Attention must be given to eating and sleeping, owing to the intense heat of the country and the constant perspiration that it causes. Our people should usually wear clothing made of fine yarn as made in Italy (where it is less needed). All stockings and breeches should be of fine yarn, though buckram can be used for those as well. The fabric normally worn in Brazil is Saragossa cloth. The fact is that the feet of many are torn by sweat. People cannot even tolerate being close to others, so they should normally be given lightweight pumps or mules. It would certainly not be out of place to issue clean shirts to them on Saturdays and Wednesdays, so that each man could have at least one spare for when he is bathed in perspiration. That is an obvious and constant need.

The question of clothing is very important and no more so than in Brazil. The truth is that nowhere do our men dress more scruffily than in Brazil. Many do not have beds, and those that have beds in many cases have no sheets, although they could have, along with everything else that I consider necessary for them.

We are perturbed by these troubling aspects. Firstly, only those that are necessary should live in Brazil, as they will have things to accomplish. Duly kept busy, they will be contented and will not be in a position to complain that they were tricked into going there. Secondly, owing to the part they will play in conversion, they will be more contented than they were when they lived in other provinces, and their work will sustain them spiritually. Apart from their being kept busy, the income from the colleges is sufficient to supply them with all their needs, both in food and in clothing. Indeed, they will be able to live just as well as those who are in Portugal or anywhere else. Normally, they will receive bread, wine, and everything else that is sent out from Portugal, all of which is not simply necessary for the body but also for the soul. Much, therefore, is to be gained by having in Brazil only those religious that are necessary, and almost all the contentious issues that have arisen there stem from these two sources.

When he is informed of how things stand in Brazil, the king will readily make concessions, especially when he is told that our religious neither eat bread nor drink wine and do not even have the fruit that is produced in Spain [and Portugal], not to mention the other inconveniences from which they suffer. Should the king be unwilling to adopt new measures, I wish at least to record that it is wrong for the Society to send out superfluous religious to Brazil merely in order to qualify for the [endowment] income. Furthermore, I consider that the Society is losing all credit with the laity and with its own religious, for the latter are undoubtedly vehemently opposed to the practice, as well as suffering from spiritual anguish. The experience of so many years has demonstrated this, for there have been so many departures and expulsions as a result. Those remaining, when there are any, are as if chained by the power of papal bulls and excommunications. Otherwise, ask the Father Superiors to explain the origin of these problems. Our religious need to be kept busy, they need to be bolstered spiritually, they need food and clothing. The land is very hot and causes neglect, not to mention a thousand other problems. Those religious who know the practice of the Society in the other provinces from which they were sent are the ones who feel this most acutely.

Were these things to be done, the province would be both well served and well supplied. Brazil would be less detested by those who go there. Indeed, it would be sought after, and they would all go there willingly.

To ensure that Brazil be well supplied and at the right time, there should be appointed a special agent in Lisbon. His task would be to make certain that on every ship that sails to the various places where our religious reside, there should be purchased and taken aboard all that they need. The best solution would be to send back from Brazil a lay brother or a priest, such as Brother Francisco Gonçalves, who is in Bahia, or Father Martim Rocha, who is in Rio de Janeiro, since it is essential to know what conditions are like in Brazil.

It is also essential for the Father Superiors to want to be supplied with [appropriate] religious under their tutelage and to devote themselves willingly to keeping them contented and in good spirits. That is more important than their personal misgivings and their reluctance to have them in Brazil. [I say that] because there continues to exist a form of expression in the papal briefs that is almost insulting. Everything that I tell you in this report is true and is not beyond the normal practice of the Society. Rather, it conforms to it. I am confident that the demands of necessity will cause the king to make due provision to the Father Superiors. Were Italian Father Superiors now to go to Brazil, I have no doubt that all these things would be immediately put into effect. Perhaps those going out from Portugal will do the same. But, as I left that country some days ago, I cannot be sure about present intentions.

Once the situation has been remedied, I do not believe that there will be the same great insistence on returning to Portugal. If it does happen, then there will be some legitimate reason. I see no reason why the Father Superiors should strive so hard to prevent it because with the regular movement of ships, there is no expense or difficulty.

When it is said that the gates should be opened to others so as to remedy the problem, there is nothing to be afraid of. Indeed, there are a thousand occasions that provide grounds for a man to be sent there, especially as nobody ever wants to return to Portugal for any reason other than the drawbacks that I have mentioned. There are other reasons that the Father Superiors might in their wisdom judge to be legitimate.

It is highly important that the agent should always come to see Your Paternity to give an account to you in person, and there should never be any dispensation from doing so. At least two great advantages would arise from such a practice: Your Paternity would learn how the Society and its religious were proceeding, and you would be receiving such news in a face-to-face interview.

Should you go to Portugal, Your Paternity should in any case order Father Rodrigo de Freitas to travel to Lisbon from Brazil. His advice is of the greatest value on all these matters. I say that without wishing to offend anyone else, for there are many others out there, and comparisons are invidious. Father Rodrigo has experience of the whole of Brazil and he has been Father Superiors in almost every part of the country. He is the procurator-general there and is the counsellor and companion of the Father Provincial. He was one of the first to go to Brazil. He is a man of great prudence and experience. The journey to and from Portugal is not as arduous for him as might be imagined because it amounts to no more than sailing to and from Pernambuco, which is something he frequently does.

We are hated in Brazil, partly because of the constant legal actions that we are always taking, partly because of the Indians, whom we protect from the Portuguese. All this should be looked into, although at this moment it does not occur to me in what way. However, in respect of the income of the colleges, if Your Paternity is going to Portugal to speak to the king and if you are armed with all necessary information, then matters should be resolved for the future. As regards other issues, I believe that we have reached a point where we are going beyond the limits by taking these things so much to heart and getting into so much intrigue that we are seeking to get our own way more by human means and by satisfying [public] opinion than by any other approach.

In Brazil anyone who writes to Rome is not popular with the father superiors. From this there stem problems, for example, a father superiors not outlining his needs to Your Paternity, or even seeking means of sending letters to those outside the Society, and so on.

The impression of Brazil that is formed in the first two years by those who judge the book by its cover is very different from the judgment that is reached through experience of its true characteristics. Because of that, many father superiors and fathers provincial at the outset pledged themselves out there and to [successive] fathers-general in Rome. Then, not wishing to go back on their word, they ceased to say what they [really] felt, such as asking for [more] religious, promising conversions and then finding themselves with more religious than they could keep occupied. For this reason, if the information that Your Paternity receives from the new fathers provincial and fathers visitor differs from what you receive from the father superiors who have been out there for some years, then you should bear that point in mind.

For my part, it is not my intention that any of the foregoing should deter Your Paternity with regard to Brazil, but that it should give you true and factual information. Likewise, it is my earnest wish that all those who are there should bear fruit and live contented lives. I trust that the means to achieve that objective are those that I have set down. Your Paternity should, however, derive much consolation from the fact that all the good things in Brazil, both spiritual and temporal, are due to the work of the Society. That is because our Jesuit Fathers help people with advice and comfort them in their work, doing just the same as they do in Portugal. Moreover, they bring about conversions. However, as there are more religious there than are necessary, as the land is so alien to the welfare of the spirit, as they are so lacking in temporal necessities, and as they are so hated by everybody there, it can be generally stated that, beyond all shadow of a doubt, there are no Fathers of our Society who suffer more and are more despised, who harvest less fruit and who lead more disagreeable lives than those in Brazil. For that very reason, they are the more in need of Your Paternity's support and good offices.

All this information is based on the experience that I have acquired in Brazil up to now and on the hopes that I have cherished there for several years. It is my firm belief that there will be no real change until the Portuguese venture farther into the interior and settle there. Once they find themselves in a cooler climate, where the air is better, where they are able to harvest crops such as wheat, where they can grow Portuguese fruit, and where the climate will buoy up the spirit, then, possibly, the problem that we have at present will cease. However, for that we shall need much faith and we shall have to wait many years.

Nor does the above mean that I want Your Paternity to recall to Portugal [all] the religious that are in Brazil. Rather, it means that no more should go out, nor should they be admitted except when needed and when the number of them out there falls below what is necessary. In the meantime, it is important that they be well provided for.

All of the above involves a survey of the entire province in accordance with the more essential aspects of its instructions. Let those instructions serve merely as a basis for Your Paternity to inquire what is happening there and how matters may be remedied. On some matters I have expressed my opinion because Your Paternity told me to do so when you ordered this report. I am well aware that once it becomes known in Brazil that I have set these matters down, by the same token some people are bound to contradict them, even though they must be privately aware that they are true, for I have not said anything that is not already common knowledge in Brazil. In particular, those from whom Your Paternity should seek an opinion on these matters are the following: Father Provincial José Anchieta, Rodrigo de Freitas, Luís da Grã, Inácio Tolosa, Gregório Serrão, Quirício Caixa, Francisco Pires, António da Rocha, António Gomes, Cristóvão Ferrão, Leonardo do Vale, Father Toledo, Jorge Rodrigues, and all the old hands out there. No doubt, Your Paternity will charge them with concealing nothing.

## 4. A Colonist's Critique of the Jesuits: Gabriel Soares de Sousa, "Os capitulos" (1592)

*The Jesuits and the colonists disputed the control of the indigenous peoples of Brazil. Both sides sought to convince the Crown that their control of the Indians would best serve the interests of the colony. The arguments of the Jesuits are well preserved in the historical record, but those of the colonists, especially their criticisms of the Fathers of the Company, were often made discreetly, and thus little evidence of them remains. This remarkable document is an exception. While in Madrid in the 1580s, the chronicler and sugar planter in Bahia, Gabriel Soares de Sousa, had supplied a list of complaints against the Jesuits to an influential Portuguese courtier.*

*The Jesuits obtained his memorial and then, in 1592, the Jesuit Provincial, Marçal Beliarte, refuted its claims one by one. The rebuttal contained the original charges as well and thus preserved Soares de Sousa's detailed complaints, revealing thereby the depth of the hostility between the colonists and the missionaries but also the tension between civil and religious authority, and between diocesan and missionary clergy.* (From Gabriel Soares de Sousa, "*Os Capítulos*," ed. Serafim Leite, in Ethnos, 2 [1941], pp. 9–35.)

*Chapters that Gabriel Soares de Sousa supplied to Dom Cristóvão de Moura in Madrid, in which he criticizes the Fathers of the Society of Jesus living in Brazil. These comments are accompanied by short replies from the Fathers, who were informed of them by a relative to whom he showed them.*

In the name of Jesus.

*[Relative:] Though the Jesuit Fathers console themselves with the words of Our Saviour, "Blessed are you when men revile you and persecute you and utter all kinds of evil against you falsely,"*[20] *the need has arisen to answer them with an account that promotes the truth. Even so, one would expect to believe that those who have left behind all that they possessed (and to which they had legitimate entitlement), in order to serve God and save their souls, would not perform such appalling acts as the author here suggests. This is what he has to say:*

[Sousa:] You place me in great danger of falling foul of our Jesuit Fathers in Bahia, were they to learn that I have passed these comments on to you. As I have told them several times that I consider the matters now contained in them to be far from edifying, some find the matter very improper and think that I show them no due respect. But in obeying your orders, while begging your protection, I now say what I have to.

*Reply. The informant is quite right in fearing that he may jeopardize his standing with our Jesuit Fathers [here] in Brazil, for they know the truth about the issues that he is addressing. These matters should have been brought to His Majesty's attention only after being more thoroughly ascertained. Furthermore, to ensure that his zeal should remain less suspect, he should have related matters simply without, as he does, passing judgment on the intentions with which they were made. That is something that he has done in many of his comments, though that right belongs solely to God.*

Item 1. In the early years in which the Fathers of the Society resided in Brazil, they were loved and well received by the settlers of this State. Indeed, the settlers worshipped them as though they were the very gods of the land. That was due to their great virtues and exemplary way of life. It was also

---

20    Matthew 5:11.

because they came to terms with what the land permits and sympathized with the people's needs, as well as helping them in their trials and tribulations with the governors-general, captains, and other magistrates, who out of respect for them did what they advised them was for the good of the country and its settlers.

*Reply. When the informant went to Brazil in 1569, the Jesuit Fathers had already been there for twenty years, for the first of them went in 1549 with Tomé de Sousa, who went to create settlements. What he says in this item, therefore, is something he did not witness but has merely heard about. It is most surprising that in view of the high regard for the Fathers that he shows here, he so freely gives credence to such favorable aspects. It seems, however, that he is doing this more for his own benefit, since when he speaks ill of them he wishes to be believed then as well.*

Item 2. The governor-general, captains, and leaders of the people sought all possible means for the Jesuit Fathers to have everything necessary for their support, giving them, from their estates, every form of produce that the land has to offer and every assistance toward other expenses, as well as providing work and shelter.

*Reply. The measures of support for the first Jesuit Fathers (and for those who went there until the foundation of the colleges) were those that King João of Blessed Memory ordered to be given. That was a certain supply of manioc and rice, plus one cruzado a month for each man, as can be found in the account books of his exchequer. To say that the governors, bishops, and so forth gave us all the supplies that the land has to offer is not right. It is true that the people gave them what they could in alms as though to the poor, according to the extent of their poverty. The first houses that the Fathers had, which were just poor little houses made of wattle and daub, with thatched roofs, were built by dint of their own sweat and toil, as they burdened their own backs with wood and water. It is true that the people helped them by lending them their slaves and anything else they could. The houses that they now have they also built, partly with the alms which King João ordered that they should receive (which for many years was not paid because of the poverty of the land) and partly with the aid given to them by King Sebastião, though mainly through their own persistent work.*

Item 3. Once the Fathers were increasing in number and needed the support of the king, they wrote to His Majesty, sometimes with such insistence that he deemed it right to help them with alms and other favors. Finally, the three colleges in Bahia, Pernambuco, and Rio de Janeiro received eight thousand *cruzados* a year from His Majesty, as well as land grants given to them by the governors, while the captains and certain settlers donated to them their estates.

*Reply. King João regarded the conversion of the heathens of Brazil as highly impor-tant, as also did the Fathers of the Society, whom he sent for this purpose with his first governor-general. In fact, the latter was duty-bound to respond favorably to their requests for assistance, and they certainly impressed this upon him, as the informant says. Even in Portugal there was no shortage of people to speak up for them, saying that they had much need of assistance from those living in Brazil. If he is speaking of what those in authority in Bahia did for the Fathers at this time, he is well placed to know it, since he always sought a position in that authority. He knows very well that the city council did not write favorably about the Fathers, quite the reverse, and that it did so with such conviction that others complain that he and one of his friends brought discredit on the letters that were issued by the city council. As well as inheriting the kingdom, King Sebastião inherited from his grandfather his zeal for conversion, and it was he who founded the three colleges of which the informant speaks, giving them an income appropriate for one hundred and thirty religious, at a rate of twenty milréis for each man, or six thousand five hundred cruzados, as is shown in the official documents, and not eight thousand, as he claims.*

Item 4. This agreement between the Jesuit Fathers and the governors, the bishop, and settlers of the State lasted until Father Luís da Grã no longer headed the Society [in Brazil]. He was Father Provincial in this country for many years. He prudently adjusted to the times and retained the regard and trust in which the Society was held in the territory, as well as the friend-ship of its settlers. He was more obeyed by all the superiors, both major and minor, throughout the country than he was by his own religious. Because of the friendliness and general acceptance that he instilled, everything was relaxed and amicable, but all that ended and disappeared when the said Father ceased to be the Provincial.

*Reply: The Jesuit Fathers have always behaved toward the settlers as they do now, but the settlers do not behave as they did when there were only a few of them. Nor did the settlers [then] do things to close the door on the sacraments with which the Fathers regularly consoled them. Such closure, now and at all times, is inevitably regretted by those who behave unacceptably toward the Indians. From this [situa-tion] have stemmed the complaints, which will continue while these wrongs persist. These have greatly increased since the hinterland was opened up by Luís de Brito[21] about eighteen years ago. The informant knows the situation well, owing to the major part that he played in it. In circumstances where the Indians have not been wronged (for the Society of Jesus seeks to place under particular protection those whom it is seeking to convert), everyone says that the Fathers have continued to be*

21   Luís de Brito de Almeida was governor-general of Brazil from 1573 until 1578.

*worshipped as though gods, for all that they themselves are more concerned about what is truly important.*

Item 5. Father Luís da Grã was succeeded by Father Inácio Tolosa, who went as Provincial to Bahia and took with him many religious from Portugal. They found that the College of Bahia was in receipt of four thousand five hundred *cruzados* in annual income from the king. There were also many cattle ranches, many properties (from which they receive a large income), a farm providing all the supplies that they needed, and five villages of freed Indians who help them enormously, not to mention sundry other benefits and services that were made available for the well-being of the college. They took the view that they had no [further] need of anyone, which was, in fact, the case. They had no intention of doing more than reaping the profits, marking out land, building houses for pleasure and recreation, and receiving regulations from the king that provided them with generous exemptions and with jurisdiction over the villages of the freed Indians. In sundry ways, they behaved with such ingratitude that they scandalized the entire State and its settlers since they did not take account of the great services that the latter had carried out for the Society. That meant that the Fathers were greatly hated by the people.

*Reply. Father Inácio found that the college had neither been built nor even begun. The Fathers lived in poor wattle and daub huts that are still standing. He began the college and put in the necessary work without offending anyone, for in this country there was no other suitable approach or enough money to buy everything, even if some amount were found. The college does not receive four thousand five hundred cruzados [annually] but three thousand, as the official documents make plain. It does have a number of cattle farms that supply the needs of the religious, and without these it would be impossible for them to feed themselves, as is well known. Moreover, this fact is of importance to the people, as there is no need to take meat from them, for they need it for themselves and there is little enough of it. The income from the properties is no more than twelve milréis. There is a farm, from which they get cassava tubers and flour for their own sustenance as well as for the people, and each year they spend more than one hundred and fifty milréis on supplies.*

*The villages that they control belong to the king and the people, and the Indians work for us, as for others in the territory, in return for wages. The Fathers do not own the villages in the way that those do who have their own, as in Jaguaripe, and as do other individuals, who use them only for their own ends, and where nobody else dares to meddle. The Fathers control no more than four villages, and those are becoming exhausted owing to the constant work caused by warfare, attacks by the English, building forts and ramparts, traveling to mines with the informant, and similar things. They marked out their land as they were obliged to do since this is ecclesiastical property. During the time of Father Inácio, a wattle and daub house with a thatched roof was built outside the city. It exists for our students to go to on their rest days. This is something that the Society seeks to do everywhere for its religious. The exemptions and jurisdiction of which he speaks were not for the benefit of our Fathers but for that of the Indians, as can be seen in the terms and conditions. One such condition was that the Indians were not obliged to pay tithes for a certain number of years but that they should spend those amounts on their own poor, their own sick, and their own social gatherings. Nor were they to work for the Portuguese in the latter's houses for more than a month at a time. There were other similar conditions that prevented such problems as their falling into vice, self-neglect, and so on.*

*Till now, thank God, the Fathers have not experienced the hatred of the people, nor is there any discernible sign of the ingratitude of which they are accused, nor any demonstration of scandal throughout the territory of Brazil, which stretches for some four hundred leagues along the coast, though the informant has never strayed beyond the boundaries of Bahia.*

Item 6. The Fathers gave the immediate order that they would themselves mark out their land as they saw fit. In that way, they encroached on many farms belonging to others and threw out the owners of the land without allowing the matter to have a judicial hearing, even though the owners had title to the land proving that they had ownership of it. When the owners sought to go to law, they were not allowed to, as the Fathers said that their only judge was in Rome. They then excommunicated the people and through their own judge conservator forced them to hand over their land. Some settlers who were ejected were so poor that they had nothing on which to survive. As a result, the whole city of Salvador and the whole of Bahia were scandalized by this, and still today complain volubly at the manner in which it was done.

*Reply. The deeds reveal the contrary, as the lands were marked out by the Crown judge, as laid down by His Majesty, and the various parties were heard. The title deeds of the college are older than the rest and have been confirmed by the king, who ordered them to be observed. The registrar of properties is obliged by law to maintain them and to act against anyone who inappropriately occupies the land and the property of the Church. In all respects, the rights of the parties were properly adjudged. After all other remedies against the objectors had been exhausted, the powers of the Church were brought to bear, and that meant excommunication. One can only believe that the informant never realized that this [allegation] could come to the attention of the Fathers and that they would be able to prove the truth of the matter, or that His Majesty should have to deal with matters of such weight, solely on the basis of what was told him in Madrid, while not being able to ascertain the truth.*

Item 7. Then at times within Bahia they forcibly wronged others, as well as in the captaincy of Ilhéus and on [the banks of] the river Camamu, where many settlers lived. They were ejected from their estates without their cases being heard, and cruel excommunications were imposed by the registrar of properties. Idiot that he was, he failed to understand what he was doing: he imposed the same excommunications on all the officials of secular justice, if either they listened to any protests from these settlers or drew up any documents regarding their demands. The object of that was to prevent the poor settlers from having any documents showing the enforcements and distress caused to them.

*Reply. The opposite is shown in title deeds and other authentic documents. The territory of Camamu of which he speaks was given to Mem de Sá by the captain of Ilhéus in 1544, and he gave it to the college as an act of piety in 1563. This is all written down in the deeds, and the land was marked out by the Crown judge. Various parties were heard, as has already been stated.*

Item 8. The settlers complained verbally to the captain of Ilhéus, who sought to do something about the matter. But they were then excommunicated and prevented from going to law. When their representatives arrived at a certain island where there was one Jesuit Father, one Lay Brother, one lay servant, and many Indians, the Father refused to let them land and ordered his men to prevent them from doing so by firing many arrows at the boat. They injured many, and all this was done so forcefully despite their not deserving such poor treatment. It proved very costly to obtain forgiveness for those who were making demands for justice, as well as for their representatives for listening to them. Many of the settlers were totally ruined, as they had invested all their capital in their land.

*Reply. The contrary is demonstrated by the documents. The magistrate in Ilhéus did not order investigation into any such offenses as alleged by the informant. Rather, he sent a bailiff at night to arrest a married man, named Pêro Simões, to get him to hand over some Indians who were said to be from some other territory. They put him in a boat, and his slaves fired a number of arrows, injuring one man. The Father and the Lay Brother were asleep in their house. A slave belonging to the captured man went to report [to them] that his master had been arrested, and the Father and Lay Brother went off to discover what was happening. They took some settlers with them and reached the boat. When they asked who it was, his captor answered that he was under arrest for not handing over the Indians. As the bailiff believed that the slaves had fired the arrows, he drew up legal reports. These were sent to the governor-general, Manuel Teles,*[22] *who sent them on to Portugal via the informant. When the Jesuit Fathers learned of this, they pressed the bishop to order his vicar-general to institute an investigation into the matter, to discover whether their Father and the Lay Brother were in any way to blame. The witnesses all agreed that they were innocent and had not [even] seen what was happening, as it was night and they were far away. As for the money invested by the settlers, it was very little, as is well known in that territory. All they had done was to clear some wasteland and grow food there, harvesting it in the years when they cultivated the land and without making any payment.*

Item 9. As there was nobody who could administer true justice in the territory, God sent vengeance for these poor people, as a number of heathens who had never encountered Christians came down from the hinterland into this part of Camamu. They destroyed all the estates belonging to the Fathers and, indeed, to those settlers who lived along the river. Where they could not burn everything, not a stone was left upon stone. They killed and maimed many, and now, today, the territory is uninhabited. It will never be populated again, owing to the scourge sent down so swiftly from Heaven.

*Reply. The Jesuit Fathers cannot work out where the informant can have got this revelation, as the heathens of whom he is speaking had been attacking the captaincy of Porto Seguro and Ilhéus for many years. His family and neighbors had charge, and still do have charge, of a significant portion of that territory. The truest assessment that one can make is that God desired by these means to punish the many unjust acts of imprisonment, as well as all the other distress and vexation that the settlers in Brazil have inflicted on the native inhabitants of this land. All of us should weep and fear on that account.*

Item 10. The Jesuit Fathers in Bahia committed a similar outrage against João de Barros, who now lives in Lisbon. They asked his permission to build a corral on his land close to his sugar mill. There they would be able to keep a few cows until another piece of land became available to them, which they were to acquire from a man who was its tenant. João de Barros allowed them to do this, believing that they were asking his permission without any malicious intent. But one moonlit night, once the Fathers had completed the corral, they brought along carts on which there was a house in sections. During the night they assembled it, roofed it, and fitted it with doors so that by morning it was fully built. As João de Barros had given them permission for the corral, his men paid no heed to the building of the house, imagining that he would be giving permission for that too. However, on his way to the city, he saw the house and was astounded at such audacity. He complained to the rector,

22  Manuel Teles Barreto was governor-general from 1583 until his death in 1587.

who replied that the land belonged to the college, that it was their property. For that reason, they were under no obligation to vacate it. If he chose to take action against the college, he should seek redress from their judge, who was in Rome. Were it not for others who urged him to be patient, he would have risked losing everything at the hands of the Jesuit Fathers.

*Reply. The land does belong to the college and has been in its possession for more than forty years, as stated in the appropriate land grant. For that reason, the college did not need to ask permission to build the corral. As to what he says about the house, that is all in his imagination. Nor were there any disputes with João de Barros, and nothing of what he says actually occurred.*

Item 11. Seven years ago, when the College of Bahia wanted some land on an island that lies a league away from the city, in order to keep cows on it, the Fathers won over Garcia de Ávila, the owner of the land, getting him to donate it to them.[23] In return, they would grant permission to him and his wife to be buried in the main chapel [of the college], along with the obligation of Mass being celebrated every day for the repose of their souls. Trusting in this agreement, he forced his wife to sign a public deed of donation of the land. That she did, in the presence of the rector. However, when the donor asked the latter to supply him with a [reciprocal] deed relating to the chapel and the Masses, he replied that that would have to be written out in the college. From there, he sent him a letter of fraternity that included the obligation to say two hundred Masses, just once and for all. At that, Garcia de Ávila lost his patience and went off to complain about the deception to the Father Provincial. He received a message stating that the Fathers were [already] on his land and were taking it over, despite the resistance of his steward, as he had not received any message about it from his master. This all led to great disputes, and the aggrieved owner sought legal redress. The Fathers of São Roque cut short their wild attempt and prevented their agent from taking matters further, as they were [too] ashamed to appear in court.

*Reply. Garcia de Ávila and his wife are still alive, the deeds still exist, and they all confirm the opposite. The Fathers asked him to sell them the land. His reply was that he was keeping it for the good of his soul. Later, at his own suggestion, on a number of occasions he told the rector that he would donate the land to him, but he was told to await the Father Visitor, to whom he offered it, asking that his wife be thanked for it. They both signed the deeds very happily, and she handed the titles of the land to the rector, without either Garcia de Ávila or his wife requesting anything, either spiritual or temporal, [in exchange]. However, as a sign of gratitude, the Father*

---

23 Garcia d'Avila (1528–1609) was the son of Governor Tomé de Sousa and eventually the largest landowner in Brazil. His extensive ranches and estates covered large tracts of the interior of Bahia.

*Visitor promised to Garcia de Ávila a letter of fraternity and one hundred Masses when he died. Then his wife, acting on advice from persons who had little liking for the Society, regretted their actions and lodged a complaint. But, as the land was [now] the property of the Church, the college could not release it. It became necessary for our father-general to issue the order that, in fact, he did issue. That is the true situation. Everything else consists of additions made by the informant. Those are the assertions that they were offered the main chapel for burial, that Mass would be said for them daily, that their steward resisted the taking over of the land (as he had no knowledge of the matter), that two hundred Masses would be said, that the Fathers of São Roque had cut matters short, and so on.*

Item 12. Similar enforcements were inflicted on many others in Bahia, Rio de Janeiro, Ilhéus, and elsewhere. In Rio de Janeiro, some appealed to the governor, António Salema, seeking the king's jurisdiction and the good of the settlers. The Jesuit Fathers put their excommunications into effect and even investigated the governor. The rector, Rodrigo de Freitas, did this by interrogating witnesses against him and in support of their position. For that reason, savage charges were sent to His Majesty by both parties, to the point where great enmity ensued between the Jesuits and the governor. Sides were taken, the faction that supported the Jesuits hating the governor, whilst the faction that supported the governor hated the Jesuits. The city of Rio de Janeiro suffered from this situation on numerous occasions, with all the concomitant offenses against God and the interests of the king.

*Reply. The informant was not an eyewitness to what he asserts. This is but hearsay brought in by ships. It swells up and then subsides as it bleeds away. It is hardly surprising, therefore, that he is wrong on so many issues, though he is much to blame in giving credence to such information and in purveying it to His Majesty as though proven, when it has been no such thing. He demonstrates that he is far less sincere toward us than is demanded by Christian charity. As he has already given account to God for what he did against the Fathers and why, there is nothing to say about António Salema, except that the prelate made him hand over the documents that he and his secretary wrote against the Fathers. Those papers enable one to see the truth of the situation.*

Item 13. The governor-general, Luís de Brito, sought to disabuse the Fathers, telling them that they could not continue with their methods of acquiring [property and land] and that they should act with a gentleness appropriate to their calling. As he sought to get them to correct their procedure in such matters, they broke with him, despite all the favors conferred, and complained about him to the king, whilst he complained about them. Mutual hatred ensued so that when he went to Mass at the college, he went to hear it in one of its churches and, when they saw him, they did not say Mass, making him wait so long for it that he got irked and went back home without hearing Mass. However, he assembled witnesses to these events. This hatred grew to such a degree that the Fathers unleashed their feelings against the governor-general from the pulpit, and he quite rightly complained about this to the king.

*Reply. As is well known, the governor-general, Luís de Brito, was the recipient of great services and favors from the Fathers of the College of Bahia. They regularly heard his confession and they all lived in great harmony. It is possible that the informant knows something from the man who disrupted that harmony, as they were very close. At all events, the disagreement arose after the governor-general opened up the interior inhabited by the heathens, and where both men established sugar plantations. There were also many boatloads of Indians whom the informant sent to be sold in the captaincies. The Fathers acted against these outrages and injustices as their position demanded. There was also another reason for the disagreement, and that is mentioned later by the informant.*

Item 14. The governors took a poor view of the tendency of the Fathers to ingratiate themselves with the Crown judges, building up strong friendships with them, much to the irritation of the governors. That led to major disputes with them. To get the Fathers to write favorably to the king about the Crown judges, the latter gave them property that they had no right to, such as Camamu. There then ensued great disputes that lasted for many years with Francisco Giraldes, the captain of Ilhéus, as they had taken away his jurisdiction.

*Reply. It does no service to past governors-general to say that as a rule they did not agree with the methods of the Jesuit Fathers, since Tomé de Sousa, Dom Duarte, Mem de Sá, Lourenço da Veiga,[24] and Dom Francisco de Sousa[25] were and are very close to them and devoted to them. There were some disputes with Luís de Brito and Manuel Teles. The informant refers to them here, and answers will be provided. Nobody can be reproached for friendship with the Crown judges, least of all the religious community, who should get on well with everybody and without offense to anyone. As to the land of Camamu, Mem de Sá took possession of it when it was his right to do so and then handed it over to the Jesuit Fathers as a charitable gift, as has already been said. The jurisdiction that Francisco Giraldes has over that land is something that he can ascertain and concerning which he can require confirmation in accordance with the existing documents. It would seem, however, that the informant is not well informed on this matter.*

Item 15. When the governor-general, Luís de Brito, brought an investigation against the Crown judge, Fernão [da] Silva, for committing serious

---

24  Lourenço da Veiga was governor-general from 1578 until his death in 1581.
25  Dom Francisco de Sousa was governor-general from 1591 to 1602.

crimes against the king's exchequer and his laws, he placed him under arrest and sent him back to Portugal. Yet, the Jesuit Fathers came out in his support, defending him and concealing his crimes. They sent many letters to the king in support of the Crown judge and against the governor-general, and from that there stemmed great animosity and scandal. After the death of both men, their sons remained bitter enemies and brought vicious lawsuits against one another. That would not have happened if the Fathers had allowed justice to be done. Since on this occasion justice was not done on earth, God sent it from Heaven, drowning at sea the Crown judge, his wife, four daughters, two sons, and three grandchildren. Everybody else from his household escaped, as did all others traveling on the same carrack, when it ran aground one stormy night at the mouth of the Bahia harbor bar.

*Reply. The rightful accusations that Luís de Brito brought against Fernão da Silva became apparent in the just sentence imposed when he returned from Portugal and in the just position that his sons hold against the Crown judge's heirs. It was, therefore, not fair to say that the Jesuit Fathers defended and concealed his crimes. As to God's judgment, which he alleges, it is not for mankind to interpret it. Similarly, it cannot be said why it pleased the good Lord that the informant, after spending seven years away from home, at great detriment to his fortune and peace of mind, should then be shipwrecked off the [River] Serigi in his own carrack and have to endure such trials and hunger on his journey back to Bahia by land. That is not to speak of everything else that is so well known.*

Item 16. After this period of contention with Fernão da Silva, the Fathers then set in train another dispute with the governor-general himself, who, as a result of a sentence imposed by the vicar-general, ordered a man by the name of Sebastião da Ponte to be removed from church. He was a criminal who, because of the gravity of his crimes, did not merit sanctuary. The church was a small chapel on an estate that, a few days earlier, a certain Lázaro de Arévalo had left to the Jesuits on the occasion of his death. The criminal sought to appeal to them, begging the favor of sanctuary and promising them a large share of his fortune. He was in the public jail when the judge conservator of the Jesuit Fathers ordered the secular justices to return him to the chapel from which he had been taken. The judge conservator then instituted unexpected excommunication proceedings against the officials of [secular] justice.

*Reply. The church of which the informant speaks belonged to the Society ever since its original foundation and not through the death of Lázaro de Arévalo, as he states. Nor did the Fathers cause this dispute. It was initiated by Luís de Brito, and they were far from being involved in such concerns. The governor-general removed the man from their church without first informing them of the matter, as he was legally bound to do. Nor did the man, for this reason or for any other, give or promise to them part of his fortune, nor can that be shown. Rather, it was the Fathers who decided to have recourse to the immunity of their church, which is exempt [from secular justice], just as they are.*

Item 17. Worse still, the Jesuits sought the help of the bishop in support of their judge conservator. As he was a friend of the governor-general, they created animosity between them, and a general interdict was imposed [on the governor-general's jurisdiction]. They burnt candles upside down at the foot of the pillory, and a crucifix was placed head down, feet upwards, which caused enormous fear in the land, to the point where people kept well away from the governor-general and the justices. That was the advice that the Jesuits gave them. The Jesuits were constantly in the bishop's palace, trying to prevent him from lifting his excommunications, and these remained in place for nine days. The clergy were armed with muskets day and night, as well as with crossbows, halberds, and other weapons. They surrounded the jail, so that the prisoner could not board a ship. They kept the governor-general shut up in his residence, as he was afraid they would kill him, and, had he not been so circumspect, there would have been many deaths and other disasters. That was because the clergy were calling out from their windows, urging the people to fight for the Church. Other clergy were out on the streets and at people's doors with drums, pressing them to go and tell the king's governor-general that the bishop and the Jesuit Fathers had joined the city in rebellion.

*Reply. At first the bishop was against the Fathers and their judge conservator but merely for as long as the only information that he received came from the governor-general. Once he knew the truth of what was happening, he took the side that he realized was right and just. As for other matters, all that can be said is that [the informant] has sought more to pursue his own goals and wishes than to respect the truth and the duty he owes to the person he seeks to inform. What he says about the crucifix and the candles burning upside down has neither rhyme nor reason, as no object would have been served by such actions. Nor did the clergy take up arms, except when the governor-general used drums and proclamations to summon everybody to his residence with their weapons. Then they did come armed, to stop the prisoner being put aboard ship instead of being returned to the church, which was what they demanded of the governor-general. When he complied, all activity stopped and peace again reigned.*

Item 18. To add to the troubles, the Jesuit Fathers handled matters so badly that they sent for all the warriors in the Indian villages, placing them both in the college and all around it, with a view to their aiding them against the governor-general in the event of hostilities. The teachers in the college's school told their pupils to fight with stones on behalf of the Church and against their own parents, brothers, and relatives. But it was the will of God that when the governor-general saw what was being organized, he chose to put a stop to it all, by deciding not to send the prisoner aboard ship and by ordering his return to the church whence he had been removed. This he did so that the excommunications and interdict would be lifted.

*Reply. If he had done that straight away, the dispute would not have lasted for the nine days that the informant mentions. What he states about the Indians and the pupils at the school is not true. One can only assume that he dreamt it and inserted it into his account because it suited his purpose to convince himself that these written statements that he handed over in Madrid could not possibly come to the notice of the Jesuit Fathers in Brazil. However, God is good and a friend and defender of His religion.*

Item 19. Bitter dissension stalked the entire country. Its governor-general and other officials complained to the king about the bishop and the Jesuit Fathers, who were sternly reprimanded in letters from His Majesty. The king was astounded that they had acted against his governor-general with excommunications. He was moved to remove from the Fathers everything that he had commanded that they be given from his exchequer and ordered that Sebastião da Ponte be taken to Portugal in chains. For his crimes and without the circumstances ever being discussed with him, he languished in the Limoeiro Prison in Lisbon for many years till death overtook him. From that can be seen how the Fathers used an "innocent" man to the point where the country was in danger of losing its settlers, with some reacting in their favor and others against them.

*Reply. The king was convinced that what the governor-general and the city council wrote to him was the truth because the documents from the bishop went to La Rochelle. Moreover, the Jesuit Fathers in Portugal took the same view, namely that the Fathers in Bahia had gone too far. However, it pleased the good Lord that the documents should [finally] arrive in Portugal. It was learned from them that the opposite was true, with the result that our Jesuit Fathers once again wrote back complimentary letters to express their satisfaction. Indeed, those letters are still extant. As to the king wishing to withdraw our income, we have no idea how the informant could know what His Majesty's decision was. Let that assertion be treated like the rest. The Fathers did not consider whether Sebastião da Ponte was innocent or guilty. Their only concern was the disrespect shown to the Church, and that was contrary to law, as has already been said.*

Item 20. The Jesuits were not content with causing the above scandal, nor with supporting the Crown judge Fernão da Silva against the governor-general Luís de Brito. Later, following the death of the governor-general, Lourenço da Veiga, the Crown judge, Cosme Rangel, planned to succeed him in the governorship. He had no right to that post and, because he was such a foolish man, the city council refused to elect him governor-general, believing that their refusal was in the king's best interests. The bishop and the comptroller of finances both signed the decision document, adding that the governor-general should not be chosen from any of the other candidates either. The result was that the Crown judge sought to move Heaven and earth against the bishop and the city council. In order to cut short the harmful consequences of this, the bishop and council evacuated the city until such time as His Majesty should appoint a governor-general and ordered Cosme Rangel to be arrested. The Jesuit Fathers supported him, however, as at that time he had given them ownership of a public street in the city, which till then he had not allowed them to include within their precincts.

*Reply. The informant says nothing about the nature of the Fathers' support for Cosme Rangel, nor how or to what extent they supported him. The street of which he speaks is both damaging to religion and of little use to the city, as is shown by the fact that hardly anybody misses it. The city gave away the street under a provision made by His Majesty and in exchange for other pieces of land of greater importance that the college released to the city. Without those pieces, the Fathers no longer possess the patch of land that they call "monastery land" and which is the best public asset of its kind that the city possesses.*

Item 21. When Governor-General Manuel Teles Barreto arrived, he showed no praise for the Jesuit Fathers for acting so sternly against the king's officials, for the latter he supported. Consequently, they took the side of the Crown judge, Martim Leitão, who with their support disobeyed the governor-general and went off to Pernambuco, where (just as in Bahia) he committed grave offenses against the interests of the king. The king ordered his arrest and the confiscation of his wealth. He is now in Lisbon for his crimes. The Jesuits supported him against both the governor-general and the country because he gave them illegitimate possession of the territory of Camamu, thus creating a thousand disputes with many people.

*Reply. The informant neither shows nor will be able to show in what respect they supported him against the governor-general. Martim Leitão did not hand over the territory of Camamu: he merely demarcated it under provision from His Majesty, who had ordered and required that this be done. Nor is it fair to blame the Society for disputes involving other people.*

Item 22. The Fathers got on so badly with the governor-general, Manuel Teles, that usually they sent him written applications for payment. On those grounds, they complained about him to the king, as he did about them. Urged by other people, he particularly made public an ugly matter in which it was alleged that the rector had got involved with a married woman. [The

Fathers] felt bound to get many people to beg him not to forward the legal documents to His Majesty, nor did he. The governor-general ordered the arrest of a certain Bartolomeu Pires for a particular crime. He was a married man and master of music in the cathedral. The bishop did not complain about his arrest, owing to Pires being a layman, though the Fathers did complain because he was their friend. Every time the governor-general went to Mass at the college, they would not say Mass, asserting that he was excommunicated for ordering the arrest of this man who, they claimed, was a minister of the Church. Their reaction scandalized the country and the governor-general even more. He made fresh complaints to His Majesty, and on those grounds His Majesty ought to withdraw from them whatever he awards them from his exchequer.

*Reply. Since Manuel Teles is now with God, as it is our duty to believe, it is not right to speak of the little affection that he held for members of the Society, whether in Portugal or in Brazil. It is surprising that the informant wishes to blind himself in respect of matters that are so clear and where the goodness of the people to whom he refers is so well known throughout the country. He could have avoided sullying himself with such an unseemly matter, but he chose not to leave it in the inkwell. It is also to be noted that the issue of the imprisonment of Bartolomeu Pires preceded that other matter, for the latter arose from it. He has related first what took place last, simply in order that people should not grasp how the one issue depends on the other. When he says that the Fathers felt bound to get many people to beg the governor-general not to send the legal documents to His Majesty, he is saying something that did not take place, for the documents were indeed forwarded. When he says that the bishop did not complain about the imprisonment [of Bartolomeu Pires], that is hardly surprising, for at that time he was away in the captaincy of Pernambuco. The Fathers knowingly did what they did because they considered that the prisoner was an ecclesiastic in accordance with the conditions laid down by the Council of Trent. His imprisonment was widely known, and the governor-general went to hear Mass after the imprisonment, though beforehand he had not been in the habit of going. The rector of this college arranged for Mass to be delayed a little so that he could discuss with his advisers what, in good conscience, he ought to do. During that short interval, the governor-general left because he did not wish to wait, though without knowing the reason for the delay. He was furious with the rector and set up the aforementioned legal inquiry against him and against the married woman. For that he will already have given account to God. This is precisely how things happened, and not as the informant says.*

Item 23. I cannot see how, in good conscience [the Fathers] can receive [their grant from His Majesty], as he has donated to them so much in charitable awards because they gave him to understand that they did not have enough to live on. Things being as they were, he kindly gave them aid. But today I do not know whether it is right that the Jesuit Fathers and the College of Bahia should receive four thousand five hundred *cruzados* from the king each year, as they have property that brings in much more. They own five, ten, even twelve cattle farms, from which, whenever they wish to make five hundred or a thousand *cruzados* in cash, they make that amount in the slaughter-houses. They also make the same amount on bullocks, which they sell to carters. They receive ample income from their land and they have an estate worked by many slaves from Guinea, from which they receive in plenty all the sustenance they need. Indoors, they have stores of all necessary fruit and vegetables. On their farms they have large herds of pigs, as well as sheep and hens. On other land, they have fishing from rafts and that provides all the necessary fresh fish. There is also a boat with a fishing-net, as well as a barge that brings the firewood that they need for the house and for the limekiln. They possess sixty oxen that pull the carts that serve the house, thirty oxen one day and thirty the next. They have good opportunities for hunting and send the heathen people from the villages that they control to hunt animals and birds. For that reason, they have no need of any supplies from Portugal, other than clothes, wine, olive oil, incense, wax for the altars, and flour for the hosts, all of which are sent from Portugal in exchange for hides and sugar.

*Reply. It has already been stated how King Sebastião founded the three colleges with income from tithes because of the duty the Crown of Portugal has to the conversion of the native heathens of this land. In the colleges, there were to be ministers who would concern themselves with that objective. It was for that reason that the king granted them the income that they have and not for the reason that the informant advances. He makes great play with his grand words about how much the Fathers possess (and this has been partly answered in the reply to Item 5). Nevertheless, those who understand the matter well and have a true knowledge of how much such things cost in this country declare quite openly that the Fathers cannot support themselves just from what they have. Indeed, the college is constantly in debt and borrowing from some in order to pay others. Even today it has debts of more than four thousand cruzados both here and in Portugal. They do not butcher their meat in the slaughterhouse but often buy cattle so that their own should not die out. That is because the lack of pasture means that they do not breed well. They do sell a few of their bullocks from their farm. As for the food and income from the land, that point has already been answered. The pigs are so few in number that they are unable to slaughter even one per week for the old and the sick. As for the sheep, they sometimes keep one for Easter. They often buy chickens for those who are ill. Fresh fish is mainly bought in the old town and from Cardoso's plantation. They tried fishing with a net but abandoned it because it was very expensive and not very profitable. It goes without saying that the college has a workshop because it is essential to keep things in running order and there is not money available to buy everything. The oxen number no more than twenty-four or twenty-six. As for what the informant says about hunting animals and birds, it is laughable. The villages are seven, twelve, or even fifteen leagues away from the city, and game is rare in this area. The wretched Indians cannot find enough for themselves. They can barely survive on what those Fathers have who teach them and live among them. So much for the college having an abundance of game! It is, however, God's judgment that the informant should be discredited in the face of such clear evidence. The Jesuit Fathers do not send hides to Portugal nor do they possess sugar plantations or even cane plantations. Sometimes they are given sugar as payment, and that they send to Portugal in return for some article for the church. They do that rarely, however, owing to the existence of so many thieves.*

Item 24. [The Jesuits] spend most on altar pieces, silver objects, and other work carried out at such enormous cost by craftsmen that they could really do without it, not spending any more on such work than on the wages of a master carpenter and a stonemason. After all, they have their own workmen and sawyers. They get the Indians from the villages to provide them with timber from the forest, sending a lay Brother in his barge [to collect it]. He also delivers oysters to them, which they use to produce lime. They have built such a splendid college that it has no rival in Portugal, and there are always eighty religious there. With the slaves, servants, and craftsmen, the college provides for some two hundred people within its walls and at no cost to the Fathers.

*Reply. Their income is not wasted on church ornaments or on decorating the college as the informant states. It does not seem fair to allot blame for this. There are few silver pieces, and most of these arrived ready-made from Portugal, whilst the rest were charitable gifts bequeathed for a chapel containing relics. There are never eighty religious in the college at one time, but sixty, though at times more and at times fewer. But, if there were as many religious as he claims, as well as the others that he mentions, the total that he says that they have is still small. To say that to provide for so many people does not cost anything would be wonderful were that the case, but may God forgive him for wishing to deceive both himself and those that he should not deceive.*

Item 25. The Fathers asked His Majesty for two thousand *cruzados* for the College of Rio de Janeiro, leading him to understand that that sum was highly necessary. In fact, the college was already built, and they also possessed extensive land grants that the captains had given to them. The college is unnecessary, as it does nothing but cause expense to the king, when he really needs it to fortify the territory. That is because in Rio de Janeiro, there are up to two hundred people, the majority of whom are of mixed

Indian and white parentage or are settlers with black wives, whose children miraculously know how to read. Yet who can there be who receives tuition in the college that it costs the king two thousand *cruzados* a year? It is surely in the interests of both God and the king that that sum should be spent on the fortification of the territory, seeing that it has no defenses.

*Reply. The informant is making many sinful observations here. He belittles the city of Rio de Janeiro, for it has many Portuguese settlers and is the most fortified city along the entire coast, as is well known. He also asserts that receives an income of two thousand cruzados from His Majesty, when, in fact, it is two thousand five hundred. He imagines that the reason for founding the college was to teach the children of the Portuguese, when it was, in fact, to provide upkeep for fifty members of the Society. They relieve the king of the obligation he has to effect conversions, as is also the case in the other colleges and as laid down in his official plans. Therefore, if as he states, there are so many people of mixed Indian and white parentage and so many black women, not to mention heathens, both freedmen and captives, then that income is not wasted in providing the upkeep for those who are helping such people to earn salvation. Moreover, they perform other duties in the service of God and the country by preaching and hearing confessions, by teaching the children to read, write, and learn Latin. They also go to provide help in Espírito Santo, São Vicente, and other settlements in the south. They maintain two Indian settlements, which form a large part of the fortification of the territory, as has been evident in the conflicts with the French and in the carracks that were captured from them with the help of the Indians. If the informant is so keen to protect His Majesty's exchequer, then he would have to make savings on the foregoing and not spend it as it has been spent. In the future, he would be able to spend it on the much-heralded mines that he has abandoned there and which in these parts hardly anyone has heard of.*

Item 26. The Jesuits also led King Sebastião to believe that it was very necessary to found another college in Pernambuco, although they already had in that captaincy an ecclesiastical foundation capable of housing thirty religious who survived very well on local almsgiving. They asked for one thousand *cruzados* just for that project. Then they demanded that on the grounds that little money was in circulation, they be paid in sugar, leading people to believe that sugar was worth four hundred réis from one year to the next, whereas, in fact, it has been worth eight hundred réis for the last twelve years. That means that they receive the king's sugar at four hundred réis per *arroba*, and the king pays the collector of the Church tithes at the price of eight hundred réis per *arroba*. Great circumspection should be brought to bear on this, just as on their assertion to the king that a college is necessary in this town, in order to teach reading and writing to those who live outside it.

*Reply. The king founded this college just like the others and for the same reason. The Fathers asked for nothing. He gave enough for twenty [religious], donating twenty thousand réis for each man, just as he did in the other colleges. As to what the informant says about sugar, this is what happened. The king ordered a valuation from year to year, and that was done under legal authority. His Majesty's comptroller-general of finances and his representative took part in this, as well as settlers and others who had taken the oath, as is laid down in the official documents. If, however, the king desired to give [the Jesuit Fathers] some other favor or donation, then the informant should not trouble himself about it and should remember the parable of the vineyard.*[26]

Item 27. There was quite enough to enable the teaching of reading, writing, and a little Latin, which could have been done without this income. Indeed, nothing else is taught, and there is not a soul in the territory who learns anything other than that. The College of Bahia was adequate for the whole State of Brazil, where, till now, no more than six or seven people have completed the course in Arts, some of whom have been received into the Society. No more than four from outside have studied theology. Only one of them completed the course and he has become a good preacher. The most fruitful outcomes are in the reading of Latin and in matters of conscience. If, in Portugal, there was formerly[27] only the University of Coimbra, why is it that the College of Bahia is not enough for the whole State of Brazil?

*Reply. The informant has not understood His Majesty's intention in founding the colleges in Brazil. It was not to provide studies for the children of the Portuguese but to create ministers for conversion. That is his solemn duty, as set down in the official documents, and the latter lay no obligation on the Jesuit Fathers to set up any schools. If there is any captaincy that has need of such ministers, it is Pernambuco. In that captaincy, there are sixty plantations full of slaves and many other people employed by the Portuguese, as well as many heathen tribesmen who have been brought in from the interior. There are many blacks from Angola, who have no other cure for their souls than that provided by the Jesuit Fathers, as is well known. As well as fulfilling that duty, the Fathers saw the great need that existed for religious teaching and recognized the great service that could be performed both for God and the settlers if they were to found schools, even though they had no duty to do that. In the schools, they teach the rudiments and mold people who give good service to both God and their neighbor. From among those, there are many canons and dignitaries in the Cathedral of Bahia and many priests along the entire coast, as well as a few preachers. Every day, more are produced and mainly in Bahia. In the other colleges,*

26  Matthew 20:1–16.
27  Until the foundation of the Jesuit University of Évora in 1559.

*they learn enough to enable them then to go [to Bahia] and read General Studies or Arts or theology. That is what is done in Pernambuco, where instruction is also given in matters of conscience to aid the many clergy who are there.*

Item 28. The Fathers have two houses in São Vicente, one in Espírito Santo, another in Porto Seguro, one in Itamaracá, and another in Paraíba. These houses are well supplied with everything they need. The free Indians whom they teach farm the land profitably and also receive aid and alms from the settlers in these areas. Their houses in Bahia, Pernambuco, and Rio de Janeiro are supplied in the same way. In these houses, the Fathers teach reading, writing, and Latin to the children of the settlers there who want to learn. They have ways of teaching that differ from those adopted in the college.

*Reply. The Fathers have no house in Itamaracá and no school in Paraíba. In none of the others do they teach Latin. The colleges supply these houses, which are linked to them, with produce from Portugal for those who live there and for the churches, because the settlers, who are poor, cannot do that. They provide them with what is available to eat but they do not run profitable farms. The teaching methods [used by the Fathers] is the same as in the colleges, as they have the same rules and system and as the Society wishes to maintain uniformity as much as possible everywhere.*

Item 29. These things result from the Fathers' poverty and their need for help from the settlers, for the latter help them to do their work by giving them provisions and supporting them with charitable donations. Moreover, such Fathers lead secluded lives, and their way of life sets a fine example, so that they are well regarded throughout the land. There are fears, however, that the colleges are a source of scandal, since other people have sought alternatives. In every captaincy, people are asking for Franciscan friars and Benedictine monks, who have begun to found monasteries, and the people are greatly devoted to them, since there is now a Benedictine monastery in Bahia and another belonging to the Capuchins. They have been well received and given assistance so as to have people on whom they can count when carrying out their work.

*Reply. Even when he speaks well of the Fathers, he fails to tell us what actually happens. Wherever there are Indians, the Fathers have many people against them, as is the case in Porto Seguro, Espírito Santo, Paraíba, and São Vicente, where they are constantly persecuted and afflicted. That is because they resist as much as they can the greed that leads men to commit considerable outrages against the Indians. They take them captive, clap them in irons, and sell them against the will of God, and His Majesty. But, as the Fathers' cause is a just one, they are prepared to suffer everything and will not give up, as there are no others who will speak up for the Indians.*

Item 30. The bishop and the governor-general were so appalled by the Jesuit Fathers that when the Benedictines arrived in Bahia, they showed the latter every favor and made their confessions to them, as did all the leading settlers of the area, and there they are buried [by them]. The bishop transferred to the abbot [of the Benedictines] many cases that were reserved to him. Beforehand, he had passed these on to the rector of the college. The Jesuit Fathers reacted so badly to this that at once they quarrelled with the monks and have never been able to establish friendly relations with them. This caused such scandal throughout the area that its inhabitants, to spite the Society, did all they could to help them, straight away founding a monastery for them. It now houses two hundred monks, which is a source of great satisfaction to the people of the area, who have also provided them with ample sustenance.

*Reply. The bishop and the governor-general, Manuel Teles, both ceased to make their confessions to the Jesuit Fathers after the arrival of the Benedictines because they both belonged to the Order of Avis.*[28] *However, Manuel Teles had no wish to die without Jesuit Fathers at his bedside, and the bishop went back to making his confession to them. As to what the informant says about the leading settlers all making their confessions to the Benedictines, it would have been very difficult indeed for them to take them from us, even were it true. As to the cases reserved to the bishop, that claim is ridiculous, as the bishop made no changes in that respect. The Supreme Pontiffs have made due and adequate provision for us all to carry out our several ministries. We have never, as he claims, quarrelled with these priests. In fact, we often visit them, and they come to our feasts, just as we go to theirs. They eat in our refectory, and we eat in theirs. We do not believe that there is anyone who supports them just to spite the Society, unless the informant is bearing witness to his own case, for he holds us in such low esteem. As for what he says about there being two hundred Benedictines, there must be some mistake as there is a zero too many. Even if we count novices and lay Brothers, they do not add up to ten.*

Item 31. The Jesuit Fathers have another scandalous and highly disagreeable practice. Whenever they have a complaint about the governor-general, the bishop, the city council, or the settlers, they immediately express their irritation from the pulpit. Their listeners seize on it, some taking it on themselves to broadcast the complaints, others forming highly dubious opinions about what has been said on the day in question, having derived nothing else from the sermon. Sometimes the Fathers leave the cathedral on major feast days without delivering a homily because they have some quarrel with the

---

28   The Portuguese military Order of Avis (derived from the Castilian Order of Calatrava) was devoted to Saint Benedict.

bishop or the chapter. For that reason, the bishop no longer asks them to provide preachers. He, his vicar-general, and the abbot of the Benedictines take it in turns [to preach], which cannot come as a surprise to the Fathers.

*Reply. Sometimes unavoidable things happen, causing Saint John to meet Herod, Elijah to encounter Ahab, Saint Ambrose to meet Theodosius, and Saint Christopher to confront Eudoxia. But the preachers of the Society have a special rule that forbids them to strike out, and they are extremely strict about this. But an injury to a finger is made to look as though it has been inflicted on the entire hand. Besides, wherever a preacher goes up into the pulpit, he has to contend with such suspicions and views. We go to the cathedral [to preach] whenever we are called on, and that happens frequently, both for major feast days and for those of the confraternities, because our homilies cost them less.*

Item 32. They send idiots to preach who hardly know any Latin and who talk arrant nonsense. Yet in their houses they have good preachers with sound Latin. They do such things because they have no regard for the people of the area, who are greatly scandalized by this behavior and by what they let the preachers say. The people become very angry and cannot be calmed down. For that reason, many of them march out of church if they have already heard Mass, just to avoid their outpourings. All they do is praise the Indians, complain about the outrages suffered by the Indians, and proclaim themselves to be good Christians. They claim that other than among the Jesuits, there is nobody that lives as a Christian or who can boast of being one. Indeed, if the Fathers were not present, they would all immediately revert to their pagan ways.

*Reply. Those who preach have to be approved by suitable [seniors], but in every profession there are those who are greater craftsmen than others. In this vocation, credit is earned, and solely earned, through the pious appreciation of one's listeners. That appreciation is something in which, to a degree, the informant is lacking when listening to our preachers. Many homilies have to be preached, and those with the best knowledge of Latin cannot preach all of them, particularly where there are schools. To express consternation at the outrages and injustices committed against the Indians is in no sense ridiculous, and from what is known about the informant, it does not surprise us that he thinks that it is. The Indians are not as bad as he paints them, and all manner of people would live in utter deprivation, were it not for those who teach them and guide their souls.*

Item 33. The first Jesuit Fathers to go to Brazil found that the Indians were highly receptive to the faith of Christ our Redeemer, and so they baptized them by the thousands every day. They wrote to Portugal and the whole of Christendom about the great service that they were performing for God, which, indeed, they were doing. However, as easily as the Indians became

Christians, so they returned to their pagan habits, making their way back into the interior and running away from our religious teaching. The Fathers used to control more than fifty villages inhabited by these Christian Indians, but now they have only three. These are composed mainly of young people who go every year to earn more and to farm. The Fathers have worked so hard and in so many ways at the conversion of the Indians. Had they been Turks or Moors, the Fathers would have reaped a great harvest of the sort they were unable to achieve with these Indians, as they are not capable of grasping what God is, nor of believing in Him. They consider that there is nothing other than life and death, which is why time is wasted on them.

*Reply. The Fathers still enjoy the ease [of conversion] that existed formerly. If any-thing prevented the alternative successful outcome that the informant describes, for all that such outcomes were not so frequent, it was the large number of outrages committed by the Portuguese, who captured and sold the Indians and took from them their land, their women, and their children. The Fathers never had more than eleven villages. If they now have three at the most, why does the informant state in Item 5 above that they have five? Only a few Indians ran off into the interior, not all of them. Those who did run away were not escaping from the Fathers' religious teaching but from the ill treatment that I have just mentioned. Of forty thousand souls or more, almost all have expired, which is why there are no more than four hundred left in the four villages that we now have. As for the remainder, who all together amount to two thousand five hundred, the Fathers have gone to very great lengths to bring them back from the hinterland, which is more than two hundred leagues from Bahia. Though we do not work so hard with them as we used to do, owing to their smaller numbers, even one soul is of such value that the Fathers do not regard the time that they devote to them as wasted.*

Item 34. The Fathers provide teaching in the Christian religion to the chil-dren who were born and reared in these villages. The children learn it very well, as they do reading, writing, and Latin, singing to the organ, playing the flute, dancing, and serving at Mass. But, when they reach an age at which they begin to take an interest in women, they soon run off into the forest and return to the pagan ways of their fathers and forefathers, ways that the Fathers can only eradicate with the greatest difficulty. Indeed, the only rea-son why the Fathers continue to help these villages is to avoid contradicting all that they have written in praise of these people to the rest of Christendom.

*Reply. The Fathers teach them neither Latin nor how to count. They are very careful to give free rein to both males and females when they come of age. What the infor-mant states is usually the case does not, in fact, happen. If a few sometimes go astray, that does not apply to all of them, nor can the reason that he advances be the expla-nation for what they do. Among former Christians, there were plenty of wicked men who deserted to the Moors and Turks, and their sin is far greater than that committed by these people. The greater their need, the better time is spent on helping and saving them. It does not seem very sensible to say that these heathens are incapable of knowing God or believing in Him. If this were true, either they are not men at all, which is an abominable thing to say, or Christ the Redeemer did not die for them, which is blasphemous. It is a figment of the informant's imagination to assert that the Fathers do not abandon them merely in order to avoid contradicting themselves. It is no surprise that the Fathers concern themselves with so few, because for the same number, and had there been fewer sinners, Christ Our Lord would have done what he did. They comfort themselves with the thought that every year they save many innocents, including not a few adults.*

Item 35. In each of these villages, there is a Jesuit Father who says Mass and a lay Brother. If they do not both know the language of the indigenous people, [at least] one of them knows it. They live there in great danger to their honor, as it is a remarkable occasion when they are ever together. One is constantly looking after the house, whereas the other is out celebrating Mass and giving religious instruction in the church or preaching, in the Indian style, in their houses, telling them what they must do the following day. They work and go about among women who are as naked as they were the day they were born. They are unable to keep an eye on each other and prevent each other from having occasion to fall into temptation. The Portuguese are given to much muttering and many foul accusations on the basis of what the Indians tell them and which they easily believe. That is because at times certain Fathers and lay Brothers have been expelled and, once expelled from the Society, have lived such execrable lives that nobody has any doubt that the Jesuits [in the villages] have plentiful opportunity to sin, not to say to commit a thousand misdemeanors. In order to live freely without fear of being found out, they do not allow any white man or man of mixed blood, married or single, to live in the Indian villages. A few such men see it as a solution to their difficulties because they hope that the Fathers will give the Indians permission to help them to clear a plot where they can grow the food they need.

*Reply. There can be no Christian heart that is not filled with disgust and outrage at such vile and distorted assumptions. Though they do not merit a reply, since the bitterness in the breast of the one who utters them is so evident, nevertheless one can say, "Tu quis es qui indicas alienum [famulum]? Domino suo stat aut cadit; potens est autem Deus illum statuere."*[29]

---

29  "Who are you to pass judgment on [the servant of] another? It is before his own master that he stands or falls. For God is able to make him stand." (Romans 14:4)

*Those who are busy with the conversion of the heathens have superiors who watch over them and they are frequently visited. They are given much spiritual support with their rules, as well as spiritual instruction and prayers [of guidance], and they frequently receive the sacraments. Most of all, they have God's protection, for, in caring for His religious Orders and to enhance their good name, He places a guiding hand on the weak among their number. It is careless and malicious to say that those who are expelled lived, while still members of their Orders, in the way that they live after leaving, which is what the informant claims. In that way, he condemns all the other Orders, both in Brazil and in Europe. As far as possible, our Jesuits are always accompanied, and there is a particular ruling regarding this. They are able to do this because they do not preach in people's houses but in church. In church, the Indian women are properly covered. When our Jesuits go to visit the sick, they go together. They are not encumbered by the running of their house, as there is very little to do there. One small black boy, living in, is enough to take care of everything. The reason that the informant gives for the Fathers not allowing anybody into the villages is quite false. [The rule] only relates to single people, under orders from various governors-general, and it exists to prevent problems. What he says is unworthy of a Christian heart.*

Item 36. To avoid such problems, when previous kings learned about them, they ordered all the governors-general to place a captain in every village to keep an eye on the Indians and to make them work on their plots of land, as they are basically lazy. They were also to command them to work on the estates belonging to the Portuguese. In return, they would be paid a certain amount each month. The plan was that in that way the Indians would be contented, and that the wages would not be so high that those paying them could not afford them. The Jesuits were solely to come into contact with the Indians in order to give them instruction in the Christian faith and to oblige them to live and conduct themselves as Christians. All that began in the time of Governor-General Mem de Sá. He sent an honorable married man to each village as captain, giving him his instructions as to what was required of him. Nevertheless, the Fathers got on so poorly with the captains. Every day, there was some dispute or difference of opinion about how to handle the Indians. The Indians got involved with the Fathers against the captains and with the captains against the Fathers to the point where the captains returned to the city and wanted nothing more to do with the Indians. The governor-general was unable to find similar people willing to accept the appointments. Those who did apply for such captaincies were not particularly trustworthy for such a responsibility, so it reverted back to the Jesuit Fathers.

*Reply. So that the Fathers could rid themselves of the irritation of the settlers, who were constantly demanding Indians [to work for them], they asked Governor-General Mem de Sá to place men in the villages to defend the Indians from the outrages being inflicted on them and also to help them in temporal matters. These men behaved in such a way that the Indians grew distressed at being put to work so hard for them and for their friends and at the liberties that they took with their wives and daughters. The other settlers complained because they did not make them available to them as well. Eventually, these men all realized what little profit they were making, became dissatisfied, and abandoned their appointments. Governor-General Manuel Teles wanted to send them back, but neither the bishop nor the city council would agree, owing to the experience that they had already had of what little purpose they served.*

Item 37. After that, the officials of the city council complained to King Sebastião and to the governors-general that the Indians would not give help to the settlers on their estates as had been agreed. Moreover, when the settlers wanted their help in warfare, the Indians refused to answer their demands, as the Fathers would not allow them to take part. For those reasons, the king ordered the Governors-General Luís de Brito, Lourenço da Veiga, and then Manuel Teles not to permit the Fathers any jurisdiction in the villages or over the Indians that inhabited them. They were only to be allowed to teach the Catholic faith. Each of the governors-general and the captains of these villages wanted to put this into effect, with the result that in private the Fathers had to confront many problems. Meanwhile, in public, they declared their opposition to the installation of captains in the villages, alleging that they would depopulate them. [Consequently,] the Fathers remained in the villages and are there still.

*Reply. Owing to these complaints and in pursuit of His Majesty's orders, Lourenço da Veiga went in person to the villages, accompanied by the Crown judge. His purpose was to see for himself how things were run there. As he found that nothing needed to be put right and that the complaints lacked foundation, he left everything as it was and gave no orders for change. The jurisdiction that the Fathers have over the Indians is no more than that of teaching them and giving them penances in church for some public misdemeanor. For that, the bishops have given permission. In all other matters, the villages have their bailiffs, and those are appointed by the governors-general. They are the ones who arrest the Indians and tie them to the stocks, doing so on the advice and direction given by the Fathers. They also set them to work and, if they fail to grow their own food, they reprimand them just as fathers scold their children. As for what the informant once more says about the captains, the answer is as above, and not what he alleges.*

Item 38. The officials of the city council complained to the king that the Fathers had no wish to obey the instructions of the courts and that they kept Indians, as they have bailiffs in the villages. They complained that the Fathers ordered the bailiffs to arrest a number of white men whom, with the bailiffs' help, they planned to hold to ransom, while getting other bailiffs to round up their slaves. They also complained that they thrashed them and put them in the stocks. When the white men complained to the courts about it, they received the answer that no action could be taken against the Fathers.

*Reply. Those bailiffs are appointed by the governors-general. Owing to the dissolute behavior of certain vagrants, the bailiffs were given the task of arresting them and bringing them into the city. It is not right for the informant to put the blame on the Fathers in this regard, for that is not their custom.*

Item 39. The Fathers usually assemble in the villages all the slaves belonging to other people and all the Indians who have got free and run away from their masters, taking refuge among their relatives in the villages. Their masters or their masters' representatives go to get them, bearing warrants from the magistrates. The Fathers answer that they should round them up and take them away, because they, the Fathers, have no obligation to do that. As the Indians have been hidden by their relatives, those who go to round them up cannot find them. If, indeed, they manage to find them, the Fathers refuse to let them take them away, declaring that they are free men and were wrongly held. The Fathers also declare that they will not let them be forcibly enslaved. Their own force in this matter has been so great that, to date, no man has been able to wrest his slave from their control, except in cases where the slave has returned to his house voluntarily. In that way, the Fathers have earned the loathing of the settlers, the bishop, the governor-general, the Crown judge, the comptroller of finances, and all other people in office, whether secular or ecclesiastic.

*Reply. Mem de Sá, who was governor-general of the State [of Brazil], made a law in which he ordered that no Indian who took refuge in the villages where the Jesuit Fathers are present should be handed over to his master until the latter could demonstrate that the slave was legitimately his. There were two reasons for that. The first was the vast and illicit conduct of those who stole Indians from others and then sold them unlawfully, not to mention buying them from those who had no right to sell them, under the rulings of the Court of Conscience. The second reason is that he issued a sentence ordering the captivity of the heathen tribe known as the Caetés.[30] That was because the Caetés had murdered Bishop Pedro Fernandes [Sardinha] and those who were traveling with him aboard a carrack that ran aground. The sentence was carried out ruthlessly and indiscriminately. Indians were captured wherever they were to be found, as though they belonged to that tribe. There were many of them in these villages who had lived there for many years and were not guilty of the*

---

30   The Caeté were a powerful Tupi-speaking people who dominated the coast northward from the São Francisco River. They were hostile to the Portuguese and were responsible for the death of Brazil's first bishop.

*murder. It became necessary to act upon this lawlessness by resorting to the [new] law. The Fathers adhered to the law, and kept to it till the arrival of Manuel Teles. With Father Cristóvão de Gouveia, the Father Visitor of this province, he agreed to a ruling that, from then on, to keep the peace in this land, and because there were no longer so many reasons as during the governorship of Mem de Sá, the Fathers should not gather Indians together in the villages, nor permit entry to any Indian, slave or freedman, who was a fugitive from the settlers. That ruling has been rigidly adhered to till the present time. If some people still complain, it is because they are still living in a world in which, prior to the agreement, nothing was ever updated.*

Item 40. The governor-general, Luís de Brito, was in the village of Santo António, with all the forces of Bahia, intent on waging war on the heathens of the Real River and of Sergipe, because they had killed many white men, bound for Pernambuco, who had run aground at that point, not to mention further harm that they had done. The governor-general sent messages via leading figures to the Fathers who were to be found in the other villages, requesting them to send warriors. The Fathers claimed that they were not in a position to do that and that interpreters should be sent to persuade the Indians. These went, and the Indians confided to them that they were quite prepared to go to war, but that the Fathers had told them privately that they must not go. A whole week was spent sending messages [back and forth], without the Fathers agreeing to the Indians setting out. Finally, the governor-general ordered a legal investigation into what was happening and asked for witnesses to come forward. He then sent a judge and two secretaries to protest to the Fathers and deliver a demand to them, at which point they altered their stance and let the Indians go to war.

*Reply. The Fathers had gathered many Indians together in three villages along the River Real. There, they had built churches and were giving instruction in the Christian faith. The Indians lived there quietly and peacefully. The governor-general, Luís de Brito, was keen to go there, with all the panoply of war, to inspect some ten leagues of land that he had in that area. The Fathers told him that the Indians were peaceful, were preparing to become Christians, and that they placed their trust in the churches that they had there. The coast from Bahia to Pernambuco was now safe for people to come and go by land because they had already made peace with thirty other villages in Sergipe. [They added that,] if he were to proceed in that manner, the Indians would run away in fear, which is, in fact, what happened. The three churches were lost, much to the dismay of those who had worked so hard to found them, and the thirty villages to which they had brought peace rose up again. The governor-general ordered the informant and other captains to pursue the fugitives, and they killed and captured many. In Portugal, this war was adjudged to be unjust, and the captives were ordered to be set free. The governor-general will, no doubt, draw up the legal investigation mentioned by the informant in whatever form he pleases, but it is plain that more credence should be given to what is said by the Fathers and by the Indians, appalled as they are by the brutal treatment that the Indians received in the conflict, for they are made to serve as beasts of burden and as a front-line barrier against opposing troops.*

Item 41. The governor-general and his successors were sometimes subjected to similar allegations, concerning which they had disputes with the Fathers. They drew up legal reports and complained to the king. The same thing happened to Governor-General Manuel Teles, with the result that there was great dissension, as they refused to hand over slaves belonging to others, wanting to set them free through their absolute power over what the Indians said. It is in respect of the Indians and the question of land that all the differences between the two sides exist, which is why the Fathers are so hated in that land. It is impossible to set down all that one could do about these issues, as there is so much.

*Reply. They could not have done the same again to those the informant mentions because Luís de Brito did not go to war again. Nor did Lourenço da Veiga, Manuel Teles, or Francisco de Sousa, as everyone knows. We have already answered what he says about the slaves. God be praised, there are no disputes about land because the courts have given to each his own. We do not believe that we are hated, nor are our good works, and the goodwill of the settlers reveals that. Although the informant does not leave aside any issue that seems relevant to him, not one of them is of any real significance, as can be seen from these replies.*

Item 42. The Fathers usually go to the estates in Bahia to hear the confessions of the people who are scattered about on all the plantations and farmsteads. There, they are made welcome guests. They hear the confessions of blacks from Guinea and of indigenous Indians. They unite in marriage those who are living in sin and who can be married. They convert to Christianity those who are not Christians. In fact, they work hard to make them all lead worthy lives. While carrying out these good works, they inquire in the confessional how they were sold, where they came from, and whether they believe that their sale was carried out legitimately. They tell the Indians that they are free men and cannot be slaves, and that if they wish to return to their villages, they will protect them there and will guarantee their freedom. The result is that the Fathers have caused and continue to cause many of these slaves to run away. They gather them back into their villages, from which their masters are unable to recover them. That leads to great dissension and hatred, and there are many settlers who refuse to allow the Fathers to visit their estates, whilst others forbid their slaves to confess to the Fathers or even speak to them when they go to their estates. The other tasks that they carry out there are not holy enough to counter such simultaneous harmful consequences. Much more could be said about the matter.

*Reply. There was nothing left for the informant to do than to meddle in sacred matters and the secrecy of the confessional. What he says does not happen, nor can he produce a single Indian who for that reason escaped from his master and headed back to the villages. The Fathers compile a register of those that they baptize, those that they join in marriage, and those whose confessions they hear. There always exists, therefore, a record, just like those kept by parish priests. When they join people in marriage, and often they join freedmen to slaves, they question them closely as to whether they are freedmen or slaves, lest the validity of the marriage be compromised owing to a mistake relating to either person. That has given rise to what the informant deludedly imagines, as this way many freedmen could be those whom he deems to be slaves. He was the one who refused to allow the Fathers onto his estate. The other settlers are very happy to call the Fathers in, as their experience tells them that the spiritual benefits received by the slaves and other workers leads them to be more peaceful, more steadfast, and better at their work. This was [even] true of the informant's estate, which the Fathers visited many times while the informant was in Portugal.*

Item 43. There is the question as to whether the Fathers interfered in the methods of selling Indians from the interior and whether they were determined that in no way should anyone put an Indian to work as a slave or even as a freedman and that they should all remain in their villages. The issue involves their blocking of the system agreed with the Board of Conscience[31] on the sale of Indians and on the best circumstances under which slaves should in all conscience be kept. In those respects, they are gravely at odds with the settlers. Fully informed by the above-mentioned court about the ways in which they conduct their lives, the king has given permission for these Indians to be enslaved. He deems that they are incapable of being free men and that they deserve to be slaves, owing to the dreadful crimes that they have committed against the Portuguese, killing and eating many hundreds, even thousands, of them, including a bishop and many priests.

*Reply. It is quite true that the Fathers have always sought legitimate means by which the settlers might improve their way of life. They did not, however, succeed in satisfying everybody, as some wish to claim that they have souls, unlike the slaves, whom they hold in low esteem. As for what the informant says about the Indians being incapable of being free men, and that they deserve to be slaves, he reveals scant knowledge of theology. Ample evidence of this, that all can recognize, is the fact that he states that the king allows the Indians to be enslaved.*

Item 44. Furthermore, the kings have been informed that the State of Brazil cannot survive without many slaves being taken from the indigenous pagan

---

31  Mesa da Consciência (Board of Conscience) was a Portuguese royal council that administered ecclesiastical and theological matters, including missionary affairs.

population and put to work on the plantations and estates. Without that provision, nobody would want to live there. That is a factor that the Fathers do
not wish to take into account, as they are the ones who profit from these heathens, as they usually get them to do their fishing, sail their boats, and go
hunting for them. On their farms, they look after the cows, mares, and pigs.
Where there is building work to do, they perform every skill for them. They
work for them as potters, making the roof tiles, floor tiles, and crockery that
are needed. They work for them by driving their ox-carts and by clearing
and tilling their land. In winter, they comb the beaches for them, looking for
amber, which is very profitable for the Fathers and something that they do
not want others to profit from. I recognize that you are already suspicious of
me and, therefore, I shall say no more, as you will not believe me. Nor shall I
repeat what I have already said, unless it is in obedience to your command.

*Reply. The only solution for the State of Brazil is to have large numbers of pagans
living in their villages around the plantations and estates. That way, there would be
men to work and to resist the enemy, be they French, English, or Aimorés,*[32] *who
have done so much harm and continue to do so. It is also necessary to restrain the
blacks from Guinea: there are many of them and their only fear is of the Indians.
The way in which to achieve that is to arrange as His Majesty has commanded, even
though it is not carried out, namely, that there should not be any slaves, as in Peru.
That is because as long as there exists the opportunity to put them in their pockets
and wear their skins, there cannot be enough Indians to go round and not be used
up [in that process], as experience has shown. The informant himself can bear clear
witness to this because large numbers [of such Indians] are his. Those others, whom
he claims that we put to work, are our slaves and are mainly [blacks] from Guinea, as
he admits in Item 23 above. There are also some freedmen whom we employ, as many
settlers do, and we pay them for their services. All together, they do not amount to
half a shipload of the ships of slaves that he has dispatched for sale in Pernambuco
and other captaincies, though this territory has a vast need for working men. As
for the amber, it would be wonderful, if this were true. The activity was no affront
to anyone, and two Indians were sufficient to carry it out. If they occasionally find
some, it is not for us but for their friends, for the decoration of their churches and
to provide for the sick. If they give us a small piece of it, it is at a fair price. The
reason for all these assertions, insofar as one can derive anything from them, was
solely to set His Majesty against us, so that he would no longer grant us any favors.
What, however, comforts us is that cor regis in manu Dei est*[33] *and not in that
of the informant, and that quodcumque volverit verset illud.*[34] *Nonetheless, we are*

---

32    The Aimorés were a Gê-speaking people who dominated the region of Ilhéus, south of Bahia.
      They were considered particularly hostile by the Portuguese.
33    The king's heart is in God's hand.
34    Whatever He ponders on, may He turn it to good account.

*greatly indebted to him for warning us to look to ourselves and to behave strictly as we should before God and before men, recognizing that there will be no shortage of people who, after the manner of the informant, will subject us to similar scrutiny. It is, therefore, essential that we should live in such a way as to emerge blameless.*

*I, Marçal Beliarte, Provincial of the Society of Jesus in this State of Brazil, having noted these chapters written by Gabriel Soares de Sousa, approached a number of Fathers with long-standing knowledge of Brazil and, in particular, of the parts that applied to them, owing to their direct experience of all these matters. I required them to give answers about what they knew concerning their own involvement and then showed their replies to other Fathers of long standing, who also had information on such matters. They all agreed with the answers given. To strengthen our case, I required them all to add their signatures to mine on this document and that, in fact, has been done. Bahia de Todos os Santos, 13 September 1592.*

> *Inácio Tolosa Marçal Beliarte*
> *Rodrigo de Freitas*
> *Quirino Caixa, Luís da Fonseca*
> *Fernão Cardim*

## 5. The Will and Testament of a *Bandeirante*

Will and testament of Martim Rodrigues (1603) and his inventory (1612).

*While the missionaries and the colonists in the sugar-planting regions of the coast battled over the control of the indigenous inhabitants, on the inland plateau of São Vicente, especially around the town of São Paulo, Portuguese colonists and their mameluco children had been exploring the interior for gold and capturing the native population, ostensibly to convert them, but enslaving them as workers as well. Formed into expeditions or* bandeiras, *their columns penetrated the interior, often following the major rivers. Eventually, they began to raid the Jesuit missions in Spanish-controlled Paraguay. These expeditions became a way of life and a source of livelihood for many of the* paulistas, *or people of São Paulo who sought their living in the backlands, as the following will and testament reveals. (From* Inventários e testamentos, *44 vols. [São Paulo: Archivo do Estado de São Paulo, 1920–77] v. 2 [1920], pp. 5–107.)*

### *Jesus (and) Mary*

In the name of God, Amen. Know all to whom this testament comes that in the year of the birth of Our Lord Jesus Christ of 1602 on 12 days of the month of March of this year in the *sertão* of the Paracatú River, I Martim Rodrigues decided to make this testament, being of sound mind and in good health and in full possession of my judgment, all of which God has given me. I do this not knowing what God has in store for me, and I make here declarations and unburden my conscience for the good of my soul.

First I commit my soul to God, Our Lord who redeemed it with his most precious blood, death, and passion, and to the Virgin, Our Lady, his blessed mother, I ask that she be my advocate and representative and to seek from her blessed Son pardon for my sins and that he receive me in glory. Amen.

Second, I declare that I am married to Suzanna Rodrigues and I am a resident of the town of São Paulo, and with her I have four legitimate daughters – Maria Tenoria, Anna da Veiga, Elvira Rodrigues, and Suzanna who are my heirs. I also declare that I have a bastard daughter named Joana Rodrigues that I have married to José Brante and I have given her a certain amount of property that my wife and I assigned to her and for which a document was drawn up that I report here.

I also declare that I have two boys that I accept as my sons who are bastards that I had in the *sertão*. . . .

I name as my executors Balthazar Gonçalves and Manuel Borrego, and my son-in-law Clemente Alvares who I ask for the love of God to care for my soul when Our Lord wishes to take me from the present life. I ask that my body be buried in the convent of Our Lady of Carmel in the town of São Paulo, and on the day of my funeral there be a sung mass with nine prayers . . . I also ask for three masses to be said in honor of the Holy Trinity.

I ask for three masses be said for Our Lady of Carmel and two for Our Lady of the Conception and two for our Lady of the Rosary, and two for Our Lady of Montserrate and these will be recited in her holy house in São Paulo. I ask for two masses to be said for blessed Holy Mary Magadalene. I also ask for prayed masses to be said in honor of St. Peter and St. Paul, St. Anthony, and St. Martinho.

I declare to unburden my conscience I ask that from my third [portion] of my estate, forty *cruzados* be taken and awarded as follows:[35]

2$,000 to the Brotherhood of the Holy Sacrament

2$,000 to the Brotherhood of Our Lady of the Rosary

2$,000 to the Brotherhood of Our Lady of Carmel

2$,000 to the Brotherhood of Our Lady of the Conception in the town of Tanhahe

2$,000 to the Brotherhood of Our Lady of Montserrate in the town of São Paulo

---

35  Portuguese law provided that the estate of the deceased be divided into three portions, one for the heirs, one for the surviving spouse, and one that could be freely disposed by the deceased. A cruzado was a coin worth four hundred réis; forty cruzados equal 16$000 réis.

Give to the Fathers of the Company of Jesus [Jesuits] 2,000 and 1,000 to the Brotherhood of St. Anthony and another 1,000 to the Brotherhood of St. Sebastian; and 2,000 to the Holy House of Mercy [Misericórdia] to be distributed to those it deems the most needy.

I declare that I took from Francisco de Espinosa, resident in the town of [São Paulo] ... a certain amount of goods and I sold a part of them and have received receipts from my creditors and from my estate. I owe him up to eighty *cruzados* ...

I declare that if anyone claims that I owe them something and can show my signature that they be believed and the debt accepted. I declare that I have in my home a book of my accounts of what I owe and they be given credit and that my debts be satisfied.

I leave as custodian and tutor of my daughters my wife Suzanna Rodrigues so long as she is unmarried and if she marries, I leave as custodian my son-in-law Clemente Alvares who I ask to do this well because I have confidence in him.

I have declared above that I have two boys, my bastard sons, and I leave my wife Suzanna Rodrigues as their curator and if she does not wish to accept this position, I ask that Clemente Alvares accept it, and that he indoctrinate them [in the Catholic faith] and that when they are of age that he will teach them to read and write and will teach them his craft [*oficio*] or have them taught other skills that he thinks appropriate.

I order that if Our Lord God wishes to take me from the present life here in the *sertão* that the gentiles of Brazil [Indians] that belong to me both slaves and "of service" not be sold, and that they be delivered to Balthesar Gonçalves who will take them to the town of São Paulo to my heirs at their expense and that if he asks to be paid for this service, he be compensated as is proper.[36]

I order that anything that remains from my portion after the aforementioned bequests are made be provided to my bastard sons ... and be divided in a brotherly fashion between them.

I also declare that five masses be said in honor of the five wounds of Our Lord Jesus Christ; two masses in honor of my Guardian Angel; a mass for God's faithful; five masses for Our Lady of Carmel; and ten masses for the souls in purgatory; and three masses for all my benefactors.

And the testator states that this testament is completed, and he ordered me, Manuel de Soveral, the scribe of this encampment [*arraial*] for the discovery of gold, silver, and other metals, to write it, and he asked that the judicial officers of His Majesty carry out its provisions and that he revokes

---

36 Indians not captured in just war and thus liable to enslavement were legally held or "administered" in a temporary servitude.

all previous wills and codicils, and that only this will be valid as his last wish. And in faith and witness of this truth, he signed, and I, the abovementioned scribe signed with him as did the other witnesses, Antonio Gonçalves Davide, Sebastião Peres Caleiro, Manuel Machado, Diogo de Oliveira Gago, Francisco Ferreira, Francisco Alvares Corrêa, Miguel Gonçalves, all residents in the captaincy of São Vicente. And, the testator declares that to clarify which of the Indians are free and which are captives that the certificates of register for each be consulted.

## Inventory of Martim Rodrigues Tenorio

The year of Our Lord Jesus Christ of 1612 on the 18th day of the month of June of that year in the jurisdiction of the villa of São Paulo of the captaincy of São Vicente on the coast of Brazil, etc. in the district that is called Ibirapoeira in the houses and property that remain of Martim Rodrigues where Bernardo de Quadros, judge of orphans of this town in confirmation of the obligations of his office, ordered me as notary to make this inventory of his property in that the said Martim Rodrigues has gone to the *sertão* and it is said that he has died there. Before me, he administered an oath to Suzanna Rodrigues, the surviving widow to state all property that remained from her husband to be evaluated in this inventory, both movable and fixed property. She promised to do so and since she cannot sign her name, she asked me, the notary, to do so for her. I, Simão Borges, scribe for orphans, did it.

### Title of "peças" [slaves]

A *negra* of the Guaya nation who says she is a slave of the expedition of Domingos Rodrigues of Paraupava who with her three children are evaluated at 22$000

#### Temiminó Slaves

Esperança with a small child (she is unmarried)

Luiza with four children; Gaspar already an adolescent [*moço*]; Marqueza, adolescent; Mecia, a young woman; and Felipa, a child of six years

Thomé, single, already grown

An old man named Martim

A young man named Balthesar

A youth named Pedro who is said to be a son of the deceased Martim Rodrigues

A black [*negra*] of the Tamoyo nation named Geneva with a child evaluated at 27$000

A young Tamoyo man named Cazão 20$000

## Clothing

| | |
|---|---:|
| A used brown cape decorated with *bertanjol* | 1,500 |
| A suit of rough cloth decorated with lace, jacket and breeches valued at | 4,000 |
| A doublet of linen, lined and quilted | 1,000 |
| A cloak of rough Florentine cloth decorated with colored lace | 3,200 |
| A loose coat of baize valued at | 3,000 |
| Some used boots of black Cordovan | 160 |
| 2 pair Codovan shoes, one black, one white | 200 |
| Some cowhide boots valued at | 400 |
| Two pair pigskin shoes | 200 |
| Some deerskin shoes | 120 |
| Some pigskin slippers and other of buckskin | 200 |

## Tools

| | |
|---|---:|
| Six scythes each valued at 2 tostões | 1,200 |
| Five hoes valued at | 1,000 |
| Another hoe, new, valued at | 240 |
| Two wedges [*cunhas*] | 200 |
| An eared hammer | 120 |

## Riding Tack

| | |
|---|---:|
| A saddle with its stirrups and seat | 4,000 |
| An old bit and bridle | 320 |
| A small ax | 80 |
| A pan valued at | 2,500 |
| A large crate and lock | 2,200 |
| Two *arrobas* of cotton | 1,000 |
| A large cedar desk | 500 |

## Cattle

| | |
|---|---:|
| A yearling with a black head | 700 |
| A tawny yearling female | 700 |
| A cow and calf | 1,100 |
| A black yearling with a white tail | 800 |
| A red cow, pregnant | 800 |

[Listing continues with a description of sixty-one head of cattle, including cows, young males, oxen, and calves evaluated at a total of 51,640]

Horses

| | |
|---|---:|
| A roan horse | 2,000 |
| A roan mare with a red female colt ... with a white blaze and another colt, tawny | 7,000 |

Swine

| | |
|---|---:|
| 26 head of swine males and females, each valued at | 10,000 |

Books

| | |
|---|---:|
| A book entitled *Retabulo da Vida de Cristo* valued at | 480 |
| *Chronica do Grão Capitão*, old, valued at | 320 |
| A book entitled *Instruccão de Confessores* valued at 4 reales | |
| A book entitled *Mysterios da Paixão* valued at | 200 |

Farm Plot [*roça*]

| | |
|---|---:|
| A new field with a *carazal* | 10,000 |
| Another field with cotton planted | 6,000 |

# 6

## THE WORLD OF THE ENGENHOS

*Sugar cane was introduced to Brazil from Madeira and São Tomé and, by the 1540s, was beginning to flourish along the coast, especially in Pernambuco and Bahia, but also in the southern captaincy of São Vicente. The sugar mills (engenhos) required land, labor, and capital. The land was seized or conquered; the labor was first obtained by enslaving the indigenous peoples, which, as we have seen, led to conflicts with the missionaries, and then by the importation of African slaves. The capital was obtained at first from Portuguese and foreign investors and subsequently was raised from other activities in the colony itself. The sugar estates were complex combinations of agriculture and industry because of the need to mill the cane imme-diately after harvesting it to produce sugar. By 1612, Brazil had 192 engenhos in operation and was exporting more than 10,000 tons a year to Europe. During the seventeenth century, Brazil was the greatest producer of sugar in the Atlantic world.*

### 1. Excerpt from a Letter from the Administrator of Engenho, São Jorge de Erasmo

*Among the first investors in the Brazilian sugar industry was the German bank-ing firm of Erasmo Schetz, which was well established in Antwerp. Schetz funded the creation of an engenho in São Vicente and employed a Flemish agent to run the operation. That man was probably Heliodoro Eobano, whose letter of 1548 is published here. This unsigned letter reveals details about the organization and oper-ations of an early sugar estate. Indigenous people were still the principal workers, but Africans were beginning to appear, especially as skilled workers. Sugarcane was supplied to the mill by cane farmers (called moradores here), a class of farmers that became characteristic of the Brazilian sugar industry. This letter suggests that the organization of Brazilian sugar estates had previously developed elsewhere, proba-bly in Madeira and São Tomé, and even in the mid-sixteenth century was already in full operation in Brazil. This letter was first published by the Belgian historian Edy Stols in "Um dos primeiros documentos sobre o engenho dos Schetz em São Vicente," Revista de História, 76 (1968), pp. 407–20.*

Laus Deo. 13 May 1548, in Santos on the island of São Vicente on the coast of Brazil.

Honorable and most generous sirs, I pledge to you my willing service! It is my pleasant duty to report to you that, with the help of God, we have arrived here safely. However, we landed in very dangerous conditions, as our ship almost sank in the river here. Much of the cargo was ruined, including some of ours, on which I am sending you a report. Fortunately, by God's grace, things have turned out well, as you will discover from the bearer of this letter.

First of all, I have to inform you that, to date, I have not received from you any reply to the letter that I sent to you from Cabo Verde. I trust that I shall receive it very soon, as we are from day to day expecting the arrival of the ship from Portugal that was chartered by our freighters and which, to date, has yet to arrive. However, a ship chartered by Martim Frera [*Ferreira*] has arrived for Luís de Góis, so that he can load it with sugar. It too did not bring any letters. People say that all the letters were thrown overboard having been read by the factor and by Joseppa Adoria [*Giuseppe Adorno*]. We all [believe that] this land is full of thieves and that they cannot be trusted. As for the land itself, it would be a good, sound place to be, if its inhabitants were honest and if there were true justice. That is because until now everything has been in the hands of scoundrels. Most of them are exiled convicts and will cheat people when the time comes for payment. The land is very suitable for the sale of goods and at a good price, but collecting payment is very difficult. If, therefore, time does not bring better inhabitants and better justice, then trade can only be conducted with those who own sugar plantations or similar estates. That is because there is no money in circulation here, and credit has to be extended for one year, though that can mean waiting a good two years for payment. As a result, plantation owners pay all their workforce in kind. With a good stock of such goods, they can load [on to ships] all the sugar produced on the plantation and do that all year-round.

We were recommended to meet Pedro Rouzée [*Peter Roesel*] here, for whom our presence was not very welcome. Thank God, we have so far received little advice or assistance from him.

Besides that, there is little to report about the aforesaid cargo, except in respect of your declaration relating to the plantation, and here that has been checked. This estate is a very fine one, though previous factors have tried too much to serve their own ends and have allowed a lot of land to fall into the hands of the settlers. Pedro Rouzée will provide a fuller, more detailed account of that, as well as of other matters that have been even better covered up, when once there is a better system of justice in this country. That is because, to date, every deal is done by [granting or receiving] favors. Some of your own land has been surrendered. As far as justice is concerned, the factor, Pedro Rouzée, was firmly in opposition. I hope that we shall soon have better news.

As for the buildings here, all those that we have are of good quality and sturdy enough to resist any adversaries. That is because Pedro Rouzée has carried out a lot of construction, namely a very large house with six frontal windows, as well as slave quarters and a smithy. All these buildings are fortified. There are also two other very fine and sturdy houses covered in roof tiles, just like those built by Brás de Rocha. These houses all stand on a hill and are all close together. The purpose of that is to ensure that our adversaries should not encounter any estate that is as strong, and that no plantation should have better houses. The result is that the [houses on the] plantation can easily be defended with three or four light cannon. The factor here has, therefore, done good work.

As for the sugar mill, it is old and close to collapse and must be rebuilt this year. The wheel is also close to collapse. It is too far too worn and is sometimes submerged by the water when the tide sweeps up the channel, which greatly hinders the milling of the sugar. For that reason, the mill must be moved upstream, and a good one built that will stand on the slope of the hill.

The factor cannot make a start till he receives news from you, to know how you feel about it. It will be a costly operation, and the mill must be made of lath and plaster walls to make it last a very long time. This year alone, the old mill has undergone structural changes and repairs that have cost more than a hundred cruzados. That was due to the poor condition it was in, and because it had to be given a new thatched roof. This has been an unlucky year for the rollers in the grinding mechanism: they had to be remade because the iron pins would not support them.

A lot of time has, therefore, been lost. Moreover, a number of settlers went away because the time was not ripe for the current sailing, and because a more suitable time is around the month of March. Nevertheless, they still came at some cost to themselves, with the result that a lot of sugar was produced, not only by this estate but also by the settlers and others. The outcome was approximately nine hundred *arrobas* of sugar, of which some four hundred *arrobas* are being sent to Portugal for our freighters.

This year, no goods were sent to the factor with which to pay our workers, yet he is bound to award sugar or a letter of credit to them. The factor has credited me for what I have done for him and for the workers to whom I have paid the sum of one hundred and twenty-three thousand five hundred réis [123$500]. That sum is for António Bicudo to collect over there [in Lisbon]. The factor could have awarded me some sugar as he has done for others, for in the current sailing he has awarded three hundred *arrobas*.

The estate incurred many debts this year. There is a great shortage of food supplies here, and none have been received from Portugal for a long time. The meat that I brought over here to the estate was totally ruined by the sea water, as we did not manage to get it out of the ships. Consequently, it remained in the water inside the ship until the ship raised anchor. To keep the estate running, there can be no better sustenance than salted meat and fish, especially dried codfish and other fish that are dried over there in abundance and at low cost, not forgetting Flemish and Dutch cheeses. Our workers derive little nourishment from local food, for all they get is manioc meal. Sometimes it is eaten with a piece of salted fish, when it is available. I hope, therefore, that better provisions will arrive very soon.

As for the slave force that we have here, they are very good, and we have roughly one hundred and thirty head of them, both male and female. Half of them do no work, as they are either children or too old to be of any use. In this country, there do not exist better slave forces because many slaves perform skilled work in the mill in the boiling and refining processes. There are also seven or eight blacks here from Guinea. The latter are all craftsmen, thus one black is the foreman in charge of sugar production [*mestre de açúcar*], a position for which our shippers customarily reward a foreman in Madeira (?) with wages of thirty thousand réis, a sum that can be a great annual saving. It would appear that this black has recently been producing better sugar than the sugar that the factor is currently shipping to Lisbon. A second black is in charge of sugar purging and, along with two others, who work as kettlemen on the boilers, increases our output by four *arrobas* a month.

We have, therefore, very few paid workers on the plantation but have many indigenous local slaves of the kind that other plantations do not have, so that they have to pay wages to [many] white workers. Yet this plantation still needs seven or eight male slaves. There is a shortfall, and we cannot manage without them. That is because in one year, we cannot succeed in making enough charcoal, so that we have to buy them from the settlers. That is a considerable expense and costs twenty-five to thirty reals per bushel. There is, therefore, no greater expense on a sugar plantation than on wood ash. I calculate that forty to fifty ducats have been spent on the said charcoal. These [seven or eight] slaves would eliminate such costs, would be present for a long time, and could carry out other tasks in the main house.

As for the land and the canes that grow on it, I have to inform you that our estate has a very good supply of them and they increase every year. The lands are cleared every year so that fresh sugarcane can be planted. This year, some thirty-two *tarefas*[1] were planted on our property, and that will produce

1 A *tarefa* is an areal measure equal to 30 *braças*, or an area of 4,356 square meters. It is also, theoretically, the amount of cane that can be milled by an engenho in one day.

more or less four hundred *arrobas*. Pedro Rouzée also planted one or two areas of sugar cane for milling in the coming July. They have been there for only a year and need to be there for seventeen or eighteen months before they are ready for milling. That, we hope, will be in July. There is also the cane planted by our neighbors [moradores], so that next year there will be roughly more than a thousand *arrobas* ready for harvesting. All of that can be garnered in, provided that the estate is well equipped and that it does not have to pay its workers with [credit in] sugar.

Pedro Rouzée has bought from a settler by the name of Barigo a fine, large piece of land situated close to our estate and which was already amply planted with sugar cane. This year, it will not be ready for milling but it can be planted [with more cane]. It will also make a slight saving, for we shall not need to buy cane from the settlers. People also say that there is a cottage on that land with a double frontage in which there is room for four or five slaves who would not do anything except clearing land to grow food for the estate. The estate itself has few such [vegetable] plots and cannot spare land for growing food in that way. However, it would be very costly if we were to buy such food supplies from the settlers. A cake made from manioc, which is the root of a bush, costs one hundred réis and can keep a person in food for three or four days. The estate, therefore, cannot release any such land [for the purpose of growing food].

But land belonging to settlers is well situated in relation to the estate. Nearly all those patches of land have been stolen [from us]. The factors have let them be taken because they were all Portuguese and conspired together among themselves. In the past, your cause has been poorly served by the courts. However, people say that those pieces of land are easily recoverable, and that if the estate is to continue, it needs such land and should profit from it. That is because there is nothing to be gained by milling the sugar cane of the settlers for them, not to mention the costs of buying charcoal and paying wages to the workers on the plantation. They say that it is essential to plant so much sugar cane that there is no need for the cane grown by the settlers. Accordingly, the factor is now about to use force to take back that land from them. Alternatively, he will set fire to their cane. They cannot take their sugarcane to any other plantation than our estate. For that reason, they will readily release those patches of land and at little cost to us. They will be forced to do so, for it is very irksome to do the milling for the settlers and also for the sugar plantations.

## 2. Cane Farmer Contracts

*The Brazilian sugar industry was characterized by the presence of cane farmers who farmed sugarcane and supplied it to the mills under a variety of sharecropping and other arrangements. Some of these* <u>lavradores de cana</u> *were independent and wealthy land and slave owners, whereas others were modest farmers who lived at the whim of the mill owners. This arrangement, however, allowed many people to participate in the sugar economy and it shared the risks and costs of plantership. The contracts between the mill owners and the cane farmers were usually oral, but on rare occasions, they were written down in a legal form and registered with a notary public. Presented here are two rare examples from the mid-seventeenth century that survive in the papers of Engenho Suassuna in Pernambuco.* (From Arquivo do Engenho Suassuna in the Arquivo da Direitoria de Obras, Fiscalização, e Serviços Públicos [Recife].)

## (a) Lavrador Contract of 1638

Know ye all who see this public instrument of a contract of sharing [*escritura de partido*] for the term of nine years and nine harvests completed that in the year Our Lord Jesus Christ of 1638 on 25th day in the month of October of that year on the borders of Suassuna and the engenho and estate of Our Lady of the Assumption of which João de Barros Correia is the master; and he being present as one party and the other being Jorge Saraiva, a cane farmer of the said engenho, both said to me as notary in the presence of the witnesses noted below the following: that the said master gives, in fact, has given to the said cane farmer a unit of cane land (*partido de canas*) in which the said master has planted fifty-five tarefas of cane along the River Suassuna Maricujé, with the obligation that the said cane farmer will plant more cane than will be necessary to provide to the engenho forty tarefas as much as the engenho can mill, placing it there at his cost; and this unit is given him for the term of nine years and nine harvests and two months to vacate and the first year and harvest will begin in 1641 and will extend consecutively for all the remaining harvests until the said nine harvests and two months to vacate are completed. And, having completed them, the said property will freely belong to the said master along with any improvements, and the said cane farmer will leave them improved and not worsened. The sugar that God provides will be divided at the fifth (*quinto*) that is, three measures to the master and two to the said cane farmer without any other obligation to the cane farmer except as stated, to transport the cane to his mill and he, the Master, will be obliged to mill the cane as much as is ready and for this he will maintain the engenho in working order (*moente e corrente*) and equipped with all necessary to make sugar; and the cane farmer can plant in the lands of the said engenho his vegetables and small plots (*roças*) that are necessary and pasture his oxen and horses, as many as he may have where he lives and if he wishes to have them in the pastures of the said engenho, he, the cane farmer, can bring them. In this way, the two parties are contracted and each obliges himself to fulfill this written agreement as is stated and declared and they oblige their persons and goods, especially the master of the engenho. And they sign the said document here. I, Simão Varela, notary public, judicial, and scribe of the town of Olinda and its district in the captaincy of Pernambuco, etc. [registered] in my book of notarial acts.

### (b) Lavrador Contract of 1656

We, João de Barros Correia, lord of the engenho Suassuna under the invocation of Our Lady of the Assumption and I, Antônio de Sousa Ferreira, resident in the parish of Santo Amaro, that we are in agreement concerning a piece of cane land, that with the favor of God, the said Antonio de Sousa Ferreira wants to plant in his lands alongside those of the said engenho in the following manner and form: that the master of the said engenho is obligated by this contract to supply all the cane necessary placed in the lands where it will be planted so long as the said Antônio de Sousa Ferreira does not have from his farming the cane necessary; in addition, the said master of the engenho will pay him one third of all the plants that the said Antônio de Sousa Ferreira produces today and forever; and, in addition, the master of the engenho obliges himself to supply one third of all the carts to transport the cane to the mill from which the sugar will be divided at the fifth, that is, of each ten parts, one will be taken for the tithe and the rest will be separated three parts for the estate and two for the cane farmer; and the master of the engenho will be obligated to mill in every harvest all of the cane it is capable of milling as long as the said lavrador desires. And the said Antônio de Sousa Ferreira is obliged to supply all the cane planted in the said lands with the above stated obligations and because in conformity and due to the desire of both parties we have agreed in this way, we have asked Father Domingos Coelho Diniz to make this contract in two copies so that each may have his own, and we ask those who sign below to serve as witnesses; they are Luís da Silva and Manuel Moreira. Written today, seven of June of 1656 years. João de Barros Correa, Antônio de Souza Ferreira, Father Domingos Coelho Diniz, Luís de Silva, Manuel Moreira.

### 3. Opportunity for Success: Ambrósio Fernandes Brandão, Great Things of Brazil

*By the early seventeenth century, as the sugar industry flourished, the relative importance of Brazil within the economy of the Portuguese empire began to rise. Voluntary immigrants from Portugal and forced immigrants from Africa carried in the slave trade began to swell the population and to complicate its social organization.*

*One of the most informative and penetrating commentaries on the colony from this period was written by a New Christian sugar planter named Ambrósio Fernandes Brandão in the form of five dialogues between "Brandônio," an old and well-informed resident of Brazil, and "Alviano," a newcomer. These "Dialogues on the Greatness of Brazil," composed in about 1618, were a kind of promotional brochure designed to celebrate the colony's potential, but they also serve as a detailed commentary on the social and political organization of Brazil and on its problems and potential. The excerpts reproduced here describe the wealth of sugar planters and merchants and reflect the growing importance of the colony within the Portuguese empire as perceived by its residents.* (Excerpts from Ambrósio Fernandes Brandão, *Dialogues on the Great Things of Brazil*, translated and annotated by Frederick Holden Hall, William F. Harrison, and Dorothy Winters Welker [Albuquerque: University of New Mexico Press, 1987], pp. 131–53).

## Dialogue III

In Which Is Discussed the Trade in Sugar, Brazilwood, Cotton, and Timber

*There are six ways to get rich in Brazil, according to Brandônio. Dialogue III describes four of these ways. Before he is fairly launched on a description of the first of them (the sugar industry), Brandônio digresses to generalize about the relative potentials of Brazil and India as sources of wealth. The Dialogue considers the profitable industries of Brazil – varying somewhat from the title – as (1) sugar, (2) trade, (3) brazilwood, (4) cotton, and (5) timber. One additional means of making money is crowded in – the gathering of ambergris. If the colonists would properly utilize the resources of their land, Brandônio asserts, it would bring in far more revenue than India.*

*This discussion of economic factors and of the India trade shows the author's knowledgeability as a financier and practical economist, familiar with large-scale business operations both colonial and peninsular. He moves with ease from the oriental trade in spices and other "drugs" to smuggling operations in Peru, methods of exporting brazilwood, or the cause of the decline in the price of cotton. He is full of aggressive plans for increasing the profit from the new land, but like many of his modern* confrères, *he complains that the government is slow to move. Brandônio's realistic account of the sugar industry reminds the reader that the author was himself a sugar-mill owner. He must have experienced at first hand the luxurious living he describes as characteristic of the wealthy class in the Northeast.*

*As a businessman, Brandônio is interested in every natural resource of his adopted country, but his interest is not purely an economic one. For instance, in his catalogue of the available timber, he names an astonishing number of trees, evaluating them not only for their commercial uses but also for their grandeur as an element in the rural scene. Obviously, this was a businessman who delighted to spend his leisure hours exploring the new land, observing as minutely as he could, taking careful notes, and, no doubt, extolling the virtues of the country to anyone who was willing to listen to him.*

*Perhaps Brandão feared that the financial data and the long lists of products would seem dull to some readers. As a relief, he has inserted several odd and interesting anecdotes, apparently from his own experience. The significance of these is often carefully underscored by the comments of Alviano, that useful interlocutor, always on hand to make sure the reader does not miss the point or take the wrong side of the argument.*

BRANDÔNIO   So as not to be thought negligent, I have been waiting for you quite a while already, enjoying the cool breeze that blows in here from the sea.

ALVIANO   An unexpected caller made me incur the guilt of being late, but it is not too late for us to begin our conversation, in which we had decided to discuss the richness, fertility, and bounty of this Brazil. I beg you, therefore, tell me whatever you know of these things, for here I am, eager to hear what you have to say.

BRANDÔNIO   The riches of this New World, and likewise its fertility and bounty, are so great that I do not know with which of them to make a start. But, since all of them deserve consideration, I shall make a salad of them, as attractive and tasty as I can. Now to begin, I will say that the wealth of Brazil consists of six things, from which its settlers grow rich, and these are: first, the production of sugar; second, trade; third, the wood they call brazil [brazilwood]; fourth, cotton and timber; fifth, the growing of food crops; sixth and last, cattle raising. Of all these things, the principal nerve and substance of the wealth of the land is the production of sugar.

ALVIANO   That wealth which comes only from making sugar cannot be of much importance, for we see that the inhabitants of our eastern India grow rich from many different things, such as a great quantity of most useful drugs, very fine cloth, gold, silver, pearls, diamonds, rubies and topazes, musk, ambergris, silks, indigo, and other goods with which every year the ships come back to Spain heavily laden.

BRANDÔNIO   It is true enough that all those things, and still others, are brought back from those parts; but, just the same, I shall endeavor to prove that taking nothing more than sugar out of Brazil is a greater thing, and brings in more profit to His Majesty's Treasury, than all those East Indies.

ALVIANO   You are bold to venture so far, and to attempt such a thing seems an act of madness, for it is as far from being demonstrable as are the heavens from the earth. I beg you, therefore, not to let anyone hear such a proposition from you, for most men would think it ridiculous.

BRANDÔNIO   I shall not be moved to retract what I have said by all those dark looks you are giving me. Rather, I intend to prove clearly what I am stating – just as I did on another occasion in the Kingdom, before their Lordships the Governors, in the year '97 [1597]. For you are not going to deny to me that every year, three, four, and sometimes five ships go from the Kingdom out to India, and come back from there laden with merchandise.

ALVIANO   That is right.

BRANDÔNIO   Likewise, you will not doubt that each one of these ships, from the time its keel is laid until it is under sail, costs His Majesty's Treasury around forty thousand cruzados.

ALVIANO   Nor do I deny that.

BRANDÔNIO   And that likewise every year, His Majesty sends out in them about two hundred thousand cruzados in cash – reales of eight and four – for the purchase of India pepper.

ALVIANO   And very often more.

BRANDÔNIO   And likewise, in wages to the soldiers and seamen who enlist to go out to India, in housing allowances for his officials, in bonuses to gentlemen and other individuals, he pays out a great deal of money.

ALVIANO   There is no doubt of that.

BRANDÔNIO   You must also be aware that every one of those ships, after it has returned safely from India laden with merchandise, brings His Majesty – aside from the pepper it carries – from forty-five to fifty *contos de réis* [45:000$000–50:000$000] (and the ships are let publicly at about that sum to persons who bid for them). At the present time, this amount is considerably less, so that His Majesty gains little from it, because of discounts that are made at the India House. Add to this fact that often no more than one or two of the ships get back to the Kingdom safely.

ALVIANO   That can be granted; but beyond that money which, as you have said, His Majesty gets from the ship contracts, his ministers collect freight charges for his Treasury on those same ships. That must amount to quite a sum.

BRANDÔNIO   The freight charges from each ship bring His Majesty's Treasury some three *contos de réis* [3:000$000], and it was at that price that a friend of mine contracted for them in '601 [1601]. Out of those three contos, the viceroy in India grants so many exemptions from freight charges to private persons that almost all the profit is eaten up by those and similar things, whence it follows that His Majesty pockets very little money from the freight charges.

ALVIANO  But how can it be that ships of such great tonnage bring in so little from freight?

BRANDÔNIO  The cause of this is the many stowage privileges that His Majesty grants on them. The captain has his own cabin and storeroom and other accommodations that are always reserved for him. Likewise with the pilot, the mate, the boatswain, the boatswain's mate, and the sailors, for all these have quarters assigned to them, and even the ship's boy and the cabin boy have their own. Thus, the quarters that are distributed in this way, and the stowage privileges that His Majesty grants, take up all the available space in which it would have been possible to stow goods that would pay freight charges. There you have the reason that His Majesty's Treasury has but little income from the ships.

ALVIANO  I understand that matter well enough but not the overall calculation you are making.

BRANDÔNIO  I am making that calculation to prove my contention that Brazil is richer, and is a source of greater profit to His Majesty's Exchequer, than all of India. Surely, you will not deny that for the ships to come back laden as they are with goods, the whole Orient must needs be gutted – what with collecting pepper from Malabar and cinnamon from Ceylon, cloves from Molucca, ambergris and nutmeg from Banda, musk, benzoin, porcelains and silks from China, cotton cloth and indigo from Cambay and Bengal, precious stones from Baiagate and Bisnaga and Ceylon. All those things from all those places must be gathered together if the ships that come back to the Kingdom are to come laden with them; and, if they were not collected thus, the ships would not have a cargo.

ALVIANO  That is clearly the case, as everyone knows.

BRANDÔNIO  Not the whole of Brazil but only three captaincies, Pernambuco, Itamaracá, and Paraíba – and of them only the inhabited parts – account for fifty or sixty leagues of coast, more or less. The inhabitants of these captaincies have not spread even ten leagues back into the bush. In just that strip of land, without the help of a foreign nation or help of any other kind, the Portuguese, by their own labor and industry, cultivate and take from the bowels of the earth enough sugar every year to lade one hundred and thirty or one hundred and forty ships, many of which are of very great tonnage. For the establishment and maintenance of all that, His Majesty does not spend from his own Treasury a single penny. All those cargoes of sugar are carried to the Kingdom and enter his customhouses, where they pay the tolls due His Majesty. Now if the cargo these ships carry were to be transported in ships the size of those that make the India voyage, twenty great ships of that tonnage would not be enough to accommodate it all.

ALVIANO   Although I cannot deny that that is so, still the duty paid on the sugar cargoes is of much less value to His Majesty's Treasury than the duties levied on the goods and drugs that come from India.

BRANDÔNIO   You are mistaken, for the ships that service the three northern captaincies I have named, without taking into account the southern captaincies, must carry somewhat more than five hundred thousand arrobas of sugar. (I would say that about one hundred thousand arrobas of this sugar is of the kind they call *panelas*.) All of these different qualities of sugar pay duty at the customhouse in Lisbon: the white and the brown pay 250 réis per arroba, and the *panelas* pay 150 réis per arroba. This is in addition to the consulage. All this, added up, amounts to more than three hundred thousand cruzados for His Majesty's Treasury. And he does not have to spend a single real from his own purse on the maintenance of this state [Brazil], for the income from the tithes that are collected from this land is enough to support it.

Now, in this connection, figure out the income he has from the other captaincies, to the south, among which is Bahia de Todos os Santos, the capital of this whole state. After making that calculation, set up an account of credit and debit, the way a shopkeeper does, and on one side write down what His Majesty spends each year on the ships that he sends to India – wages of soldiers and seamen, housing allowances for his officials, and bonuses to private individuals – and add the cash that he sends out to buy pepper. Now put down on the other side what India renders His Majesty, and also the price at which he lets the contract for the ships that come from there. And note carefully how much you will have to add to make that equal the income that he collects from Brazil, from only the three captaincies I mentioned, and you will see how much this latter exceeds the income from India. Thus, I do not need any other proof to demonstrate the truth of what I claimed.

ALVIANO   That income which you are crediting to Brazil appears excessive, for not all sugar pays the full duty. We know, for instance, that some sugar pays no duty at all because of the exemption that His Majesty has granted to persons who set up new sugar mills.

BRANDÔNIO   That's true; but the exemption that His Majesty grants on new sugar mills does not last more than ten years, and when these are over, it expires. Granted that those mill owners and small planters who export sugar on their own account always pay less duty; still, there are only a few who do that. And it cannot be claimed that [the loss] amounts to very much. Furthermore, in my reckoning, I purposely did not include in my total the income from the brazilwood that the same three captaincies export to the Kingdom; this amounts to more than forty thousand cruzados a year. That is what His Majesty's ministers collect in the

Kingdom from the brazilwood contractors. Similarly, I have excluded from the income of the customhouses of the state [Brazil] the duties paid on cotton and timber in the customhouses of the Kingdom, which amount to a very large sum. Balancing one thing against the other, you will find that the income from these sources is greater than the loss from the exemptions you pointed out.

ALVIANO   As a matter of fact, I was so convinced of the opposite of what you have so clearly shown and proved that my mind is still reeling, and what you have said seems a dream to me. Nonetheless, I know for a fact that in Portugal I have seen mansions built by men with large incomes from fortunes they made in India, and I found none – or almost none – who have similar houses and enjoy incomes from wealth brought back from Brazil.

BRANDÔNIO   But that is the greatest proof of their wealth! For the men from India, when they leave there to return to the Kingdom, carry with them all the property they own, for none of them own any real estate in India worth mentioning. All their capital is invested in movables, which they take aboard ship with them. With the money from the sale of these goods in the Kingdom, they acquire the incomes and build the mansions you spoke of. But the settlers in Brazil have all their wealth invested in real estate, which they cannot take back to the Kingdom! And when somebody does go back there, his land must needs stay behind. You must have known many such men in Portugal. It is not possible for them to retain great holdings here and buy more property there, and they prefer to have it in Brazil, where they derive a great income from it. To sum it up, you will come across many men in this country who are worth fifty, one hundred, and even two hundred thousand cruzados, and very few such in India. And if the people who live in Brazil were more enterprising, they could avail themselves of still more things that would make them rich and increase His Majesty's revenue from Brazil.

ALVIANO   I should very much like to have you tell me just what things would give so great a return.

BRANDÔNIO   I was understating the case when I said that Brazil could be richer and yield more revenue for His Majesty's Treasury if the King or the gentlemen of his Council would only turn their eyes toward it. For if they would, then Brazil could make the Dutch and other foreigners who send ships to India cease their shipping and their trade, without His Majesty's having to draw his sword against them or to spend a single real to bring it about.

ALVIANO   That will have to be done by magic, for I do not see how ordinary measures can achieve it.

BRANDÔNIO   It can be achieved without magic, if only His Majesty and the gentlemen of his Council make up their minds to it.

ALVIANO   Then tell me how it can be done.

BRANDÔNIO   It is well known that the Dutch do not send their ships to India at the expense of the States [General], but rather that the merchants themselves pay the costs and expenses of fitting out the ships that sail there. The capital to build the ships and buy the goods they carry is subscribed by many persons who wish to invest in this. Some put in more, others less, according to the amount of cash they have on hand. An account is drawn up and the contribution of each man is represented by a certain number of shares. When the voyage is over and the ships have come back safely, the cargo is sold, and expenses are paid from the gross returns. From what is left, they calculate the percentage of profit and make good accordingly to each one of the subscribers, who gets back the capital he invested plus that percentage.

ALVIANO   You are quite right, for a good friend of mine who spent a long time in Flanders told me that that is the way they do it. But what has that got to do with Brazil's being able to make those nations give up their trade?

BRANDÔNIO   It has a lot to do with it. We already know that the largest and most valuable cargo that their ships seek in India is pepper. The cloves, amber, nutmeg, chinaware, benzoin, and other things that they bring back are merely accessories, and not the mainstay of their trade. For a very little of each one of those is enough to glut the northern markets, and those foreigners cannot bring back cinnamon, cloth, or indigo because these items are not found in the parts of India where they trade. And so it is pepper that they want, pepper that they go to fetch, and pepper that gives them a profit from their overseas trade.

ALVIANO   What are you getting at?

BRANDÔNIO   I say that His Majesty ought to do just what King Dom Manuel, of glorious memory, did to stop the trade in pepper that was brought overland, by way of Cairo, to Venice, whence it was distributed and sold over all of Europe.

ALVIANO   And what did the King do?

BRANDÔNIO   After the seaway to India had been discovered, and wishing that the pepper should pass through the hands of the Portuguese alone, and that only their ships should bring it to Europe, the King determined to close off all that trade through Venice, and he did it in this way: he sent trustworthy men to that city to find out exactly how much a quintal of pepper cost there and the price at which it had to be sold if the dealers there were to make a profit on it.

After he was well informed on all this, he sent his pepper to Flanders with some Portuguese agents to sell it at such a low price that if the Venetian pepper had been sold at the same price, those merchants who dealt in it would have ended up losing much money. Thus, everyone who had to have pepper hastened to buy the King's because it was cheaper. Now, since the Venetians could not let their pepper go at such a price without taking a great loss, because it had cost them so dearly, they gave up their trade in it.

ALVIANO   Come, out with it now, whatever you have in mind!

BRANDÔNIO   I tell you that all the land in this Brazil is so disposed to growing pepper that great quantities of different kinds of it grow wild in the fields without being cultivated at all. It is not the same kind as that which comes from India, which doesn't grow here because there are no proper seeds for it. But, if we had the right kind of seeds, that quality of pepper would grow profusely.

ALVIANO   That I do not doubt, for I myself know that the land here is well disposed for growing pepper. When the birds eat it, the pepper grows wherever they leave their droppings, even on the trunks of trees. But you must finish clarifying the point you are getting at with all these arguments.

BRANDÔNIO   These arguments lead up to what I have in mind. And this is that His Majesty should send a ship to India for the sole purpose of bringing back pepper seed in casks, or in something else in which it could travel safely. Now this caravel should run along the coast of Brazil and deliver the seed to all the captaincies. The captains-major should parcel it out amongst the settlers, obliging them to plant and process it. In this way, more pepper could be obtained from Brazil than from the Malabar Coast.

ALVIANO   But couldn't the pepper that the India ships ordinarily bring be used for planting?

BRANDÔNIO   No, because that pepper – so they say – has had lye passed through it, which keeps it from germinating. So, now, if there were a great deal of pepper in this Brazil, it would end up costing His Majesty little or no trouble, and even less money, to transport it to Portugal. Imitating King Manuel, he could send it to market at such a price that the Dutch would wind up losing a great deal of money if they tried to sell theirs, which they had to go to India to get. Therefore, since they would derive no profit from their commerce, the Dutch would have no reason to persist in it, and that would put an end, without expense and without bloodshed, to a struggle that has cost Portugal so much. And His Majesty, although sending his pepper to be sold more cheaply, would lose little, if he did not actually make money, because

it would cost him less to transport it to the Kingdom and to buy it in
Brazil.

ALVIANO   The reasoning behind your proposal is so convincing that surely
no one can doubt that the results would be what you predict. Indeed, I
wonder that you do not at once take ship for the Kingdom and lay the
proposal before His Majesty, for so much great good would come of it
for all the State of India.

BRANDÔNIO   I have already discussed it with a minister who held a high
position in His Majesty's Treasury. Although he thought it a marvelous
idea, his answer was that the present procedure in the pepper trade is
so firmly established in Portugal that it would be very hard to replace
it with another system. And since I realized that such an attitude is an
ancient evil in our Portugal, beyond all remedy, I brought the conversation to an end, as I shall right now, leaving the job to those whose duty
it is to correct such things, if they have a mind to.

ALVIANO   You are right! To try to set the world straight is an error on the
part of people like us who have so small a station in it; so let us get
back to our subject. If I remember correctly, you were going to tell me
what constitutes the riches of Brazil, the chief source being, you said,
the production of sugar.

BRANDÔNIO   And that is right, for sugar is Brazil's chief distinction and
source of wealth. In its cultivation, the system followed up to the present
time has been this: the captains-major, who are tenants of His Majesty,
each one in his own captaincy, divided – and even now still do divide –
the land among the settlers, giving to each one as much as he has the
means to cultivate. Then, the persons to whom these lands are given
build sugar mills on them, if they have the capital to do so. If they lack
capital, they sell the land to persons who *are* able to build. One must
have great resources and capital to get a sugar mill into operation. For
a mill powered by water, like most of those that have been built so far,
or even one of those that are called *trapiches* and are turned by oxen,
costs pretty close to ten thousand cruzados [4:000$000] by the time it is
all built.

ALVIANO   You seem to be saying that there are other kinds of sugar mill
than those that are powered by water and the *trapiches* that are turned
by oxen.

BRANDÔNIO   That's right. The water-powered mills, you see, are built on
fast-flowing rivers. In addition, tanks are put up to hold back the water
so that the mill can grind with even greater power. In these mills, the
sugar cane is ground between two large rollers that are turned by a
wheel on which the water strikes with great force; then the bagasse is
pressed beneath heavy timbers, called *gangorras*. Oxen are used to make

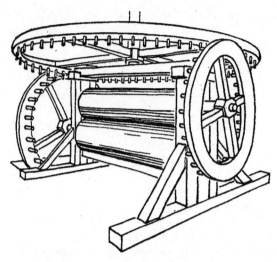

The older type of cane press, with two rollers placed horizontally. Hamilton Fernandes, *Açúcar e álcool ontem e hoje* (Rio de Janeiro: Instituto de Açúcar e de Álcool, 1971), p. 27. *Courtesy of the Edward E. Ayer Collection, The Newberry Library, Chicago.*

them press tight together; this releases and expels from the bagasse all the juice the cane holds. The juice is collected in a tank and then turned into great copper cauldrons, which are placed on top of furnaces in which fires are lighted. By the heat of these, the sugar is cleansed, boiled, and purified. To refine and fortify it further, they have to stir in some lye, made from ashes.

There are other mills that do not use water, and these are the *trapiches* I spoke of. They grind the cane with a contrivance of wheels that is set up for this purpose, turned by oxen, but in the rest of the sugar-making the same process I have described is followed.

But a newly invented press, which they call *palitos*, has recently been introduced. This does not require such a big setup and likewise uses either water power or animal traction. This invention is considered so fine that I think all the old-style mills will be scrapped and only this new device will be used.

ALVIANO   One must always prefer what can be done with less labor and expense, and since this new contrivance of the *palitos* achieves exactly that, I am sure everyone will adopt it. But I would like to know how they make a loaf of that fine white sugar which is sent to Portugal and which we see out here.

BRANDÔNIO   The process is this: after the sugar-cane juice is cleansed and thickened in the cauldrons, it is transferred to boilers that are also made

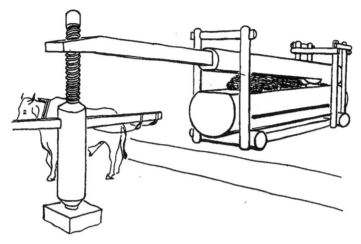

The *gangorra* described by Brandônio presses out the residue of juice from the cane. Hamilton Fernandes, *Açúcar e álcool ontem e hoje* (Rio de Janeiro: Instituto de Açúcar e de Álcool, 1971), p. 25. *Courtesy of the Edward E. Ayer Collection, The Newberry Library, Chicago.*

of copper. Here, it is heated until it reaches the point of coagulation and takes on body. From there, they put it into earthenware molds, inside of which it gains consistency and hardens. After it has cooled, they take it to a large building called the clarifying house, which is outfitted just for this purpose. Here, the molds are set into holes cut in a plank. Then they pull out the plug in the bottom of the mold, and through it the treacle drains off into gutters of the same planking, which they place underneath to catch it. The treacle that drains off from the molds in this way runs into a big tank, and from it they later make the molasses, and still another quality of sugar that they call *batidos*. And when the molds have stopped draining, they pour over the sugar some water that has particles of clay suspended in it. That is what makes it white, the way we see it.

ALVIANO   It is hard for me to understand how the clay, which seemingly ought to soil the sugar and turn it black, can whiten it instead.

BRANDÔNIO   The first sugar makers did not know about that for many years either, and they used to spoil it the way they made it. At last, a chicken disclosed the secret: it happened to fly up onto a mold of sugar with its feet covered with clay. All around that part where its footprints were impressed, the sugar turned white. That was how they learned the secret power of the clay to turn things white, and they put it to use.

The newer type of cane press, with three vertical rollers (*palitos*). It could be powered either by water or by oxen (*trapiche*). Hamilton Fernandes, *Açúcar e álcool ontem e hoje* (Rio de Janeiro: Instituto de Açúcar e de Álcool, 1971), p. 31. *Courtesy of the Edward E. Ayer Collection, The Newberry Library, Chicago.*

ALVIANO   The chicken was not a bad teacher, to reveal in that fashion how they could correct the dark color of the sugar, for there is such a great difference in value between the white and the dark sugars. And, if a mill produces a great quantity of the good quality, it cannot fail to bring the owner a profit.

BRANDÔNIO   There is a vast difference between the good sugar mills and the bad ones. Assuming that their owners can afford the necessary personnel and equipment, good mills can become supremely valuable if they have three other things; namely, plenty of good land to plant cane on, enough water so that the press will never have to stop, and a quantity of wood in thick stands of timber. Neither the cane nor the wood should be far from the mill, but rather so located that both things can be transported easily. Now, when sugar mills are of this quality and have all the necessary personnel and equipment, they generally produce every year up to six, seven, eight, and even ten thousand arrobas of *macho* sugar, besides the treacle, molasses, and syrups, which always come to about three thousand arrobas. When the sugar can be tested, some of it generally turns out to be very good, another lot inferior, and some of it extremely bad, depending on whether the master workmen who make it are good or bad at their trade. Smaller mills usually produce five, four, or even only three thousand arrobas of sugar, and such mills are of little profit to their owners.

ALVIANO    And what personnel and equipment must a mill have if it is to produce much sugar?

BRANDÔNIO    It must have fifty slaves working – and good ones; fifteen to twenty yoke of oxen, with the necessary wagons and harnesses; plenty of copper utensils in good repair; reliable foremen; ample firewood, molds, and lye. If any one of these things is lacking, then right away the production of sugar falls off because of it.

ALVIANO    Now tell me if all the sugar that is produced belongs to the mill owner.

BRANDÔNIO    If all the cane from which it is made belongs to the mill owner, then all the sugar is his too. But this is seldom the case because of the large capital and great equipment needed to plant cane fields and run a mill. Thus, most of the owners generally parcel out their cane fields in *partidos* [tracts], which they do in this manner: the mill owner contributes the land and even some assistance beyond that. The smallholder on his side undertakes to plant the cane and afterwards to cultivate and cut it and carry it to the mill, all according to the terms of their agreement. When the cane has been pressed and the sugar refined, the tithe on it is paid first of all from the gross product. After that is paid, a division is made on the basis of thirds, fifths, or even halves. Division by thirds means that two-thirds of the sugar goes to the mill owner and one-third to the smallholder. Division by fifths means that three-fifths goes to the mill owner and two-fifths to the smallholder. Division by halves means that each party gets the same amount; but division by halves – being of scant profit for the mill owner – is rarely met with, except in the case of a person to whom a favor is owed or who plants the cane on his own land. But whatever type of contract exists, there is no division of the treacle – the molasses and syrups – for all these belong freely and *in solido* [wholly] to the mill owner, who has no obligation to share them beyond paying on them the tithe that is due to God.

ALVIANO    And when the division is made that way, how much sugar would the mill owner receive?

BRANDÔNIO    He would always get from four thousand to four thousand five hundred arrobas of *macho* sugar, besides the treacle and syrups, which will amount to from two thousand five hundred to three thousand arrobas.

ALVIANO    How much does it cost a mill owner to produce enough sugar each year so that his own share will be the amount you mention?

BRANDÔNIO    One of these mills – I mean one of the really good ones – will always have expenses of three thousand five hundred to four thousand cruzados. If any of its slaves die, so that others have to be bought, expenses will be even higher.

ALVIANO   That is a lot of money, and if that much has to be put out, the profit a sugar mill brings its owner cannot be so great as people have told me it is.

BRANDÔNIO   But it is still a good profit. It often comes to five or six thousand cruzados, free and clear. And if the owner ships his sugar to the Kingdom himself, his profit will be much greater. Not only does he get a higher price for it in Portugal, but he can avail himself of the right of exemption. This means that if his mill is a new one, he has ten years during which he does not have to pay any duty at all in the customhouses. When that time is up, he nonetheless enjoys in perpetuity a half exemption. This means that he pays the customhouse only half the regular duty, just as if his sugar were sent over by a smallholder, for smallholders have that exemption.

   Some of the mills enjoy greater exemptions than others. Those that are situated in a proprietary captaincy pay the proprietor a yearly water tax of three to four percent of all the sugar they make, and that amounts to a lot. But mills in the captaincies owned by the Crown are exempt from paying His Majesty such a tax – which is no small privilege!

ALVIANO   Nonetheless, the mills situated in Potosí, which press the earth from which silver is taken, must have quite a different income from that of the mills you have been boasting of to me, which produce sugar. At least, I would rather have the income from one of the former.

BRANDÔNIO   You are mistaken there, for I have seen figures on that, worked out by men who were well acquainted with both operations. They found that the income from sugar mills was ever so much greater. Proof enough of that is that we see very many exceedingly rich owners of sugar mills, whereas most of the men who own silver mills are very poor and in debt.

ALVIANO   That cannot be the fault of the silver mills but must be the result of the excessive expenditure that those men are accustomed to incur for themselves and their houses. I have been told that they are tremendously extravagant.

BRANDÔNIO   In that respect, the sugar-mill owners of Brazil are not one whit behind them, for many of them also go to the greatest expense, with many richly caparisoned horses and liveries, and with the costly clothing that they and their children ordinarily wear. For in this state, every four days there are bullfights, jousts with staves, tilting at the ring, and similar sports, on which both organizers and participants spend a vast amount of money. They are, furthermore, very liberal in giving expensive presents. And I have heard men who have had much experience at the Court in Madrid say that even there they do not dress better than do the mill owners, their wives and daughters, other rich men, and the merchants of Brazil. I will give only one very strong proof of this wealth: in the Captaincy of Pernambuco, there is a House of Mercy that every year spends thirteen or fourteen thousand cruzados, more or less, to discharge its obligations. All of this is given in alms by the inhabitants of that captaincy, for the hospital does not have any income of its own to speak of. Indeed, its superintendents [*provedores*] – a different one is appointed every year – spend more than three thousand cruzados out of their own pockets. All the other captaincies have charity hospitals that spend much money, but the one in Pernambuco spends more than the others.

ALVIANO    That is a strong argument in support of your claim for the great wealth of Brazil. And since you have said enough about the first source [sugar] of that wealth which you attributed to the entire province, let us go on to the second source, which you say is trade.

BRANDÔNIO    Many men in Brazil have acquired a great amount of wealth in cash and property through trade, though the most successful are merchants who have come out from the Kingdom for that purpose. This trade is conducted in two ways. The first way is that they come out with a round-trip passage, sell their goods, invest their profits in sugar, cotton, and even very fine ambergris, and then return to the Kingdom, sometimes in the very same ships they came in.

The second way is for merchants to live in this country and keep retail shops. Their stores are filled with expensive goods, including all kinds of the best linens, the richest silks, the finest fabrics, and marvelous brocades. There is a lavish use of all these out here, which brings great profits to the merchants who sell them.

ALVIANO    Now, the merchants who live here and keep shop, do they perhaps order their stock from the Kingdom, or do they buy it from persons who bring it out from there?

BRANDÔNIO    Many of them do order their stock sent out from the Kingdom, but most of them buy from other traders who bring goods out. They pay forty or fifty percent of the purchase price in advance, depending on the kind and quality of goods and whether they are scarce or plentiful out here. And on these merchants depend yet others who operate on a smaller scale.

ALVIANO    And what type are they?

BRANDÔNIO    There are many persons who make their living and become very rich just by buying goods from the merchants in towns or cities and carrying them back to sell on the sugar plantations and farms that lie far out. They often make more than one hundred percent on them.

In the Captaincy of Pernambuco, I once saw a certain trader make a deal that I did not approve of and considered illicit. He went out and bought a shipment of Guinea slaves for quite a sum of money, paying cash for them. Then, the very same instant, without actually having received the slaves, he turned around and sold them to a farmer, on credit over a certain period, which was less than a year, at more than 85 percent over the price he paid for them.

ALVIANO   Now, where I come from that is called, in good Portuguese, *usury!* It is a curious thing, withal, that one could make so much money right on the spot, from one minute to the next, without taking any risk.

BRANDÔNIO   Well, it can be done. And it happens so often that many traders of that sort and many of the storekeepers here are owners of great property in sugar mills and farms. Many of them live on their estates, and some of them are married.

ALVIANO   Men who can prosper so in a foreign land must have great abilities.

BRANDÔNIO   You must realize that Brazil is a crossroads of the world. I mean no offense to any other kingdom or city when I call it that. At the same time, it is a public academy in which one may easily learn every manner of civility, polite discourse, courteous behavior, how to make a good business deal, and other accomplishments of similar importance.

ALVIANO   It ought rather to be just the contrary, for we know that Brazil was settled first of all by persons of evil ways and men who had been banished from Portugal for their crimes, and therefore persons of scant civility. Their not being of gentle birth surely was enough for them to lack all refinement.

BRANDÔNIO   There is no doubt of that. But you must realize that the first settlers who came to Brazil had many opportunities to get rich in a hurry on account of the liberality of the land. As they prospered, they promptly shed their evil nature, which the necessity and poverty they had suffered in the Kingdom had brought out. And the children of those men, having those riches and enthroned as rulers of the land, sloughed off their old skin just the way a snake does, and adopted in everything the most polished manners. I must add that later on, many gentlemen and persons of noble birth came out to this state. They married here and became attached to the colonists by family ties. Thus, there was developed among them all a mixture of fairly gentle blood. Furthermore, all kinds of people come from all parts of the world to do business in Brazil, and they transact this business with the residents of the country. Now, the latter are usually very shrewd, either because of the highly favorable climate or because of the auspicious heavens. So they pick up from the foreigners whatever they think useful.

They carefully preserve this knowledge and put it to use in their own good time.

ALVIANO  To be able to imitate and to steal abilities from those who have great ones, why, that is to wrest the club from the hands of Hercules!

BRANDÔNIO  That's just what the people in Brazil do, to the point that the sons of Lisbon and those of other parts of the Kingdom come here to learn fine manners and with them make themselves new men, thanks to the refinement that formerly they lacked.

But it appears to me that long ago we lost the thread of our discussion, in which we were considering the profit that trade brings to those who engage in it in this Brazil.

ALVIANO  But this other discussion, by which we were briefly distracted, should not displease those who may hear of it, especially the Brazilians. But, leaving that aside, you have yet to tell me if Brazil has any commerce beyond that with the Kingdom.

BRANDÔNIO  Oh, yes. Brazil does a great trade with Angola and the Rio de la Plata. Ships with all kinds of goods are sent to Angola and come back carrying slaves to be sold here, and the men who deal in slaves make a big profit. Further, the ships bound for Angola from the Kingdom put in at the Captaincy of Rio de Janeiro, where they take aboard cargoes of manioc flour, the chief foodstuff of the land, which is cheaper there. Carrying it to Angola, they exchange it for slaves and ivory, which they bring back in great quantities.

ALVIANO  All that concerns Angola. But I wish you would tell me about the business that is done with the Rio de la Plata.

BRANDÔNIO  Many *peruleiros* come up regularly from the Rio de la Plata in carracks and in caravels of small tonnage. They bring a vast sum of *patacas* of four and eight reales, and worked and unworked silver in cones and in bars, both gold dust and grain gold and some wrought into chains. They take these things to Rio de Janeiro, Bahia de Todos os Santos, and Pernambuco and exchange them for the different kinds of goods they need. Leaving all their silver and gold behind them here, they stow their goods aboard and make the return trip to the Rio de la Plata. And even our local merchants have an interest in this trade, for it is of no small profit to them. A few of these *peruleiros* settle down in Brazil, and use their money to make loans on notes, or to loan money at interest, or to buy sugar; or they take it with them to Portugal.

ALVIANO  That is not a bad business, when you pick gold and silver as its fruit! But all of the trade which you have discussed, and from which so much profit is derived, seems to end up in the hands of foreigners, and the profit goes to them and not to the settlers.

BRANDÔNIO    For the most part that is so, because the people of this country
are busy looking after their sugar mills and improving their farms, and
they don't want to get involved in trade. The few who do so are satisfied
just with sending their sugar to the Kingdom and ordering sent out from
there whatever they need for their farms. But in everything else, they
leave the door wide open to the merchants, who carry on their business
most profitably. As an excellent illustration of this, I can tell you of a
case which I myself witnessed.

   In the year '92 [1592], a small businessman came straight to Pernambuco from the Algarve, his ship laden with wines from Alvor, a little
olive oil, a lot of raisins and figs, and many other things that are always
brought out from there. He had invested a capital of 730$000, according
to his bill of lading, which I saw. This man stayed out here six months,
sold his stock for cash, and made close to seven thousand cruzados
[2:800$000] on it. He invested this in the finest white sugar, paying 650
réis per arroba. Now, because he bought that sugar so cheaply, he must
surely have doubled his money once again when he sold it back in
Portugal.

ALVIANO    I admit that a country where businessmen can make a profit like
that must be very bountiful.

BRANDÔNIO    You can see how bountiful it is from just one thing that I shall
tell you. There is a private citizen of good standing, a settler in the
captaincy of Paraíba in this Brazil, who – though owning no more than a
single sugar mill – boldly promised to give everyone who would build
a house in the city [Filipéia], which then was just being laid out, 20$
[20$000] for each house of stone and mortar more than one story high,
and 10$ [10$000] for a house of one story. And he kept his word over
a long period, during which many houses were put up, without there
being any profit to him other than the gratification of his desire to see
the city grow. And now, to complete this story, I will tell you that he
undertook, further, to build the city's House of Mercy, a thing of vast
expense because of the size and grandeur of its church, which now is
almost finished. Having given you that one example, I want to go on to
a discussion of the third commodity on which the settlers of this state
make money – and a good deal of it – which is brazilwood.

ALVIANO    I beg you to do so.

BRANDÔNIO    Brazilwood, from which this whole province takes its name,
as I have already explained, yields a red dyestuff, which is excellent for
dyeing wood and silk, and for making paints and other things. Though
it is found throughout all the state, the best and most valuable brazilwood is cut in the captaincies of Pernambuco, Itamaracá, and Paraíba,
for it far surpasses in coloring strength the wood found elsewhere. Thus,

only the wood from the three captaincies mentioned is considered good enough to be sent to the Kingdom. There it sells for four and sometimes five milréis per quintal, depending on how abundant the supply is.

ALVIANO   Tell me now, how do the settlers in this Brazil make money on the wood, and how much does it bring His Majesty's Treasury?

BRANDÔNIO   Brazilwood is His Majesty's own drug and, as such, is protected so that no one may deal in it except the king himself or those who have received his license under contract. A long time ago, anyone was permitted to trade in it, paying His Majesty's Exchequer one cruzado on every quintal he cut. But since the feeling was that there were many abuses under that system, the order establishing it was revoked so that the trade should be handled only under contract, as is the case today. About forty thousand cruzados are paid to His Majesty's Treasury for a contract, which is let in the kingdom. It is specified that in any one year, the contractors may not take out from this state, especially from the three captaincies I have mentioned, more than ten thousand quintals of the wood, although if they cut less in one year, they may make it up in the next.

ALVIANO   I had no idea that brazilwood was the source of so much revenue for the Exchequer without His Majesty's having to spend a single real for it, whereas he must spend so many cruzados in India to purchase other drugs.

BRANDÔNIO   All Brazil is a source of revenue for His Majesty's Exchequer, without entailing any expense – a fact that ought to be very much appreciated!

ALVIANO   And what profit do the settlers make on the wood?

BRANDÔNIO   A great deal, for many settlers make their living simply by going into the forest and hauling the wood out with oxen to a waterway, where they sell it to persons who have a license to ship it.

ALVIANO   Now tell me how they cut this wood.

BRANDÔNIO   Well, it's like this: they go some twelve, fifteen, and even twenty leagues out from the captaincy of Pernambuco in search of the greatest stands of it, for it cannot be found any closer at hand, since the demand has been so great. There, amidst great forests, they find it. The tree has a smallish leaf and thorns along the trunk. The men who engage in this occupation take many slaves from Guinea with axes. After the tree is on the ground, they remove all the outer layers, for the brazil is in the heartwood. In this way, a tree of tremendous girth supplies a piece of wood no larger than your leg. After it is trimmed, they pile it up. From there, they cart it in wagons, five or six logs being tied together, until they get it to storage sheds, where barges can come alongside to take it aboard.

ALVIANO    It must be a hard job to cut timber that way. Unless the yield is
    great, the merchandise will end up being very expensive.
BRANDÔNIO    Oh yes, the yield is great. Many of these men cut one to two
    thousand quintals of brazil every year and haul it out with their ox
    teams. After they have got it to the storage sheds, they sell it for seven
    to eight tostons per quintal, and sometimes for more than that. They
    make a lot of money on it, and many men have made their fortunes that
    way.
ALVIANO    If that's the way it happens, we can say that God gives the settlers
    in Brazil gold and silver in their fields, and that from something they
    have neither planted nor tended they pick the fruit.

## 4. Instructions on How to Manage a Sugar Mill and Estate

*These guidelines were prepared in 1663 by the sugar planter João Fernandes Vieira
for the senior administrator of Engenho do Meio in the floodplain of the Capibaribe
River in Pernambuco. Fernandes Vieira had risen to prominence during the Dutch
occupation of northeastern Brazil and had himself served as administrator of sugar
estates during that period. He eventually owned at least five such properties. In
1645, Fernandes Vieira, heavily indebted to the Dutch West India Company, took a
leading role in the Luso-Brazilian revolt against the Dutch occupation. By the 1660s,
he was a leading figure in the restoration of Portuguese control, governor of Pernambuco, and one of the wealthiest men in the captaincy. He knew the sugar industry
well, and his own practical experience as an administrator makes this document
particularly informative about common practices on Brazilian sugar estates. In his
instructions, the care and command of the slave force is placed first, indicating the
importance and centrality of the labor force in the making of sugar. (This document
was first published by the noted Pernambucan historian J. A. Gonsalves de
Mello as "Um regimento do feito-mor de engenho de 1663," Boletim do Instituto Joaquim Nabuco, II [1953], pp. 80–7.)*

REGIMENT that the Administrator of the Engenho should follow to satisfy
his obligations and unburden his conscience, and doing otherwise, he must
explain himself to God and is obliged to give restitution to the owner of the
estate.

    Confess the Slaves [*negros*] – He will be obligated every year to order
everyone under his control to confess each Sunday and on saint's days, and
he will order them to hear mass, and the children born he will order to be
baptized in their time, and if any sick slave [is] in need of a confessor, he will
send for one, and every Saturday and at night he will order the slaves to be
instructed in their prayers.

Slaves Who Become Ill – As the blacks become ill, he will try to heal their bodies and provide whatever is lacking on the estate, and if the illness is dangerous, he will send the slave to the person who handles my affairs in Recife, if he believes that the slave cannot be cured on the estate.

Housing the Slaves – He will be obligated to go each morning to the slave quarters to see if the slaves are ill and to provide to them anything that is lacking and he will require that their houses be well swept with their sleeping platforms and mats in order; and he will require them to plant their gardens on saint's days and when the engenho is not milling, he will give them Saturdays for their planting in the winter.

Punishing the Slaves – Punishment of slaves should not be done with a stick nor should slaves be struck with rocks or bricks but when deserving of punishment, they should be tied to an oxcart and punished with a whip, and after being well-lashed, they should be cut with a razor or knife and then treated with salt, lemon juice, and urine and then placed for some days in chains; and if it is a woman being punished, she will be whipped in a shirt of baize and it should be done inside a house [privately] with the same whip.

Rationing the Slaves – In the winter, he should not awake the slaves before daybreak for any reason and only after daylight he should give them their ration of cane juice when it is available without fail.

Care with Slave Fights – He will take the greatest care to prevent hatreds among the slaves to prevent them from killing each other and try to promote friendships and when this does not occur, they should be sent to another estate. He should not permit them to eat meat of animals that have died and must be especially careful when oxen have died that they do not eat them.

Care for the Sick – When slaves develop a fever, he should wait forty-eight hours before ordering them bled. He should try to relieve them of the illness and get rid of it by ordinary means; and he should ask them what they have eaten or drunk in order to see if poison may be involved, and he should take them promptly to someone who knows about these things to see if they should be bled. And if a swelling of any kind appears and there is a suspicion that it may be a carbuncle, he should send the slave immediately to the house of Baltesar Leitão de Vasconcelos on my behalf to do me the favor of curing him. In similar cases, avoid using Master João or barbers because they do not know how to cure this and often have said it is a carbuncle and have killed the slave.

Count the Slaves – the slaves should be counted every day and those missing found by all means.

Care of the Oxen – He will take great care with the ox herd of the estate and send them to pasture with the best herdsmen and count the herd each day and look immediately for any that are missing. In the same manner, cure them of any illness or infestation [*bicheira*] that they may have and take care that those that work one day do not work the next and he will pay attention that they do not suffer the work too greatly and that young oxen are broken in slowly and prepared for the carts so that all are ready to work. To each cart, man give two, three, or four teams of oxen according to their availability so that each carter knows the teams he has to work, and he who holds the office of captain or the cart men should have all needed to control them, and whoever disobeys him should be punished.

Visit the Woodlands – He will be obliged to visit the woods of the estate and defend them, to go there and see where the boundary markers are placed and not allow anyone to remove wood without permission; and to know this, he should have the woods inspected each week by an overseer or a slave of his confidence, and if anyone is found cutting wood, he should seize their tools and stop them from transporting the wood, and if they are caught a second time, a complaint of theft should be initiated with justice officials.

Visit the Waterworks – The same obligations apply to inspect the water tanks (*açudes*) and channels and keep all in good repair as necessary and he should never trust only in ordering that this be done but in going himself to make sure it is done.

Take Charge of the Firewood – When firewood is prepared for the mill, he must turn over a measure of six palms high by six palms wide and twelve palms in length and he will go every week to see the firewood that is prepared and that it is of the proper measure and mix of thick and thin pieces and even if there is an assistant overseer assigned this task, the administrator will do this to make sure.

Fence the Cane Fields – He will seek to properly fence all the cane fields and crops of the estate and will see to it that the [dependent] farmers of the estate do likewise for it is not just that anyone eats the produce that costs so much effort to grow.

Care with the Houses – He will take great care with all the buildings of the estate and will order them repaired and roofed and will do the same with the slave quarters and will make sure that the [cane] farmers of the estate do the same for those under their control.

Care with the Pottery Works – He will try at all times to have a pottery works with a free potter when there is no slave to do this job and everything the said potter makes with his own hands, he will keep himself to sell to whomever he wishes, and if the estate has need, it will take what it needs, paying the potter as is the custom of which he will receive his share be it in dishes, sugar forms, and all else he makes, except roof tiles and bricks since these are made using slaves belonging to the estate and are only given to the potter when he fires roof tiles and bricks which take two days. And if the mudpits are close to the pottery, the people can carry it in baskets or on boards, and carts are needed only when the distance is great. He will always have a surplus of tiles and bricks for any need and as many forms as may be needed.

Care of the Purging House – The purgery must always be well furnished with cisterns, chains, funnels, rows for forms [*andainas*] and lianas [*timbó*] to repair the forms, and he must take special care that the forms do not break.

Care of the Saw Mill – The saw mill of the estate will always be working and the carpenter will always have more than enough wood to make crates, boards, and carts, and he will continue to make them and will have a surplus of yokes made and everything else needed for the carts.

Collection of Cordage [*envira*] and Vines [*cipó*] – He will try in the period when there is the least to do to have much *envira* collected to make rope. Here, should always be a surplus on hand and also good quality vines to bind the fences together when necessary and using the same care, have lianas for the forms to make sugar.

Wood for the Gears [*dentadura*] – He will seek to have a surplus of wood for the gears of the axles and of the flywheels and will always have them ready, wood for the *cunhas* and some ready, and the other parts and equipment ready.

Ash for the Temper [*decoadas*] – He will take care each year to collect the ashes from the slave quarters and the pottery and place them where they will not become wet, and there should always be eighteen containers to prepare temper and there should be some extras always ready because they break and before the ash is added, they should be well prepared with lianas.

Care of the Distillery [*casa de aguardente*] – With the distillery, much care should be taken, using all the raw rum [*cachaça*] and if it is made well, it should be for transport, and if many containers are made for the juice [*garapas*] and all the necessary barrels should be asked for from the person who handles my affairs in Recife with all diligent care.

Attention to Plantings – If at the estate's expense plantings [of foodstuffs] are made, he should see to them with great care so that they are not lost nor that any animal should get to them to eat them.

Bridges of the Estate – He will have the bridges and entrances of the estate made and in good repair with their gates covered and if there is a road outside the estate, he will not allow anyone to enter except in case of necessity.

Clean the Pastures – He will always have the pastures clean and the estate drained. He will seek to have a good garden with many grape arbors, fig trees, briars, and enclosures that can be made of vines.

Division of the Sugars – The sugar made on the estate will be divided with all clarity and honesty with the cane farmers, giving them an equitable division. He will always strive that the sugar be of the best quality and that it does not go to the trash or that they stop making it because of some minor problem. And if the sugar master or the purger is in error, the administrator will call on others from outside to investigate what error has taken place so it can be fixed, and the purger will always deal with the sugar with much care so that it can be made in as little time as possible.

Crating the Sugar Well – The sugar belonging to the estate will be crated perfectly so that if it is necessary to remove the lid so that the whole crate can be seen, it should be done; in making muscavado, he should be very careful and it is better to have two arrobas of muscavado than to lose good white sugar. Some four to ten crates should be ready.

Care of the Corrals – The corrals where the cattle sleep should be large and to take them in the morning, there should be another smaller corral so that there should be no effort in taking the oxen. The carts should always be kept in time of sun and rain beneath some building and to the carters there should always be grease [sebo] and he should order that during the harvest it should be used as a lubricant on the mill when it is working, and this should be done with great care. The temper for the sugar should always be good and the sugar master should be admonished not to wet the sugar excessively, and if it is made without water, I will value it even more. Put little or no oil in the heating pans [tachas] because experience has shown that it is harmful to the sugar.

Do Not Do Anything without the Order of the Governor – Do not give anything belonging to the estate without my order when I am where I can be asked, and when my agent in Recife is not available; and any matter of importance that takes place on the estate will be reported to me or to the said agent to be reported to me.

Report the Death of Slaves and Oxen – He will report the death of all slaves that die on the estate and the cause of death and do the same with the oxen so that everything is clear, and he will register the birth of the children that are born.

Care of the Coppers – The most important thing on an engenho are the kettles [cobres] with which he must take great care so that they are not damaged by fire. The same attention should be given to the tools so they are not stolen or lost.

Make a Roll Each Night – For the best satisfaction of his obligations, the Administrator should make each night a list of all to be done the next day and for all to be done well and easily, he should be a Christian fearful of God, mindful of the estate that has been entrusted to him, respected by the neighbors, courteous, seeing to the necessity of others, affable and reasonable with those under his jurisdiction, and not taking advantage of this under his orders.

If the Administrator does all of the above, not only will his conscience be clear but he also will reap the credit and will oblige me to help him gain more profit beyond his salary, God willing.

Beyond this, no excuse is to be permitted because as I have said, when there is doubt, I should be asked, nor do I want more than is written here even though it might seem better because the best practice is always to follow the orders of the owner.

And the said Administrator can sell molasses, low-grade sugar, and other byproducts of the mill as well as dishes from the pottery in order to help the sick and to attend to the other needs of the estate, and he can order that a slave woman of the estate raise chickens so that they can be available to be eaten by the sick.

Written at this Engenho do Meio on 23 June 1663.

And the Administrator at this Engenho do Meio will give to Senhora Izabel Ferreira all that she requires and will adjust accounts accordingly.

João Fernandes Vieira

## 5. The Commerce of Brazil

*The export of Brazilian sugar connected the colony to Portugal and the rest of Europe. Ships from Holland, Hamburg, and other Hanseatic cities, and even Ragusa in the Adriatic, carried much of the sugar trade in the sixteenth century, and although after 1590 controls of this commerce became much tighter, such commerce continued under Portuguese license. In this document, a ship from Gadansk (Danzig) seeks a permit to sail to Brazil, undoubtedly to load sugar. The way in which Brazil's commerce could be used as an attraction to other nations for Portugal's benefit is made clear here in the colonial council's recommendation.* (From Arquivo Histórico Ultramarino, Codice 41, fs. 101v–102.)

### Discussion of the Conselho da Fazenda

On the landing of the ship called the *White Greyhound* (*Galgo branco*), which is in the river of this city for which João Mainante, native of Danzig, vassal of the King of Poland has petitioned.

By a communication of the Governor of the 29 of last March of this present year [1636], there comes before this council a petition of João Mainante, master of the ship called the *White Greyhound* now in this port to be presently discussed, having it in mind that His Majesty wishes that these people be treated with all possible kindness and favor. In this petition, the said João Mainante states that he is a native of Danzig, a subject and vassal of the king of Poland and he came directly to this city with a cargo of wheat for its relief and sustenance during a period of much shortage, and while unloading his vessel he had been prohibited from going to the parts of Brazil, which was a great inconvenience to him being as he was a subject of the king of Poland, and by whose order and command he came with his ship as Almirante in the company of Nicholas Larquer, also in a ship of the said king of Poland, who carried letters for His Majesty and for Princess Margarida [regent in Portugal] in which they were asked not to cause this difficulty or keep the ships from sailing but rather to give them every favor and support. And by the documents that he provided, they show that he is a subject of the king of Poland. He asks Your Majesty order that his ship be landed since he is a vassal of the king and that there are in this port ships from Asia more suited for that voyage.

The said petition and documents are being sent to the Provedor of the Customshouse so that he may be informed, and that was done and Mainante said that he was a vassal of the king of Poland. And he [Mainante] says that the ship in which he came, having brought wheat for the benefit of this city, he asked to be excused from the embargo so that he could proceed to Brazil. And because his departure is not so imminent and the delay will be long and with costs to Your Majesty's Treasury and that in the meanwhile other ships will arrive that can make up for the absence of this one, and that it seems to him that he should be excused.

It seems that given the reasons that the petitioner alleges in his request and the information provided by the Provedor of the Customshouse and according to the papers presented to this council that he is a vassal of the king of Poland, and that Your Majesty and the Governor had been contacted about the good treatment and passage of the petitioner, Your Majesty should order that his ship be released because in addition to the other reasons mentioned, this will move the king of Poland to send to this kingdom many ships and goods from which will result many taxes for the Treasury of Your Majesty. Lisbon, 11 of April of 1636.

## 6. The Crisis of Brazilian Sugar

*By the mid-seventeenth century, the Brazilian sugar economy confronted a series of structural and political challenges. The occupation of much of northeastern Brazil by the Dutch (1630–54) and the subsequent war to recover that territory (1645– 54) destroyed many sugar estates and placed a heavy tax burden on the remaining plantations. Meanwhile, competition emerged in the Caribbean, as islands such as Barbados, Jamaica, and Guadeloupe and mainland colonies such as Surinam began to export sugar to Europe; this lowered the price of sugar but raised the price of slaves because of the new demand for laborers. By the late 1680s, the price of sugar in Lisbon was only a third of what it had been in 1654. These generally unfavorable conditions for Brazil's exports were exacerbated in the 1680s by droughts and epidemics in the colony. This lamentable situation moved the town council of*

*Salvador to petition the Crown for tax relief in 1687. The town councilors could not know at that point that with the outbreak of war in Europe in 1689, new opportunities would be created for Brazilian commodities. However, the recovery in the 1690s proved to be short-lived, and there was a downward trend of agricultural exports thereafter until the mid-eighteenth century. The letter of the Senate (or town council) of Salvador included here reveals the contemporary perception of the Atlantic market, an understanding of the south Atlantic links between Angola and Brazil, and the importance of the slave trade. It also indicates unhappiness with the level of governmental taxation and an emerging recognition of Brazil's vital role within the economy of Portugal and its empire as a whole. (From* Cartas do Senado da Câmara da Bahia, 1638–1692 *[3 vols. Salvador, 1950–3], vol. 3, pp. 49–51, as translated by C. R. Boxer,* Portuguese Society in the Tropics *[Madison: University of Wisconsin Press, 1968], pp. 186–8.)*

## 20. The Senate of Bahia and the Crisis in the Sugar Trade, 1687

*Letter from the Senate to his Majesty Concerning the Need to Find a Means to Encourage an Increase in the Exports of the Products of this Land, Owing to the Way They Have Slumped Due to Their Dearness and High Taxation, 12 August 1687*

At the demand of the most eminent of the People of this city of Bahia and impelled by our duty as the head thereof, We come to the Royal Feet of Your Majesty in order to represent the universal sorrow of us all at the slump in the products of Brazil – sugar and tobacco. It is said that the foreigners no longer need them since there is a surplus from what they themselves cultivate in the Indies, selling the refined sugar in Italy and the tobacco in India. And exports of these commodities from Portugal are now reduced to a very small quantity, which we still retain because of the superior quality of our sugar over theirs, and because they need some of every kind to drive a better business. This would seem to be true, for the Customs Houses no longer clear these commodities, and the people who went [to Portugal] in the fleet of the last year of 1686, wrote and ordered their agents in Brazil to send them their capital in money or in bills of exchange; for sugar and tobacco are neither wanted nor bought by the foreigners, and for Portugal eight thousand or ten thousand chests of sugar and as many more of tobacco suffice yearly. We are compelled to recognize the truth of this since in this present fleet, the merchants refrained more than ever before from buying these commodities, and they only accepted sugar and tobacco in payment of their goods when they were bound by previous contracts to do so.

Matters being in these straits, Sire, it seems that we can regard the trade of Brazil as given over and lost, nor must Your Majesty's Council consider

232 • Early Brazil

it in any other way. This is all the more reason why every effort should be made to find a remedy before it is too late, even though those who are in Portugal write us, and those who come thence tell us, that this trade is already lost, since there is no hope of making a profit therein, nor of exporting these commodities from that kingdom. Those who discuss the cause thereof state that both as regards Brazil and Portugal, the collapse of the sugar was due to the duties that were laid on it on top of the old duties and the seven vintens per arroba for the convoy-tax when the Companhia Geral was founded, at a time when the emergency of the war justified this and when the sale price of sugar oscillated between 30,000 and 30,500 arroba, thus enabling it to bear the new burden. And as regards the tobacco, the decline is due to the rigid monopoly thereof and the heavy duty of one vintem per pound that was imposed on it, in addition to the other duties that had been levied on it at the same period of the war and of the convoy. That the English and the other peoples of the North, resentful of the high price of 30,500, resolved to go and cultivate these products in the Barbados and on the mainland of the Indies. That if it had been realized at the time what harm that diversion of this business boded for us, and the prices of our sugar and tobacco had been lowered to reasonable amounts, then it might well have happened that those nations would not have been so eager to grow those products for themselves, for despite everything, their sugar is not of such fine quality and prestige as ours. But this was not done, and we now realize that this trade is lost to us:

Wherefore, Sire,

We beseech, prostrated at the Royal Feet of Your Majesty, that you would order to be considered in your [Overseas] Council some remedy to ensure that this State does not perish completely, nor that of Angola, nor the interests of Portugal and of Your Majesty, so important for both these two conquests; because if there is no longer any demand for field-labor in Brazil, then the slave trade of Angola will likewise perish. This much is obvious.

Considering how to find a remedy for this state of affairs, we can suggest no other than that the cause thereof should be removed – the high price of 30,500, which was current in the years from 1645 to 1655. It is true that this price has declined since many years ago, but this would not matter so much if the duties had been lowered as well. The same applies to tobacco and the rigidities of its monopoly, so that if greed of gain leads to some smuggling and evasions, the resulting profits should not be reaped by foreigners but by the native-born vassals. These were called sons by the Lord Kings, Your Majesty's ancestors, and it is only right that Your Majesty should hold us in equal regard, and more especially those of Brazil because of the willing generosity with which they serve Your Majesty, to a degree far beyond their resources, for there are very few who do not owe more than they are worth to the traders who come from Portugal, due to the excessively high prices that are charged for slaves, copper utensils, iron, pitch, *ireu* [?], and stuffs of silk and wool, as the ministers who serve and have served in this High Court can inform Your Majesty, since many bankruptcy and insolvency cases have passed through their hands. Furthermore, to this should be added the annual contribution of more than 100,000 cruzados, comprising a levy of 40 percent on a total of 1,280,000 cruzados, which this city alone has to contribute toward the dowry of the Lady Queen of England and the peace with Holland. Not to mention another six hundred added to the usual taxes to pay for the upkeep of the garrison (which is not the least important cause of our poverty) – so that if our products have no reliable export market, it must inevitably happen that we will not be able to carry these burdens and that Your Majesty's vassals in the whole state of Brazil will all be ruined. Moreover, it seems to us that this will be harmful to all the vassals in the kingdom of Portugal, since it follows that they, too, will then have fewer export markets for their own products. All this is very well known and understood by the fidalgos who have governed this State, and by the law officers of the Crown who have served here, for which reason we have ventured to expound it thus to Your Majesty, so that not only as our King and liege Lord, but also as our Father, you may rescue us all from the misery in which we lie. May God preserve the Royal Person of Your Majesty as these your vassals desire and need. Joam de Couros Carneiro wrote it in the municipal council at Bahia on 12 August 1687.

[Signed] *Antonio Guedes de Paiva | Manuel Pereira de Goes | Domingos Dias Machado | Francisco Pereira Ferraz | Domingos Pires de Carvalho.*

# 7

# GOVERNMENT AND SOCIETY IN DUTCH BRAZIL

*Portugal was ruled by the Spanish Hapsburgs from 1580 to 1640. During that period, it profited from the advantages of new markets and opportunities in Spain and its empire, but its commerce and colonies also became a target for Spain's enemies. The rebellious provinces of Holland formed the Dutch West India Company in 1621 to aid in the political and economic struggle against the Hapsburg Crown. Portugal and its colonies and commerce, now ruled by the Spanish Hapsburgs, became prime targets for the Dutch. Pernambuco and subsequently much of the northeastern coast of Brazil were captured after 1630; the Dutch created their own colony in northeastern Brazil and held it until they were expelled in 1654. The report included here provides an overview of that colony during the years in which the Dutch, under the able direction of Governor Johann Maurits von Nassau, sought to make the Brazilian colony a success by extending religious toleration to Catholics and Jews. (From José Antônio Gonsalves de Mello, ed., Fontes para a História do Brasil Holandês, 1. Economia Açucareira [Recife, 1981], pp. 96–129.)*

## 1. A Brief Report on the State That Is Composed of the Four Conquered Captaincies, Pernambuco, Itamaracá, Paraíba, and Rio Grande, Situated in the North of Brazil

### Government by the Dutch

His Excellency Johan Maurits, Count of Nassau, as governor-general, captain and admiral-general, together with the noble members of the High and Secret Council, acting on behalf of their High Powers, the States-General of the United Netherlands, of His Highness the Prince of Orange, and of the noble directors of the General West India Company, constitute the supreme government of those areas of Brazil that have already been conquered or that will be conquered in the future. To them is subordinated the Board of Political Counsellors, which was established to administer justice.

The aforesaid Board of Political Counselors, which should consist of nine members, is at present greatly under strength, with insufficient counselors to conduct its business. Heer Ippo Eysens was killed in October 1636 in Paraíba;

Heer Cornelis Adriaensz Jongknecht has also died, just after his return from an expedition to the south; and shortly afterwards, Heer Johan Robbertsen died at Cape Santo Agostinho. Heer Jacob Stachhouwer has become a private citizen, Heer Paulus Seroskerchen has obtained permission to return to the Netherlands, and finally Heer Hendrick Schilt has been dismissed from office. There are currently only three political counselors, namely Heeren Willem Schot, Balthasar Wyntgis, and Elias Herckmans. The last-named has to date been living in Paraíba, of which he is director, and consequently has been unable to attend meetings of the board. Heer Wyntgis used to live on [the island of] Itamaracá as director of that captaincy, but, owing to the board's reduced numbers, we have commanded him to take up residence here, in order to accompany Heer Willem Schot in the exercise of justice. We have appointed a number of assistant counselors to work alongside these counsellors in dealing with criminal matters and with other issues of major importance. Nonetheless, judicial and other concerns, which are the very purpose for which the college exists, are not being exercised as they should be, and as is so necessary for the good of the settlers.

The period for which Heeren W. Schot and B. Wyntgis were contracted to serve has now expired, and each of them has bought a sugar plantation. They therefore request to be relieved of their positions, though they are both willing to continue in office until such time as the Assembly of the Nineteen[1] should send other political counselors to take their places. That release from duty cannot be denied them for any longer than it will take for their replacements to arrive. Your Lordships will readily appreciate how essential it is for us here to restore board membership to full strength.

As justice is the main concern of the Board of Political Counselors, it is highly expedient that those functions should be exercised by jurists. Not only should such jurists have learned legal theory at law school but, as far as possible, they should also have worked in the courts for a number of years and have been taught and experienced how justice works in practice.

Membership of the subordinate boards of justice is achieved here by the holding of elections in all the captaincies and areas of jurisdiction, as is laid down in our instructions. That means that in those places where there are suitable Netherlanders to serve as magistrates alongside the Portuguese, five magistrates are elected, of whom two are Netherlanders and three are Portuguese. In the remaining areas, we have to regulate matters according to circumstances. Thus, in the areas of jurisdiction that are Olinda, Itamaracá, and Paraíba, the magistrates' bench is made up of five members each, whereas in Sirinhaém and Rio Grande, it consists of only three. In those latter instances, the lower numbers are in response to the requests of the settlers. They assert

1  The Heeren Negentien were the nineteen directors of the West India Company.

that, as there are so few of them, they should not be overburdened with these duties, until such time as Netherlanders settle there, and suitable people are found to serve alongside the Portuguese, though in Sirinhaém, of the three magistrates there, one Netherlander has already been elected.

The magistrates' benches were instituted a few months ago and have been in operation ever since. However, till now it has not been possible for them to proceed according to the ordinances and methods of the Netherlands and Western Frisia. There are two reasons for that. The first is that it is a very difficult task to get an entire people to change its laws, its system, and its approach and learn a new method. The second derives from the difference in language and the difficulty in translating our ordinances from Dutch into Portuguese. However, we are busily engaged with that undertaking and we shall soon issue Portuguese translations of our ordinances in respect of judicial matters, inasmuch as they relate to those benches of magistrates.

Apart from the aforesaid magistrates' benches, there also exists in every district a board of legal guardians and administrators for orphans. It is an elected body and is composed of two Portuguese and one Netherlander. There is also a secretary. It has been constituted in accordance with the rules that apply to administrators for orphans in Amsterdam. *Mutatis mutandis*, the rules have been translated into Portuguese for the use of speakers of that language.

We also have the Board of Management of the Misericórdia of Olinda. Its task is to supervise and administer the property, houses, lands, and black slaves belonging to the Misericórdia. It does its work in the city of Olinda. Its board of management consists of seven members, of whom three are Netherlanders and four are Portuguese chosen from the brotherhood of the Misericórdia.

## The Reformed Religion

In respect of the Reformed Religion in the conquered territory, the Word of God in all its purity and with general consent is preached to the reformed community in the Dutch language by Ministers[2] Kesselarius and Dapper here in Recife.[3] It is also preached by Minister Plante, who is currently serving in the army. Minister Polhemius officiates on the island of Itamaracá and in Goiana, whilst Ministers Cornelis van der Poelen and Doreslaer do the same in Paraíba. Also here in Recife is Minister Soler, who preaches in French

---

2  These Calvinist ministers are in some texts referred to as *predikanten* (preachers).
3  As expressed in full in the original, this city bore the name Recife de Olinda (literally, Reef of Olinda).

and Portuguese. Minister Batchelar preaches in English in Paraíba. Minister Johannes Oosterdagh has also received orders to work with the army.

There are many places and garrisons, such as Rio Grande, Cape Santo Agostinho, and the townships of Porto Calvo and Penedo, which have no ministers, with the result that such work has to be carried out by those who visit the sick.

Furthermore, many Netherlanders have bought sugar plantations or work with sugarcane or in other occupations in the interior. Consequently, owing to where they live, they are unable to attend divine service. It is, therefore, most essential that ministers or suitable candidates [for the ministry] should come out here from the Netherlands and be sent to preach at sundry places in the surrounding countryside. Such places, for example, are the sugar plantations of Paraíba, Goiana, the meadowlands of the River Capibaribe,[4] and the plantations of Cape Santo Agostinho. It is also essential that such plantations should be required to make a financial contribution toward the upkeep of these ministers. The Netherlanders would be very willing to do that, and those in Goiana have already made representations to us about this very matter. That is because it grieves them to go on living, as they have done for such a long time, without hearing the Word of God and without even having a single sick visitor. The Portuguese are scandalized by this, saying that we call ourselves the reformed community, and yet our people live in such places without ever visiting a church or a chapel and without practicing any form of religious observance.

### The Catholic Faith

As for the Catholics, they benefit from the terms laid down in the accord signed when Paraíba was conquered, that is to say that they are free to exercise their religion and to make use of their churches and monasteries. Their clergy includes three Orders: the Franciscans, the Carmelites, and the Benedictines.

The Franciscan friars are the most numerous and possess five friaries. The first is in the town of Frederica in Paraíba, the second in Igaraçu, the third in Olinda, the fourth in Ipojuca, and the fifth in Sirinhaém. They are all fine buildings. In addition, they have a small friary in Capibaribe, above Massurepe. The Franciscans own no land, receive no [specific] income, and live off the charitable gifts that people give them.

The Carmelites own two friaries, a fairly insignificant one in Paraíba and another in Olinda that would be a splendid building if it were finished. We

---

4   The fertile valley of this river is still known as the *Várzea* ("meadowlands") and is named as such in the original text.

are not aware that they possess any other property except a few houses in the city of Olinda. Those houses were either built and leased by them or were built by others, with the owner receiving a small annual income from the latter, which he or his successors pay to the Order.

The Benedictine monks also have two monasteries, the first in Paraíba, where [before the conquest] they had started a handsome structure, and the second in the city of Olinda. The latter is very fine indeed but was greatly damaged by the fire. This Order owns a fine sugar plantation on the Barreiras estate in Paraíba. It stretches along both sides of the river down to below the forts. There are a number of small islands on the river, including the Restinga fortress. In Pernambuco, this Order possesses a splendid sugar plantation by the name of Massurepe. It has extensive territory and is currently milling its sugar cane.

Apart from these Orders, there are also many clergy that they call the Fathers. These priests celebrate Mass and live from the money that they earn in payment for the Masses or from what they are given by the sick or from other sources. The Fathers possess lands and incomes that constitute their own private property. In addition to their religious work, they also occupy themselves with their plantations, which they cultivate with their black [slaves]. In each captaincy or in a given area, they are subordinated to a vicar, and there is also a vicar-general who used to live in Olinda, where he was the superior of all clergy in these four northern captaincies.[5]

In addition to those who belong to the Reformed Religion or who adhere to Catholic superstition, there are, among the settlers in this land, many Jews and people with Jewish tendencies. Formerly, for fear of justice or the Inquisition, they concealed their beliefs and pretended to be Christians. After the conquest, however, they began to make public their religion. They joined the Jews who have come from the Netherlands and accompany them in their superstitious practices.

## Jews

The Portuguese, who are Old Christians, are scandalized with the freedom granted to the Jews, or rather, that they strive to achieve that freedom. The Jews who come from the Netherlands behave with a certain audacity, not only in their aggressive arguing about their superstitious beliefs but also in the way that they slander the Christian religion. For those reasons, we have been forced to give them a stern warning to put an end to such behavior, under pain of severe punishment; indeed, we have forbidden it. We have commanded the head bailiff to break up their conventicles, which were

5  These were Pernambuco, Itamaracá, Paraíba, and Rio Grande.

becoming more and more public in the town of Recife and were greatly scandalizing the reformed community and their ministers. Strict orders have been issued, requiring them to conduct their ceremonies behind closed doors and in such secrecy that they should not be heard and not cause any further scandal.

The Jews consider that they are entitled to greater freedom than the Papists, as we are more assured of their loyalty. We are well aware that, as they profess their Judaism publicly, in no way would they wish or be able to go back to being under Spanish control. On the contrary, they would strive to maintain and defend this State, whereas the Portuguese Papists have revealed that they are not entirely loyal to us and that they would cast us aside at the first opportunity.

## Catholics

But let us return to Christian affairs. The Papists' religious Orders, as we have indicated, have shown considerable zeal in building their handsome monasteries. But that is not all. In addition to the monasteries, in every town there is a mother church and other churches and chapels, so that there is no shortage of churches in the towns. Furthermore, it is a rare estate that does not have its own church or chapel, with sufficient capacity for a reasonable assembly.

The Portuguese inhabitants are extremely obstinate with regard to their religion and are imbued with such stupid prejudices that they do not even wish to listen [to the views of others]. The same has to be said of their priests, who have filled them with these prejudices and refuse to hear about any other religion. They have hardly any knowledge of the basic rudiments of the Christian religion, and the road to salvation is entirely hidden from them. All they know is how to mutter their Ave Marias while telling the rosary beads that each one of them either wears around his neck or carries in his hands. For them, a man is not a good Christian unless he openly carries his rosary in his hands or wears it round his neck. They regard those of the Reformed Religion as great heretics and hate them, not only on religious grounds, but mainly because they [the Catholics] were the ones who were defeated. For that reason, what the Portuguese have done till now and the obedience that they show are the results of fear and constraint. They have no liking for our State, except for a small minority who genuinely welcome us.

## Free Men and Slaves

As for the inhabitants in general, they consist of free men or slaves. The free men are Netherlanders, Portuguese, and Brazilians.

## The Netherlanders

The Netherlanders are composed of two groups: those who are obliged to work and those who are private citizens or have been discharged from work. We shall come to the first group later on.

Those Netherlanders who are exempt from work are the ones who came from the home country as private citizens or who became private citizens once they were here. For us to have available soldiers who are not a drain on the resources of the [West India] Company, we have already discharged from service a considerable number of officers and soldiers. That we do when once we are certain that they have completed, their tour of duty, that is to say, when once they have served for four full years out here, excluding the time spent on the voyage. However, that is insufficient to colonize such a vast territory. In addition, many of them look to be discharged solely in order to return to the home country aboard merchant ships as and when they see fit. That is something that we have noticed from time to time.

The private citizens, who till now have come here from the Netherlands, are mainly merchants and their employees, while those of lesser substance are tavern keepers and small-time traders. To them is due the huge growth of Recife and António Vaz.[6] It is now twice as big as it was before and has a constant building program. But that too is insufficient and is trivial in relation to the size of the population that is actually needed. It is, therefore, essential that greater efforts and resources be applied to attract more Netherlanders to this land. That is of particular importance to the [West India] Company, for it is the best way of ensuring the defense and progress of this State and of bringing about a reduction in the charges that it has to meet. The more immigrants come to live here, the more the land is cultivated, the more prosperous it will become, and the greater will be the benefit to the Company. If this conquered territory were filled with Netherlanders, the Company would be safe from the disloyalty of the Portuguese inhabitants. Indeed, if the enemy were to attempt to invade, those inhabitants would not be able to be of any assistance to the enemy, nor would they dare to, nor could they provide them with any food supplies, as is their current practice. In that way, the Company would also take control of the territory and would cause the Portuguese to be less of a danger toward our State. If need be, the Dutch inhabitants could serve as reliable soldiers, many of them having already borne arms as officers or in the ranks. The Company would thus be relieved of the financial burden of maintaining large garrisons, which would otherwise need to be kept to defend the very lengthy coastline here. It would then only have to remain on guard against enemy attacks from outside its boundaries and

6  A nearby island.

could be assisted [by men] from the territory; whereas, at present, when it comes under a dangerous attack, it has to take immediate steps against foes from both within and without.

It is, however, important to bear in mind that the kind of people that are sent here is not a trivial matter, nor are the terms on which they come, simply because sending settlers out in accordance with the old ruling in this matter is, in our view, quite inappropriate. Indeed, it would do the Company more harm than good. Furthermore, it is also inappropriate to give the settlers parcels of confiscated and cultivated land, along with the privilege of their being exempt from all tithes and other charges for a period of five years. The reason is that such land may be sold for good money and charges readily collected from it. Nor may parcels of land belonging to any one of the Portuguese inhabitants be sold off to the [Dutch] settlers. Consequently, the latter may only receive land that has not been cultivated or worked on and that has not belonged to any previous owner. Such land lies well into the interior, beyond all the inhabited areas and the cattle farms, and it is doubtful whether the [new] settlers would be very pleased with them. If they were to dwell so far from the sea, how could they help us, were the enemy to attack us from the sea? Yet, if marauders were to come from the rear, bursting through the scrubland, such settlers would, in effect, constitute excellent perimeter guards, with the onslaught falling on them first. That would be the sole advantage that we could expect, for, if we were to have such a Dutch advance post against the marauders and prowlers out in the bush, our enemies could not encroach upon our territory by stealth nor make their way across it at any point.

It is bound to be wearisome for the settlers to cut down the thick scrub and to clear and till the land. Such work has little appeal for the majority of Netherlanders in Brazil, for their objective is to make an easy living. The same will apply to the [new] settlers, mainly because those who are the most hardworking rarely figure among such settlers. Rather, they are feeble and feckless, brought in from one place or another, men who back in the Netherlands are too lazy to get down to solid work. If such settlers arrive with no means of support of their own, they will be even less useful to the Company because they will need to be provided with food and other items. That was the case with those who arrived with John Harrison, as well as with those other folk that the Delegates placed as settlers on the island of Itamaracá. The result of that settlement was that they ended up owing huge sums to the warehouses, debts that they will never pay. There was no particular progress with farming [there], and the settlers were reduced to penury, most of them becoming soldiers.

It is also important to note that quite the wrong effect is produced by sending out settlers to receive free land and housing in accordance with the [old] regulation. That is because many people here who have bought sugar plantations (many of which are not much better than untilled land and which have few buildings on them) are now beginning to complain and to argue that they have the same rights as the [new] settlers, that they should be regarded as [new] settlers themselves and that they too should receive their sugar plantations just as freely. Furthermore, some of the inhabitants of Recife consider that under the terms of the [old] regulation, land should be allotted to them free of charge, whilst others, who have purchased their houses, maintain the same in respect of those properties. Were this to happen, the Company's finances would go awry. We request the Assembly, therefore, to give future consideration to its best course of action in this matter.

Those wishing to profit from farming in Brazil should not travel out here empty-handed. On the contrary, they should [first] amass sufficient capital to arrange for the construction of the workplace that they need. Such workplaces are necessary out here and cannot be brought from the Netherlands. They should also have sufficient capital to buy black slaves because, without those, no profit can be achieved in Brazil. The Portuguese have a saying: "Whoever wishes to take Brazil out of Brazil should first bring Brazil into Brazil"; that is, whoever wishes to make his fortune and heap up capital in Brazil must first bring considerable resources with him to Brazil.

It is wrong, therefore to send poor people out to inhabit Brazil, unless those settlers have at least a leader who can make a [significant] contribution in some way. Every day, we notice that the old[er] soldiers, who know the land well and have become used to it, when once they become civilians, cannot thrive unless they accept the authority of a plantation owner or otherwise subject themselves to someone who is prepared to help them. We are referring here to those soldiers who intend to live by working as farmhands.

The most suitable new settlers are individuals who arrive here with some capital and who are able to purchase slaves. Such people can set themselves up from their own resources, [working] until they produce profits with which they can reimburse themselves. Such people can make considerable profits in this country.

Meanwhile, those Netherlanders who have started to settle in Brazil and who have been buying sugar plantations are working very hard to work the land again and to rebuild the sugar mills. That involves no little expenditure. By dint of great effort and considerable financial outlay, many mills are ready to crush cane this year or, at the very least, the land is unbelievably well planted with sugar cane. This year, the Company will derive huge profits and will do so especially next year and in ensuing years.

## The Portuguese

As for the Portuguese who have remained here in obedience to the High Powers, the members of the States-General and of the West India Company, and who have, therefore, kept their lands and sugar plantations, as well as those who have bought from us a number of confiscated sugar plantations, they have revealed themselves to be no less industrious than the Netherlanders, for all that they were considerably impoverished by the war and could not survive on their own resources. They have, however, received generous help from our merchants, who have taken little profit from the plentiful goods they had at their disposal. Our merchants willingly support the owner of any sugar mill or cane plantations, providing the farmers with all the goods and even the money that they need, only collecting the debt at the following harvest. Some of them have given an even later deadline where that has been the only way of promoting cultivation of the land. In addition, the price of sugar has currently risen so high as to encourage everybody to plant cane with all due vigor. It also inspires great confidence in the merchants in their attitude toward those who own sugar mills or cane plantations.

## The Brazilians

The third kind of free men are the [indigenous] Brazilians, who live in their villages and are inspected by Dutch captains. They eat manioc and a few other fruits, taking as much as they think is sufficient for their nutrition. In other respects, they lead carefree lives and have no inclination to amass wealth. They content themselves with owning a hammock in which to sleep and a few gourds to drink from, as well as a bow and arrows, flour, good water, and the game that they hunt in the woods for food. They work solely to earn enough cloth with which to cover their bodies and those of their wives. They believe that it is sufficient for their wives to don a shift that reaches down to the ground and for the men to obtain clothing that permits them to wear breeches and a doublet, though without a shirt.

Were it not for this last tendency, it would not be possible to get them to work. It is solely to earn cloth that they go to work, and they have no wish to do any further work when once they have earned enough for ten yards of coarse cloth or for some ready-made clothing. Normally, that corresponds to some twenty to twenty-four days' work. With just that, they then go back to their villages, saying that they have enough and need nothing else. They refuse to undertake any further work unless they are forced to by the Dutch captains.

The main tasks carried out by the Brazilians are chopping wood for the sugar mills, planting cane, clearing the cane plantations, driving or steering carts, looking after cattle and other similar jobs. They will not carry out such tasks if, apart from being fed, their payment is not first placed in their captain's hands, to be handed over when the shift is over and the work finished.

Currently, they live in many places but they are without religion, for lack of people to instruct them via their own language and to lead them in prayer. Indeed, we have no suitable person to send to their villages. They sent the Catholics away and have no wish to let them back again. It would, therefore, be appropriate if there were people in their villages capable of giving instruction to the Brazilians, especially the children. The aim would be for them to learn our language and, in due course, to be taught the rudiments of the Christian religion. For that purpose, we intend to employ the Spanish schoolmaster who has recently arrived.

They actually plead with us to send them our ministers. They say that they would be pleased if one or two of our ministers were to converse with them, give them instruction, baptize their children, and join their young people in marriage. In the villages of Paraíba, our minister Dorislaer is busy learning their language and giving them religious instruction. He has made such progress that he can now converse with them in Portuguese and, to a certain extent, preach to them and admonish them. Our ministers hope that the outcome will be very successful.

## The Slaves

We have talked about the free men. We now pass to discussing the slaves, of whom there are three categories: those from Africa, those from Maranhão, and those who were born locally.

Those from Africa come from Angola or from other places where the Company has dealings. Those from Angola are regarded here as the best because they are better at devoting themselves to work and also because when they are recent arrivals, they are more effectively taught by our long-serving blacks, as they understand one another's language.

However, those that the Company acquires on the Ardra coast[7] are slow-moving, obstinate, and disinclined to work, though, when they want to do it, they work even harder than the Angolans. At first, they refuse to accept any strict instructions and all rebel in the field against the stewards who are directing them. The stewards rain blows down on them and that causes them to speak a language that our long-serving blacks do not understand. Nor do the Ardra understand what anyone says, with the result that there is massive incomprehension. The situation will eventually improve since as soon as these first arrivals learn our language and grasp what work they

---

7 The Ardra came from Allada in Dahomey, nowadays the Republic of Benin.

are being employed to do, they will then be in a position to teach those who come later.

It is impossible to achieve anything in Brazil without slaves. Without them, the mills cannot crush the cane nor can the fields be tilled. The presence of slaves is essential to Brazil, and in no way can we operate without them: if any man feels offended by this, his is a useless scruple.

As Brazil cannot be cultivated without blacks, and as it is essential that there should be a large number of them (simply because everyone complains about not having enough blacks), it is most important that every means possible is brought to bear to ensure the traffic along the coast of Africa. The Company has the greatest interest in this matter because, apart from selling them at a good profit, the Company receives annually one third of the work of each black, so that the black works not only for his master but also for the Company.

As for the slaves from Maranhão, the Portuguese traffic in them, just as they do in Angola.

There was a third category of slaves, namely the indigenous Brazilians of this area, most of whom were located in Traição ["Treachery"] bay at the time when Bouwen Heynsen was there, and they were enslaved by the Portuguese. However, we have given them back their freedom, wherever we have been able to find them.

### The Portuguese Way of Life

Generally speaking, the Portuguese are easygoing with regard to their houses and the way in which their homes are run. They are quite happy with houses made from clay, as long as their sugar mills and their plantations function well.

They possess few items of furniture, apart from those that are necessary for the kitchen, as well as a bed and a table, for those are indispensable. Their greatest luxury consists in serving themselves at table from silver tableware. The menfolk seldom wear expensive clothes, dressing in normal fabrics or cloth even, with their breeches and doublet tailored with great slashes through which taffeta is revealed beneath. The women, however, dress expensively and bedeck themselves in gold, though they wear few or no diamonds but adorn themselves with lots of costume jewelry. They always wear hats when they go out and are carried in a hammock, over which a rug is draped. Alternatively, they are borne along enclosed in a costly sedan chair, duly dressed up, so as to be seen by their women friends and acquaintances. When they go out visiting, they send a message ahead, and the lady [hostess] seats herself on a splendid silken Turkish carpet that is spread out on the floor. There she awaits her lady friends, who sit down on the carpet at her side, just like tailors do. Their feet are shod because it would be most shameful to allow anyone to see their [bare] feet.

With regard to pictures and other ornaments to cover the walls, the Portuguese show no interest whatsoever and have no appreciation of painting.

They do not eat a wide range of dishes, as they are satisfied to nourish themselves with a little flour and dried fish, though they do have chickens, turkeys, pigs, sheep, and other animals. Such food they add to the flour and fish, especially when they invite friends to dinner.

They have excellent fruit, such as oranges, lemons, melons, watermelons, two varieties of bananas, pineapples, potatoes, two varieties of passion-fruit, custard-apples, and the most delicious of all fruits, *mangaba* plums.[8] They also eat sundry legumes, as well as maize, rice, and other crops from which they make a variety of sweet dishes. The latter are very good for them, and they eat great quantities of such sweetmeats.

The Portuguese mainly drink spring water, which is both healthy and pleasant. They dip pieces of sugarloaf into it and then suck them, which is a healthy and refreshing experience. They also make a honey drink, which is what the blacks drink most, whilst the indigenous Brazilians greatly enjoy a drink made from cashews.

There are many Portuguese who do not drink wine. On the other hand, there are many who drink a lot of wine. It is said that every year, five thousand casks of wine come to Recife to be consumed here. Few of the women drink wine, and many of them have never tasted wine throughout their lives.

Portuguese men and women are not very attractive. Their faces and bodies are rather wizened and their skin is swarthy. Normally, the womenfolk, even when quite young, lose their teeth and, owing to their leading such sedentary lives, they are not as nimble as Dutch women. Indeed, they wobble about on their high-heeled shoes as though their legs were in shackles.

The men guard their women very possessively and always keep them shut away, acknowledging in that way just how prone their compatriots are to leading other men's wives astray.

## Trade

We have said enough about the above subject [the Portuguese way of life] and now move on to commenting on the trade carried out in this territory.

Brazilian exports to the Netherlands comprise sugar, brazilwood, tobacco, sugar-coated sweetmeats, leatherwork, and sundry very fine varieties of timber for different purposes. This land also exports excellent cotton and ginger, and some here have now begun to manufacture indigo dye,

8 The fruit of the mangabeira *(Hancornia speciosa)*.

namely Daniel de Dieu and Jacob Velthuysen. They have already made a start with trial samples, though as yet they have not quite hit on the right way to produce it. If, in the Netherlands, someone could be found who understands how to manufacture indigo dye, then over here there would be no shortage of people ready to grow the indigo plant in abundance because it grows here everywhere [in the wild].

Likewise, annatto dye can also be produced here simply because small trees exist here and there from which it can be extracted. The same applies to cochineal. However, what we have mentioned above refers to trial samples whereas, to date, we have yet to see any samples of cochineal.

On the accompanying invoice there is a list of those goods that it would be best to export to us from the Netherlands: they are the ones that are most sought after and that attract the earliest payment.

## Crafts and Skills

We shall now mention the crafts and skills that are practiced out here. First place belongs to the boiling of sugarcane juice and to everything related to the process by which sugar is produced. There are lots of carpenters, stonemasons, blacksmiths, boiler men, pottery workers, not to mention tailors, cobblers, saddlers, jewelers, and a number of cotton spinners. The carpenters, stonemasons, blacksmiths, and boiler men earn at least three florins a day, and the master craftsmen four or five.

Men who do not work on the sugar plantations occupy their time, in addition to any craft that they might have, planting manioc or other agricultural produce, such as tobacco or something like that. Others are starting to set themselves up in the surrounding areas in order to plant legumes and every kind of Dutch seed. Some of these are already well underway, like lettuce, radishes, cucumber, turnips, watercress, and all the native vegetable produce, such as pumpkins, melons, water melons, maize, and so on. Food is generally dearer in Brazil than anywhere else in the world, and especially dear in Recife. That very fact spurs people on to sow and plant all that they can.

## The Company's Employees

We have already mentioned that all the Company's employees, from the lowliest to the most elevated, have been required to feed themselves at their own expense. They have come to terms with that, and even the soldiers prefer to receive their wages and allowance to getting their former food ration. That is because they find it more convenient to shop for native produce in the markets, especially as fresh meat is butchered daily. Nevertheless, their wages do not run to purchasing much food from the Netherlands, except for broad beans, peas, and barley. Indeed, they prefer local broad beans and other native produce.

We had continued to give the soldiers their bread ration, debiting their allowance by the equivalent amount. However, as we discovered that [the price of] our flour was greatly increasing, we decided to award the soldiers their allowance in full and to cancel the bread order, other than ship's biscuit. However, when times are hard, it will be possible to supply them with manioc flour. It is [, nevertheless,] our intention to supply [wheat] flour to our fortresses. The soldiers fully accept this arrangement, as they could hardly get by without bread. Indeed, they can use their money to buy plenty of [manioc] flour.

## [Other] Products

This land not only provides the food supplies mentioned earlier but also nearly everything that is needed for the construction of houses and ships. The exceptions are iron, pitch, tar, and bitumen. To build houses, it is possible to quarry freestone from the hillsides and the reefs [along the coast] or to use bricks that are fired here. Timber for building is also very abundant in the conquered territory, though it is a very costly exercise to chop and hew it in the places where it is required.

There are limekilns here also, where as much lime can be produced as necessary. Charcoal is likewise produced in quantity, as the Portuguese blacksmiths only use charcoal. However, when our smiths have to tackle large and heavy enterprises, they cannot resort to charcoal. Even though a great deal of charcoal is produced, saltpeter and sulphur are [also] needed for the manufacture of gunpowder.[9] Here, we also make cables from the inner bark of trees. The Portuguese use the same bark for cannon fuses. Sundry ships and caravels have been constructed here; the only imported materials used are the sails, the ironware, bitumen, pitch, and tar.

## The Course of the War in Brazil

We have commented sufficiently on the land and its inhabitants. We shall now concern ourselves with the questions of warfare and the defense of the coastline, beginning with a statement on the current situation of the enemy.

According to the latest news, Count Bagnuolo is about to break camp in Sergipe del-Rei and pull farther back, owing to the report that he has received of the expedition led by Heer Johan Ghijselin and the very noble

---

9 Gunpowder was used not just in warfare but also to blast away rock.

Sigismund von Schkoppe, who are in charge of our forces. We are, however, informed that the enemy still has some two thousand armed and semi-armed men, composed of soldiers and fugitive settlers.

In a letter that, six weeks to two months ago, Count Bagnuolo[10] wrote to His Excellency,[11] he requested that there be sent to him the wife of Luís Barbalho and the wife of Captain António de Freitas, assuring us that Luís Barbalho had reached Bahia with his regiment. We expressly sent an intelligent young man to take our reply to the count. He is His Excellency's bugler; his task was also to observe and take note of whatever he could. He duly reported to us everything he was able to find out. His report tells us that Luís Barbalho had duly arrived, according to what people said, with four thousand men. However, we are perfectly aware that Portuguese regiments consist of no more than three hundred, four hundred, or [even] five hundred men. Doubtless the regiment in question cannot amount to more than that, as we learnt that the men had arrived aboard three caravels. In Sergipe, people were also making much of a great fleet that they were expecting, on board which many thousands of men were due to arrive. But, as Barbalho landed with [just] one regiment, we assume that the said armada has yet to arrive; indeed, that its sole purpose will be the defense of Bahia. Moreover, it was rumored that Barbalho had been entrusted with commanding the Bahia militia. At all events, his wife has vehemently urged that she should not be forced to leave here, as she did not believe that her husband had reached Bahia, and that if he had, he would have written to her. Consequently, she has remained here, awaiting further instructions.

The rumor here is that Count Bagnuolo will retreat as far as the Ávila tower, which is situated some fifty kilometers north of Bahia (or Salvador). Captain António de Freitas has told his wife to land there to meet him. If, therefore, the retreat is not yet an accomplished fact, there can be no doubt that it will take place as soon as our troops approach [theirs].

Moving on now to our own concerns, we sent a letter to Your Lordships (of which we enclose a copy) via an Englishman brought here from São Tomé. In that letter, we explained our reasons for sending an expedition against Elmina castle,[12] as well as mentioning the successful outcome granted to us by Almighty God. The expedition was led by the very noble lord Colonel Hans van Koin and by Sergeant-Major John Goodlad, known as Bongarçon. All our ships and troops (other than those left behind as a

---

10  Count Bagnuolo was a Neapolitan general in the service of Philip IV of Spain. His mission was to expel the Dutch from Brazil.

11  Johan Maurits, Count of Nassau.

12  Situated on the Gold Coast of Lower Guinea, this castle, known to the Portuguese as São Jorge da Mina, was an entrepôt where the Portuguese traded in gold and slaves. It fell to the Dutch in 1638, as is outlined in the text.

garrison) have arrived back here at the expected time and have completed the undertaking in every detail. In order to inform your Lordships of every aspect, we are enclosing copies of the letters submitted by the general about that coast and listing the artillery, military supplies, and everything else that was found there.

In the selfsame letter, we also reported on the expedition that we sent to Ceará under the leadership of George Gartzman, accompanied, as sergeant-major, by the valiant Captain Hendrick van Haus. They made their way in two sailing-ships, with a force of one hundred and fifty men. However, we are unable to add anything about subsequent events as we have received no further news so far.

Notwithstanding these [two] expeditions, we have not neglected the preparation of an armed attack on the enemy at Sergipe del-Rei. As his dangerous illness did not allow His Excellency to go in person, we appointed [as leaders] Heer Johan Ghijselin and the very noble Sigismund von Schkoppe. The ships, the troops, the munitions, and the food supplies with which the expedition set out in search of the enemy are all carefully listed in the minutes of this Council, as Your Lordships will find.

## Fortifications

We shall now describe the fortresses, castles, and smaller forts along our coastline. Some of them existed before the conquest, and others have been constructed by our troops in order to defend the coast.

## Pernambuco

Starting in the south, we have, first of all, Fort Maurits. It was built by our troops at Penedo, on the north bank of the River São Francisco, about twenty-five miles from the sea. It is a pentagonal fort and is perched on a rocky escarpment, eighty feet above the river. One side is so steep as to be totally inaccessible, whilst on the other side, where the enemy could conceivably attack, the fort is defended by three bastions. The land is low-lying in the surrounding area, except for a small eminence, about the height of a man, and that is covered by water throughout the summer.[13] The fort has lofty ramparts and deep, dry ditches, as Your Lordships will be able to see from the maps that His Excellency has already sent you (or is yet to send you). It is extremely well defended.

On the other side [of the river], facing Fort Maurits, our troops have built a small wooden fort, and a battery of three six-caliber cannon has been installed in a tree.

13   The author probably meant "winter" (the rainy season).

On the same side of the river, farther downstream, near the rivermouth, there is a redoubt named "Keert de Koe."[14] Its purpose is to dominate the river at that point, to keep it free and to protect our shipping, as well as to have a footing there. It is located in a swamp.

These forts are reasonably provided for in respect of artillery, munitions, and food supplies, and three hundred men are stationed there at present.

The expenditure on these fortifications (now completed) amounts to twenty thousand florins. It is now proposed that Fort Maurits should be clad in mortar, which will cost as much again. We are in a quandary over this and have not been able to decide how to proceed. We shall see later what the appropriate action is.

The next fort is that of Porto Calvo. It was greatly strengthened after the conquest, yet it still remained as much of an irregular shape as it was beforehand. It is essential to surround it with a counterscarp with a solid palisade. This fort still has all the artillery and nearly all the ammunition that was found in it. Just a few unnecessary pieces of artillery were removed and dismantled. It is now fully equipped and garrisoned by two companies of soldiers. The fort sits on a high and isolated hilltop, without any other hills in the vicinity that overlook it. Rivers run along two of its sides. Inside the fort there is a well that provides excellent water. It is some eighteen fathoms deep and is lined with square-cut freestone that reaches upward from the bottom of the well to its rim.

If we continue northward from Porto Calvo, the first fortification that we come across is at Cape Santo Agostinho.

We now have no defensive construction there. Regarded as worthless, the fortification that the enemy built around the church dedicated to Our Lady of Nazareth, sited on the highest hill at the cape, was razed to the ground long ago.

The redoubt at Pontal,[15] which we were able to defend against every enemy attack, has now been so damaged by the sea that one of its sides has collapsed and been borne away by the waves. Our every effort to shore it up to preserve it has proved unavailing.

Fort Ghijselin stands facing it on an island and is likewise so damaged by the sea that despite the constantly renovated shoring that exists in front of it, the battery and all the front of the fort have collapsed. As we had no further use for this fort after conquering Cape Santo Agostinho, and as it merely served as a pointless garrison for idlers, we finally decided to gut it completely and leave the sea to take it over in its own good time.

In order to keep the harbor in our possession, it will be essential to build a fort at Pontal, though sited more inland than was the redoubt. In that way,

---

14  Literally, "where the cow turns back."
15  The word *pontal* means "spit of land," thus indicating the location of this redoubt.

we can avoid its being exposed to the sea, and at the same time it will act as protection for the harbor, making it more secure, as well as enabling us to keep the battery on the sandbar, for that has always been there. It is true that the battery could not be defended, if some enemy were to land there with sufficient forces. It is open from the rear and cannot be enclosed. Consequently, the enemy could reach that point by stealth because the battery is located below two elevations, from where it would be susceptible to direct musket fire. It is impossible to counteract this danger by building a rampart, no matter how high. To defend the battery, there is just one redoubt, situated on one of the two elevations. From there the other elevation can be fired on and so, to a certain extent, the battery on the sandbar can be defended.

Nonetheless, all this is of the greatest importance for, if we have a fort at Pontal, the harbor will be useless to our enemies. We shall always be in a position to provide the Pontal fort with every assistance, bringing in food supplies, munitions, and troops, via either the major sandbar or the smaller one, provided that we keep those sandbars under our control.

There can be no doubt that if we have a fort at Pontal, the enemy will not attempt to attack the harbor. [After all,] it is not such a convenient harbor as to merit a great effort to take it, especially as ships with a great draught cannot sail in, and as both the way in and the way out are perilous.

After Cape Santo Agostinho, we come to the forts of Recife.

The first of these is Fort Prince Willem, situated in Afogados.[16] It is a quadrangular fort with four bastions and is very well positioned because it secures the road through the meadowlands and defends the crossing from the island of António Vaz to Afogados. It is located on the highest part of a plain and in that way it dominates the land around it for as far as cannon-fire can reach. On the northeastern side, it possesses deep ditches. To the southeast, however, the ditches are very shallow, and the land is higher, enabling the enemy to advance by [digging] approach works. It is most important that this fort be surrounded by a counterscarp, or otherwise it will be too weak to defend. It is built from unusual earth that dries as hard as stone in the summer but in winter, when it rains, it becomes as soft as mortar, with the result that the water cuts channels in it to the point where it becomes very costly to make the essential repairs to preserve the fort.

The next fort was Fort Emília, located on the island of Santo António.[17] It stood in front of the *hornaveques*[18] of Fort Frederik Hendrik, but it too was abandoned as useless, and orders were given to demolish it.

---

16  Afogados is an area on the mainland, to the west of the island of António Vaz.
17  Strictly speaking, the island of Santo António forms part of the island of António Vaz, constituting its historic easternmost quarter.
18  This kind of fortification (deriving from German *Hornwerk*) was horn-shaped and consisted of a curtain or rampart extending between two half-bastions.

The next fort is Fort Frederik Hendrik, [also] known as the Fort das Cinco Pontas.[19] It possesses five regular bastions and is located at one end of the island of Santo António. From there can be seen all the ships at anchor in Recife's harbor. This fortress, therefore, acts as the [principal] defense of the harbour. It is built on an elevated spot overlooking the route that the enemy must take to have any opportunity of attacking the clusters of houses on António Vaz. It also protects the waterholes, which are the only ones that provide water to Recife and António Vaz in times of necessity and siege.

In the early stages, the ramparts of this fortress were no more than twelve or thirteen feet high. Indeed, when His Excellency and the members of the Supreme Council arrived here, the walls of the fort were in such a ruinous state that a fully armed horseman could clamber over them. The stockade and the palisades were rotting and lying on the ground. The whole construction was in a state of collapse, and the ditches were quite dry, owing to the movement of the sands. We gave orders that the ditches should be made wider and deeper, that the ramparts should be made thicker and raised to the level of the former parapet, and that a new [and higher] parapet be built on top of them. We also ordered that the outer edge of the ditches be surrounded by a counterscarp and that the fortress be solidly shored up on the side overlooking the sea. The result is that the fortress is now strengthened and can be defended. All of this will cost the Company some twenty thousand florins for the new parts alone.

This fortress has also acquired on its south side a solid *hornaveque* that used to stretch in the direction of the former Fort Emília, as well as another smaller one that ran in the same direction and is overlooked by it. All of this is in reasonable condition.

Within arquebus-range from Fort Frederik Hendrik, to the northwest, there stands a redoubt next to the Capibaribe. This redoubt acts as an advance post, enabling us to ascertain whether the enemy is trying to cross the river.

Next comes the great cluster of buildings on António Vaz, where His Excellency lives. It is girt about by a very lofty rampart. This rampart boasts two bastions on the west and northwest sides and is linked to the ditch of Fort Ernestus by a defensive wall that encloses it. To the south, alongside the beach, there stands a half-bastion. From there, a wing or [further] defensive wall stretches away, skirting the river and passing in front of His Excellency's residence, before ending where it joins the ditch of Fort Ernestus again, in front of which it stands open.

This quarter is divided into streets and patches of land, where many people have begun to build and where many houses have already been

---

19   Literally, the "Fort of the Five Angles." Nowadays, it houses the museum of the city of Recife.

completed. The streets are arranged in such a way that they all open on to Fort Ernestus, the ramparts of which tower above them.

Fort Ernestus is sited around the friary of Santo António. If it were completed, it would be a quadrangular fortress with four bastions. It is complete on its north, south, and west sides. As for the east side, however, it is merely closed in by the old wall of the monastery, and that wall is now threatening to collapse. We have debated whether it would be right to demolish the wall and complete the fortress with a pincer-shaped earth rampart. However, the cost has led the work to be postponed because this part of the fortress is not subject to any danger and because it is essential for the ditches to be made deeper, not only around the major residential area but also around Fort Ernestus. They are of little use as they are. With the earth removed from the ditches, we plan to build a counterscarp around both these developments.

To the north of Fort Ernestus stands Fort Waerdenburgh on terrain that juts out from the mainland. It is quadrangular, but the shortage of available land has prevented its having more than three bastions. These are sited on the north, west, and east sides, but without one on the south. A ditch separates if from the mainland so that it is surrounded by water. It is subject to the river's impact and always requires costly shoring up to preserve it. As it appears that this fort is not really needed, and as it is understood that a mere redoubt is sufficient to protect that area, it has been decided to allow the river to carry on ravaging it. It will then be converted into a redoubt.

There then comes [the island of] Recife. The members of the High and Secret Council, as well as the Political Counsellors, all reside here. It constitutes the main port for all major shipping throughout the captaincy of Pernambuco. It is there that the Company has established its headquarters; and it is there that all the general warehouses lock away all foodstuffs, artillery, military supplies, and merchandise.

This port possesses an admirable layout, consisting of a continuous stretch of rock, on which there is a mole or dike, forty yards wide or more and some five miles in length. It runs from the lesser sandbar (the *Barreta*) along the whole length of Recife, thus creating inside it a port where many ships can dock.

Work is taking place to surround and enclose Recife with a strong, flanking palisade, as the shortage of land [on the island] does not allow it to be enclosed within ramparts, either on the outer side facing the sea or on the inner side where the river flows past. This palisade will certainly cost from eight to ten thousand florins. We hope to collect this from [the owners of] houses, land, and warehouses here in Recife, private citizens and Company alike.

Further on, on the route to the city of Olinda, there stand a battery with a stone wall facing seawards and an earth redoubt facing inwards in the direction of the river. The base of the redoubt rises out of the river and was assembled from unwhitewashed stones. These two structures are linked together by a strong wooden palisade. Nearby is the exit from the harbor.

Outside Recife, we first come across the old castle of São Jorge. This castle is in ruins, and the administrators of the hospital requested its use as an infirmary, promising to repair it internally and to preserve it at their own cost. They would use it until such time as it were needed for military purposes and for the defense of Recife. We decided to grant their request, both because that would save the Company expense and because this castle is of no practical use at present and will probably remain so in future. Nevertheless, all its cannon remain in place.

Facing the castle of São Jorge, standing on the rocky reefs, close to the sea and the entrance of the harbor bar, there is another splendid stone castle that we call the "castle of the sea." The sea has to some extent damaged it. It pounds against it with full force and with every incoming tide and has torn away some of the stonework at its base. We have arranged with the master stonemason who first built it to engage the help of Portuguese stonemasons to fill in the hole and secure the castle against the sea, for that is indispensable to prevent future damage.

In front of the castle of São Jorge, on the sandy strip that extends in the direction of Olinda, there stands Fort Bruyne.[20] It is quadrangular and, on the side facing the sea, it has merely small, half-bastions. On the side facing the river, its bastions are entire and have been fully completed. The fort is in good order and in a perfect state of repair, but it needs a ditch and palisades. In front of it there stands a somewhat damaged *hornaveque*. A musket-shot away from this *hornaveque* there stands a redoubt that acts as an advance post.

All these forts and constructions are well supplied with artillery and ammunition, in accordance with the circumstances pertaining to each one. They are also fully garrisoned with troops in accordance with the soldiers that we have available. However, we are much in need of gun carriages and batteries. We remedy this, as far as we can, by getting the Portuguese to fell the right sort of timber in the woodlands and for that we pay them. Thus, we are able to make excellent gun carriages, and they are cheaper and more durable than those made in the Netherlands simply because they require no iron bolts [to hold them together].

---

20  Nowadays, this fort is referred to as Fort Brum and is a military museum of some note.

## Itamaracá

If we continue northwards, the nearest fortification is to be found on the island of Itamaracá. Inside the harbor bar, we first encounter Fort Orange, located on a sandbank that is separated from the mainland by a creek that can be forded at low tide. This fort dominates the entrance of the harbor, since ships on entering have to pass within arquebus-range. It is a square fort, has four bastions, and was recently repaired and made higher. However, it has only a shallow ditch and no stockade or palisade. It is essential that the last-named be installed and that the ditch be dug deeper (whilst its outer side needs a counterscarp). In front of this fort, on the north side, where the enemy could encroach, there stands a *hornaveque*.

The small town of Schkoppe, located on the same island, has been fortified for many, many years. Indeed, it was already fortified when we captured it. There was no alternative but to abandon the extensive parapet built by the Portuguese, as we had insufficient troops with which to garrison it. We left it to fall into ruins, but the little church that is to be found on the south side of the city has been connected to the battery that flanks the river. In that way, it is secure from any sudden incursion from the enemy or, indeed, from troops on the land side. Nonetheless, all of that is insufficient to stop a powerful enemy force coming from outside simply because all the fortifications are outmoded. On the far north of the little township, where the entrance is over the Itapissuma bridge, there is a tiny redoubt that acts as an advance post, but it offers no real defense.

At the northerly tip of the same island, at the entrance to the north sand-bar, there is also a redoubt with a battery that dominates the said entrance. It stands on a rocky eminence (a factor that precludes deep ditches) but it does have a palisade. This redoubt is a total ruin and needs to be rebuilt.

## Paraíba

Following on from these fortifications, we come to the three that are located along the River Paraíba. The first of these is situated on the south side of the sandbar, the second is on the north side, and the third is about a cannon-shot away from those two, standing between them, roughly in the middle of the river on a sandbank that creates a small island called the Restinga.[21]

The fort on the south side is entirely our construction: the old fort of Santa Catarina was demolished, as it was very small, cramped, and could not offer much resistance. Just outside the same spot, we have built this other one.

---

21  Literally, "sandbank."

On the land side it has a fine bastion, with its curtains running toward the beach. On either side, there is a half-bastion that is related to the other in a pincer formation. The perimeter of the fort is such that it is very spacious, and it possesses fine, lofty ramparts. However, owing to the shifting sands, as is the case on all the beaches, it is not feasible to have deep ditches. At all events, it is a very powerful fortress. Before our government came into being, this fortress was already contracted for and its construction had got well ahead. Nevertheless, we were the ones who met the bulk of the costs, namely thirty-one thousand florins.

The fort on the north, named Santo António, is quadrangular and possesses four bastions. It remains in the condition in which it was captured from the enemy. The sole exception is that, as it was greatly scarped when they built it and was, therefore, in danger of collapsing, we found it necessary to mitigate the slope on the outer side in order to give it a more practical shape.

The former Portuguese structure on the Restinga, in the middle of the river, has been demolished and replaced on the same spot with a fine redoubt equipped with half-bastions. A splendid battery is sited on the curtain that overlooks the channel in the river along which ships have to proceed. This site is as strong as any other in Brazil; it is almost within culverin-range of the island and is surrounded by water.

In the township of Frederica, the Franciscan friary has been moderately fortified in order to provide refuge and protection for the inhabitants of the town should they be attacked by marauders or prowlers, as has already been the case.

## Rio Grande

North of the Paraíba forts there comes Castle Ceulen in Rio Grande, located on the rocky reef at the entrance to the harbor bar. Built of freestone, it is a very lofty castle and possesses very thick and sturdy ramparts. At its front, on the land side, it has the shape of an *hornaveque*, that is to say a curtain with two half-bastions, equipped in the old style with cannon turrets and casemates. In front of the other three sides are pincer formations.

This fortress is surrounded by lofty dunes that are merely at arquebus-range. They are so high that if one stands on them, it is possible to see right through the crenellations to the terreplein [on the other side] and, therefore, to fire musket balls at the very feet of those inside the castle. When we laid siege to it, we set up our artillery on these dunes and plied the castle with such a cannonade that nobody could remain on the parapet. This defect has now been remedied. We have erected on the front rampart a second earth parapet that stands on top of the original stone one. This second one is proof against cannonfire and, consequently, the entire upper section of the fortress is covered over and protected.

As this fortress is surrounded by water at high tide and has to stand up to the impact of the sea, it is slightly damaged at the base. Repairs will be carried out by constructing a new base made of stone and lime.

The castle is well equipped with artillery: apart from the two cannon that were captured when it was taken, we have installed two more four-caliber cannon. These were found on the caravels that were moored in the river when we laid siege to the castle. In general, all the constrictions, forts, and castles that we have described above are well supplied with artillery and ammunition.

In would be very helpful for us to state at this point just how many cannon exist in each fort, whether they are made of iron or brass, and what is their weight and caliber, not to mention presenting a complete inventory of all the munitions and ancillary objects. However, up to the present time, we have been unable to assemble all the data, though we shall complete the task as soon as possible.

All the forts are reasonably well garrisoned with troops. But to take our army into battle with the necessary strength, everywhere we [have to] rally together as many men as we can. Even then, we are unable to assemble a force of more than three thousand to three thousand, three hundred men. Consequently, we are starting to feel that our forces are insufficient.

### Military Matters

We have read the letters that were brought in the latest ships to arrive from the Netherlands. From them we have learned that the Amsterdam city council, as a result of our requests and in advance of the meeting of the [Assembly of the] Nineteen, had invited the other [eight] municipal councils to arrange that all nine of them should undertake to recruit one hundred and fifty men. We are extremely grateful for this news. We respectfully ask Your Lordships to bear in mind that if we dispatch an expedition of major importance against any distant location, we shall still need to leave our forts sufficiently well garrisoned to be able to defend themselves, resist the invasion of marauders, and protect our farms and inhabitants. Accordingly, if we are to receive here the aforesaid one thousand, three hundred and fifty soldiers as recruits, even then we shall be unable to field a force of more than three thousand troops. That is because the number of men diminishes daily and at an incredible rate, either because of those who return to the Netherlands or fall ill, get injured, or simply die, or because of those who become civilians. We trust, therefore, that the Assembly of the Nineteen, that will now have met, has given due attention to our most recent request and taken the decision to send the entire number of recruits that we are asking for. We also trust that it will command the defaulting municipal councils to send the remaining soldiers, for their numbers were fixed by the previous decision, which, in our view, corresponds to what was reported in the joint memorandum.

It is also important for arrangements to be made to enable us to receive all manner of military supplies. With that end in view, we have on occasion sent to the noble directors of the Assembly of Nineteen the lists of our shortages over here. On this occasion, we are sending a list of requirements that we request be met with all due dispatch, subject to the deduction of what may already have been forwarded.

We are also sending a list of those ships that are presently here at anchor. The majority of them will make their way back again because they cannot be kept and maintained here any longer. Your Lordships will receive them as they return, one by one, with their cargoes of sugar.

It should be borne in mind that we shall [soon] be left with very few ships at anchor here. Should it happen, nevertheless, that an enemy armada is launched against us from Portugal, it would be desirable that we could offer resistance to it at sea and defeat it before the enemy could get an opportunity to land anywhere. Clearly, if we could strike such a blow, the Company would be firmly established here forever, and the enemy would never again dare to trouble us along this coastline.

We are aware that the municipal councils have resolved that all nine of them shall be committed to sending out one ship each. We therefore request Your Lordships to note that by the end of summer, all the ships that are here at present will have departed with their cargoes of sugar. Consequently, it seems appropriate to us that Your Lordships should double the number established by the aforesaid resolution and send us eighteen galleons, plus nine other sailing ships capable of putting up a fight, deducting from that total whatever ships Your Lordships shall calculate are still available to us here. It is most important that the aforesaid galleons and sailing ships should arrive here not just well supplied with artillery and munitions but also with supplies of food, not to mention [ample reinforcements of] soldiers and sailors. There has been a great shortage of sailors: crew members have to do all the work on board the ships, and no matter how good and well equipped the ships may be, they are quite ineffective if there are insufficient crewmen to move all the tackle and carry out the duties that we have a right to expect aboard our ships. Your Lordships will be aware of how many disasters occurred a year ago along this coast because the ships' captains can offer the excuse that they have insufficient crew. It is important that due provision be made in this regard so as to forestall any further such excuses.

Above all, it is essential to bear in mind that the ships should be fully seaworthy and comprehensively equipped. The ribs of every ship should be thoroughly nailed down, and the whole vessel should be well caulked and amply supplied with sails, anchors, cables, and so on. The object is to ensure that they remain in a good state of preservation during the time that they spend on this coast, without their needing to undergo major repairs. We say that simply because we calculate that whatever the Spaniards plan to undertake is bound to occur at the present time. If we have such ships at our disposal and can thus rout the enemy, we shall then be able to carry on with a smaller number of ships and shall let them return to the Netherlands with their cargoes of sugar.

## Income from the Conquest

If the State of Brazil merits the vast expenditure that it currently receives and will continue to need, the reason becomes obvious when we enumerate all the income and profits that the Company will be able to derive from the conquered territories.

First place is occupied by the sugar trade, from which the Company derives: 1. the Church tithe; 2. the share pertaining to the donatary of the captaincies of Pernambuco and Itamaracá, which is worth one and a half percent; 3. tax of twenty percent; 4. freightage, average, and marine escort charges; 5. tax and freightage charges on goods imported from the Netherlands for consumption in Brazil and [as barter] to purchase sugar, etc.

We reckon that when this country flourishes again (as it has already begun to), there will be a great leap forward next year. In the year after that, almost its full potential will be reached. In the conquered captaincies, there will be the following sugar plantations:

| | |
|---|---|
| In the first district there will, without doubt, be more than | 15 plantations |
| In the Sirinhaém jurisdiction | 18 plantations |
| In that of Olinda | 67 plantations |
| In that of Igaraçu | 8 plantations |
| Total number of sugar plantations in the captaincy of Pernambuco | 108 |
| In the captaincy of Itamaracá | 20 plantations |
| In that of Paraíba | 20 plantations |
| In Rio Grande | 2 plantations |
| | [42] |
| Total number of sugar plantations in the four captaincies | 150 |

Sugar plantations that will not mill this year:

| | |
|---|---|
| Half of the plantations in Alagoas and Porto Calvo | 8 plantations |
| In Sirinhaém | 11 plantations |
| In the jurisdiction of Olinda | 20 plantations |
| In Igaraçu | 1 plantation |
| On Itamaracá | 8 plantations |
| In Paraíba | 2 plantations |
| In Rio Grande | 1 plantation |
| Total number of those that will *not* mill this year | 51 |
| Number of sugar plantations that *will* mill this year | 99 |

The above ninety-nine sugar mills are not [yet] in a position to crush sugarcane to the extent that they were wont to do formerly. That is because in those places that were in the war theater or were subject to enemy invasions last year, the cane plantations were destroyed and the sugar mills were greatly damaged. Thus, if we wish to calculate the amount of sugar produced this year, that is to say, produced by the mills in the current harvest, we imagine that the total is unlikely to reach more than two thousand, five hundred *arrobas* of "male" sugar per plantation. By that, we mean white and muscovado sugar jointly, whilst the molasses from those sugars will amount to one thousand *arrobas* per plantation. That gives the following results:

| | |
|---|---|
| Plantations | 99 |
| Each one mills | 2,500 [*arrobas* × 99] |
| | 49,500 |
| | 198,[000] |
| Total of white and muscovado (as muscovado forms part) | 247,500 *arrobas* |
| [Less] the Church tithe | 24,750 *arrobas* |
| | 222,750 |
| [Less] donatary's share, now received by the Company | 3,340 *arrobas* |
| | 219,410 |
| [Less] tax of 20 percent | 43,882 *arrobas* |
| Sugar remaining to be traded | 175,528 *arrobas* |

According to this calculation, the Company can expect from the current harvest, apart from the Church tithe that is auctioned off:

| | |
|---|---:|
| From the donatary's share | 3,340 *arrobas* |
| From tax | 43,882 |
| | 47,222 |

That means, at twenty *arrobas* per chest, two thousand, three hundred, and sixty-two chests of white and muscovado sugar, not to mention the molasses that will provide the Company with four to five hundred chests.

If Your Lordships add together the one hundred and seventy-five thousand *arrobas* of "male" [first-grade] sugar and the thirty to forty thousand *arrobas* of molasses,[22] all of which remain for the merchants to load onto the ships, plus what they will pay for freightage, average, etc., then Your Lordships will see the gross profit for this year.

[There follows a] list of auction contracts, charges imposed for sundry crossings, bridge charges, charges for fishing permits, abattoirs, weighing [of goods], wine and other beverages, dry goods, various Church tithes, etc., that are auctioned off in Brazil for a period of twelve months (and have been sold for greater or lesser periods, but are here scaled as for twelve months):

| | |
|---|---:|
| The crossing between Recife and António Vaz | 700 florins |
| Idem between António Vaz and Afogados | 400 florins |
| Idem between Fort Bruyne and the mainland | 1,840 florins |
| Passage over the great bridge to the plain on Itamaracá | 100 florins |
| Idem over the Itapissuma bridge to Itamaracá | 240 florins |
| Idem in Catuama, at the northern sandbar on Itamaracá | 100 florins |
| Crossing between Recife and Afogados | 1,800 florins |
| Idem at the lesser sandbar, between Recife and Cape [Santo Agostinho] | 2,556 florins |
| Idem at the boatyard on the River Paraíba | 7,930 florins |
| Fishing permit between the city of Olinda and River Doce | 150 florins |
| Idem to the south of Cabedelo in Paraíba | 336 florins |
| Abattoir charges in Recife | 1,500 florins |
| Idem on Itamaracá | – |
| Idem at Cape [Santo Agostinho] | 200 florins |
| Idem in Paraíba | – |
| Weighing charges in Recife | 11,400 florins |
| Idem on Itamaracá | – |
| Idem at Cape [Santo Agostinho] | 200 florins |

22 In view of the earlier statement that each of the ninety-nine plantations could be expected to produce one thousand *arrobas* of molasses, it is clear that the sundry deductions do not alone account for the difference. Much of the molasses (or syrup) was probably used up in the refining processes.

| | |
|---|---:|
| Idem in Paraíba | 1,663 florins |
| Charges on wine and other beverages, etc., in Recife | 27,400 florins |
| Idem on Itamaracá | 1,800 florins |
| Idem at Cape [Santo Agostinho] | 500 florins |
| Idem in Paraíba | 2,500 florins |
| The Church tithe on sugar in Recife and the captaincy of Pernambuco | 85,000 florins |
| Idem in the captaincy of Itamaracá | 13,000 florins |
| Idem in Paraíba | 26,000 florins |
| Other Church tithes in Recife and Pernambuco | 7,765 florins |
| Idem on Itamaracá | 1,350 florins |
| Idem in Paraíba | 2,600 florins |

This is what we wish to communicate to your Lordships, with due regard to what was resolved in your latest letter regarding the present situation in Brazil. We would also mention what appears in the accompanying document.

Recife, 14 January 1638
J. Maurits, Count of Nassau
M. van Ceullen
Adriaen vander Dussen
S. Carpentier, Secretary

# 8

## BURDENS OF SLAVERY AND RACE

*Slave flight and resistance was a constant feature of Brazilian life. The formation of escaped slave communities called mocambos or quilombos took place everywhere in Brazil, but during the period of the Dutch occupation, a group of escaped slave communities formed into a conglomerate kingdom in a mountainous area in southern Pernambuco in what is today the state of Alagoas. Despite expeditions mounted against this community of Palmares [place of the palms] by the Dutch and then by the Portuguese, the defenders put up an active guerilla defense throughout the seventeenth century. In the 1680s, expeditions of backwoodsmen from São Paulo as well as local troops were used against the escaped slaves, but only in 1694 were the last resistors defeated and their leader, Zumbi, killed. The following letters and accounts provide an idea of the tactics used to combat the fugitives and the threat that a community of escaped slaves seemed to present to the stability of the slave system as a whole.*

## 1. The War against Palmares: Letter from the Governor of Pernambuco, Ferão de Sousa Coutinho (1 June 1671) on the Increasing Number of Insurgent Slaves Present in Palmares

(Reprinted from Richard Morse, *The Bandeirantes* [New York: Alfred Knopf, 1968] and translated from Ernesto Ennes, *As guerras nos Palmares Coleção Brasiliana*, vol. 127 [São Paulo: Companhia Editora Nacional, 1938], pp. 133–4.)

Sire. For some years the Negroes from Angola who fled the rigors of captivity and the sugar mills of this captaincy have established numerous inland settlements between Palmares and the forests, where difficult access and lack of roads leave them better fortified by nature than they might be by human art. These settlements are growing daily in number and becoming so bold that their continual robberies and assaults are causing a large part of the inhabitants of this captaincy who live nearest the mocambos to leave their land. The example and permanence of the mocambos each day induces the other Negroes to flee and escape from the rigorous captivity which they suffer and to find freedom amid fertile land and the security of their own dwellings. One might fear that with these advantages they could grow to such numbers that they might move against the inhabitants of this captaincy, who are so few in relation to their slaves. To avoid this danger, I intend to go to Pôrto Calvo with the entrada of this summer, which is the most suitable place from which to wage this war. From there, using bodies of men that will continually relieve each other, I will order roads opened to the above Palmares by means of which their settlements can be besieged and razed consecutively until all are destroyed and this captaincy is left free of the misfortune which so severely threatens it. For many are the obstacles confronting me in this plan, owing to the difficult terrain and the lack of roads and transportation for provisions, which throughout this State can be carried only on the backs of Negroes since there are no roads for wagons nor even for more than men traveling in single file. . . . And Your Highness may be sure that this State is in no less danger from the audacity of these Negroes than it was from the Dutch. For in their very houses and plantations, the inhabitants have enemies who can overcome them if they should decide to follow the pernicious example and admonitions of those same rebels, who maintain contact with them, and who now have blacksmith shops and other workshops where they can manufacture weapons, since they already possess some firearms which they took from here. Also, this *sertão* is so rich in metals and nitrate that it furnishes everything for their defense provided they have the skills, which it may be feared many fugitives do possess who are trained in all the crafts. And because irreparable harm generally results when such dangers are ignored, I decided to take measures against any which might arise from these.

May God succor me to free this captaincy of this disturbance, which for me will be the highest tribute of all the services which I hope to render Your Highness. May Our Lord protect the most lofty and powerful person of Your Highness as is the wish of us your vassals. Olinda, the first of June, 1671.

FERNÃO DE SOUSA COUTINHO

## 2. Combating Palmares (c. 1680)

(Excerpt from A. de Magalhães Basto, ed., "Alguns documentos de interesse para a história do Brasil": anon. "Breve manifesto de nutiçiozas utilidades pertenssentes a este Estado do Brazil," in *Brasília*, 7 [1952], pp. 151–87 [pp. 182–3].)

## Chapter 3. The Blacks and Their Quilombo

Many years ago, in Pernambuco, large numbers of runaway black people built a huge township in the interior of Alagoas, known as the "Quilombo of Palmares." There they remain, behind sturdy fortifications and stockades, bursting out to make their raids on so many townships, causing great harm and damage to their inhabitants. Many times, the governors of Pernambuco have issued orders for these blacks to be defeated, causing great expense to the Royal Exchequer and great anxiety to the inhabitants and the garrisons. When our forays appear successful, no sooner are a mere handful of blacks released in Pernambuco or in Bahia than they immediately run away and form up again with the rest in their shanty town. For our sins, weary as we are with sending out expeditions, they have actually made a pact with us, permitting them to inhabit their abode, even though there are a few conditions in our favor, as we try to make the best of a bad job.

Having said that, these incursions could easily be stopped, with little effort, at little cost to the Royal Exchequer, and with no further anxiety on the part of the inhabitants and garrisons, as I shall go on to explain.

Not many years ago, when I was in the captaincy of São Vicente, [I met] a certain Cornélio de Arzão, a man of great ability. He had gone to that town as captain-major of the expeditions that were [subsequently] sent against the heathens in the Orobó hills and against many other people of the same ilk. I was told that if His Majesty, whom God preserve, were to agree to invest in an expedition to capture these blacks, then Arzão and his men would guarantee success. They also promised to crush the blacks' forces in short order and to prevent them from ever forming up again.

I would like to support this with the following arguments. Apart from the presence in their forces of many indigenous warriors, *mamelucos*, *caboclos*,[1] mulattos, and other kinds of half-castes, these soldiers fight with a discipline not noted in others. Other such expeditions fail for lack of food supplies, either because the distance is too great for those carrying them or because long delays between meals weaken the troops. The first thing that these men do, however, is to pitch their camp and simultaneously encircle the enemy. They then immediately plant maize, beans, and other vegetables and harvest these after a short period. While these are still growing, they derive their customary sustenance on such expeditions from molasses mixed with bread and herbs and from wild fruits. In the meantime, they are always careful to ensure that their enemy does not escape. When once there is ample food dealt out to their warriors, there is a call to battle and the

---

1 The terms *mameluco* and *caboclo* both apply to cross-breeds of white and Amerindian parentage.

encirclement is tightened, until the beleaguered foe either surrenders or is destroyed by force of arms. As they are more skilled than the blacks and are better at survival in the interior, they defeat the blacks with very great ease. That is not only because the vast majority of these men fight with firearms, but it is also because the indigenous population has a natural aversion and hatred for black people. The latter are at a disadvantage, both in the use of bows and arrows and even more so in the use of firearms because of their lack of gunpowder. The inhabitants of Alagoas, Camaragibe, Porto Calvo, Barra Grande, Sirinhaém, and other nearby townships are all prevented from selling or giving any gunpowder or lead shot to the blacks. That is despite the blacks' claim that they wish to live in peace when they go to buy gunpowder. Otherwise, some of the inhabitants of these coastal townships could sell or give them the gunpowder and the other things that they ask for, either for their own selfish reasons or because they have no wish to offend them.

When the task is completed, all those Brazil-born black people capable of running away could head for remoter areas like Maranhão, where they are much needed. Neither could they run away from there because the indigenous population that lives close to the townships would never allow them to do that. Otherwise, they could make their way [round] to the south of São Paulo, to Buenos Aires. That is because the inhabitants of São Paulo will not allow them access, owing to the fact that in other places, as was the case in Rio de Janeiro, in just a few days they formed up again. It was in Rio de Janeiro that a number of blacks [rounded up by] the Carrilhos expeditions escaped again after a few days, causing even greater trouble because they took away with them others who had been working peaceably in their masters' houses.

## 3. Excerpts from the Will and Testament of Paulo de Almeida, a Former Slave [1752]

*Many of those people enslaved escaped that status not by rebellion or flight to quilombos but by manumission. Freed persons of color became a large segment of the population. The complexities of slavery are apparent in this legal document in which Paulo de Almeida, a former slave in Bahia, draws up his final will. Almeida had been able to purchase his freedom through the practice of coartação in which slaves were allowed to buy their liberty after a price had been set on them. Like many former slaves, he eventually acquired property of his own, including slaves. The format of the will and testament and its standard Catholic provisions are quite common, but Almeida's recounting of his life, his possession of a number of slaves, some of whom were from his own region of Africa, and his marriage to a woman formerly his own slave seem to indicate that slavery may have had alternate meanings and uses for those people formerly enslaved.* (From Arquivo Público do Estado da Bahia, Pirajá, seccão judiciaria, maço 2170, n. 1.)

In the name of the Most Holy Trinity, Father, Son, and Holy Spirit, three persons in one, The True God

Know all to whom this public instrument and certificate of testament comes, that in the year of the birth of Our Lord Jesus Christ of One thousand seven hundred and fifty-one on the ninth day of the month of January of the said year, I, Paulo de Almeida, a free black man, being healthy and in the perfect judgment that our Lord has given me, fearing my death and wishing to place my soul on the path to salvation, and not knowing what God wishes to do with me and when He wishes to take me to Him, I make this my will and testament in this way.

First, I commit my soul to the Holy Trinity that created it and I ask that the Eternal Father by the death and passion, of His only son will receive it as he received His son who was dying on the True Cross, and to my Lord Jesus Christ by His divine wounds, that in this life gave me the benefit of His precious blood and His sacrifices that He give that grace in the life that awaits us that is glory; and I ask that the Virgin, Our Lady, the Mother of God and all the saints of the celestial Court, especially my Guardian Angel, and the saint of my name and all the saints to whom I have a particular devotion intercede for me with Our Lord Jesus Christ now and when my soul leaves this body, because as a true Christian I have tried to live and die in the Holy Catholic Faith and to believe in what the Holy Mother Church of Rome teaches, and in this faith I hope to save my soul, not by my merits but by the merits of the passion of God's only son.

I ask that in the first place my wife senhora Brites de Almeida and in second place my son, Cosme de Almeida, and in third place Senhor Antonio da Cunha for the service of God, Our Lord and to do me this favor, will serve as my executors.

Item. My body will be buried in my parish or where I die, wrapped in white burial sheets and carried to my parish to be buried, and the Reverend Vicar will be compensated in the usual way and will say four masses for my soul, each of 320 réis to be said on the day of my death or the following day.

I declare that I am a native of the kingdom of Angola of the land of the Congo and I came to this city of Bahia and from here was sent to the *sertão* and there I was the slave of Antonio de Almeida, and on his death a price for my freedom [*coartado*] was set at 100 milréis which I paid, and I was granted a letter of liberty and this I have been in possession of for more or less thirty years.

I declare that I was married the first time with Catherina Antonia, my companion and we were both slaves of the said Senhor Antonio de Almeida and he freed us both for money that we gave him, and my first wife is now deceased for many years from the present life, and from that marriage there were various children and all are now dead.

I declared that I am married in the form of the Sacred Council of Trent the second time with Brites de Almeida, a black woman now free who was for some time my slave to whom I gave her liberty, and afterwards I married, from which matrimony we had three children, that is two boys and a girl, the boys are called Martinho de Almeida and Cosmo de Almeida and the girl Domingas de Almeida, and all three I accept as my forced[2] heirs of my possessions.

I declare that the goods I possess [include] a black man [*negro*] named Manoel of the Angola nation from the land of Congo and I leave the slave Manoel with the price of his liberty set at 100 milréis and when he pays the 100 milréis, my executors will grant him his letter of liberty.

I declare that I also own another slave called Pedro of the Congo nation and he is married to another slave of mine named Isabel, also of the Angola nation who has a Brazilian-born [*crioulo*] son named Domingos who is also my slave; and I also have a black slave woman named Antonia of the Angola nation who has a little Brazilian-born daughter Maria who is also my slave. And I also own a Brazilian-born *parda* woman Anastacia who is the daughter of my wife who she had before she married with me, and I had freed her while she was in a relationship with another man, and thus the said child is my slave.[3]

And I also have a wheel to peel manioc with its copper and I have a pair of gold buttons worth 8 milréis and I have a cross of gold worth 5 milréis and these buttons and cross are pawned and in possession of Father Luis, the slave of Antonio Correia and also I have a pair of gold earrings and two pair of small gold buttons and two small bracelets of small red coral, and in my chest I have 20 milréis in cash, and I have whatever else is found in my house.

I declare I owe noting to anyone nor is anything owed to me.

I declare that my executors order that twenty masses of charity of twelve *vintens* be said for my soul in my parish. . . .[4]

---

2  Forced heirs are those who are entitled to inherit by law and cannot be excluded from the will.
3  It would seem that Paulo de Almeida freed his wife but kept her daughter legally as a slave. The reference to the daughter as a *parda* (light color) implies that her father was white or mulatto.
4  Missas de esmola de twelve *víntens:* meaning is unclear.

I declare that I leave to my Guardian Angel and the saint of my name four masses of charity of twelve *vintens* to be distributed in a brotherly fashion to each saint and two other [masses] to be in my parish.

I declare that my executors should order a mass of charity of twelve *vintens* be said for the soul of my former master Antonio de Almeida.

I declare that my executors order four masses of charity of twelve *vintens* each be said for the most needy souls in Purgatory.

I declare that I grant to my executors who accept the responsibility of my will four years within which to give an accounting.

I declare that my possessions that are not sold publicly and belong to my portion of the estate be sold privately.

I declare that after my bequests are made and my debts paid, the other costs incurred by my executors that I ask that for the love of God that masses be said for my soul with alms of twelve milréis for each and I thus leave my soul as the universal heir of my portion.

[the document closes with legal formula]

X (signed by the testator Paulo de Almeida).

# 9

## PUBLIC AND PRIVATE POWER

*In theory, the Brazilian colony was governed from Lisbon by centralized royal authority vested in governors, magistrates, and other royal officials, but the earlier system of donatary captains had remained in place in some regions, and local government was often controlled by the municipal councils of the port cities. Thus, powerful individuals, families, and interest groups such as the sugar planters or the merchants often exercised considerable influence on government and the law. The growth of the colony's population and its burgeoning economy in the later sixteenth century had created a number of challenges for the administration of justice. Municipal magistrates and a royal judge sent in 1549 were not able to keep up with the increasing amount of litigation and the prosecution of crime. After an aborted attempt in 1588, a royal court of appeals (Relação) with ten judges (desembargadores) was established in 1609. Its judges not only enforced the law but also made and interpreted legislation and served the governor in an advisory role, as well as taking on other administrative functions. Competing authorities such as the bishops or the donataries resented the proximity and power of the High Court, and so, in the aftermath of the Dutch seizure of Salvador (1624–5), pressure was brought on the Crown to abolish the High Court. It was abolished in 1626 and not reinstituted until 1652. The following anonymous document laments the court's demise and reveals the inequities and continuing problems in the judicial system.* (From Biblioteca Nacional de Lisboa, Colecção Pombalina 647, fols. 69–72).

## 1. Arguments of the Inhabitants of Bahia against the Suppression of the High Court (1626)

His Majesty has the responsibility of ensuring that his subjects are treated justly. Yet there was [formerly] no justice in the State of Brazil, nor could there be, as there was only one senior Crown judge. After taking detailed advice, the very Catholic and prudent King Philip, the first king of Portugal to bear that name,[1] ordered that there should be established a High Court in Brazil. To that end, he twice sent learned judges out to these Indies.

---

1  Philip II was king of Spain from 1556 to 1598 and also became Philip I of Portugal from 1580.

Driven by the same pressing need and sense of duty, His Majesty's father[2] sent a High Court to this country in 1609. It was very effective and, owing to its establishment on the basis of sound advice, it frustrated the intention of the bishops and of others to suppress it. Their object was to promote their own personal interests, without regard for the public good. Hiding behind a mask of private greed, they even argued that for reasons of State, the High Court was unnecessary in Brazil. Out of respect for the aforesaid former sovereign, it seems right that it should be kept in being, all the more so because without a High Court, justice cannot be administered, and the State would collapse in chaos.

Brazil is situated at a distance so remote from His Majesty that not only the poor cannot approach him but also even the wealthy, as we have noticed in individual cases. Moreover, the very difficulties and dangers of the sea voyage underline that fact. As the State of Brazil is governed by a governor-general and a senior Crown judge, they are effectively its monarchs, along with the bishops, the donataries, and other powerful figures, all of whom act in all matters with absolute power, so that His Majesty is king in name only. Men faithfully obey them, and the poor are simply ruined, without having anyone to whom to complain with regard to the injustices and ill use to which they are subjected. They simply get arrested and have their possessions confiscated without judicial redress.

Furthermore, the notaries fail to write down their applications or forward their grievances. The ships' masters are unwilling to carry such grievances for them and, if they do, they bring them back again, racked by fear of those whose interests are at risk from the complaints that are being made.[3] That [even] occurs in Portugal, where from the remotest part of the country one can reach the [Royal] Court in ten days without any danger and with little difficulty. But, rather than journey one thousand, six hundred leagues across a sea full of pirates and at the mercy of so many perils and [dire] events, Brazil's inhabitants prefer to endure persecution and injustice and to lose their property. They would rather do that than travel to Portugal to appeal against such injustice because the expenditure involved is normally greater than any profit that they might make from going to Portugal. As is well known, boosted by the confidence that they gain from such a situation, tyrannical ministers persist in their abuses and summon up courage to commit even greater outrages, before the High Court comes to Brazil.

---

2 The father in question was Philip III of Spain (Philip II of Portugal), who ruled over both countries from 1598 to 1621. The monarch reigning at the time at which this document was written was Philip IV of Spain (Philip III of Portugal), who ruled over both countries until the Portuguese Restoration of 1640.

3 The text is defective here.

I have no idea what good reason could be advanced by those whose object it is to suppress the High Court. If they are driven by any enthusiasm for justice when they say that there was no justice when the High Court was here, then how can they assert that there can be any justice without it? The following example illustrates this.

Was there ever seen such unrestrained dominance here in Brazil as that exercised by the governors, the senior Crown judges, and the comptrollers of the finances of the deceased and absent, not to mention the comptrollers of His Majesty's Exchequer? Yet, before the inauguration of the High Court, all justice lay in their hands. Were there ever such excesses and outrages, such misappropriation of State funds as each one of them practiced? In the past, High Court judges did not even receive one hundred milréis, which was insufficient even to pay for their food. Even when they came here in more prosperous times, their salary was [only] three hundred and fifty milréis, plus their perquisites. If we compare that with what the current authorities receive and with the misdeeds that all of them together have committed, we shall find that each one of the senior Crown judges and financial comptrollers has committed more misdeeds and made away with more money than all the High Court judges put together. This can be seen from the records of the proceedings concerning Licentiates Ambrósio de Siqueira and Francisco Sutil de Siqueira, who were, respectively, senior Crown judge and comptroller of the finances of the deceased. Those records are to be found with those relating to Brás de Almeida and others in the official criminal archives in Lisbon.

One man alone can easily be led astray by self-interest, love, hate, or fear. But a High Court cannot be corrupted, even if two men are unreliable, because the others remain steady. Even though some may feel inclined to commit some outrage, their sense of shame makes them hold back, as does their realization that the others will perceive what they are about. If High Court judges can forget their duties and responsibilities, do what they should not do, and bow to the requests of a dishonest governor-general, what is to prevent a single senior Crown judge from doing likewise? That is because, if he were to bow to his requests, he would receive honors and favors [from him].[4] Such a situation can give His Majesty cause to remove him, commanding him in the end to live out of reach of any harassment and ill treatment that may be inflicted on him by either the governor-general or the people. That is because he may become a victim of the people's displeasure and be persecuted by them if he does not accede to the governor-general's behest.

---

4  The text is defective here.

In our own times, as we have seen, governors-general and others, both from Angola and São Tomé, have embarked for Portugal, taking with them their Crown judges for not administering justice as they would wish the law to be applied. Although His Majesty declared himself to be well served by all those who made the journey, the governors went unpunished. Consequently, honest and saintly men are needed who will dare to administer justice in such remote areas. That is because they will be subjected to every form of outrage and persecution from those whose perception is perhaps so blind or whose self-interest is so great that they are unable to admit to the benefits that a High Court can bring. They fail to see that without a High Court, there can be no justice in these parts.

If, when there is a High Court, the senior Crown judges, in pursuit of their own ends, collude with the governors, captains, and other powerful men in the land, in order to intimidate High Court judges into revoking their verdicts, what will they do when there is no High Court?

If the Crown judges are normally so opposed to the other judges as to want them to revoke their verdicts, if they daily enter into judicial disputes with them, and if they constantly do whatever they see fit, then what will they do when there is no [judicial] body in the land to reject their unjust verdicts and decrees?

If the chancellor and other [High Court] judges who suspect the motives of the Crown judges and recognize how to curb their judicial disputes and adversarial behavior nonetheless cause excessive trouble themselves, what will happen when there is no High Court and when there is just one man of dubious character and qualifications to pass judgment on such suspicious activity? He is bound to do only what he wants to do.

If certain [High Court] judges, in order to avoid dying as martyrs in the cause of justice, just say and do what the governors, bishops, and captains want of them, and if they approve their actions, what will a senior Crown judge do, working on his own?

If ordinary justices and the city council commit misdeeds in the eyes of the High Court, as we have seen, and if the High Court blocks and revokes their verdicts, thus leading to judicial dispute with its judges, what then? Will they be so bold and so [lacking in] respect as to put them aboard ship? That is what happened on 14 August 1626, much to the dismay of the people of Bahia. What then would they do to a senior Crown judge acting on his own?

If anyone asserts that the High Court judges are just so many thieves and that they commit injustices as well, my answer is that those injustices are not a consequence of the High Court in itself but, rather, that they are due to the wretched approach and lack of Christian values on the part of its judges. Nor is that sufficient reason for suppressing the High Court. Let those who are unscrupulous judges be thoroughly punished, as an example to others, and let their places be taken by other learned men, of whom there are plenty. Let honest judges be rewarded by His Majesty: then all judges will be good judges. If irresponsible behavior were to be grounds for suppressing all High Courts, there would be none left, because in all of them there have been good judges and bad judges. Similarly, in the Appeals Court in Lisbon, there have been those who have gone astray and been relieved of their posts, yet the Appeals Court has not been suppressed. The same action could be taken in respect of the Brazilian High Court, were any [judges] to be found guilty [of bad faith]. This should not be a cause for surprise because even among the Disciples of Christ, there was a certain Judas. As among all those who are not apostles, there are always some who fail to do as they ought, it is all the more likely that in this particular matter there would always be somebody to complain that justice was for sale and could never really be found.

If governors, their secretaries, and others in their service, even in the presence of the High Court, commit such well-known excesses, what would they get up to in the absence of a High Court? If governors, captains, and donataries, as well as other ministers, fail to deliver justice when a High Court judge takes up residence among them every three years, what would happen if a senior Crown judge were to do the same in accordance with a list of regulations that the next governor-general were to give him? If a captain-major on a poor salary, though fearful of the presence in residence of a High Court judge, forgets his fear and amasses thirteen thousand, two hundred cruzados in three years, what then? If this culprit is not punished during the period in residence of a disinterested High Court judge, if he is not punished by the High Court in the appropriate manner for being the protégé of the governor-general, what will that judge do if he charges and tries a senior Crown judge for doing the same thing as the [other] man charged?

If, rightly or wrongly, the good aroma of amber resin or the evil smell of a black man [as bribes] can achieve so much, if closeness to that smell can impede justice in a High Court, what will be the outcome if that smell reaches [the nose of] just one man, who not only smells it but really likes it? What kind of verdicts will he issue? His word will be law.

If the Jews take control of this State and achieve all that they want from the governor-general and certain ministers when there is a High Court here, what will they get up to when there isn't one? Though there was a High Court present, those people did what they did so openly during the Dutch invasion,[5] as everybody knows, and as His Majesty had warned. Yet, as they have remained unpunished for their scheming and the money [that they made], what will they get up to in the absence of any High Court? Will

5  The Dutch occupied Bahia from 1624 to 1625.

they be allowed to have mosques [i.e., synagogues] like those that they have in Damascus and elsewhere?

If those who made this proposal [to suppress the High Court] were motivated by the words of Judas, then they were also motivated by the intentions of Judas, namely that the money spent on the High Court should be given to impecunious soldiers. Let me state, as I have already done, that His Majesty is responsible for ensuring that his subjects are treated justly and that no monarch is so poor that an extra four or five thousand cruzados either enrich or impoverish him, especially as his Majesty is so powerful. Furthermore, without justice, the world will collapse in chaos. Consider what has been done in the city of Bahia [i.e., Salvador] since its recovery [from the Dutch]. As justice cannot be appropriately administered, and as the High Court is held in check in so many well-known ways, will His Majesty's subjects find that there is any? Consider [also] what has happened since there was news that the High Court was to be suppressed, for after its suppression, its verdicts have been set aside. Magistrates against whom appeals and grievances have been lodged do as they please. Ordinary justices and city councillors have reacted indignantly at the [High Court's earlier] revoking of their verdicts and unjust municipal ordinances. They act illegally, browbeaten by a certain donatary, who dislikes having High Court judges on his territory. As he has no wish that a High Court should exist, this donatary got the officers of the city council to arrange that a man in his service should be given power of attorney for the city of Bahia. That was at the very time when the flotilla of Dom Fradique was preparing to sail.[6] Once this representative reached Portugal, his very first request was that the High Court should be suppressed. [He supported his petition] with false information and with documents signed by people in litigation [against the High Court] and by the secretaries of noblemen. That can be seen from an examination of his petition, which also falsely asserts that by this [suppression] His Majesty would be spared considerable expense.

As there were eight judges sitting in the High Court (the largest number ever to have sat together), the cost amounted to six thousand, seven hundred and fifty cruzados. Its chancellor or any other High Court judge could act as comptroller-general of the Exchequer. If the High Court remained, therefore, one thousand cruzados would be saved. With the suppression of the High Court, His Majesty has to have [i.e., pay for] a comptroller-general of the Exchequer, a Crown judge, and a comptroller-general of the finances of the

---

6 The joint Spanish and Portuguese fleet under Don Fadrique de Toledo recaptured the city from the Dutch in 1625.

deceased, and roughly only four thousand cruzados are saved.[7] These costs were [otherwise] met by the chancellery, at no cost to His Majesty.

In respect of the salaries of the chaplain, the physician, the barber, and the chief customs officer and their perquisites, as well as the other expenditure of the High Court, His Majesty did not meet those either, as they were included in the expenditure of the High Court, which was duly funded. It could even help with other costs, so that such funding met the chancellery's tithes. Even then, there was money left over.

If His Majesty wishes to reduce any expenditure on the part of his Exchequer in respect of the High Court, since the litigants have alleged such expenditure in order to suppress it, let him command that the number of years in exile to which convicts are sentenced be commuted to half that number (they seldom serve the full sentence anyway). Instead, they should pay costs toward the expenses of the High Court, even if they have a case to argue. Let him also make a second decree, namely that in this captaincy, a public inquiry should be set up into misdemeanors against the community, just as there is in Lisbon. In that way, a great service will be rendered unto Our Lord, as well as contributing considerable sums toward the aforementioned expenditure and thus to the chancellery. Ten High Court judges could then be afforded, and still there would be money left over. His Majesty would thus reduce his expenditure while simultaneously delivering justice to this wretched country, for without justice, it runs the risk of countless disasters.

His Majesty has been misinformed because, even if he were to meet the entire cost of the High Court from his Exchequer, with the assistance of the High Court his income would grow all the more. Even with the High Court present, if there were all kinds of skullduggery, not to mention lack of executive action and excessive perquisites at the expense of the Royal income (for every sort of embezzlement is practiced against it), what would happen if it were suppressed?

His Majesty could also require that appeals and grievances arising in Angola should be brought to the High Court. As ships sail every month from there to Bahia, such a measure would perform both a great service to Our Lord and a great favor to the settlers in that country because of the great distance there is from there to Portugal. In addition, the income to this chancellery would be augmented.

In Peru and the Indies, His Majesty has many chancelleries [*audiencias*]. In [the viceroyalty of] Peru, there are five of them: one in Chuquisaca, one

---

7    In short, to dispense with the cost of the High Court would only produce a partial savings, owing to the extra cost of the three officials mentioned, whereas the chancellery of the High Court would have met that expenditure.

in Lima, another in the city of Quito, yet another in Chile, and the fifth in Panama. There are many more in the Indies.

The Canaries are four islands with a very small population and are situated quite close to Spain, yet His Majesty maintains a High Court on one of the islands to spare his subjects the immense inconvenience of a four or five days' journey to Spain for their appeals to be heard. That is all the more reason, therefore, for him to maintain a High Court in Brazil, which is nowadays so heavily populated. The population is constantly increasing, and Brazil is a long way from Portugal, as has already been mentioned.

Were His Majesty and his advisers to be aware of what is happening nowadays in this country since the suppression of the High Court, he would immediately send one out here with a large number of High Court judges. He is a Catholic monarch and would not wish his subjects to be devastated for want of justice. Brazil's jails are full of prisoners without hope of release. Some who are released after verdicts are passed on them (for the Crown judge to hear their appeals) experience a nail-biting wait for the results of the appeals to arrive from Portugal. Such results arrive sometimes late, sometimes never, owing to the mishaps that still occur at sea, whereas in the High Court, matters were dealt with from one day to the next: those involved were either released or punished. There was no long torment. May it please Our Lord to grant justice once more to this unhappy country. When there is justice, all will be well. If there is not, everything will go to rack and ruin, as at present.

# 10

## RELIGION AND SOCIETY

*The missionary clergy, especially the Jesuits, exercised a powerful influence on Catholic religious life in the colony. Brazil was organized around the continued efforts of the missionary clergy among the indigenous peoples and the presence of a diocesan clergy, which administered to the majority of the population. The two spheres, however, were never fully separated, and the members of the religious orders like the Jesuits, Carmelites, Benedictines, and Franciscans – usually referred to as the "regular" clergy – often took an active part in other aspects of religious and cultural life. Then, too, there were various forms of local practice, "superstition," and heterodoxy carried from Europe that encountered Native American and African practices and beliefs in Brazil. The documents presented here reveal two sides of religious life. The first text is a report on Jesuit activities in northeastern Brazil that underlines the multiple and varied activities of the missionary orders in the colony. It makes clear that the Jesuit activities were not limited to the Native American inhabitants of Brazil. The second text presents two depositions made before a visit of the Inquisition to Brazil, both of which reveal the existence of heterodox thought.*

### 1. Jesuit Missions: Information for the Lisbon Committee on the Missions, 1702, on General and Economic Matters

(From Serafim Leite S.J., ed., *História da Companhia de Jesus no Brasil*, Rio de Janeiro and Lisbon, vol. 5 (1945), pp. 569–73).

The following is a brief report on the missions carried out this year in the territory of Bahia and in the Diocese of Pernambuco. A report on those in Rio de Janeiro will be sent separately, should news about them arrive in time. Otherwise, they will be sent in a year's time.

In Pernambuco, Fathers Cosme Pereira and Francisco de Araújo carried out a mission lasting four months and in eighteen places, starting out in Cape Santo Agostinho and ending in Alagoas. The fruits of this mission were the revalidation of thirty-three marriages to which there had been impediments and listening to five thousand, one hundred and ninety-five ordinary confessions. In addition, they heard four hundred and seven general and necessary confessions pertaining to entire lives or to those who had not confessed for many years. There were another thirty heard as a special act of devotion. Holy Communion was distributed to four thousand, nine hundred and seven people. Religious instruction was imparted with particular care to black people. This was also of no little benefit to white people, amongst whom there is just as much ignorance. In that way, the Fathers sought to persuade masters to treat their slaves better, to moderate the punishments that they mete out to them, and to give them all that they need in order to feed and clothe themselves. Many occasions of sin were abandoned, duly remedied by stable marriages. Many made peace with one another, and many deaths were thus avoided, deaths that would certainly have ensued, if the presence of the mission had not caused enemies to become reconciled. By night and by day, it was a major task because certain women in poverty sought absolution at night, and because everybody wanted to make their confession to the missionaries rather than to the [local] secular priests.

Fathers José Bernardino and Francisco de Lima spent five months making their way between the sugar plantations of Bahia. From there, they moved on elsewhere, till finally their round trip amounted to one hundred and fifty gruelling leagues. They made regular stops and carried out their duty of preaching, giving instruction, and hearing confessions in both Portuguese and the language of Angola. This they did in forty-eight churches, apart from the chapels that they also visited. Though short of sleep, they had to satisfy crowds of people who came to them more at night than by day and for the reasons already mentioned. Frequently, they experienced sleepless nights, for there was no alternative. Sometimes very poor people had journeyed for three days without food and without respite, simply in order not to miss the chance to earn the plenary indulgence and to open their burdened consciences to the Fathers. On such occasions, the parish priests also heard confessions, for this was a true visitation made to their flocks, because the missionaries attracted them from afar and gave them great consolation, whereas sometimes a Father Visitor would frighten them away and leave them unconfessed.

The feuds that were peacefully resolved numbered forty-eight. Three parish priests who till then had been greatly disliked by their parishioners came to be acknowledged with all due deference and love. A number of parents welcomed back children whom they had thrown out of their houses for disobeying them. Nearly seventy potential scandals were intercepted; some of them would have led to dispossession or even death. Some men rid themselves of slave women with whom they were developing unsavory relationships, selling them to people who lived a great distance away, to avoid ever seeing them again. Others married their concubines and heaped gifts upon them as an expiation of their guilty behavior. Many marriages were reinstated, and with the necessary dispensations. Much stolen property was given back: it so happened that on the selfsame day, five Father Confessors all got up from the confessional with a considerable amount of money with which to hand back what had been stolen.

One hundred and seventy-eight Angolan slaves were baptized. Some received baptism in the absolute sense because they were living just as they had arrived, that is to say, unbaptized. Others were conditionally baptized because, though adults, they had received too little religious instruction and had not grasped the full implications of receiving water on their heads and salt in their mouths, prior to their being shipped to Brazil.

Masters were effectively persuaded to give female slaves decent clothing with which to cover themselves. That was done to discourage their masters from seeking what would be offensive to Almighty God and, more importantly, from wantonly preventing them from going to Holy Mass on Sundays and Holy Days. Many masters in fact did this, both the owners of sugar plantations and tenant farmers who were growers of tobacco and sugarcane. While the mission was present, some slaves paid no heed to the threats and punishments that they received and gave up work for a while, in order not to miss the benefits that the mission conferred.

Using exorcisms sanctioned by the Church, the Fathers cast out sundry demons from people's bodies. In particular, one such demon answered the priest in Latin, having entered the bodies of three children, one by one, because their father had given them over to the Devil in a torrent of rage, as a lot of fathers are wont to do. It was also necessary to remove a great deal of superstition to which some people were prone. Others had to be cured with words and drinks that would make them more gentle and amiable. Quite a number of objects used for inflicting curses on people were handed in to the Fathers.

The number of ordinary confessions that the missionaries heard at this time amounted to six thousand, three hundred and ninety, quite apart from those heard by other priests, which would be as many again. The general and necessary confessions, for those concealing their sins, came to two hundred and twenty-four. Those heard as a special act of devotion or to remove specific scruples totaled two hundred and eighty-seven. It was a result of particular Divine Providence that the missionaries were drawn to certain houses where there was a profound need for such absolution. In many places, the Fathers dispelled a sense of shame that was felt by certain women at not going to Holy Mass because they were not as well dressed as other women of lesser standing. The Fathers also dealt with the case of a certain man who was in litigation with some cleric who, in his view, had harassed him unjustly. They got him to make an effort to go to church to hear Holy Mass, to go to confession and to receive Holy Communion. For five years, because of the said cleric, the man had hated everybody and could not bear to see them, go anywhere near them, or even discharge his Lenten duties. In one village, where they were all fishermen, the villagers believed that their failure to catch any fish was due to the fact that they had paid no heed to the excommunications received for the stealthy thefts that they had carried out. Yet fishing was their livelihood and their normal means of sustenance. With a common accord, all the people who had had things stolen responded to the Fathers' persuasive words by forgiving the fishermen for any thefts committed up to that time. Afterwards, the fishermen asked the missionaries to bless their nets, their boats, and the sea. This they did with such joy and expressions of Faith that they brought tears to the Fathers' eyes and, with that, the complaints ceased forthwith. The protection afforded by Our Lady was evident wherever the missionaries went and on those occasions when they had great need of her intercession, as when they needed to overcome obstinate and perverse attitudes and change people from wolves into lambs and win from them the desired deference and repentance.

In the new villages in Açu in the territory of Jaguaripe in Pernambuco, Fathers João Guincel and Vicente Vieira suffered very greatly, not only in the assaults that were made against their Payacu Indians but especially also in those made by the cowherds. The latter, whenever the Tapuyas build a village anywhere, at once seek to install cattle ranches near them. When they do this, they cause considerable difficulties for the Indians and treat them with contempt. There is no means whereby the Indians can stop them. Indeed, the cowherds instigate other tribes to cause trouble for them as well, when they ought, as Christians, to be helping the Fathers to attract them to the Faith and to win them over to it. However, as the garrison from São Paulo is located in the same area, the Indians will have a force to defend them and relieve them of their anxieties, for the cowherds greatly obstruct God's work. Fathers Filipe Bourel and Manuel Dinis experience fewer difficulties of this kind and so they find it easier to teach their barbarians the Catechism and deal with them in an orderly fashion.

Fathers Ascenso Gago and Francisco de Araújo are already experiencing the fruit of their endeavors in the largest village in the province. It is up in the Ibiapaba Mountains, beyond Ceará, and was formed from three other smaller villages. Each of them keeps its own leaders, so everybody is contented and they all remain united. Till now, they have maintained the peace that they negotiated with two other Tapuya tribes who in former years caused them considerable trouble.

Plans already existed to send other Fathers to Montevideo but, as His Majesty, whom God preserve, has decided to send a garrison there, their journey has been suspended. As had been arranged, they stand ready to obey and set off elsewhere at the first opportunity to wherever is deemed to be necessary. Bahia, 5 July 1702.

[List of Indians]

There follows the list of the [Indian] villages that are under the care and direction of the Fathers of the Society of Jesus throughout Brazil [with the exception of Maranhão and Pará]. His Majesty commanded in his letter of 18 April 1702 that such a list be forwarded to him. The approximate details are as follows:

### Pernambuco

| | |
|---|---:|
| In the village of Guajuru there are some | 250 |
| In Guaraíras there are no more than | 300 |
| In Urutaguí little more than | 150 |
| By the headwaters of the Jaguaripe over | 1,000 |
| Around the Podi lagoon in Açu | 1,000 |
| In the Ibiapaba mountains, where three villages have come together, over | 4,000 |
| The total for Pernambuco is at least | 6,700 |

### Bahia

| | |
|---|---:|
| In Camamu there are some | 300 |
| In Sirinhaém many have died, leaving | 50 |
| In the village of Espírito Santo up to | 300 |
| In São João de Porto Seguro they amount to | 500 |
| In Pativa there are some | 300 |
| In the enlarged village of Ilhéus nearly | 900 |

### Tapuyas in the Interior of Bahia

| | |
|---|---:|
| In the village of Natuba more than | 600 |
| In the village of Saco more than | 700 |
| In the village of Cana Brava almost | 800 |
| In the village of Juru more than | 400 |
| [Total of] those pertaining to Bahia | 4,850 |

### Captaincy of Espírito Santo

| | |
|---|---:|
| In the village of Reis Magos more than | 500 |
| In the village of Reritiba more than | 600 |
| All together | 1,100 |

## Rio de Janeiro

| | |
|---|---:|
| São Lourenço few more than | 100 |
| São Barnabé nearly | 400 |
| Itinga up to | 300 |
| Cabo Frio more than | 1,000 |
| Total | 1,800 |

## São Paulo

| | |
|---|---:|
| In Emboug, Capela, and the plains of the Paraíba, more than | 1,000 |
| Grand total for all the above Brazilian villages | 15,450 |

The two villages in Açu, namely the one alongside the Jaguaripe and the one around the Podi lagoon, are new and are receiving baptism; those not yet baptized are receiving appropriate instruction.

The Indians that inhabit the [three] united villages in the Ibiapaba mountains have nearly all been baptized, both those that speak Tupi and those that speak Portuguese. Apart from those, the Fathers are currently visiting a number of Tapuya tribes and winning their confidence, persuading them to abandon pillaging and to congregate in villages, so that they too can receive religious instruction.

The Indians in Açu, the Quiriris from the interior of Bahia, and the Paiaiás are Tapuyas who speak different languages. Nearly all of them have been baptized. Those who speak Tupi are all Christians.

Our Jesuit Fathers are to be found in all these villages. In some of them are [other] religious as well. There are also youthful students who are learning the language, without which they cannot go on to study philosophy. They are tested, under oath, by four examiners and either pass or fail.

As our college in Olinda maintains six villages, of which four have grown up since the endowment received from the Foundation, representations are being made to His Majesty that he needs to award an annual subsidy to cover the costs that would arise, if it were to happen that the six thousand cruzados that he sent did not take effect. That sum was forwarded, on His Majesty's orders, to fund a hospice or residence with three cattle farms for the upkeep of the missionaries working in the Ibiapaba mountains in Ceará. It went with a letter on 8 January 1697 to the governor of Pernambuco, Caetano de Melo de Castro. To date, nothing has been done about it, for the reasons that are now being set before His Majesty.

Bahia, 5 July 1702
João Pereira [Provincial]

## 2. The Inquisition in Brazil: Two Cases

*No permanent tribunal of the Portuguese Inquisition was established in Brazil, but individuals charged with heresy, apostasy, and various moral or religious crimes were sent from Brazil to Lisbon for trial. On a number of occasions, a "visit" or temporary investigation conducted by visiting inquisitors was sent to Brazil and operated in the colony. From 1591 to 1593, such a visit was made to Bahia and Pernambuco. During a period of grace, persons could confess to the inquisitors and expect to receive a lighter punishment. The two confessions translated here made during the period of grace reveal not only what weighed heavily on someone's conscience and the form in which such testimony was collected but is also revealing of the intimate life and thoughts of people in colonial Brazil. The first case contains the confession of a woman attracted to a heretical millenarian cult that began among the Indians but that also attracted persons of African or European background. The second case deals with bigamy and provides a glimpse into domestic life and the relations between men and women in the colony. (From* Santo Ofício da Inquisição de Lisboa. Confissões da Bahia, *Ronaldo Vainfas, ed. [São Paulo: Compañía das Letras, 1997], pp. 144–9).*

### (a) Confession of Luísa Barbosa, an Old Christian, during the Period of Grace, 23 August 1591

She described herself as an Old Christian and native of Bahia. She was the daughter of Álvaro Gonçalves Ubaca and of his wife Maria Barbosa. She was married to Belchior Dias Porcalho, was approximately thirty-seven years old, and lived here, in the city of Bahia.

In her confession she said that when she was some twelve years of age, a superstition had arisen in this captaincy among the native Christian Indians of Brazil, a superstition that, among themselves, they called the "sanctity" [*santidade*]. Since that time, this superstition has frequently been noticed in this captaincy.

According to the indigenous Brazilians, Christian or otherwise, this "sanctity" was a god of theirs. This god told them not to work because food and other supplies would always be available naturally, and that those who did not believe in the "sanctity" would be turned into sticks and stones. White people would be turned into game for them to hunt. That "sanctity" of theirs was kind and saintly, whereas what the Christians taught was worthless. That was what these people said, among many other forms of nonsense.

Her mother being dead, the penitent had at that time been expounding these beliefs in a house belonging to Mécia Pereira, the wife of António da Costa. In fact, black people, both Christian and pagan, as well as indigenous Brazilians, who were to be found in Mécia's house, all repeated to one another the above-mentioned elements of this superstition, as well as many other aspects that she cannot recall. This applied equally to those to be found in the house of the penitent's father and elsewhere.

She had herself been indoctrinated into these beliefs at a tender age, at a time when she had had little experience. For two years and some months, she had accepted this mistaken doctrine, repeating its erroneous views and believing in the "sanctity." It had seemed to her to be true, to be beyond all doubt. She had discussed matters with the followers of these mistaken beliefs, had agreed with them, and had told them that she truly accepted them.

Once the followers of this superstition had been suppressed and punished, she had realized that it was all false and erroneous and had made her confession to the Fathers of the Society of Jesus, who had absolved her. She now seeks forgiveness and mercy from this [inquisitorial] board.[1]

When questioned as to whether, when she had believed in the aforesaid aspects of the superstition, she had ceased to believe in the Christian Faith and all the good things that it taught, she replied that she had always continued to accept Christian teaching as good teaching and had never abandoned the Christian Faith, even though she had simultaneously accepted the other absurd beliefs, owing to her tender age.

Questioned further, she stated that all those adherents of the superstition with whom she had spoken and associated were now dead, and that she was unaware of any that were still alive.

At once, the Visitor-General recommended to her that she should frequently go to confession and listen to preaching.

### (b) The Confession of Antónia de Barros, an Old Christian, during the State of Grace, 23 August 1591

[The penitent][2] declared that she was an Old Christian and that she was a native of Benavente.[3] She was the daughter of Diogo Martins Perdigão, who was one of those who ran the township, and of his wife, Maria de Barros, both of whom were now dead. She was approximately seventy years of age, dwelled here in Bahia, and had been the wife of Álvaro Chaveiro, who worked as a fisherman and boatman between Benavente and Lisbon.

---

1 The board was presided over by the Visitor-General, Heitor Furtado de Mendoça, whose visitation to Bahia and Pernambuco lasted from 1591 to 1595.

2 Examined by the Visitor-General, she was discharged for having made her confession while in a state of Grace. Having abjured her sins before the inquisitorial board, she was given spiritual penance (ANTT, II, proc. 1279).

3 This township is situated on the River Sorraia between Santarém and Lisbon.

Confessing her sins, she declared that she had arrived from Portugal some thirty-two years earlier, having been exiled to Brazil for five years by the secular justices on account of the adultery of which her husband had accused her.

Back there in Portugal, she had begun a relationship with an Old Christian named Henrique Barbas. He was the son of Vasco Barbas, a prominent citizen of Vila Franca [de Xira]. She had accompanied him to Brazil and they had come ashore in Porto Seguro.

Just a few days after their arrival in that captaincy, though both she and the aforesaid Henrique Barbas knew perfectly well that Álvaro Chaveiro, her legitimate husband, was still alive in Portugal, she, the penitent, and Henrique Barbas had got married.

Henrique Barbas had arranged false witnesses, who swore that Henrique Barbas was a bachelor and that she, the penitent, was a widow. They also swore that they had witnessed the death and burial in Benavente of her husband, Álvaro Chaveiro. This was a lie and a falsehood. Two years after the penitent had married Henrique Barbas at the church door, with permission from the [ecclesiastical] ordinary, issued on the basis of the declaration made by the false witnesses, her husband, Álvaro Chaveiro, was still alive in Benavente, as later news and messages confirmed.

After her marriage, with Church approval, to her second husband, Henrique Barbas, when both she and he knew that her true husband was still alive, they went on living in Porto Seguro for more than fifteen years as man and wife.

Yet, Henrique Barbas beat and thrashed and generally abused the penitent to the point where she fled the house and took refuge in the church in their township. There she began to declare openly that Henrique Barbas was not her legitimate husband, simply because when she had married him in Porto Seguro, her true husband, Álvaro Chaveiro, had still been alive and had lived for a further two years.

Consequently, she separated from him. Still a bachelor, he now lives in the captaincy of Espírito Santo, on the coast of Brazil. For her guilt in this matter, she was now seeking the forgiveness and mercy of this board, while in a state of Grace.

When asked who were the false witnesses, she replied that they were already dead.

When asked where she was married to her first husband, she answered that she and her first husband were joined in matrimony by the prior of Benavente (whose name she does not remember) in the mother church, Nossa Senhora da Graça. They had taken the customary vows required by the Church. Her sponsors had been Tareja da Gama, sister of the count of

Vidigueira,[4] in whose service she, the penitent, then worked, and Maria Teixeira, also a noblewoman, both of whom were now dead. Her husband's sponsors had been Luís Mendes and Manuel de Vasconcelos, sons of the aforesaid Tareja da Gama, both of whom had gone to serve in India. Also present at the marriage had been many other people, whose names she could not now remember.

When she was asked who in Porto Seguro joined her in marriage to Henrique Barbas, she stated that the latter had arranged the false witnesses (as mentioned above), and that thereby they received permission to marry. She added that they were joined in marriage by Father Diogo de Oliveira in the Church of Santo Amaro, and that they both took the customary vows in accordance with the rites of Holy Church. Her sponsor at the marriage in Porto Seguro was Maria Barbosa, whilst Henrique Barbas's sponsor was Gonçalo Pires, the husband of Maria Barbosa. Many other people were present at the marriage, but she could not now recall who they were.

As she had nothing further to add, she was ordered to maintain secrecy on account of the oath that she had taken and to return to the board when she was sent for.

As she did not know how to sign her name, the notary did that on her behalf and at her request.

4  The first count of Vidigueira was Vasco da Gama. The fourth count, Francisco da Gama, mentioned here, pursued a distinguished career and was twice viceroy of India.

# 11

## FRONTIERS

*Although the heartland of the Portuguese colony of Brazil remained the coastal strip, by the seventeenth century, slave hunting, cattle ranching, and prospecting had opened up small settlements and trails into the interior. On the perimeter of the major areas of settlement, a number of kinds of frontiers developed. The northern captaincies of Maranhão and Pará constituted a separate colony in many ways. They had been the target of French, Spanish, and other European projects at colonization, but with the foundation of cities such as São Luiz (1614) and Belem (1616), a Portuguese presence was fully established, and the area was created as a separate administrative unit, the State of Maranhão, in 1621. Despite that action, the European population remained small because these areas continued to be something of an economic backwater, even though attempts were made there to develop sugar plantations. Colonists remained dependent on Native American workers and thus clashed with the missionaries in the region, repeating in a way the struggles between colonists and Jesuits that had characterized the Brazilian coast in the sixteenth century. The Jesuits replaced the Franciscans as the major missionary order in the region in the 1640s. They led a campaign against colonist abuses that resulted in a 1655 law limiting enslavement of Indians, but this legislation was ineffective, and the struggle continued between missionaries and colonists well into the following century. Jesuit Father Antônio Vieira, author, preacher, diplomat, and missionary, was sent to Belem as Jesuit Provincial in 1652. His letter to the Crown translated here makes clear the region's problems.*

*Another kind of frontier developed in the interior. Westward from the coastal settlements of Brazil, especially in the northeastern captaincies of Bahia and Pernambuco, cattlemen had opened up vast stretches of the arid backlands or sertão, sometimes creating properties of great size. Large drives of cattle brought the livestock down to the coast to supply the needs of the colony as described in document 2 and, in doing so, expanded the scope of the colony.*

*It was, however, the search for precious metals that finally moved the population inland on a large scale. Travelers, colonists, and royal officers had long searched for gold or other precious metals. Companies of trailblazers and backwoodsmen had traversed the interior in search of mineral wealth and of Native Americans who could be used as workers. Setting out from São Paulo and from other towns, these men explored the interior and pushed the frontier of occupation westward. By the 1670s, with the sugar economy in decline, the search for precious metals became intense, but it was only in 1695 that relatively large strikes were made in the mountainous area called Minas Gerais. Gold fever swept through the colony and the empire. Neither Brazil nor the Portuguese empire would ever be the same again. The most famous early account of the mining region was penned by André João Antonil (Giovanni Antonio Andreoni), an Italian Jesuit who came to Brazil in 1681 and became Provincial of Order and rector of the Jesuit College of Salvador. In 1711, he published* Cultura e opulência do Brasil por suas drogas e minas, *an analysis of the major economic activities in Brazil including the newly discovered mines, but his descriptions of the routes to the mines were so accurate that the book was banned and almost all the existing copies destroyed.*

## 1. The State of Maranhão: A Letter from Father António Vieira S.J. (1653)

(From J. Lúcio de Azevedo, ed., *Cartas do Padre António Vieira*, Lisbon, vol. 1 (1970), pp. 296–305).

To King João IV from Maranhão, 20 May 1653

Sire,

Your Majesty was pleased to entrust me with the very special task of converting the pagans of this State[1] and with maintaining and increasing therein the presence of our Holy Faith. For that reason, I would be greatly failing in my duty to Your Majesty and to the demands of my conscience, if I were not to report to Your Majesty the sad lack of spiritual values that is so prevalent here. I shall, therefore, indicate, as summarily as I can, the causes of these difficulties and how they can and must be remedied.

The inhabitants of this new world, for that is what it may be called, are either Portuguese or native Indians. Some of the Indians are pagans who live in the interior and speak a vast range of different languages. Other Indians are for the most part Christians and live among the Portuguese. Of the latter Indians, some are free men and live in their villages, whilst others are partly free and partly captive, living and serving the Portuguese in their houses and on their plantations. Without them, there is no way in which the Portuguese can provide for themselves.

The Portuguese in these parts, Sire, suffer from spiritual needs that border on the extreme. They profoundly lack religious instruction, profoundly

---

1 From the 1620s to 1777, the Estado de Maranhão was ruled separately from the rest of Brazil.

lack the sacraments, and many of them never attend Holy Mass nor listen to any preaching because there is none available to them. They have no knowledge of which are the Holy Days to keep and, even if they do know them, they fail to keep them. Nor is there anybody to oblige them to do so. This state of [spiritual] deprivation is still greater in their wives, their sons, and their daughters, who not infrequently die without confession.

The main cause of this situation (if we are to leave aside other remoter causes) is the shortage of priests, particularly of parish priests. In the entire captaincy of Maranhão, there are only two churches that have a priest, one on the mainland and the other on the island. The island is seven leagues long and seven leagues wide and every part of it is populated. Consequently, it is impossible for a single priest to attend to all those who need him, mainly because he has to go on foot, as there is no kind of mount in the whole area. Moreover, apart from the great shortage of priests, those here are, for the most part, men of little learning and even less zeal for the saving of souls. That is because they either come out here as exiles or because having scant ability for earning their living anywhere else, they have come to earn it here. In addition, in spiritual matters, this State belongs to the bishop of Brazil, who resides in Bahia, which is five hundred leagues away, with the Dutch in between [in Pernambuco]. Its only resources come from Portugal, so that the flocks here can be neither heard nor visited and in effect exist without a shepherd.

The solution to this most grievous problem is for the number of churches and priests to be greatly increased, especially in the most appropriate places. The solution includes the presence here of an ecclesiastical figure, noted for his learning and enthusiasm, to act as the administrator of the entire State. Alternatively, he could supervise spiritual matters in a different way, as in Rio de Janeiro. Another way would be to make up for all these deficiencies by sending out a sufficient number of religious who would regard it as their bounden duty to save souls and who would be ever watchful in observing that duty. That is because what has caused great harm to this State is the presence here of religious with a largely unsuitable way of life and training.

The Indians who live in the houses of the Portuguese, owing to the poverty in which they find themselves and to the inborn barbarous natures of nearly all of them, are affected even more adversely by all the examples of spiritual deprivation that I have mentioned. Many of them live and die as pagans, without their masters or their parish priests seeking to baptize them or even to care about the situation. Of those who have Christian names and received Christian baptism, they received these without knowing what they were receiving. They live lives that are just as heathen as they were beforehand. Very, very few of them, even the most astute among them, fulfill their Lenten duties. There are Christians who are sixty years of age who have never made their confession. Most of these people, when they are asked when they last made their confession, say that it was to Father Luís Figueira, who has not been here in this State for seventeen years. It is a very normal occurrence for them to die without making their confession. That applies mainly to those who do not live in the town. Also normal is the abuse of their not being given Holy Communion even at the hour of their death.

The great causes of this harmful perdition of souls lie in the very shortage of priests and, in the main, of religious who would regard it as their bounden duty to study and to get to know the language here. Without a knowledge of the language, priests cannot achieve very much, and only those who know it are able to administer the sacraments in the right manner. I refer to the sacraments of baptism and confession, which are those that are most needed.

The solution is to install a sufficient number of the aforementioned religious to give instruction to the Indians, to baptize them, and to rebaptize those that were badly baptized, and to administer the other sacraments to them, as they now [have started to] do with great success. But their numbers are too low to reap so great a harvest.

This harmful problem is common to all the Indians. Those who live in the houses of the Portuguese were only too often victims of unjust captivity, a factor suffered by so many of them, as Your Majesty has frequently been informed. That is possibly the principal cause of all the punishments meted out in all our conquered territories.

The causes of this problem and its harmful effects can be simply attributed to greed, mainly the greed of powerful men, who send expeditions into the interior, as well as to unauthorized and unjust wars that cannot possibly be justified. Even though they bring back some Indians who are genuine captives, because they were [found] roped up together, ready to be eaten, or because they were working as slaves in their own areas, most of the Indians are, nevertheless, free men who have been captured by force or by deceit. They sell these men [as well] and make use of them as though they were genuine captives.

Sire, the solution that Your Majesty and the kings your predecessors sought to bring to bear on this tyranny was to impose a total interdict on expeditions into the interior. They sought to prohibit the purchase of Indians and to declare free all those who had already been purchased, whatever the means by which that was done. Sire, those remedies are indeed the most effective of all those that may be proposed. Nevertheless, it is extremely difficult and almost impossible to put them into practice, as experience has constantly demonstrated, most particularly in the disturbances experienced this year. All these originated in the claim that the Indians are the sole means whereby the settlers can survive and that without them, they would all perish.

It would seem that the most appropriate and practicable method (which has already started to be put into effect) is for the various forms of captivity to be investigated, so that those who are really free men should be freed, and those who are genuine captives should remain captive.

However, for this investigation to be carried out with all due justice and integrity, it is insufficient for the officers of the municipal council to pass judgment on it, even if they do so with the help of the High Court judge. Rather, it is essential for the High Court judge to approve the investigations himself and to arrive at a decision on the various cases and their hearings. In that way, without consciences being in any way burdened, those that are adjudged to be genuine captives may remain captive. Furthermore, as the High Court judge, João Cabral de Barros, is such a learned man and as he acts so justly and with such integrity in all matters, it would seem that all the trust that Your Majesty would place in a great minister can [likewise] be placed in him.

As to the future purchase [of Indians], if expeditions do have to take place with that sole objective, the selfsame drawbacks will be encountered. However, as it is appropriate that such purchases should take place, if only for the redemption of their souls, the means by which they could be justifiably carried out is as follows. Firstly, the expeditions into the interior should be carried out solely for the purpose of converting the pagans and to make them subject both to the Church and to the Crown, just as Your Majesty has commanded me. Secondly, if, on such expeditions, Indians are found roped together or are genuine slaves, they should be purchased. That must be approved by the Jesuit Fathers that accompany the mission in question, among whom there should be at least one theologian and one good interpreter. To that end, which is as it should be, the captain whose task it is to lead the expedition should be chosen not just by the captain-major or governor but also by the municipal council, the religious leaders, and the vicar-general. That is because as the captaincy is owned by the captain-major, he will simply send someone who will serve the captain-major's interests rather than those of God and the public good.

The Indians who live in their villages and who are deemed to be free men are more captive than those who live in the private houses of the Portuguese. There is just one difference: every three years, they have a new master, namely the governor or captain-major who comes out to these parts. He uses them as though they were his, while treating them as the property of others. In that way, their circumstances become far worse than that of slaves, as they are normally put to work on the tobacco plantations, which is the most cruel form of labor [even] in Brazil. They are brutally sent to work for people and to carry out tasks to which they only go because they are forced to. There they die in utter wretchedness. Married women are removed from their villages and are set to work in private houses, despite the disservice to God and the protestations of their husbands, who after such removals often separate from their wives. The Indians are given no time to till and cultivate their fields, with the result that they, their wives, and their children suffer and perish. In short, they are in every respect treated as slaves, enjoying freedom solely in name. *Mamelucos* or men of similar ilk are placed in their villages as overseers and are the ones who commit these injustices, so that the wretched Indians are nowadays virtually wiped out. Yet, lest that should happen completely, they have transferred their villages this year to new locations where they can lead lives free from such intolerable subjection. Doubtless they did that because one of our Jesuit Fathers, who is a fine interpreter, persuaded them, on our behalf, to await a new decision on the part of Your Majesty.

It is clear that the causes of this problem and its harmful effects are simply brought about by the greed of those who govern. Such men are wont to claim that Your Majesty sends them out here so that they may better themselves and reward themselves in your service; they claim that there is no other way of achieving that objective than this.

The solution to all these problems, and there exists no other, is for Your Majesty to command that no governor or captain-major may grow tobacco or any other crop either for himself or through some proxy. Nor may they put the Indians to work or divide them into gangs except to build fortifications or other things in Your Majesty's service. Nor may they install overseers in the Indian villages, thus permitting their own headmen to govern them. They are, after all, the rulers of their tribes. Let them send them to work for the Portuguese for the customary wages, and let them do so willingly and as free men, without being subject to force. As for spiritual matters, let religious visit their villages or even reside in them, if that can be done, for that is their practice. After many experiments, that is the form that has been adopted as the best means of ruling over the villages in Brazil. It means that neither viceroys nor governors can interfere with the Indians, except to send for them when needed in Your Majesty's service, either in peace or in war. That is the only way in which it will be possible to preserve the villages, to add to their number, and to arrange that their Indian occupants live as Christians.

According to the information available, there are many Indians in the interior. They live close to the rivers; indeed, alongside the River Amazon they are beyond count. All these Indians suffer from a truly deep spiritual need. Under pain of sin, their need demands that, in Christian charity, preachers of the Gospel should promptly be sent to help them and to show them the path to salvation. Sire, that obligation becomes a double obligation for Your Majesty and for Your Majesty's ministers (on whom it impinges by virtue of their office). That is because it is not just a question of charity but also of justice, owing to the contract that Your Majesty's most serene predecessors made with the Papacy, when they undertook to command that the Faith be preached in every land that they conquered.

The main reason why we have had so little success with the Indians is that they have been treated so tyrannically. One captain had ten blazing brands tied to the fingers of a village headman, to force him to give him slaves, saying that he would leave him to burn if he did not do that, and so they were handed over. This and similar outrages have caused the Portuguese to be hated in the interior and have brought discredit upon the Faith, as the pagans have concluded that we merely use it as a pretext for our greed. Consequently, many of them have withdrawn even farther into the bush. Others, after approaching us, become disillusioned. Still others make war on us and cause us as much damage as they can. All of them (and this is the most regrettable aspect) go in their thousands to Hell.

The solution lies in our putting into effect all the remedies that have been proposed. Those Indians who have been wrongfully made captive should be set free. Those in the villages should lead lives that are genuinely free, cultivating their crops and willingly working for their wages. Expeditions into the interior should be made on a truly peaceful basis, without any hint of pretense. The Faith of Jesus Christ should be preached to the Indians, without any further aim than what He came into the world to seek, namely [the saving of] souls. There should be a significant number of religious to learn the [native] languages and to dedicate themselves to that mysterious task with genuine enthusiasm. If all that were done, there is no doubt that the combination of Divine Grace with this display of human effort would lead to the Indians readily accepting our friendship, embracing the Faith, and leading Christian lives. When once the good treatment received by the first Indians became generally known, many others would be attracted in their wake. Consequently, apart from their spiritual well-being and that of their descendants, the State would have many Indians to serve and defend it, just as they were the ones who made a major contribution to its restoration.[2]

Sire, I consider it important for me to draw these matters to Your Majesty's attention, both to comply with my duty and to assuage my conscience. With all due respect to Your Majesty, my particular concern is to find a solution to these most grievous problems that beset such a vast number of souls, in respect of whom Almighty God will surely hold Your Majesty to account. That situation becomes all the more significant after this report reaches Your Majesty's royal hands, since it is based not just on hearsay but

---

2  Maranhão was occupied by the Dutch from November 1641 to February 1644, their expulsion owing much to the Indians.

on what I have both seen and experienced. As Your Majesty knows so very well, it is forwarded by one who came to Maranhão solely in the service of God and to His greater glory and who, under God, has never sought anything other than to serve Your Majesty.

What I have declared is the same as what is felt by all those who, with genuine enthusiasm for the service of God and the public good, as well as with wide experience of this State, desire its spiritual and temporal progress. Those who would declare the opposite can only be those who are ruled by their own selfish interests and who have destroyed the State in every way.

Accordingly, Sire, we prostrate ourselves at Your Majesty's royal feet on behalf of all the souls in Your Majesty's immense territories who continue to descend to Hell, for want of those who could give them instruction. Prostrate before Your Majesty, both they and we, the few religious who are out here, make the following entreaty by the blood of Christ through which they were redeemed. We beseech Your Majesty to send us more fellow religious, so that we can continue and add to what has already been set in motion. If, in Portugal, there are not enough of those who are so needed (as there are not), let others be sent from countries that are above scrutiny, as has always been permitted. In that way, if we add their enthusiasm and hard work to ours, we shall all be able to undertake and continue this great campaign, for which the powers of those currently here are inadequate. We promise Your Majesty, in the name of that Lord who grants and sustains all kingdoms, that this undertaking, pursued with all piety and justice, will be the most solid basis upon which Your Majesty can establish [the kingdom of] Portugal, for the preservation and extension of which we all continually offer our sacrifices. All the souls who by our efforts attain salvation will make the same entreaty to Almighty God.

António Vieira
Maranhão, 20 May 1653.


## 2. The Ranching Frontier

*As the sugar industry developed and the coastal cities grew, there was an increasing demand for oxen, beef, and hides. Large tracts of land were opened for ranching in the interior of the northeast and eventually on the grasslands of southern Brazil. A "civilization of leather" was created among the ranchers and cowboys of the interior as the ranching frontier was extended inland. The short description presented here by the Italian Jesuit Giovanni Antonio Andreoni, who wrote under the name of Andre João Antonil and lived in Brazil at the end of the seventeenth and beginning of the eighteenth centuries, captures the importance of the cattle drives for the economy of Brazil and the way in which the ranching frontier was closely tied to the cities and the export economy. (From André João Antonil, Cultura e opulência do Brasil por suas drogas e Minas [1711], Andreé Mansuy, ed. [Paris: 1968], pp. 480–4).*

## Of the cattle drives that ordinarily travel each year from the stock pens to the cities, towns, and agricultural zones of Brazil, both to the butcher shops and to supply industry

To give an adequate idea of the cattle drives that come each year from the corrals of Brazil, it is enough to note that all the rolls of tobacco that are shipped anywhere are wrapped in hides. And since each roll weighs 8 *arrobas* [256 lbs] and those of Bahia ... total each year 25,000 rolls and those of Alagoas (Pernambuco) another 2,500 rolls, it is easy to see how many head are needed to provide for 27,000 rolls.

Moreover, another 50,000 tanned hides go from Bahia to Portugal, and 40,000 from Pernambuco and 20,000 from Rio de Janeiro (I do not know if these include those originating in Colonia de Sacramento or are only those from Rio de Janeiro and other captaincies of southern Brazil). A total of 120,000 tanned hides (*meios de sola*).

What is certain is that in the city but also among the majority of the better-off rural population live during those days in which it is permitted on meat from the slaughterhouse and from what is sold in parishes and towns; and the great number of blacks that live in the cities live on the blood and entrails of cattle, and in the backlands beef and milk are the common food of everyone.

Moreover, since there are so many sugar mills in Brazil, each year the drives supply the oxen to pull the carts (for their sugarcane) and those needed by the cane, tobacco, and manioc growers, and by the wood cutters and sawyers. And so it is easy to infer how many head are needed each year for all this work. Thus, I leave this to the judgment of whoever reads this chapter and I believe that this is better than trying to fix a precise number because not even the many merchants found all over Brazil can give a figure, and if they did so it would seem incredible and thought to be fantastic.

### *Chapter III*

**How the herds are driven from the *sertão* of Brazil. The usual price of the cattle killed and for those who are sent to work**
The herds that are usually sent to Bahia usually include 100, 150, 200, or 300 head. And also most every week some arrive at Capoâme, a place about eight leagues from Salvador where there is pasture and where the merchants buy them.[3] And in some periods of the year, there are weeks in which herds

---

3   A league equals about 3.5 miles. Capoâme, located near the present-day city of Camaçari, was founded in 1614. Its function as a cattle fair was taken over by Feira de Santana in the nineteenth century.

arrive every day. The men who drive them are whites, mulattos, blacks, and Indians who all hope for some profit from this work. They drive them by some going ahead and singing for the cattle will follow them, and others follow the cattle, driving them and making sure they do not stray. Each day, they travel four, five, or six leagues depending on pastures where they have to stop. Where there is no water, they have to travel fifteen to twenty leagues, moving day and night without rest until they can find a place to stop. At some river crossings, one man will don a cattle hide and head and swim his horse across the river so that the herd will follow him.

Whoever gives his herd to a trail boss to take it from Jacoabinas [modern-day Jacobina] to Capoâme, which is a trip of fifteen to seventeen days, will pay a cruzado per head and the trail boss will cover the cost of the drivers and guides and the costs of the trip. So if the drive has two hundred head, the boss will be paid so many cruzados if all the cattle arrive at the destination, but if some stray or are lost, the payment will be reduced by their number. To the Indians that travel from Jacoabinas to Capoâme, they pay four to five milréis and to the man who leads the herds with his horse, eight milréis. When the distances are greater, the payment is proportionally larger. So those who come from the São Francisco River and beyond to Capoâme with the herds of others ask for six or seven *tostões* per head or more depending on the distance.

A head of beef ordinarily sells in Bahia for four to five milréis, tame oxen for seven to eight. In Jacoabinas, they sell a head for 2,500 to 3,000. In the corrals of the São Francisco River, which are best suited to sell their cattle to Minas [the mining region], they sell them at the gate of the corral for the same price as in the city. And all that we have said here of the cattle herds of Bahia can be applied with little difference to those of Pernambuco and Rio de Janeiro.

## 3. The Discovery of Gold

From André João Antonil, *Cultura y opulência do Brasil por suas drogas e minas* (Lisbon, 1711), translation from Richard M. Morse, ed., *The Bandeirantes: Historical Role of the Brazilian Pathfinders* (New York: Alfred A. Knopf, 1965), pp. 130–6.

### Concerning the gold mines called "general" and their discoverers

A few years ago, when Artur de Sá was governor of Rio de Janeiro, the discovery of the general mines of Cataguases began. They say that the first discoverer was a mulatto who had been at the mines of Paranaguá and Curitiba. He had gone to the *sertão* with some Paulistas to fetch Indians, and on reaching Mount Tripuí, he went down to the stream, today known as Ouro Prêto, with a wooden bowl to get water. After scraping it along the riverbank, he saw that it contained some nuggets the color of steel which he could not identify. Neither could his companions recognize or evaluate what he had so easily picked up. They simply supposed that it was some metal which was poorly formed and therefore unrecognizable. When they arrived at Taubaté, however, they did not fail to ask what kind of metal this might be. And without further examination, they sold some of the nuggets to Miguel de Sousa at half a *pataca* for each *oitava*, without their knowing what they were selling or the buyer what he was buying. They finally decided to send a few nuggets to the governor of Rio de Janeiro, Artur de Sá; and when they were examined, they turned out to be the purest gold.

Half a league from the Ouro Prêto washing another mine was found which is called that of the Ribeiro de Antônio Dias; and another half-league from there, the mine of Ribeiro do Padre João de Faria; and near this, a little more than a league away, the mines of Ribeiro de Bueno and Bento Rodrigues. And a moderate three-day march by daylight from there was the mine of the Ribeirão de Nossa Senhora do Carmo, discovered by João Lopes de Lima, and still another called Ribeiro Ibupiranga. And all these mines took the names of their discoverers, who were all Paulistas.

There is also a stopping place on the way to these general mines, eleven or twelve days distant from the first ones if one makes good time until three o'clock each afternoon. This place takes its name from the River das Mortes, so called because some men died there while swimming across it, and others killed each other by gunshot while fighting over the allocation of wild Indians which they had brought from the *sertão*. And gold is found in this river, as well as in the streams that flow from it and those that flow into it. This stopping place serves for lodging those who are going to Minas Gerais, and here they supply themselves with necessities because those who are now settled here have farms and sell livestock.

I do not mention the mine of the Serra de Itatiaia (which means white gold, which is gold not yet well formed), which is a moderate eight-day journey by daylight from the Ouro Prêto washing. For the Paulistas show no interest in this mine as they have others of completely formed gold and much greater output. And they say that these general mines are at the latitude of the captaincies of Espírito Santo.

. . .

## Concerning the yield of the washings and the different qualities of gold taken from them

. . . There was a year during which more than 100 *arrôbas* of gold were taken from all these mines, or washings, excluding that which was and still is taken surreptitiously from other washings which the discoverers did not report.... And if the King's fifths reached seventeen or twenty arrôbas even though so much untaxed gold is concealed, it is easy to see that the gold taken out each year exceeds one hundred arrôbas without any exaggeration, and that during these past ten years, more than one thousand arrôbas were taken out.... Only the fifths owed His Majesty have been diminishing conspicuously, whether because the gold dust was diverted to other regions, or because it did not reach the royal smelting house, or because some, using a more despicable ruse, stamped the gold with false seals. Yet even so, His Majesty did not fail to realize a large profit through the mint at Rio de Janeiro; for by buying the gold at twelve *tostões* per oitava and in two years minting three million in national and provincial gold coin, he made a profit of six hundred thousand *cruzados* in advance.

## Concerning the people who go to the mines and take gold from the streams

The insatiable thirst for gold impelled so many to leave their lands and take to such arduous roads as those leading to the mines that it would be difficult to calculate the number of persons who are now there. However, those who have stayed there for a long period during these last years and have visited all the mines say that more than thirty thousand souls are employed, some in prospecting, others in directing the prospecting of the gold washings, and others in doing business, selling and buying the essentials not only for life but also for pleasure, with greater activity than in the seaports.

Every year, great numbers of Portuguese and foreigners arrive with the fleets to go to the mines. From the cities, towns, coastal regions, and *sertaões* of Brazil go whites, mulattoes, and blacks, and many Indians whom the Paulistas make use of. There is a mixture of people of every condition: men and women; young and old; poor and rich; nobles and plebeians; laymen, clerics, and religious of various orders, many of whom have neither convent nor house in Brazil.

With regard to temporal power, there have so far been no restraints or even a moderately well-ordered government. Only a few laws are kept, pertaining to the claims and the allotment of the washings. Beyond this, there are no ministers or justices who handle or might have authority to handle punishment of crimes, which are not rare, particularly homicide and theft. With regard to spiritual matters, since the prelates have hitherto been uncertain about the question of jurisdiction, the representatives of one or another group, whether local priests or visitors, have found themselves quite perplexed; and they have caused no little perplexity to others, who in the end do not know to which pastor these new flocks belong. And when the right to appoint priests is determined, few of them will be feared and respected in those parishes which move from place to place like the children of Israel in the desert.

The King's superintendent of mines was the Crown Judge José Vaz Pinto, who after a final two-year term returned once more to Rio de Janeiro with a handsome capital. And I suppose that through him, the King must have been kept fully informed on what is happening in the mines, and that he has indicated the disorders and the remedy for them when such is possible. Also present at the mines are a Crown procurator and a Crown representative (*guarda-mor*) on a stipend. Until now, there have been smelting houses in Taubaté, in the town of São Paulo, in Parati, and in Rio de Janeiro; and in each of these houses are a superintendent, a notary, and a founder who casts the gold into bars on which he stamps the royal seal, signifying the fifth that was paid to the king on that gold.

If there were mints and smelting houses in Bahia and Rio de Janeiro (since these are the two poles which eventually attract all the gold), His Majesty would make a much greater profit than what he has till now. And he would make a much greater one still if the mints, well equipped with the necessary apparatus, always had money on hand to buy the gold that the miners bring in and are delighted to sell without delay.

We have just learned that His Majesty is sending a governor and ministers of justice to the mines and ordering a regiment of soldiers levied so that everything will proceed with more control and order.

### Concerning the allotments or distribution of the mines

To avoid the confusion, tumult, and deaths that would arise from the discovery of the gold washings, the following method of allotment was agreed upon. The discoverer has the first claim as discoverer and a second as a miner. Next follows the king's share and then that of his representative. The rest are distributed by lot. Those known as whole claims are thirty square braças, and such are those of the king, the discoverer, and the royal representative. The others that are drawn by lot have an area proportionate to the number of slaves brought for prospecting, with two square braças allowed for each slave or Indian so used. Thus, a man with fifteen slaves receives a whole claim of thirty square braças. To be admitted to the distribution by lot, one must submit a petition to the superintendent of these allotments, who receives an oitava of gold for filing the petition, as does his notary. And it sometimes happens that five hundred petitions are presented, which means that the superintendent and the clerk take in one thousand oitavas. And if, because some claims fail to produce, all the miners do not extract from them an amount equal to what they paid, they therefore look for other claims as soon as new washings are discovered. The king's claim is sold straightway to the highest bidder. Anyone can sell or exchange his claim, and this has given and continues to give rise to many different arrangements, for one miner may extract much gold from a few braças while others extract little from many braças. There was one man who sold a claim for more than a thousand oitavas from which the buyer extracted seven arrôbas of gold. This goes to prove that whether or not gold is found in a claim is simply a turn of good or bad fortune.

### Concerning the abundance of provisions and all the necessaries found today at the mines and the slight attention paid to the extraordinarily high prices

Since the land that gives gold is completely barren of everything needed to sustain human life, as are most of the routes leading to the mines, one cannot imagine what the miners suffered at the beginning for lack of provisions. More than a few were found dead clutching an ear of corn as their only sustenance. However, as soon as the abundance of the gold extracted became apparent, and the largess with which everything sent there was paid for, lodging places were built and soon merchants began to send to the mines the best that arrived by ship from Portugal and other parts: not only provisions but also luxuries and elaborate clothes, as well as a thousand trinkets from France which also found their way there. In this regard, all parts of Brazil began to send everything the soil produces, with profits not merely large but excessive. And as there is no currency but gold dust at the mines, the least that could be given for anything would be oitavas. Shortly, the cattle herds from Paranaguá, those from River das Velhas, and those from the plains of Bahia were sent to Minas Gerais, along with everything else that the settlers imagined might fill a desire, including every kind of product, natural and manufactured, foreign and domestic....

And these high prices so prevalent at the mines were the reason why the prices of all things rose so much elsewhere, as is felt in the ports of the cities and towns of Brazil; and why many sugar mills were divested of their necessary slaves; and why the inhabitants suffer a great scarcity of provisions, which are almost all taken to be sold where they will yield greater profit.

### Concerning the harms done to Brazil by the greed which followed the discovery of gold in the mines

There is nothing so good that it cannot occasion many evils through the fault of him who fails to make good use of it. And even against things sacred the greatest sacrileges are committed. Is it any wonder then that gold – being such a handsome and precious metal, so useful for human commerce and so worthy of being made into the vases and ornaments of the Temples for Divine Worship – be transformed by the insatiable greed of men into a continual instrument and cause of many harms? The fame of mines so abundant in Brazil attracted men of every rank and from all places, some with means and others vagabonds. Those of means, who came by much of their wealth through prospecting, behave as a result with hauteur and arrogance; they always travel accompanied by bands of musketeers who need little pretext to commit any violence and to take great and thunderous revenge without any fear of the law. Gold induced these men to gamble unrestrainedly and to spend enormous sums on frivolities without blinking – to buy, for example, a Negro trumpeter for a thousand cruzados, or a mulatto woman of easy virtue for double that price to compound with her continual and scandalous sins. The vagabonds, who go to the mines to extract gold not from the washings but from the tubes in which the gold washers collect it and save it, were guilty of the most shocking treacheries and the cruelest killings. These crimes went unpunished because at the mines, human justice did not yet have a tribunal or the respect that it enjoys in other places where there are qualified ministers reinforced by numerous and reliable prisons. Only now that the governor and ministers are going there can some relief be expected. Even the bishops and prelates of several regions profoundly regret that no heed whatever is paid to their censures, which would return to their dioceses and convents the goodly number of clerics and religious who roam about there in defiance or as fugitives. The fact also that the very best provisions that could be desired go to the mines caused such a sharp increase in the prices of everything sold that the owners of sugar mills and the planters find themselves in very bad straits. For lack of Negroes, they can no longer produce sugar or tobacco as they so abundantly did in times past when theirs were the true mines of Brazil and Portugal. And the worst is that the larger part of the gold extracted from the mines is sent as dust or in coins to foreign kingdoms, while the smaller part remains in Portugal and the cities of Brazil, except for that spent on necklaces, earrings, and other baubles, which are seen worn today by mulatto and Negro women of easy life much more than by ladies. No prudent person can fail to admit that God has allowed the discovery of so much gold in the mines in order to punish Brazil with it, just as in the wars that are now so plentiful, He is using iron to punish the Europeans.

# INDEX

305